A PLEA
FOR THE
ANIMALS

A PLEA
FOR THE
ANIMALS

THE MORAL, PHILOSOPHICAL, AND
EVOLUTIONARY IMPERATIVE TO TREAT
ALL BEINGS WITH COMPASSION

MATTHIEU RICARD

Translated by Sherab Chödzin Kohn

SHAMBHALA • BOULDER • 2016

Shambhala Publications, Inc.
4720 Walnut Street
Boulder, Colorado 80301
www.shambhala.com

© 2014 by Matthieu Ricard
Translation © 2016 by Shambhala Publications, Inc.

Previously published in French as *Plaidoyer pour les animaux: Vers une bienveillance pour tous.*

9 8 7 6 5 4 3 2

Printed in the United States of America

♾ This edition is printed on acid-free paper that meets the American National Standards Institute z39.48 Standard.
♻ This book is printed on 30% postconsumer recycled paper.
For more information please visit www.shambhala.com.

Distributed in the United States by Penguin Random House LLC and in Canada by Random House of Canada Ltd

Designed by Lance Hidy

LIBRARY OF CONGRESS CATALOGING-IN-PUBLICATION DATA

Names: Ricard, Matthieu, author.
Title: A plea for the animals: the moral, philosophical, and evolutionary imperative to treat all beings with compassion / Matthieu Ricard.
Other titles: Plaidoyer pour les animaux. English
Description: First English edition. | Boulder: Shambhala, 2016. | Previously published in French [in 2014] as Plaidoyer pour les animaux: Vers un bienveillance pour tous. | Includes bibliographical references and index.
Identifiers: LCCN 2016003252 | ISBN 9781611803051 (hardcover: alk. paper)
Subjects: LCSH: Animal rights. | Compassion.
Classification: LCC HV4708 .R5313 2016 | DDC 179/.3—dc23
LC record available at https://lccn.loc.gov/2016003252

TO PEMA WANGYAL RINPOCHE
AND JIGME KHYENTSE RINPOCHE,
TIRELESS DEFENDERS OF THE
ANIMAL CAUSE, WHO HAVE
BY NOW SAVED THE LIVES OF
MORE THAN THIRTY MILLION
ANIMALS DESTINED FOR
HUMAN CONSUMPTION

TO JANE GOODALL AND ALL
THOSE WHO, INDIVIDUALLY
OR AS PART OF GROUPS,
HAVE DEDICATED THEMSELVES
TO SPEAKING OUT IN THE
NAME OF ANIMALS AND
TO PROTECTING THEM

"Animals are my friends . . .
and I don't eat my friends."
     —*George Bernard Shaw*

"A person doesn't have two
hearts, one for animals and
another for humans. One either
has a heart or one doesn't."
     —*Alphonse de Lamartine*

CONTENTS

INTRODUCTION

Some people are born with a natural tendency to be compassionate. From an early age, they show spontaneous kindness toward those around them, including animals. This was not the case for me. I was born into a Breton family, and until I was fourteen years old I often used to go fishing. I also remember when I was very young my friends from the local school and I once grilled ants by focusing the sun's rays on them with a magnifying glass. Looking back, I am ashamed of this, but it upsets me even more that such behavior struck me as normal. When I was five, my father took me to see the bullfights in Mexico. It was a celebration. The music was exciting. Everybody seemed to feel this was a great occasion, that all of this was wonderful. Why didn't I leave in tears? Was it a lack of compassion, of education, of imagination?

It never occurred to me to put myself in the place of the fish, the ant, or the bull. Was I just a hard-hearted guy? Or was it simply that I had never thought about these matters, that my eyes had yet to be opened?

It took me some time to come to a kind of awakening. I lived for a few years with one of my grandmothers, who had all the qualities one could wish for in a grandmother. Like a lot of people I knew who in other ways were good parents and good children, she was very fond of fishing. When we were on vacation, she often spent her afternoons fishing on the shores of a lake or in the harbor at Le Croisic in the company of elderly Breton ladies who still wore the traditional white lace Bigouden headdress. How could these people possibly have wanted to inflict pain on anything or anybody? Hooked at the end of the line, the little wriggling fish being pulled out of the water glittered in the light. Of course, there was the painful moment when they suffocated in the wicker basket and their eyes glazed over, but I looked the other way.

A few years later, when I was fourteen, a girlfriend asked me point-blank: "Really? You go fishing!?" Her tone of voice and the look she gave me—stunned and disapproving at the same time—were eloquent enough.

"You go fishing?" Suddenly I saw that whole scene in a different light: a fish pulled from its vital element by an iron hook stuck through its mouth, then suffocating in the air the way we drown in water. In order to lure the fish to the hook, did I not also skewer a worm as living bait, thus sacrificing one life to destroy another? How could I have let my mind block out this reality of suffering for such a long time? Sickened to the heart by these thoughts, I gave up fishing on the spot.

No doubt, when compared to the drastic events that wreck the lives of so many human beings in the world, my preoccupation with those little fish might seem ludicrous. But for me this was a turning point.

At the age of twenty I had the great good fortune of meeting Tibetan spiritual masters, who from that time on have inspired every moment of my existence. The central point of their teachings has been the royal way of love and universal compassion.

Although for a long time I had not been able to put myself in others' places, training with the masters, little by little I learned altruistic love, doing the best I could to open myself—to open my mind and heart—to the plights of others. I trained myself in compassion, and I reflected on the human condition and the condition of animals as well. Without a doubt, I still have a long way to go, and I will continue to do my best to make progress in my understanding of the teachings I have received.

It is far from my intention, as you will have gathered, to rebuke people who in one way or another cause animals to suffer. They often do it without thinking, as I myself used to do. It truly is difficult to make the connection between the latest consumer items, including food and medicines that sometimes save our lives, and the suffering that is usually involved in their fabrication. Cultural traditions also play a major role in our perceptions of animals, our companions on this planet. Some societies have developed collective patterns of thought that encourage the view that animals exist to serve humans, but the outlook of other traditions has long been that every being, human or nonhuman, must be respected.

This book is a logical and necessary follow-up to my book *Altruism: The Power of Compassion to Change Yourself and the World.*[1] Its purpose is clearly to demonstrate the justifications and the moral imperative for extending our altruism to all sentient beings, without any quantitative or qualitative limitations. Certainly there is so much suffering among human beings throughout the world, one could spend one's whole life just alleviating a tiny fraction of it. Despite that, however, concern for the fate of the 7.7 million other species of animals that inhabit this planet is neither unrealistic nor misguided, because most of the time there is no need to choose between the well-being of humans and the well-being of animals. We live in an essentially interdependent world where the fate of each being, of whatever kind, is intimately linked to that of all the others. So what we are suggesting here is not concern for animals *only* but concern for animals *also*.

Such an approach does not involve humanizing animals or animalizing humans; rather it is a matter of extending benevolence and kindness to all. Reaching out in this way is more about taking a responsible attitude toward all that is around us than about making choices concerning what we should do with the limited resources we possess for action in the world.

This book invites us to face up to something: in spite of the sense of wonder the animal kingdom inspires in us, we are responsible for an ongoing massacre of animals on a scale unequaled in the history of humankind. Every year, sixty billion land animals and a thousand billion marine animals are killed for our consumption.

Moreover, as we will show, this mass killing and its corollary—the excessive consumption of meat in the wealthy countries—is madness on a global scale. It perpetuates hunger in the world, increases the world's ecological imbalances, and is even harmful to human health.

Industrial-scale meat production and overfishing of the seas are without doubt the main problems, but a general lack of respect for animals also leads to other depredations. Scientific experimentation on animals results in the death or suffering of great numbers of them.

Other problematic activities are trafficking in wild animals, hunting and fishing for sport, bullfighting, circuses, and other forms of regarding animals as mere instruments for our use or pleasure. In addition, the impact of our lifestyle on the biosphere is considerable: at the current rate, by 2050 30 percent of *all* animal species will have disappeared from our planet.[2]

We continue to live in ignorance concerning the harm we inflict on animals; very few of us have ever visited an industrial breeding site or a slaughterhouse. We maintain a kind of moral schizophrenia that has us lavishing pampering our pets and at the same time planting our forks in the pigs that have been sent to the slaughter by the millions, even though they are in no way less conscious, less sensitive to pain, or less intelligent than our cats and dogs.

This book is a plea and an exhortation to change our relationship with animals. This plea is not just moral finger-pointing but is based on evidence, the work of evolutionists, ethologists, and philosophers who are respected throughout the world. Some of the studies we call on in this book bring to light the intellectual and emotional richness, too often ignored, that a great proportion of animal species are endowed with. These studies also show the continuum that links all of the animal species, including us, and makes it possible to retrace the evolutionary history of the species that populate the planet today. Starting with the era of the ancestors we share with other animal species, little by little, by a long series of steps and minimal changes, we arrived at the stage of *Homo sapiens*. In the course of this slow evolution there was no "magical moment" that would justify our conferring on ourselves a special nature that makes us fundamentally different from the many species of hominids that preceded us. Nothing occurred in the evolutionary process that would justify our claim to a right of total supremacy over the animals.

The most striking quality that humans and animals have in common is the capacity to experience suffering. Why do we still blind ourselves, now at the beginning of the twenty-first century, to the immeasurable suffering that we inflict on animals, knowing that a great part of the pain that we cause them is neither necessary nor unavoidable? Certainly we should know that there is no moral justification for inflicting needless pain and death on any being.

I

A BRIEF HISTORY OF THE RELATIONS BETWEEN HUMANS AND ANIMALS

The evolution of living beings is characterized by an ongoing attempt to maintain the continuously challenged balance among cooperation, competition, and indifference. The biosphere as a whole is ruled by the principle of interdependence: having evolved together, vegetable and animal species depend closely on one another for survival. In accordance with differing situations, this interdependence can lead to either cooperation or competition among members of a single species or between one species and another. Predation is a mode of behavior in which one species survives at the expense of other species. But a great number of species do no more than ignore or avoid each other, because there is no advantage to cooperation and they are not in direct competition for survival.

The evolutionary appearance of behaviors of growing complexity produced forms such as territoriality, synchronization of rhythms of activity, commensalism (an association of individuals of different species that is profitable for one of them without danger to the other), parasitism, herding, living in colonies (within which females come together at a breeding site but care only for their own offspring), and ultimately the form known as eusociality, the highest level of social organization. Eusociality is characterized by hierarchical structures, collaboration, exchange of information, division and specialization of roles among members (queen, workers, warriors), the existence of a reproductive caste and other castes that are sterile, and cohabitation of different generations in a "nest" where the adults care for all the young collectively. Among the eusocial species are bees, ants, termites, mole rats, and certain species of shrimp.

Increasing complexity of animal societies led to the appearance of cultures that reached a higher level of sophistication in the societies of the human species, thanks to the cumulative transmission of knowledge and customs from one generation to the next. As intelligence developed, most particularly in the human species, the capacity to form a mental representation of the situations and mental states of others became possible. This gave rise to cognitive empathy in relation to the mental states of others as well as the kind of emotional empathy that allowed individuals to enter sympathetically into the feelings of other individuals. Individuals also became capable of establishing long-term relationships based on an appreciation of the value of others and characterized by reciprocity.

Over the course of 99 percent of our history, human beings have lived from hunting and gathering, constantly moving from place to place, evolving with few possessions within a minimally hierarchized social system based on cooperation. The first human societies lived in widely scattered small groups, far enough from one another that they had almost no reason to make war. The lack of archaeological evidence for war during this hunting-and-gathering phase suggests that war was rare or altogether absent during the greater part of human prehistory.[1] Contrary to the image conveyed by history books and the media, which sometimes lay more emphasis on drama and conflict than on the realities of everyday life, nature is not "red in tooth and claw," as Alfred Lord Tennyson put it.[2] During this period the majority of living species lived in a relatively peaceful manner, even though there might have been spectacular episodic manifestations of violence. Even among the big cats, the hunt occupies only a small fraction of their time. Ethologist Shirley Strum tells us, "Aggression was not as omnipresent and important an influence in evolution as might have been thought."[3]

During the last glacial period, a great part of the northern hemisphere was covered with glaciers several miles thick, which prevented the formation of large-scale human social groups as well as the practice of agriculture. Nevertheless, the mean temperature was only 4 to 5 degrees centigrade lower than today's, which shows to what extent differences in temperature that seem minimal at first glance are capable of creating radically different life conditions.

About twelve thousand years ago, at the beginning of the Holocene era, a period characterized by remarkable climatic stability, humans were able to cultivate the earth and began to store goods and provisions and domesticate animals. During this same period, the domestic wolf and then the dog made their appearance in the company of humans. They were followed by sheep and goats. Nine thousand years ago in certain regions of Asia, it was cows' and pigs' turn to be domesticated. Then came horses, camels, and fowl. Finally, three or four thousand years ago in Egypt, it was cats. In the New World, lamas, alpacas, turkeys, and guinea pigs became humanity's animal familiars. Plants were also being domesticated, and numerous varieties derived from wild plants came into being. People had wheat and barley in Europe, rice in Asia, and corn, potatoes, and beans in the New World.[4]

Societies became hierarchized; chiefs appeared. There was agriculture and the slaughter of animals. Barter and then regular commerce spread over the entire earth. As various societal developments occurred, people learned to live in societies in which no one knew everyone: They established rules and social contracts to defend against abuses and to facilitate interactions among members of society. Disputes and personal vendettas evolved into organized wars between groups of individuals who had no personal relationships to each other, and then conventions were established to reinstate peace and to maintain it.[5]

Barely ten thousand years ago, just before the sedentarization of the hunter-gatherers and the agricultural boom, the human population of the planet stood at between 1 and 10 million.[6] From that point on, with the demographic explosion and the expansion of technological methods that followed, what had once been no more than a means to survive and prosper gradually developed into our present overexploitation of tillable land by monoculture, deforestation on a scale without precedent,[7] and finally the transformation of animal breeding into an industry of meat production that costs the lives of hundreds of millions of animals every year. In the 1950s, we were taken by surprise by the "great acceleration" that marked our entry into the anthropocene era, the human era, in which human activities have begun to have a major impact on the planet as a whole. Indeed, since 1950, the world population (which went from 2.5 billion in 1950 to 7 billion today), emissions of carbon dioxide and methane, deforestation, the use of pesticides and chemical fertilizers, and the consumption of fresh water have not only greatly increased, but the rate of their increase has considerably accelerated. We have gone beyond the limits of planetary resilience, and the biosphere is now in a danger zone.[8] The loss of biodiversity has been particularly heavy. At the rate things are going, as much as 30 percent of all mammals, birds, and amphibians are in danger of extinction by the end of the twenty-first century.[9] As a result of human activities in the twentieth century, the rate of extinction of species has accelerated from a hundred to a thousand times higher than the average rate of extinction, in the absence of major catastrophes (such as the one that led to the disappearance of the dinosaurs). In the twenty-first century, it is expected that this rate will again multiply by ten. Of course, extinctions of species are irreversible.

In *The Politics of Species*, Raymond Corbey and Annette Lanjouw speak of "respectful coexistence," referring to the possibility of sharing resources and space with all other species on Earth, of respecting their needs along with our own. "Respectful coexistence" is an expression that implies an acknowledgment of the moral and social relevance of animals. It connotes an attitude of concern and consideration for the needs of other species as well as a sense of care and respect for them.[10]

Transformation of Our Attitude toward Animals

After becoming sedentary, human beings became able to domesticate animals in a systematic fashion. At the same time they also began killing a certain number of the animals they raised. This began a relationship to animals that is quite different from that of the hunter, for whom the animal is not a familiar individual but an unknown prey, even though its behaviors may be well known. James Serpell, a professor of animal ethics at the University of Pennsylvania, observes that only cultures that have domesticated animals defend the principle that animals are inferior to humans. This position is an indication of malaise with respect to the act of killing an animal and at the same time an arbitrary justification for doing so. Hunter-gatherer peoples do not consider animals inferior beings but instead regard them as equals, perhaps even superiors, beings who are different from us but are capable of thoughts and feelings analogous to our own.[11] The Chewong of Malaysia, as the ethologist Dominique Lestel reports, do not divide the world into humans and nonhumans. In their view, the members of each species have a perspective on the world that is their own. Thus the Chewong perception of the world is organized into a "way of the tiger," a "way of the bear," and a "way of humans." What the animal species perceive as true for them is as true as what human beings perceive is true for them. Through imagination and empathy, human beings become capable of forming an idea of the experienced reality of animals.[12]

There are many cultures in which a perceived kinship with animals is formalized into a system of beliefs in which the family, clan, or tribe attributes its origin to a mythical animal considered to be an ancestor. This anthropomorphic perception of animals provides hunter peoples with a conceptual framework that enables them to understand their prey, to identify with it, and to anticipate its behavior. On the other hand, it creates the following moral conflict: if the animal is considered an equal, then killing it is murder.

The hunters of Siberia, for example, believe that reindeer have the capacity for reasoning and even attribute speech to them. This is the case for many tribes of hunters, in particular in regions where the conditions of life are hard and resources are scarce.[13] They sometimes attribute the capacity to regulate the supply of game to a Great Spirit. As the British anthropologist Tim Ingold points out, even though reindeer are considered to be consenting victims, the act of killing them is surrounded by an elaborate procedure meant to avoid offending the spirit of the reindeer or endangering the future supply of reindeer. The hunter is the recipient of the physical substance of the animal— its meat, skin, and bones—but its spirit is considered to be immortal, cycling eternally between deaths and rebirths.[14] Among these peoples, a sense of guilt at the killing of animals and the need to expiate it are frequently present. In certain African tribes, hunters are required to perform rites intended to make amends for the murder that soils their conscience. In other tribes, the hunter supplicates the animal to for-give him and not to bear him any ill will.[15]

The ethical problem is more serious for the traditional stock breeder than for the hunter, because his or her relationship with animals is different. The hunter possesses remarkable knowledge of the behav-ior and character of his or her prey animal, but he never has the occa-sion to interact with it socially. Therefore there is very little occasion for him to develop attachment toward particular individual animals. By contrast, in traditional societies the breeder lives in contact with his or her animals and becomes personally attached to them. In that case, slaughtering the animal or causing the animal to suffer inevita-bly brings about feelings of guilt and remorse, since they are a grave betrayal of a preestablished trust.

Once domesticated, the animals become servants or slaves of their master and are at his or her mercy. According to the historian Keith Thomas, devaluing the domestic animals that we exploit, regarding them as inferior beings, becomes a means of justifying in our eyes the treatment we inflict on them.[16] This was also the opinion of Darwin, who noted that "Animals, whom we have made our slaves, we do not like to consider our equals."[17] In this way, humans demonstrate our capacity to selectively turn our moral norms on and off in accordance with our own interests. A dog has no need to justify its act when it kills a rabbit; a cat shows no sign of remorse when it plays with a half-dead mouse. These behaviors and the suffering they cause are inher-ent in the relationship between a predator and its prey. For humans, these questions are not so simple.[18] Certainly there are exceptions, but in general it is difficult for men and women to kill animals or cause them to suffer with total indifference. Paradoxically, this inhibition seems to stem from the difficulty we have in making a clear distinction between animals and ourselves. Indeed, many studies have shown that most human beings tend to perceive their domestic animals and pets as their children and to treat them that way. They take responsibility for them; they feed them; they protect them from danger and the ele-ments, keep them clean, pamper them, and take care of them when they are sick.[19]

In industrial animal production, tens of thousands of chickens or thousands of pigs are confined in immense hangars. The feeling of repugnance at killing an animal is then diluted by de-individuation and by the rapidity of the large-scale slaughter that occurs. Even so, however, it is replaced by a sense of horror at the number of the killings being carried out. A person whose job was to bleed pigs confided to Jocelyne Porcher: "Loading the pig on the truck is done quick, the transport is done quick, the killing is done quick, then eating it is done quick too, right? Yep, that's the way it goes."[20] She calculated that just this one bleeder by himself, in his twenty-four-year career, had slit the throats of between six and nine million pigs. As the employee of a large U.S. chicken producer put it, "You are murdering helpless birds by the thousands (75,000 to 90,000 a night). You are a killer."[21]

All of this is obviously not without consequences for people's moral values. In the opinion of researcher Elizabeth Fisher, "By keeping them and feeding them, humans at first entered into bonds of friendship with animals—then they killed them. To reach that point, they first had to kill a part of their own sensibility. . . . The enslavement of animals seems to have served as a model for the enslavement of human beings, in particular the large-scale exploitation of female captives for child-bearing and labor."[22] The American philosopher Charles Patterson also cites the example of the Sumerians (four centuries before Jesus Christ), who castrated male slaves and put them to work "like domestic animals."[23]

The Justifications of Animal Exploitation: The Religions of the Book and Western Philosophy

On the whole it is uncomfortable to live with a constant feeling of bad conscience. Having decided to utilize other living species for their own ends, humans had to find moral justifications for this exploitation. Some religions base anthropocentrism of this sort on the divine will. According to the mainstream view of the Christian religions, animals do not have a "soul" and are only on earth for the use of humanity. God made humans in his image and said, "And let them have dominion over the fish of the sea and over the birds of the heavens and over the livestock and over all the earth and over every creeping thing."[24] As the writer Milan Kundera remarks, "Clearly, Genesis was written by a man, not by a horse."[25]

In general, Judaism and Islam are no more tender with animals than Christianity, but there are also notable exceptions. The Jewish tradition describes itself as more concerned about the suffering of animals than Christianity does. According to the Torah, "It is forbidden to inflict pain on any living creature. On the contrary, it is our duty to soothe the pain of any creature."[26] In the Talmud, we also read, "Great importance is attached to humane treatment of animals."[27] According to certain Torah specialists, the only reason God gave humans permission to eat meat after the Flood was on account of their weakness, but the ideal would be for them to be vegetarian.[28]

Aristotle stated that animals exist in order to serve human beings as well; moreover, he defended keeping them in servitude. According to him, "plants exist for the benefit of animals, and wild beasts for the benefit of humans. . . . Since nature does nothing uselessly or in vain, it is undeniably true that it made all the animals for the benefit of human beings."[29]

In the Roman world, anthropocentricism was king. For Cicero, "quite obviously the hosts of animals were created for the needs of man, some for his use, others for his nourishment."[30] It is strange to see the way in which great minds so glibly set forth such categorical points of view ("quite obviously") without feeling the need to provide the slightest proof, even empirical, for their positions. Enunciated vociferously enough, dogma takes on the force of truth.

To return to an argument made as far back as the third century by the Neoplatonic philosopher Porphyry, the author of several treatises advocating vegetarianism: crocodiles devour humans and are of no use to them—does this mean that humans were created for the benefit of crocodiles?[31] And if by chance extraterrestrials who are more intelligent and powerful than we are were to land on our planet and announce that their God had created human beings for their use, what would we have for an answer to them? And what if, to pursue this idea further, they found human meat so delicious that they claimed they could not do without it? That is what Milan Kundera imagined in his *The Unbearable Lightness of Being*:

> The reason we take that right for granted is that we stand at the top of the hierarchy. But let a third party enter the game—a visitor

from another planet, for example, someone to whom God says, "Thou shalt have dominion over creatures of all other stars"—and all at once taking Genesis for granted becomes problematical. Perhaps a man hitched to the cart of a Martian or roasted on the spit by inhabitants of the Milky Way will recall the veal cutlet he used to slice on his dinner plate and apologize (belatedly!) to the cow.[32]

Christ demonstrated, in his life and teaching, that charity consists in the love of Man—of all human beings, including one's enemies. He thus fulfills the commandment in Leviticus "Thou shalt love thy neighbor as thyself."[33] On the other hand, as Renan Larue has shown in his historical study "Vegetarianism and Its Enemies,"[34] it is difficult for Christian thinkers to promote compassion and goodwill toward animals for the simple reason that, in the Gospels, Christ himself seems to have shown little concern for them. In the canonical Gospels it is said, for example, that a man came to Jesus begging to be delivered from the demons that possessed him.[35] When Jesus cast the demons out, they asked his permission to enter into a herd of about 2,000 pigs that were grazing on the mountain side. When permission was granted, the demons possessed the pigs, who promptly rushed down the hill and were drowned in the sea. Granted the historicity of the account, it is evident from the Gospel story that the exorcism of the possessed man was more important to Jesus than the lives of thousands of pigs. Likewise, after the resurrection, Christ appeared to his disciples, who were returning from an unsuccessful fishing expedition. Standing on the shore, he indicated the place where they should cast their nets. Later the fish were cooked, and he distributed them to his disciples with some bread.[36]

Confronted by the Manichees, who refrained from killing animals and causing them to suffer, Saint Augustine declared that the moral basis of vegetarianism is absurd and it is to be censured inasmuch as "Christ has shown that it is a pure superstition." The Son of God, he said, never killed human beings, even when they were guilty. By contrast, he killed animals even though they were perfectly innocent. "If he considered that human beings and animals formed a single society,"[37] he would never have killed them. Man therefore has no duty toward the animals, Augustine reasoned, and should carefully avoid any misplaced feeling in their regard. Augustine concludes, "It is by a very just ordainment of the Creator that they [animals] have been subordinated to our use."[38]

As Saint Thomas Aquinas later confirms, "love of one's neighbor" does not include animals. He asks the question "Whether irrational creatures should be loved out of charity,"[39] and his answer is no: animals are not our neighbors, since they are deprived of reason and are without a spiritual soul. In his view, the only possible objection to cruelty toward animals resides in the fact that it might encourage cruelty toward humans; there can be no moral objection to the cruel treatment of animals per se.

This became the official position of the Roman Catholic Church. Pope Pius XII, for example, refused to grant his permission for the formation of a society for the prevention of cruelty to animals because such a permission would have implied that human beings have duties and obligations toward inferior creatures.[40] For a long time, caring for ailing animals was prohibited because medicine and medical care was reserved for human beings; this made it shameful to provide such care to inferior beings.[41] The first veterinary medical school of the Western world was founded in Lyon in the reign of Louis XV. The king's aim was not to protect the animals themselves but to preserve them from, among other things, the bovine plagues that were the ruination of his peasants. Thus the primary aim of veterinarians was to improve the rural economy by caring for the health of animals.[42]

In the Orthodox Church, there are seasons in the year when food of animal origin is forbidden (vegetalism) and when even the use of materials derived from animals is proscribed (veganism). But if the Desert Fathers, and the monastic order in orthodox Christianity, encourage vegetarianism, it is purely for ascetic reasons. Vegetarianism when practiced for moral reasons is condemned by the Church Fathers. Saint Augustine and Saint Bernard of Clairvaux, among many others, make a clear distinction between "good vegetarians," who abstain from flesh for penitential reasons, and "bad vegetarians," who preach compassion for animals and refrain from killing them.[43]

Among philosophers, the status of animals knew one of its blackest periods with the advent of Descartes's theory of "animal automata."

Not only do animals exist only for the benefit of human beings, but on top of that, they do not feel anything. Descartes tells us:

Animals are no more than simple machines, automata. They feel neither pleasure nor pain, nor anything else at all. Although they are capable of crying out when they are cut by a knife or of going through contortions in their efforts to escape contact with a hot iron, that does not mean that they feel pain in these situations. They are governed by the same principles as a watch, and if their actions are more complex than those of a watch, that is because the latter is a machine fabricated by humans, whereas animals are infinitely more complex machines made by God.[44]

This mechanistic vision permitted the scientists of the time to ignore the pain of the animals they used in their experiments. Thus at the Jansenist seminary at Port-Royal, "they beat the dogs with perfect indifference and mocked those who lamented for these creatures as though they felt pain. . . . They nailed the poor animals to planks by their four paws so they could vivisect them and observe the circulation of blood, which was a major subject of discussion."[45]

Voltaire rebelled against such practices:

The barbarians take hold of this dog, which so far surpasses humans in friendship; they nail it to a table and they dissect it alive in order to show you its mesenteric veins. You discover in it *all the same organs of feeling that are in you. Answer me, mechanist: did nature arrange all the apparatus of sensation in this animal in order that it should feel nothing?* Does it have nerves in order to be without sensation? Do not suppose this kind of incongruous contradiction in nature.[46]

In his *Lecture on Ethics*, Kant aligns himself with Thomas Aquinas, declaring, "Animals have no consciousness of themselves and as a consequence are no more than a means to an end. This end is man. Thus the latter has no immediate duty toward them. . . . The duties that we have toward animals are only indirect duties toward humanity."[47]

This vision is even found in the work of contemporary existentialists.

A notable example is Jean-Paul Sartre, when he writes: "Animal free-dom is not a concern, because the dog is free only to worship me. The rest is appetite, mood, physiological mechanism; in growling and turning away from me, it falls back into determinism or into the dark opacity of instinct."[48] Or the philosopher Jean Marie Meyer, who said, "Man alone is an end in itself, so he alone can claim the right to 'respect.'"[49]

As we shall see in chapter 6, which is entitled "The Continuum of Life," science has now shown that many animals have self-consciousness. Moreover, unless we adopt the creationist point of view, there is no reason to think that their purpose is the benefit of man.

Spinoza also maintains an instrumentalist view of animals. He writes in his *Ethics:* "The law that prohibits the killing of animals is based much more on vain superstition and on feminine pity than on sane reason. . . . There is no reason there that we should not pursue what is useful to us and thus no reason not to make use of animals in a way that suits our interests."[50]

In essence, as James Serpell puts it:

> For more than two thousand years, European religion and philosophy have been dominated by the belief that some supernatural and omnipotent being has placed humanity on a moral pedestal, very much above the rest of creation. On the basis of this point of view, we have exercised absolute dominion over the rest of living beings, and we have even held the belief that their only reason for being was to serve our own egoistic interests. . . . The point of view of the early Christians, according to which animals were created solely for the benefit of humanity and the Cartesian idea that they were incapable of suffering are only mutually compatible variations on the same theme. Both have furnished human beings with a permit to kill, a permit to use or abuse other forms of life with complete impunity.[51]

Dissenting Voices

From the time of antiquity and all through the centuries, voices have risen in the West that have attempted to draw attention to the cruel and arrogant character of our relationship to animals and have manifested profound revulsion toward our use of them for our own ends.

Pythagoras was not only a vegetarian, but he also refused to wear clothing of leather or wool. According to Appollonius of Tyana, he "was never willing to wear fabrics derived from the hides of animals, and he abstained from eating meat and from all sacrifices that cost the life of an animate being."[52] As Renan Larue[53] tells us, rejecting animal sacrifices for moral reasons meant challenging the religious order as well as the political order that was closely associated with it. In place of blood offerings, which in his eyes could not possibly give pleasure to gods supposed to be full of kindness, Pythagoras suggested offerings of honey, incense, chanting, and other nonviolent offerings. The position of the vegetarians who were the disciples of Pythagoras, as well as of Orpheus, aroused scorn and sarcasm. The idea of extending the concept of murder to all animate beings drew sniggers from Euripides, Aristophanes, and even the great Plato, who characterized their doctrine as "childishness."[54] At the dawn of the Christian era, abstinence from meat was regarded as a superstition and was prohibited in Rome by the emperor Tiberius. Despite all this, the prestige of Pythagoras conferred an intellectual standing on this abstinence that it had never enjoyed before.

Ovid transmitted this same message in his *Metamorphoses:*

There are crops; there are apples weighing down the branches; and ripening grapes on the vines; there are flavorsome herbs; and those that can be rendered mild and gentle over the flames; and you do not lack flowing milk; or honey fragrant from the flowering thyme. The earth, prodigal of its wealth, supplies you with gentle sustenance, and offers you food without killing or shedding blood. . . . Oh, how wrong it is for flesh to be made from flesh; for a greedy body to fatten, by swallowing another body; for one creature to live by the death of another creature![55]

A few decades later, in his work entitled "On the Eating of Flesh," Plutarch shows himself to be an ardent defender of animals and deplores the loss of sensibility that accompanies the act of feeding on animal flesh:

You ask me for what reason Pythagoras abstained from eating the flesh of beasts; but for my part, I can only ask you with astonishment what motive or rather what boldness the first man could have had who brought to his lips the bloody limbs of a dying beast, who had dead bodies and cadavers served on his table, and devoured body parts that shortly before had bleated and bellowed, walked and saw? How could his eyes have borne the sight of murder? How could he have watched the throat-cutting, the skinning, the tearing apart of a weak animal? . . .[56]

We are touched neither by the beautiful colors that some of these animals exhibit, nor by the harmony of their songs, nor by the simplicity and frugality of their lives, nor by their skill and their intelligence; and with cruel sensuality, we cut the throats of these unfortunate beasts, we deprive them of the light of the heavens, we take away from them the minimal portion of life with which nature ordained them. Do we believe, moreover, that the cries that they utter are inarticulate sounds and not pleas and just complaints on their part?[57]

Plutarch also ridiculed those who argued that man is primarily a carnivore:

We declare, then, that it is absurd for them to say that the practice of flesh-eating is based on Nature. For that man is not naturally carnivorous is, in the first place, obvious from the structure of his body. A man's frame is in no way similar to those creatures who were made for flesh-eating: he has no hooked beak or sharp nails or jagged teeth, no strong stomach or warmth of vital fluids able to digest and assimilate a heavy diet of flesh. . . . If you declare that you are naturally designed for such a diet, then first kill for yourself what you want to eat. Do it, however, only through your own resources, unaided by cleaver or cudgel of any kind or axe. Rather, just as wolves and bears and lions themselves slay what they eat, so you are to fell an ox with your fangs or a boar with your jaws, or tear a lamb or hare in bits. Fall upon it and eat it still living, as animals do. . . . No one eats the flesh just as it is; men boil it and roast it, altering it by fire and drugs, recasting and diverting and smothering with countless condiments the taste of gore so that the palate may be deceived and accept what is foreign to it.[58]

Among Catholic thinkers, there have been some exceptions to the general rule. Saint Francis of Assisi, known for his compassion for animals, asked "all the brothers of the world to respect, venerate, and honor every living thing; or rather, everything that exists." He preached to birds and returned live fish he was given to the water. Famously, he is said to have convinced the wolf of Gubbio not to kill man or beast. But Saint Francis was not a vegetarian, and a few moments before his death, he expressed a wish to eat trotters. Accordingly, his fellows cut off two feet of a nearby pig.

Priest and philosopher Jean Meslier expressed strong views against cruelty to animals:

It is an act of cruelty, of barbarism, to kill, to strike unconscious, and to cut the throat of animals, who do no harm to anyone, the way we do; because they are sensitive to injury and pain just as we are, regardless of what is said vainly, falsely, and ridiculously by our new Cartesians, who regard them as purely machines without soul and without feelings. . . . This is a ridiculous opinion, a pernicious principle, and a detestable doctrine, because it clearly tends to stifle in the hearts of men all feelings of kindness, of gentleness, and of humanity that they might have toward these poor animals . . . . Blessed are the nations that treat them kindly and favorably, who are compassionate toward their miseries and their pains; but cursed are the nations that treat them cruelly, who tyrannize over them, who enjoy shedding their blood, and who are avid to eat their flesh.[59]

However, Meslier was hardly representative of Christianity because, paradoxically, he had become an atheist. He even considered indifference or cruelty to animals by Christians as one of the proofs of the nonexistence, or the malice, of their God.[60]

In England, the first known sermon in favor of animal protection

was pronounced in 1773 by the Anglican pastor James Granger, pro-
voking a nationwide controversy. The pastor said afterward that a
number of his flock thought he had gone mad.[61] Another pastor, Hum-
phrey Primatt, made a link between the devaluation of certain human
beings and that of animals:

> The white man . . . can have no right, in virtue of his color, to
> reduce to slavery and tyrannnize the black man. . . . For the same
> reason, no man can have a natural right to mistreat or torment a
> beast. . . .[62] Whether we walk on two legs or four paws, whether
> our head is turned toward the earth or is erect, whether we are
> bare-skinned or covered with hair, whether we have a tail or not,
> horns or not, long ears or round ones; whether we bray like an ass,
> talk like a man, whistle like a bird, or are mute like a fish, nature
> never intended these distinctions as bases for the right of tyranny
> and of oppression.[63]

In the present day, the theologian and priest Andrew Linzey, holder
of the ethics, theology and animal welfare chair at the University of
Oxford, has published several works in which, countering the traditional position of the Church, he proposes to grant real rights to animals. In his essay "Animal Rights," he does not hesitate to call into
question the usual interpretation of Genesis: "Humanity has given
in to a sort of idolatry, imagining that God is primarily interested in
the human species. This is a staggering absurdity. Why did God create
the wasp? Certainly not for our use. And the dinosaurs? How could we
have exploited them? For my part, I find it quite reassuring that God
has other concerns."[64]

In another work, entitled *Animal Gospel,* Linzey rails against
humanist chauvinism:

> As soon as you start to challenge the despotic treatment of
> animals—whether it is killing for sport, the brutality of the export
> trade, or (to take the most up-to-date example) the absolutely
> obscene massacre of thousands of seals to obtain their penises so
> they can be sold as aphrodisiacs in Europe and Asia—you are con-

fronted again and again by this humanist dogmatism: if it's to the advantage of humanity, then it must be right."[65]

For Linzey, this means that

Animals should not be considered as merchandise, resources, instruments, or useful objects at the disposition of humans. If humans want to claim to be the masters of creation, then this mastery can only consist of serving. There can be no mastery without service. According to the theological doctrine of animal rights, therefore, humans should be the serving species—the species to which the power, the opportunity, and the privilege has been given to give themselves, indeed to sacrifice themselves for weaker, suffering creatures."[66]

Linzey became the apostle of "active compassion toward the weak and against the principle of might makes right." He made common cause with the Archbishop of Canterbury, Robert Runcie, for whom the concept of God "precludes the idea of a second-class creation." If "the universe as a whole is a labor of love," and "nothing that is done with love is of little value," a purely humanist and utilitarian conception of animals is forbidden to Christians, according to Linzey and Runcie.[67]

There is also a new trend at the highest level of the Church. Unlike his predecessors, John Paul II invited Christians to respect animals and encouraged animal protection associations. It is also concerned by the protection of the environment. As for Pope Francis, in his encyclical *Laudato si*, he explains: "When our hearts are authentically open to universal communion, this sense of fraternity excludes nothing and no one. . . . We have only one heart, and the same wretchedness which leads us to mistreat an animal will not be long in showing itself in our relationships with other people. Every act of cruelty towards any creature is 'contrary to human dignity.'"[68] He goes on: "The Catechism firmly states that human power has limits and that 'it is contrary to human dignity to cause animals to suffer or die needlessly.'"[69]

Some Jews have become fully conscious of the reduction of

animals to the status of "things"—or "production machines" in the meat industry—and they consider vegetarianism, even veganism, as an inescapable moral imperative. At the beginning of the twentieth century, Isaac Kook, the Grand Rabbi of Palestine, claimed that God loves all creatures and that, before the Flood, he originally intended vegetable food for their consumption. He concluded that the slaughter of animals is a shameful act, and that it is wrong to take the wool from sheep and deprive calves of their mothers' milk. For him vegetarianism was a moral duty.[70] Jonathan Sacks, the Grand Rabbi of the Jewish Communities of the British Commonwealth, has himself become a vegetarian, like David Rosen, former Chief Rabbi of Ireland and honorary president of the Jewish Vegetarian and Ecological Society and a vigorous critic of industrial animal breeding. He is of the opinion that the treatment inflicted on animals by modern methods of commercial production is so cruel that meat produced under these conditions cannot be considered kosher. "Moreover," Rosen tells us, "the wastage of natural resources and the damages caused to the environment by the production of meat constitute a convincing moral argument from the point of view of Judaism for adoption of a vegetarian diet."[71] The scholar Samuel H. Dresner, author of a book well known in the American Jewish community entitled *Jewish Dietary Laws*, acknowledges that "eating kosher meat is a sort of compromise. . . . Ideally people should not eat meat, because to obtain it, an animal must be put to death."[72] One can only share this point of view once one has realized that kosher slaughtering methods are extremely cruel to animals, as can be seen in the images of the documentary film *Earthlings*.[73]

Islam

In the Muslim world, vegetarianism is on the whole an exception. However, a few followers of Islam are of the opinion that ultimately vegetarianism would be the best way to observe the precepts of Islam, since is it not halal to treat an animal like a machine, and animals—who are also creatures of God—deserve our compassion. In *Animal Welfare in Islam*, the scholar Al-Hafiz Basheer Ahmad Masri highlights the teachings of Islam that urge compassion toward animals.[74] He quotes the prophet Muhammad: "He who takes pity [even] on a sparrow and spares its life, Allah will be merciful on him on the Day of Judgment."[75] Regarding hunting and animal fights: "The Prophet was reported as saying: 'Do not make anything having a life as a target,'" and "God's Messenger(s) forbade inciting animals to fight each other."[76] The grand mufti of Marseille, Soheib Bencheikh, has offered the opinion that the sacrifice of a sheep on the occasion of Eid al-Kebir "is neither a pillar of Islam, nor a main obligation comparable to prayer or fasting on Ramadan." He goes further to say that Islamic law permits replacing sacrifice with "making a gift in a country where the inhabitants are not able to eat their fill, and this is closer to the spirit of sharing that is involved in this practice."

Elsewhere, there is a tradition of vegetarianism among certain Sufis. Sufis recommend vegetarianism, especially during periods of retreat, as a means of purifying the body and soul and of mastering the "inner I" (nafs). It seems that the most complete example of vegetarianism comes to us from a woman, Rabia al-Adawiyya. Born in 717 in Basra, she was a great Sufi mystic who spent most of her life in meditation in the deserts of Iraq. Her biographers relate that she lived surrounded by gazelles and antelopes who approached her without fear. A very well-known anecdote recounts how one day a great Sufi master, Hasan al-Basri, came to visit her in her hermitage. He had hardly come near when all the animals ran away. Surprised, Hassan asked Rabia the reason. "What did you eat for lunch?" she asked him. "Onions fried in lard," he admitted. "So, you ate of their flesh, and you're surprised that they run away from you?"

A very little-known fact in the history of Islam is that in the tenth century a group of Muslim philosophers, intentionally anonymous, took the simple name Pure Brethren (Ikhwan al-Safa) and composed a tale entitled "The Case of the Animals versus Man before the King of the Jinn." This story portrays representatives of the animals decrying the pitiful fate that had been imposed on them by humans ever since they were created. It is a poignant denunciation of the mistreatment and slaughter of animals:

We were fully occupied in caring for our broods and rearing our young with all the good food and water God had allotted us, secure and unmolested in our own lands. . . . Ages passed and God created Adam, father of mankind, and made him his vice-regent on earth. His offspring reproduced, and his seed multiplied. They spread over the earth—land and sea, mountain and plain. Men encroached on our ancestral lands. They captured sheep, cows, horses, mules, and asses from among us and enslaved them, subjecting them to the exhausting toil and drudgery of hauling, being ridden, plowing, drawing water, and turning mills . . . . Whoever of us fell into their hands was yoked, haltered, and fettered. They slaughtered and flayed him, ripped open his belly, cut off his limbs and broke his bones, tore out his eyes; plucked his feathers or sheared off his hair or fleece, and put him onto the fire to be cooked, or on the spit to be roasted, or subjected him to even more dire tortures, whose full extent is beyond description. Despite these cruelties, these sons of Adam are not through with us but must claim that this is their inviolable right, that they are our masters and we are their slaves, . . . all with no proof or explanation beyond force alone.[77]

The eleventh-century Muslim philosopher Abû-l'Ala Al-Ma'arri, who was a convinced vegetarian, declared: "I'll be satisfied if, when I appearing before God, I will charged with nothing more than my abstaining from meat."[78]

In the sixteenth century, Akbar, the great Muslim emperor of Mughal India himself, was so impressed by Jainism and the doctrine of nonviolence that he published numerous imperial orders forbidding the slaughter of animals as well as fishing, and he encouraged his subjects not to eat meat for a minimum of six months per year.

It is more than past the time for both the Islamic and Jewish religious authorities to reform their systems of halal and kosher slaughter, which cause the dreadful suffering seen in their slaughterhouses. This ought to be done if for no other reason than the financial one that one system of slaughter would be cheaper than two: the one normal system (if what takes place in the slaughterhouses could be said to be normal) and the other, halal or kosher system. As a result of the present situation in which two systems are in use, according to a report made to the French Ministry of Agriculture in 2011: "Although the demand for halal or kosher meat ought only to amount to 10 percent of the total number of slaughters, it is estimated that the actual volume of ritual slaughters reaches the level of 40 percent of the total for cows and nearly 60 percent for sheep. Thus what should have been no more than a minor exception has become quite general."[79]

The Viewpoint of the Asian Traditions

Much written material has been devoted to the relationship between humans and animals in Western cultures, but relatively few works have reported on the Asian cultures, which have radically different points of view. I am referring to the points of view of Hinduism, Jainism, and especially Buddhism.

Hinduism

Today India is the country in the world where vegetarianism is most widely observed. Let us note that Indian vegetarianism prohibits the consumption of eggs but permits consumption of dairy products. It is estimated that vegetarians represent about 35 percent of the population, which means that there are roughly 450 million vegetarians in India. India has recently instituted a system that calls for visible labels on products that are made with strictly vegetarian ingredients.

Hinduism includes within it a multitude of religious movements, which have different outlooks concerning vegetarianism. The dawn of civilization in India, the Vedic period (ca. 2500–1500 B.C.E.), was not a vegetarian era. Vedic cults called for bloody animal sacrifices. It seems that the notion of *ahimsa* (nonviolence), with vegetarianism as its corollary, appeared sometime in the seventh to sixth centuries B.C.E. under the joint influences of Buddhism, Jainism, and the Hinduist Upanishads. The Upanishads fundamentally challenged the notion of animal sacrifice, which was still being practiced. The following lines can be found in several Hindu texts of this period:

The blood of the animals you slay
Form a sea at your feet.
If in this way you reach the higher realms
What would it be that sends you to hell?

Similarly, the epic *Mahâbhârata*, composed between 300 B.C.E. and 300 C.E., proclaims:

> The meat of animals is like the flesh of our own children.... Does it need to be said that these creatures, who are innocent and in good health, are made for the love of life? But behold they are sought after to be killed by the miserable sinners living in slaughterhouses. For this reason, O King, O Yudhishthir, know that renouncing meat is the greatest refuge of the religion of heaven and happiness. Ahimsa is the greatest of principles. It is also—that, too—the greatest of penances. It is also the greatest of truths among all the proofs of benevolence.[80]

Toward the first century of our era, the "Laws of Manu" (*Mānava-Dharmaśāstra*) adopted a complex and ambivalent attitude toward the consumption of meat. The rules proclaimed in this code of laws continually alternate between permission to eat meat and unconditional vegetarianism. Meat, including the meat of cows, could be eaten by the two highest pure castes, if it had been ritually sacrificed to a deity. The consumption of meat that was not the product of sacrifice was condemned, and considered punishable by experiencing suffering in one's next life identical to the suffering that had been inflicted on the killed animal: "The one whose flesh I eat in this world will eat my flesh in the next."[81] But in other places the Laws condemn eating food containing meat in other terms, appealing for compassion considering the sufferings endured by slaughtered animals: "You can never obtain meat without committing violence against creatures endowed with the breath of life. Killing creatures endowed with the breath of life will cause you to go to hell. Therefore, abstain from eating meat. One who has attentively observed how meat is obtained, the fashion in which incarnated creatures are bound and slain, ought to abstain from eating *all* meat."[82] Over the course of centuries, these laws gained a following, especially in the upper castes. At the present time, brahmins, and especially those who officiate in temples, are strict vegetarians.

In roughly the second century, the Yogashastras, a collection of spiritual and moral rules, reinforced the notion of respect toward all forms of life by establishing vegetarianism as a basic norm, especially for the "pure" castes. In addition, in the first or second century C.E., Thiruvalluvar, a weaver by trade and a sage and philosopher who was part of the Shaivite tradition of South India, wrote in the *Tirukkural:* "One who eats the flesh of an animal in order to fatten his own flesh— how could such a person practice authentic compassion?"[83]

The Vishnaivite sects, and in particular the devotional current centered on the person of Krishna, also emphasize strict vegetarianism. As for the numerous Shaivite sects, they hold divergent views on vegetarianism, and each defines its own dietary rules, whether meat-eating or not.

Within Hinduism, the followers of Bishnoism, who live in the desert regions of Rajasthan, are the ones who have taken benevolence toward animals and respect for all forms of life, animal or vegetable, to the furthest point. This community, which numbers between 600,000 and 800,000, was founded in the fifteenth century by the Hindu sage Jambheshwar Bhagwan, who taught twenty-nine principles (*bishnoi* means "twenty-nine" in Hindi), among which are the practices of meditation morning and evening, and forgiveness and compassion. The Bishnois devote considerable attention to the care of animals. They build shelters for old and sick animals. During community festivals, they refrain from building fires at night so that insects will not be attracted by the light of the flames and be burned. They also abstain from cutting trees. In the sixteenth century, hundreds of Bishnois tried to prevent the powerful Maharajah of Jodhphur from cutting down trees. They paid with their lives for this ecological revolt before its time. Gazelles and antelope are protected by the villagers against the attacks of aboriginal hunters. They nourish and shelter these animals, who walk around in their villages without fear. One-tenth of their grain harvest is reserved for feeding animals, which moreover are not exploited in any way.[84]

In the first half of the twentieth century, Mahatma Gandhi, who struggled for the independence of India while observing fundamental principles of nonviolence, gave fresh impetus to vegetarianism. He frequently stressed the link between vegetarianism and nonviolence, two attitudes that inevitably lead to the benefit of others. "Never would I consent to sacrifice to the human body the life of a lamb," he said, adding, "I hold that the more powerless the creature, the more right it has to be protected by man from the cruelty of man."[85]

Jainism

Of all the great religions, only Jainism has always preached strict vegetarianism and absolute nonviolence toward animals. This religion, which originated in the sixth to fifth centuries B.C.E., was very widespread in ancient India. It still has around five million followers and often exerts a major influence on Indian society.

Following their ideal of nonviolence, or ahimsa, the Jains denounce sacrifices, arranged animal fights, hunting and fishing, and also the consumption of meat. They have built numerous shelters for animals and run a charity-supported hospital for birds in Delhi—the Birds Charitable Hospital—which can accommodate as many as six thousand birds.[86] There, a doctor in an impeccable white frock, a volunteer like all the others, can be seen treating an old rooster suffering from pneumonia; another might be cutting out a cancerous tumor or setting the broken bone of a kite or a pigeon. If a bird cannot be cured and released, the hospital hospice will keep it until it dies.

The Jains take this approach to an extreme. They regard it as their duty to avoid treading on insects or other crawling creatures when they walk. Jain monks tie a cloth over their mouths in order to avoid swallowing insects that might be in the air they breathe. For similar reasons, they filter the water they drink. They even avoid eating vegetables that grow under the earth (potatoes, carrots, etc.) for fear of injuring subterranean fauna such as worms and insects.

In all conservative Jain homes, fires for cooking are not lit in the morning until forty-five minutes after sunrise so that insects will not be drawn into the flame. For the same reason, cooking fires are put out forty-five minutes before sunset.

Buddhism

According to Buddhism, "buddha nature" is present in every being, latent even in beings who do not have the mental faculties necessary to manifest it, such as animals. The special quality of human beings is their ability to draw on buddha nature fully. Realizing the great advantage this gives us indubitably makes us place tremendous value on being human, but it far from gives us a reason to look down on other life forms. In fact, this realization encourages Buddhists to feel greater compassion for beings who are foundering more deeply in ignorance than they are themselves, and it incites them to do everything in their power to alleviate the sufferings of these beings. From the point of view of Buddhism, then, *it is out of the question to use human intelligence for the purpose of exploiting other beings.*

In the *Lankavatara Sutra,* one of the sermons given by Buddha Shakyamuni 2,500 years ago, we read: "Alas, what sort of virtue do these beings practice? They fill their bellies with the flesh of animals, thus spreading fear among the beasts who live in the air, in the water, and on the earth! Practitioners of the Way should abstain from meat, because eating it is a source of terror for beings."[87]

When a Buddhist enters the Way, he utters the following sentence: "In taking the Dharma as refuge, I promise not to harm any being." It is clear that this promise also applies to animals. We may guess that the Buddhist rejects the idea, maintained by the monotheistic religions, that humans were brought into being to occupy the summit of creation, and other creatures were made to satisfy their needs, to feed and amuse them. By contrast, the Buddhist takes the view that all beings have the fundamental right to exist and not to suffer.[88]

Shantideva, a Buddhist master of the eighth century, gives us the essence of this idea in these famous verses:

Since I and other beings both,
In wanting happiness are equal and alike,
What difference is there to distinguish us,
That I should strive to have my bliss alone?

Since I and other beings both,
In fleeing suffering are equal and alike,
What difference is there to distinguish us,
That I should save myself and not the other?[89]

The Dalai Lama gives the following commentary on these verses: "We must protect others from suffering just as we would ourselves and be concerned for their well-being just as much as for our own. When we protect our body, we consider it as one whole entity and protect all parts of it equally. So also all beings form a single whole, for we all have in common the same suffering and happiness, and all the parts of this whole should be treated in the same way."[90]

How Should We Define "Sentient Being"?

A being that is called "sentient" is a living organism capable of distinguishing between well-being and pain and between different ways of being treated—that is, between different conditions that are either favorable to its survival or harmful. It is also capable of reacting in an appropriate fashion, meaning that it is capable of avoiding or moving away from anything that might put an end to its existence and also of seeking out whatever might be favorable to its existence. In Tibetan Buddhism, for example, sentient beings are designated by the word 'gro ba, which means "to go" in the sense of going toward that which is favorable and away from that which might be harmful.

Endowed with subjectivity or not, the natural tendency of an earthworm is to stay alive. To have such a tendency, it is not necessary for a being to possess the intellectual faculties necessary to form concepts such as "pain," "existence," or "finitude." Thus Buddhism makes a distinction between the instinctive reaction of a tiny animal that moves away from a stimulus that is potentially harmful to it and the purely mechanical reaction of a flower that tilts toward the sun through the process of phototropism.[91] The movements of plants are entirely determined from the outside. A plant has no choice—at a given moment, only one direction of movement is possible for it. While the metabolism of a plant reacts instantly, an animal may defer its action.

In the case of the most rudimentary organisms, such reactions obviously do not reflect thought-out activity or a subjective experience of well-being or suffering, but nevertheless they are part of a *continuity* in which a gradual growth in complexity leads to the development of a nervous system that first permits perception of sensations of pain and then the subjective awareness of pain. Acknowledging the existence of such a continuity should lead us to see value in all forms of life and to respect them.

Buddhism and Vegetarianism

All Buddhists are not vegetarians, and Buddhist texts do not unanimously condemn the consumption of meat. Certain sutras of the Great Vehicle, the Mahayana, however, do so unequivocally. An example is the *Lankavatara Sutra*, which states: "So as not to become a source of terror, bodhisattvas established in benevolence should not eat food containing meat. . . . Meat is food for wild beasts; it is unfitting to eat it. . . .[92] People kill animals for profit and exchange goods for the meat. One person kills, another person buys—both are at fault."

Similarly, in the *Great Parinirvana Sutra*, the Buddha says, "Eating meat destroys great compassion" and advises his disciples to avoid the consumption of meat "just as they would avoid the flesh of their own children." Numerous Tibetan masters also condemn consumption of the flesh of animals.[93]

Fifty years after the death of the Buddha, Emperor Ashoka, who embraced Buddhism and vegetarianism at the same time, promulgated several edicts calling for animals to be treated kindly. Most notably, he had precepts engraved on a stone pillar enjoining his subjects to treat animals with kindness and forbidding animal sacrifices throughout his territory.[94]

Chinese and Vietnamese Buddhists are strictly vegetarian. Many Tibetans live on high plateaus, vast plains that are unsuitable for anything but raising herds of yaks, goats, or sheep. Until recently, renouncing eating meat in such conditions would have meant living purely on butter, yogurt (in the summer), and tsampa, the traditional Tibetan dish made from roasted barley flour.[95] These conditions have led the inhabitants of these plains, nomads for the most part, to live off their herds. Moreover, most Tibetans are very fond of meat.

In spite of this, they are quite aware of the immoral aspect of their behavior and attempt to compensate for it by killing only the number of animals strictly necessary for their survival. Exiled in India and Nepal, more and more Tibetan monasteries have stopped authorizing the use of meat in the meals prepared in their kitchens.

For the Buddhist in general, to be vegetarian or vegan (especially in industrialized countries) is a means of manifesting his or her compassion toward animals. In contrast to the view of Hindu vegetarians, for Buddhists meat is not impure in itself. In principle, Buddhists would find nothing wrong with eating the flesh of an animal that had died from natural causes.

Going beyond merely being vegetarian, many Buddhist practitioners have regularly followed the practice of buying animals marked for slaughter and then freeing them in their natural habitat or handing them over to shelters where they are well treated. For example, we read in the autobiography of the Tibetan hermit Shabkar (1781–1851) that over the course of his life he saved the lives of hundreds of thousands of animals. In Tibet animals that are "redeemed" in this fashion end their days in peace with the rest of their herd. This practice is still current among the Buddhist faithful. In Bhutan, where Buddhism is the predominant religion, hunting and fishing are prohibited throughout the country.

European Admiration for India and Vegetarianism

The sophist Philostratus of Athens recounts in his biography of Apollonius of Tyana that this Neo-Pythagorean philosopher of the first century C.E. paid a visit to the brahmins of Taxila and thereafter became an advocate of vegetarianism. Apollonius proclaimed that "the earth provides all that is necessary for humanity; and those who are happy to live in peace with creation as it is ask for nothing more from it," whereas meat eaters, he goes on, "deaf to the cries of mother earth, sharpen their knives against her own children." Apollonius tells us that this is just "what the brahmins of India taught."[96] Similarly, the hermit Saint Jerome, who lived in the fourth and fifth centuries, declared that the example of the brahmins was worthy of being followed by Christians. During the same period, Palladius, the bishop of Helenopolis, depicted the brahmin Dandamis as disdaining the gifts made to him by Alexander the Great, replying to the great man, "The earth provides me with everything, just as a mother gives milk to her child," before adding with irony that "it is better to be thrown as food to wild beasts than to make of oneself a tomb for other creatures."[97]

In *The Bloodless Revolution*, the English historian Tristram Stuart describes how, beginning in the seventeenth century, a number of

European travelers began discovering Indian civilization and were fascinated by the doctrine of ahimsa, nonviolence. These travelers were astonished to note the existence of hospitals for animals and shelters for elderly beasts, things that were totally unthinkable in the Europe of this time. They became aware of the prevalence of vegetarianism in Indian society and the widespread benevolence of Indians toward all animals, even the most humble. As Gérard Busquet explains in his *Vaches sacrées et chiens maudits* (Sacred Cows and Cursed Dogs), these European travelers were amazed to see wild animals such as deer, antelope, cranes, and storks wandering peacefully around the villages. These Westerners, having come from societies where all animal life, apart from domestic animals, was avidly hunted down or pitilessly exterminated, could not comprehend this kind of benevolent attitude dictated by the religious and cultural factors prevailing in southern Asia.[98]

Some of the travelers mocked the customs of the Indians, but others were impressed by their system of morality, which was completely unknown in the West. The existence of a very advanced civilization that showed such great respect toward animals posed a radical challenge to the Christian idea of humanity as the ruler of creation. The surprising revelation of this view of animals engendered a crisis in the European conscience of the time. Many intellectuals were attracted to the Asian moral approach, and a number of works appeared that helped to popularize these "exotic" views with the general public. Discussions began to take place that heralded our debates of today on the subject of vegetarianism and the treatment of animals.

The Animal Liberation Movement

Two movements appeared in Europe. The first promoted a "scientific" vegetarianism, claiming that it was better for health than a diet containing meat. Three of the great philosophers of the seventeenth century, Descartes (who, as we have seen, legitimized the slaughtering of animals, of which he had the most inhumane notions), Pierre Gassendi, and Francis Bacon came together in agreement that vegetarianism is the diet that suits humans the best. Bacon cataloged the many vegetarians known in history who were famous for their remarkable longevity: the Essenes, the Spartans, the Hindus, and many Christian ascetics.

The second movement put itself forward as the champion of compassion toward animals, which its followers felt should be considered sentient beings just as human beings are. The English merchant and writer Thomas Tryon, who had looked on with horror as his Christian compatriots whipped the slaves on the plantations of Barbados hour after hour through the day, also became an ardent advocate of the animal cause. In 1683 he published an imaginary dialogue between an Indian brahmin and a Frenchman that became quite popular.[99] In it, he praised the moral greatness of the brahmins, their virtuous temperance, and their respect for animal life. He concluded that, if one shows a lack of compassion toward animals, one ends up lacking compassion toward human beings as well.

Tryon opposed Hobbes, who averred that human beings have rights over animals simply because they have the power to exercise them. The idea that he put forward was that "might makes right." Tryon, on the other hand, proposed to grant animals the right to live independently of human interests, and he exerted pressure on the English parliament to recognize "the rights of man and of innocent and defenceless creatures who have no protectors in this world."[100] He spoke of the unity of living beings as "co-citizens of the world."

Letters Writ by a Turkish Spy, a novel comprising fictional letters in seven volumes (the first of which was published in French in 1686 and was attributed to Giovanni Paolo Marana), portrays an Ottoman man, the spy Mahmoud, who is discovering the history, customs, and mores of Europe.[101] This novel, which was immensely successful, was an indictment of established religions, as ruthless as it was ironic. Moreover, it contained a condemnation of the manner in which Christians had made use of the Bible to justify their "gluttony, their cruelty, and their arrogance" with regard to animals. In this way it played a role in the promotion of vegetarianism in Europe.

Bernardin de Saint-Pierre, a writer and a friend of Henri Rousseau's, was a convinced vegetarian. Also a convinced vegetarian was the great Swedish naturalist Carl von Linné, who opposed his colleague George-Louis de Buffon, to whom killing animals was a "legitimate and innocent" practice.[102]

The great scientist Isaac Newton wanted to extend the commandment "love your neighbor as yourself" to include animals. He was highly praised by Voltaire for having shown that it was completely contradictory to both recognize that animals have feelings and at the same time cause them to suffer.[103] As we have seen, Voltaire did not mince words about the idea that animals were put entirely at humans' disposition by the Lord: "In the end it is only too certain that the disgusting carnage that is continuously on display in our butcheries and in our kitchens does not seem to us to be an evil thing; but on the contrary, we regard this often pestilential horror to be a blessing of the Lord, and on top of that we have prayers in which we give thanks to him for these murders. But what could be more abominable than to continually nourish oneself on corpses?"[104]

Arthur Schopenhauer was inspired by India and Buddhism, among other influences. He had a strong sympathy for animals that caused him to rail against the positions of Kant and Descartes, as well as against the anthropocentrism of the Judeo-Christian tradition in general: "It is claimed that animals have no rights; we convince ourselves that our conduct with regard to them has no bearing on morality— or to speak in the language of *that* morality—that we have no duties with regard to animals. This is a revolting doctrine, a crude and barbarous one, which has its home in the West and its roots in Judaism. But in philosophy, we base it on the hypothesis of an absolute difference between man and animal, accepted in spite of the evidence."[105]

In an unpublished essay called "On the Vegetable System of Diet," the great English poet Percy Bysshe Shelley declared that causing animals to suffer so as to be able to eat their flesh was "detrimental to the peace of human society."[106] In his poem entitled "Queen Mab," Shelley imagined that a day in the future will come for man when "no longer now / He slays the lamb that looks him in the face, / And horribly devours his mangled flesh."[107] An ecologist before his time, he says elsewhere that "the meat on which rich men gorge is literally grain stolen from the mouth of the poor," since the amount of nutritive plant matter necessary to fatten a cow could provide ten times more food for subsistence if edible vegetables were planted in its stead. He maintained that at the rate the human population was bound to increase, it would become necessary in time to adopt a vegetarian diet, for only such a diet would be able to meet the increased needs of humanity. Malthus, who thought that abandoning the consumption of meat was a desirable eventuality, rallied to Shelley's point of view. In 1881 the playwright George Bernard Shaw, inspired by the writings of Shelley, became a vegetarian and was soon followed in this by Leo Tolstoy.

Many of the thinkers who spoke out in favor of the animal cause—Voltaire, Shaftesbury, Bentham, Mill, and Shaw—were also the ones who were the most ardent advocates of respect for the rights of man. These ideas were taken up in a more rigorous manner in 2003 by Colin Tudge, a researcher at the London School of Economics, who showed that the world will run short of tillable land if the growing levels of meat production are not reduced.[108]

The Darwinian Revolution and Its Consequences

Darwin profoundly transformed our vision of the relationships among the various forms of life by showing in a masterly fashion that, in the course of millions of years of evolution, species exhibit only gradual transitions from one to the next. This brought about a major upheaval in our outlook, because what Darwin had demonstrated is that the differences between human beings and animals are far from being as fundamental as had been presumed: "We have seen that the senses and intuitions, the various emotions and faculties, such as love, memory, attention, curiosity, imitation, reason, etc., of which man boasts, may be found in an incipient, or even sometimes in a well-developed condition, in the lower animals."[109]

In his journal, he also writes that "man in his arrogance thinks he is a masterwork, worthy of the act of a god. It is more humble, and in my opinion, more true to see him as having been created out of the basis provided by the animals."[110] Here for the first time we see the emergence of the idea that the difference between humans and animals is only one of degree and variation, not a difference in nature. Darwin also shows himself to be solicitous of the well-being of animals and insistent on respect for them. Notably, he states: "Humanity toward inferior animals is one of the noblest of virtues with which man is endowed, and it is part of the final stage of the development of moral sentiments. It is only when we become concerned for the totality of sentient beings that our morality attains its highest level."[111]

As Schopenhauer tells us, a movement championing animals was born in the nineteenth century. Schopenhauer writes: "In Europe, also, day by day a feeling for animals is awakening." His essay concludes, "Compassion for animals is so intimately connected to kindness that we can well say that anybody who is cruel to animals cannot be a good man."[112]

In the twentieth century, at the end of the 1960s and in the 1970s, a new animal movement arose, the effects of which have continued to grow down to the present day. This movement has set the stage for a major change in the attitude toward animals in Western societies. A half century after the publication of Upton Sinclair's novel *The Jungle*, there came *Animal Machines: The New Factory Farming Industry*, in which Ruth Harrison once more described the abominable conditions that then prevailed and continue to prevail in the meat production industry. A short while after this book appeared, the Oxford Group was formed, which brought together a number of intellectuals and public figures around the psychologist Richard Ryder. Ryder published several articles and pamphlets decrying abuse of which animals are the victims. In 1970 one of his essays introduced a new term, *speciesism*, which he put forward to call attention to the fact that our attitude toward animals derives from the same kind of mentality as racism or sexism. He described his "eureka" moment as follows:

The 1960s revolutions against racism, sexism and classism nearly missed out the animals. This worried me. Ethics and politics at the time simply overlooked the nonhumans entirely. Everyone seemed to be just preoccupied with reducing the prejudices against humans. Hadn't they heard of Darwin? I hated racism, sexism and classism, too, but why stop there? As a hospital scientist I believed that hundreds of other species of animals suffer fear, pain and distress much as I did. Something had to be done about it. We needed to draw the parallel between the plight of the other species and our own. One day in 1970, lying in my bath at the old Sunningwell Manor, near Oxford, it suddenly came to me: SPECIESISM! I quickly wrote a leaflet and circulated it around Oxford.[113]

At the beginning, no one paid any attention to this pamphlet—until Peter Singer, a student at Oxford, got in contact with Richard Ryder and then went on to launch the concept of "animal liberation." In 1975 Singer wrote a book on this subject that reached an international audience. The title of the book, *Animal Liberation*, became the name of the movement.[114] Other voices arose that enriched the debate, in particular those of the principal theoretician of the animal rights movement, Tom Regan, and of primatologists Jane Goodall and Frans de Waal, who took the movement further by showing that animals feel very varied and complex emotions, including empathy. More recently, we have also heard from the writer Jonathan Safran Foer, and many other writers are speaking of animal ethics, animal rights, and in general of our relationship to animals.

The Rise of Nongovernmental Organizations Dedicated to the Protection of the Environment and Animals

The emergence of NGOs as actors in social life and politics in the areas of environment, development, social action, human rights, and the rights of animals will certainly be remembered as a most significant phenomenon of the end of the twentieth century. According to Rémi Parmentier, one of the founders of Greenpeace International,

> Among the NGOs active in the protection of animals, we must distinguish two schools which agree in most cases but conflict with each other in some others: those whose mission is the pro-

tection of biodiversity in an environmental context (Greenpeace, the WWF, EIA,[115] or Oxfam) and those whose mandate is the protection of animal life as such (the IFAW [International Fund for Animal Welfare] and Sea Shepherd are two representative examples). At the end of the day, whether it is in speaking out for the protection of the animals with whom we share our lives or for the ecosystems that sustain all life on earth, both schools demand, each in its own way, that we critically reconsider the belief according to which humanity is at the center of the world.[116]

Kindness, altruistic love, and compassion are qualities that do not harmonize well with bias. Restricting the field of our compassion not only diminishes it quantitatively but also qualitatively. Applying our compassion only to certain beings, human beings in this case, makes it a lesser and a poorer thing.

There is no doubt a great deal left to do, but it is beyond argument that the Western world is becoming more and more aware of the fact that it cannot pretend to uphold decent and coherent moral values and at the same time exclude from the ethical field the majority of the sentient beings who populate the earth.

2

OUT OF SIGHT, OUT OF MIND

Without doubt it would take a great deal of time and energy and a lot of resources to put an end to the various forms of violence, abuse, and discrimination that continue to trouble our fellow human beings. But today these practices are increasingly disapproved of and more and more widely seen as unacceptable.

But the various ways in which animals are mistreated still are most often ignored, tolerated, or even approved. Why are they ignored? Because the overwhelming majority of these abusive practices are inflicted on animals far from public view, in industrial breeding facilities and in slaughterhouses. And the agro-industrial and food-processing industries exercise tacit but very tight censorship, making sure that no shocking images are allowed to get beyond the walls of their torture chambers. Today in the rich countries, the animals one sees are not the animals one eats. A study carried out in the United States revealed that, in urban environments, most five-year-old children did not know where the meat they ate came from. To the question, "Do you eat animals?" the majority of them emphatically replied, "No!" as though they were shocked by the very idea.[1] The fact is, children almost always feel natural sympathy for animals and are very affectionate toward the ones they spend time with.

Leo Tolstoy and his whole family were strict vegetarians. His daughter recounts that a meat-eating aunt who was invited to lunch notified the Tolstoys that she would absolutely insist on eating meat. When she got to the table, she found a living chicken tied to her chair and a sharp knife next to her plate![2] It has been shown that the great majority of human beings feel profound revulsion at having to kill one of their fellow humans,[3] but killing an animal is also a disturbing act. In order to avoid the aversion of a consumer to seeing the live animal he or she is going to eat or being reminded of all the sufferings it must have endured before arriving on the consumer's plate, the flesh of the animal, having become "meat," is presented as an innocuous manufactured product. As a result, the consumer no longer makes the connection between her food and the being that has lost its life to provide it.

Paul Claudel noted in 1947:

> In my youth, the streets were full of horses and birds. They have disappeared. The inhabitants of the big cities no longer see animals except in the form of the dead flesh sold to them at the butcher's. . . . Nowadays, a cow is a living laboratory. . . . The wandering and adventurous chicken is now incarcerated and scientifically force-fed. Its egg-laying has become a matter of mathematics. . . . What is left of the animals is useful machines, living storage for raw material.[4]

A good number of children do not become accustomed to eating meat except as a result of their parents' insistence. In addition we have the deliberate efforts of the food industry to deceive the public about the nature of modern farms. An impenetrable screen is created between the public and reality. In books that contain pictures and drawings of animals on the farm, we see them frolicking gaily and living in tender relations with their little ones in spacious places where life is sweet.

See No Evil, Speak No Evil: How to Keep the Issue off the Table

With very rare exceptions,[5] what happens *every day* at industrial meat-production sites is *never* shown on television. A few remarkable documentaries; such as *Earthlings*; *Food, Inc.*; and *LoveMEATender*;[6] produced despite considerable obstacles, are never telecast on the public networks. Every time Shaun Monson, the director of *Earthlings*, contacted television channels to get his film shown, he received the reply that his images ran the risk of shocking children and other sensitive viewers. In 2009 PETA, the largest international organization working to reduce mistreatment of animals, was ready to pay $2 million (the price of a one-minute TV ad during a U.S. football game on Thanksgiving Day) to the NBC television network to show a relatively innocuous publicity spot depicting a family about to eat their traditional Thanksgiving turkey. In the spot, when one of the parents asks the little girl to say grace before the meal, she recounts the cruel fate the turkey had to face in being slaughtered. The only images were those of the family at the table, but the network refused to broadcast the spot.[7]

It is of course not at all the case that the media and television shy away from images that might offend sensitive souls. They continually broadcast images of war, terrorist attacks, and natural catastrophes with the goal of providing information and, in some cases, of arousing our compassion and encouraging us to come to the aid of victims. As for horror movies, although of course they are not recommended for children, they are nevertheless shown on television all through the year, without that seeming to pose the least problem to the consciences of the programmers.

In the rich countries, with a few exceptions—in rural locations, among small-scale breeders, hunters, fishers, and others who are in contact with nature—the fate of the creatures we eat is concealed by means of a multitude of precautions. Everything is done to keep the consumer in ignorance. Industrial agro-businesses (aka, Big Ag) and the food-production industry play on the fact that we like to eat meat, always more of it, and as cheaply as possible. With this in mind, they work with the fluctuation of supply and demand to continually ensure solid profits for the whole of this sector.

The heads of the industries in question say that they have no reason to be ashamed of their activities. But if their consciences were at rest, why would they go to such trouble to conceal what they do? They know very well that, if consumers saw what takes place on the industrial breeding sites and in the slaughterhouses, the demand for their products would diminish spectacularly.

Thus it is hardly surprising that the leaders of these industries systematically keep their sites off-limits to journalists and other people who want to visit them, and they make sure that their factories are guarded like top-security military installations.

As Aymeric Caron remarks, "Has anyone ever known a school to organize a field trip to a slaughterhouse? Never. Why? Where does this sense of shame come from that obliges us to keep silent in front of our children about the fate that we impose on animals? Throat-cutting, electrocution, and evisceration—are these scenes that would be obscene in the eyes of innocents? The answer is yes."[8]

In brief, we do not reflect on these matters very much, because we are given very little opportunity to become aware of how serious they are. According to the philosopher Élisabeth de Fontenay:

> The amnesia that creates our reality by blotting out our ordinary practices and the everyday cruelty that is part and parcel of them carries a very simple name: indifference. We are not bloodthirsty and sadistic; we are indifferent, passive, blasé, aloof, uncaring, callous, vaguely complicit, and bloated with humanistic good conscience; and we are made that way by the unfeeling collusion of monotheistic culture, technoscience, and economic imperatives. Once again, the fact of not knowing what others do for us, of not being informed, is far from constituting an excuse; rather it represents an aggravating circumstance for beings endowed with consciousness, recall, imagination and responsibility, which is what with quite good reason we pretend to be.[9]

In the case of experimentation on animals, the places where it is carried out are set up in such a way that the public never sees the living animals that are brought in nor the dead ones that are carried out. Peter Singer reports that, in the United States, a guide for the use of animals in experiments advises laboratories to install an incinerator, because the sight of tons of animal corpses thrown out like ordinary garbage "would certainly not increase the esteem of the public for the research center in question."[10]

False Advertising

The big companies connected with animal production, as Jocelyne Porcher points out, can no longer even be dignified with the name of "breeders."[11] They are not content with merely concealing their activities, but they go beyond that to carrying out campaigns of disinformation. In an attractive ad, Kentucky Fried Chicken (KFC) proclaims that it is "attentive to the wellbeing and humane treatment of chickens" and "only deals with suppliers who promise to respect the strict norms that we have established and who share our commitment to animal wellbeing." These pretty words are sadly deceptive. As reported by Jonathan Safran Foer, investigations have clearly established that, at the two main suppliers of KFC—Tyson Foods and Pilgrim's Pride, the two biggest chicken-processing companies in the world, which kill more than five billion fowl a year—employees were tearing the heads off live birds, spitting chewing tobacco juice into their eyes, spray-painting their faces, and violently stomping on them as well as throwing them violently against the walls and ripping off their beaks.[12] These aberrant behaviors are unfortunately more frequent than we imagine.

The idyllic advertisements of Frank Perdue, another major U.S. chicken-processing firm, averred that the chickens on its "farms" are pampered and "led a very nice life."[13] A well-known animal advocate, Henry Spira, revealed in a full-page ad in the *New York Times* that Frank Perdue raised his chickens in buildings 140 meters in length that housed 27,000 chickens, and that his system of mass production alone killed 6.8 million chickens per week.[14]

The philosopher Jean-François Nordmann cites the case of a billboard for a delicatessen called Noblet, which depicted a large pig in tears being consoled by a little girl: "Don't cry, big fellow, you are going to Noblet."[15] The animal artist Sue Coe recounts that the enclosing wall around John's Slaughterhouse and Meat Packing Plant, the largest factory for the processing of meat in Los Angeles, is entirely covered with painted scenes showing an idyllic countryside where manifestly happy pigs and cows gambol and play. In a verdant setting, under a blue sky adorned with fluffy white clouds, we see children at play, appealing dogs, a farm with lovely red barns, flowering trees full of birds, and animals romping in green pastures. These kinds of scenes cover not only the walls but the windows as well. The result is that is it impossible to see the inside of the slaughterhouse. The reality inside the walls of these hangars, Sue Coe writes, is quite different:

> The sky might be blue, but who can see it? There is not a blade of grass. The stifling heat is foul with the smell of meat. . . . It seems that the pigs are certainly not swooning with pleasure as suggested by the murals painted on the walls. It's a pity that "Farmer" John did not also provide peaceful sound effects to cover their cries. . . .
>
> The mass of pigs is pushed along in an indescribable crush that leaves behind the ones who can no longer walk or are dead. Blood drips from their mouths and noses, others have broken backs. Sometimes they are left for days in the heat without water—until they die or are dragged to the slaughter. . . . This whole process is concealed. Animal flesh is now a commodity for consumption just like soft drinks, toilet bowl detergents, and sliced bread.[16]

The slaughterhouse walls are not made of glass. And who would want to look through them if they were? More than a century ago, Ralph Waldo Emerson observed, "You have just dined, and however scrupulously the slaughterhouse is concealed in the graceful distance of miles, there is complicity."

Cognitive Distance and Rationalization

Sometimes we take care of our domestic animals as though they were our own children. Sometimes we hunt animals down and kill them for our pleasure. Sometimes again, we wear their fur with vain pleasure. We pass from one attitude to another without thinking twice about it, with no sense that there is anything at stake, but for the animals themselves, it is a matter of life and death. In her book *Why We Love Dogs, Eat Pigs, and Wear Cows*, Melanie Joy invites us to a moment of reflection:

> Imagine for a moment the following scenario: You are a guest at an elegant dinner party. You're seated with the other guests

at an ornately set table. The room is warm, candlelight flickers across crystal wine glasses, and the conversation is flowing freely. Mouthwatering smells of rich foods emanate from the kitchen. You haven't eaten all day, and your stomach is growling.

At last, after what feels like hours, your friend who is hosting the party emerges from the kitchen with a steaming pot of savory stew. You serve yourself a generous portion, and after eating several mouthfuls of tender meat, you ask your friend for the recipe.

"I'd be happy to tell you," she replies. "You begin with five pounds of golden retriever meat, well marinated, and then . . ." *Golden retriever?* You probably freeze midbite as you consider her words: the meat in your mouth is from a *dog*.

What now? Do you continue eating? Or are you revolted by the fact that there's golden retriever on your plate, and you've just eaten some? Do you pick out the meat and eat the vegetables around it? If you are like most Americans, when you hear that you've been eating dog, your feelings would automatically change from pleasure to some degree of revulsion.[17]

While most Westerners love their dog almost like another member of their family, the same is not true in certain Asian cultures, where dogs are not only eaten but also subjected to terrible cruelties. In China, Vietnam, and Cambodia most notably, millions of dogs and cats are killed every year for food. Worse, according to a popular Chinese belief, if a dog is tortured before being killed, its meat has more flavor. Thus it is not at all rare for dogs to be hung up by their hind legs and beaten severely before being cut to pieces or immersed while still alive in boiling water. They are sometimes skinned alive. Their skins are removed from the top down, as if a piece of clothing. Investigators from the association One Voice reported having seen people in a restaurant beating a curled up and moaning dog with a club until it lost consciousness. Then they bled it outside on the sidewalk. Its blood spread under cages full to bursting with more terrorized dogs waiting to undergo the same treatment.[18] A growing number of Chinese disapprove of these practices, but they still go on quite commonly throughout the country.

According to the psychologist Albert Bandura, our ability to turn our normative moral judgments on and off explains how it is possible for people to be cruel one moment and full of compassion the next.[19] Our moral sense can be turned off in a number of ways, and doing so has cumulative effects: it is habit-forming. People come to associate a desirable result with the reprehensible acts needed to accomplish it, and this enables them to close their eyes to the suffering these acts cause. This cognitive incongruity leads to a progressive loss of sensitivity to the suffering caused by the acts in question.

The philosopher Martin Gibert comes to the following conclusion:

> What is at once surprising and rather depressing is that we are all fundamentally in agreement on the questions of animal ethics. Nobody denies the horror of industrial breeding or of the slaughterhouses. Nobody seriously believes that it is morally acceptable to mistreat and kill sentient, intelligent, and social beings like pigs just because bacon is yummy. If we add to that the environmental considerations, everyone without exception should be vegan, or at least promote and encourage veganism. Whence the question arises: Why is this not the case?[20]

The Use of Euphemistic Language

In food-production and meat-processing systems, when somebody talks about "taking care of the piglets," what it really means is cutting off their tails without anaesthetic. It is said that the piglet does not feel any pain, only "nociception." Imagine that somebody was about to cut off your little finger and they told you, "Don't worry, there's no pain: it's just nociception." The term *nociception,* invented by Charles Sherrington in 1906, refers to the avoidance reflexes triggered by noxious stimuli (mechanical, chemical, or thermic) that threaten the integrity of the organism. It also refers to the purely physiological reactions brought about by these stimuli. By contrast, "pain" is spoken of when the nociception is modulated by cognitive and emotional factors. As Élisabeth de Fontenay points out:

> Unfortunately, it is the INRA [Institut National de la Recherche Agronomique] in France that conducts the majority of the work on

this issue, the goal of which is to reduce the pain caused by techniques used in breeding and slaughtering. Yet still quite recently, the researchers of this agronomic research center refused to recognize that animals experience pain and in their regard spoke only of nociception. It is extremely important that we not let these issues be hijacked by the zootechnicians. Individuals arising from many species not only have environments, they also have worlds, worlds that correspond to their subjectivities and which have areas of conflict with ours.[21]

In a so-called "rationalized" breeding program, when "unproductive" animals (that is, pigs that are not gaining weight fast enough) are eliminated, sometimes with the greatest brutality, it is called "technical slaughter."[22] To call things by their real names would offend the sensibilities of consumers and harm the reputation of the firm. As for hens, once they have laid three hundred eggs in one year and begin to lay less frequently, they are "reformed." This amounts to transforming them into bouillon cubes, ravioli, or chopped meat for cats and dogs. In general their bodies are not in good enough condition to be presented as cooking chickens.

The emotions and reactions of animals are always described using sanitized vocabulary. According to Peter Singer, cleaned-up terms make it possible for science students, who are not sadists, to pursue their experiments without feeling empathy for the animals they are using.[23] Their jargon speaks of electric shocks or prolonged deprivation of drink or food as techniques of "extinction." And when an animal is subjected to a painful situation that it tries by all means to avoid, this situation is known as a "negative stimulus." Moreover, as reported by a veterinarian, animals used for research are sometimes referred to by the phrase "standardized biological research tools." This kind of vocabulary obviously does not prevent an animal from being what it is—that is, a sentient being. As Mary Midgley remarks, "A bird is far from being only a machine; it is not a machine at all. No one manufactured it."[24]

In the English language, as the writer Joan Dunayer explains, the correct grammatical form for speaking of an animal (with the exception of a pet) is not "he" or "she"; it is the neuter pronoun "it," which refers to things. And in French, one would ask a fisher or trapper, "Have you caught anything?" but never "Did you catch anybody?" The commonplace quality of this kind of usage shows to what degree our vision of nonhuman sentient beings remains limited. If the maître d' at a restaurant asked you, "How did you find that person's flesh?" that might run the risk of ruining your appetite.[25]

This disguising of reality, remarks the neuroscientist and philosopher Georges Chapouthier, leads to our using a whole series of neutral terms to cover up the fact that, when it comes down to it, and as unpleasant an idea as it may be, people are eating corpse. The fact that the pieces of corpse that are being served are so nicely called "filet mignon" or "veal filet" or "sirloin" help the buyer or consumer assume an outlook in which she truly forgets that the "main course" that she is eating is a piece of flesh. "The manner of disguise may sometimes be symbolic," writes Chapouthier, "as is the case in a certain number of savage sports, such as fox hunting and bullfighting. In the latter a colorful display of sights and sounds is put on so that the torture of the animal by the humans disappears behind a symbolic combat that pits a superior being of light and beauty (the human) to a base and evil inferior being (the animal). The symbolic showmanship, here too, is an attempt to cause the reality of the facts at hand to be forgotten, to disguise what is real."[26]

We do not eat corpse, we eat "butcher's meat." We do not "kill" the animals used in scientific research, we "use up laboratory materials." Animals may either be called "domestic" or "wild" beasts. When a man behaves in a brutal fashion, it may be said that he is "bestial." When he is benevolent and kind, he shows his "humanity." With this usage that we have developed, Chapouthier concludes, "we drown atrocity in language perfumed with rosewater."

As Brian Luke points out, "An enormous amount of social energy is spent to prevent, undermine, and overcome our sympathies toward animals, so that vivisection, breeding, and hunting can continue."[27] The heads of the meat industry as well as the consumers make use of this same energy to hide the sad reality of the process that transforms living beings into products for consumption.

Is it acceptable just to look the other way? When one brings up the subject of animals and the way we treat them, Jean-Christophe Bailly notes in his *Le versant animal (The Animal Side)*, our remarks not only fall flat but they provoke a kind of irritated embarrassment, "a little as though one had inadvertently crossed a line and blundered into something improper or even obscene."[28] Would it not be better to have the honesty and the courage to face this no-go zone of embarrassment and call upon the potential for humanity that each one of us possesses?

The Truth from the Mouths of Babes

When Brazilian Luiz Antonio was a little boy, three years old, his mother put cooked octopus on his plate. In the video she took, he looked attentively at his dish and began a more or less Socratic dialog with his mother. Pausing after each phrase, he reflected and then passed on to the next stage of his reasoning, which strikes as disarmingly lucid:

LUIZ: This octopus . . . it's not a real one, is it?

MOM: No.

L: So, it's really . . . it doesn't talk, it doesn't have a head, right?

M: It doesn't have a head. There's just his little legs that were cut off for you.

L: Huh? But . . . the head is in the ocean?

M: The head is at the fish market.

L [puzzled]: The man cut it off? Like that? [Luiz makes a cutting gesture.]

M: Yeah, he cut it off.

L: Why?

M: So you could eat it. Otherwise you'd have to swallow it all up whole.

L: But why?

M: To be able to eat it, my love. The same way a cow is cut into pieces and a chicken is cut up into pieces.

L: Huh? A chicken? No way, nobody eats chickens!

M: Nobody eats chickens?

L: No . . . they're animals!

M: Really?

L: Yes!

M: Well then . . . we'll eat some gnocchi and some potatoes.

L: Okay . . . just some potatoes and rice.

M: Okay.

L: Octopuses are animals.

M: Yes.

L: Fish are animals . . . chickens are animals . . . cows are animals
. . . pigs are animals.

M: Right.

L: So! When you eat animals, they die!

M: Well, yes.

L: But why?

M: So we can eat them, my love.

L: But why do they have to die? . . . I don't want them to die . . . I
want them to stay standing up.

M: Okay then. So we're not going to eat them anymore, all right?

L: Okay! . . . Those animals . . . we have to take care of them . . . not
eat them!

M: [says nothing, then laughs tenderly]: You're right, son. So go
on and eat your potatoes and rice.

L: Good . . . Why are you crying?

M: I'm not crying . . . You just touched my feelings.

L: I did something good?

M: [laughing and crying at the same time]: Go on, eat. You don't
have to eat octopus, okay?

L: Okay![29]

In two minutes and forty seconds, in a video that was watched by
millions of people, we see Luiz carry out a faultless piece of reasoning
without letting himself be thrown off track: he cannot simultaneously
love animals and accept that they die to be served on his plate. The
force of his words comes from the fact that no one in the world would
dare accuse a child of three of being an extremist being manipulated
by an animal rights organization.

But does it have to be a child who reveals the naked truth? Are the
majority of adults incapable of carrying out this same reasoning, or

have they relegated it to the dark dustbin of their bad conscience? Or are they suffering from a shrinkage of the visual field of their compassion?

In her novel *The Abyss*, Marguerite Yourcenar describes the revulsion of her main character toward eating meat: "It repelled him to be digesting death's agony."[30] Many children do no not want to eat the meat they have on their plates, seeing it as the flesh of the animals they encounter in their everyday lives. But their parents insist, giving the excuse that it is good for their health. It is not until the end of the discussion that little Luiz's mother breaks down in tears, moved by the accuracy of his argument, which sees things as they are.

A friend told me about a little girl who was present when a pig, beloved by her family, was having its throat cut. Seeing that it was bleeding after the first cut of her father's knife, she cried out, "Daddy, Daddy, call Mama so she can put a Band-Aid on!"

Jane Goodall, the well-known primatologist and specialist in studying chimpanzees, recounted to me that, the day when her five-year-old grand nephew found out where chicken meat came from, he decided without hesitation that he would no longer eat chicken. And that was the last time he did. Then one day, when he was visiting an aquarium, he declared, "I'm not going to eat these pretty fish anymore." After that, he visited a part of the aquarium that had less brightly colored fish in it, and he watched them for a long time and then concluded, "You know, in fact, I'm not going to eat *any* fish anymore."

But often, the parents win the child over to their point of view, and the child gets used to eating flesh. You can get used to anything. We have turned suffering into an acceptable commonplace, we have desensitized ourselves to the suffering of others. We have learned to distance ourselves, withdraw ourselves, from the spectacle of the suffering that we cause, directly or indirectly. We have achieved moral dissociation between certain harmful activities we commit and the rest of our existence, and this allows us human beings to perpetrate deeds that our conscience disapproves of without detesting ourselves because of it.

3

EVERYBODY LOSES

Effects of Industrial Breeding and
Meat Eating on Poverty, the
Environment, and Health

Before even considering the moral questions involved, people who like
eating meat—and are willing to come to terms with the fact that we
massacre billions of animals per year so we can eat them—should, for
the sake of themselves and their children, worry about the real-world
consequences of excessive consumption of meat and its corollaries,
industrial livestock breeding and industrial fishing.[1] Animals are the
first victims, and certainly they ought to be protected for their own
sake. However, the fact that sixty billion land animals and a thousand billion marine animals are killed every year for our consumption
also has a deleterious effect on the environment and, thus, on human
beings. Every year, 775 million tons of grain and 200 million tons of
soy (90 percent of world production), which could be used to feed the
inhabitants of the countries where they are grown, are set aside to
feed livestock used for meat production in the developed countries.
This of course aggravates the already grave situation of the poorest
populations of the world.[2] Moreover, the conclusions of scientific
research presented by several synoptic reports to the United Nations
(GIEC and FAO)[3] as well as by the Worldwatch Institute and several
other organizations indicate that this disproportionate emphasis on
the industrial production of animals has significant negative impacts
on the environment. That means that it will have significant negative
impacts on the conditions future generations will face, and it is already
having negative effects on human health. The following few statistics
should enable the reader to form his or her own judgment:

- Animal breeding contributes 14.5 percent of the greenhouse gas emissions linked to human activities, putting it in second place after construction[4] and before transport.
- To produce 1 kilogram of meat (2.2 pounds) requires 10 kilograms of food materials, which could be used to feed the populations of the poor countries that produce them.[5]
- Sixty percent of the available land in the world is used for animal breeding.
- Animal breeding by itself consumes 45 percent of all the water used for the production of food materials.
- By reducing the consumption of meat, 14 percent of annual human premature deaths in the world could be avoided.

Entering the Anthropocene Era

Up until the Industrial Revolution, human influence on the environment was limited and easily absorbed by the natural environment, which could recycle the by-products of human activities. The development of agriculture and animal breeding was gradually transforming the planet, but it remained unthinkable that human activity could create disturbances on a planetary scale.

In our day, the rate of change is continuously being accelerated by ecological disturbances provoked by human activity. In particular, the "great acceleration" that has been taking place since 1950 has defined a new era on our planet, the anthropocene era (literally, "the era of humans"). This is the first time in our history that human activities have profoundly modified (and up to now, degraded) the total system that maintains life on earth. We never "decided" to overexploit the earth; the changes that brought us to the present point took place very gradually along with our increasing prosperity, almost without our noticing them. As Jared Diamond has shown in his book *Collapse*, many prosperous societies have gone into decline and disappeared because of overexploitation of their environments.[6] What will the consequences of overexploiting the entire planet be? We already know that some of them will be very painful.

According to the Swede Johan Rockström and twenty-seven other internationally renowned scientists, including the Nobel Prize winner Paul Crutzen, in an article that appeared in the journal *Nature* in 2009,[7] going beyond the planetary limits of Earth could be devastating for humanity. However, if we remain within certain limits, it may still be possible to preserve a secure environment within which human beings can continue to prosper.

But the period of time in which this will remain possible is very limited. Study of the resilience of the terrestrial system and its complex dynamic have enabled scientists to point to definite "thresholds" beyond which we are in danger of producing potentially irreversible imbalances. Today, two-thirds of the most important ecosystems on the planet are overexploited,[8] and according to the formula arrived at by Pavan Sukhdev, director of the global study group TEEB (The Economics of Ecosystems and Biodiversity), "We are in the process of consuming the past, present, and future of our planet."[9] Thus the biosphere has entered a danger zone, and big agro-business and the industrial breeding of animals for meat and dairy production are among the principal risk factors.

Nearly two-thirds of the land available for cultivation is used for animal breeding (30 percent for pasture and 30 percent for the production of feed).[10] According to the FAO, animal breeding is responsible for 70 percent of the deforestation currently in progress. A Greenpeace report estimates that 80 percent of the deforestation of the Amazon region is caused by the increase in the number of cows pastured there.[11] And we know that the humid tropical forests account for 50 percent of the biodiversity of the planet.

Meat for the Rich Countries Costs a Lot for the Poor Ones

The equation is simple: one hectare of land (about 2.5 acres) can feed fifty vegetarians or two meat eaters. Producing 1 kilogram (2.2 pounds) of meat takes the same amount of land as growing 200 kilograms of tomatoes or 160 kilograms of potatoes or 80 kilograms of apples.[12] According to another estimate made by Bruno Parmentier, an economist and former director of the École Supérieure d'Agriculture in

France, one hectare of good soil can feed up to thirty people with vegetables, fruits, and grains, whereas if this same acreage is used for egg production, milk, or meat, it can feed only ten people.[13]

To produce 1 calorie of beef by means of intensive breeding, it takes 8 to 26 calories of vegetable matter that could have been used to feed humans directly.[14] By planting oats, one can obtain 6 times more calories per acre than by using this same acre to produce pork, and 25 times more calories than by using it to produce beef. Clearly the yield of land used to produce meat is deplorable. Thus it is not surprising that Frances Moore Lappé described this sort of agriculture as a "backwards protein factory."[15]

As we have seen, animal breeding consumes 775 million tons of grain and corn per year, which would be enough to adequately feed 1.4 million of the poorest human beings.[16] In 1985, during the famine in Ethiopia, while the population was dying of hunger, this country was exporting grain to feed English livestock.[17] In the United States, 70 percent of grain production is used for animal breeding, whereas in India this figure is only 2 percent.[18]

Thus eating meat is a privilege of the rich countries that is only made possible at the expense of the poor ones. During the past thirty years, the amount of meat eaten in the world has increased exponentially, and at the same time the number of undernourished people has doubled. According to the FAO and the Action Contre la Faim (Action Against Hunger), more than 900 million people currently suffer from malnutrition, and a child dies every six seconds for lack of food; at the same time we produce enough calories on a global scale to feed everyone.[19]

Jocelyne Porcher carries out research at the INRA and is one of our most eminent specialists on the global food question. She explains:

> The industrial systems for animal production have profit as their only aim. They have no other vocation. They do not have the primary objective of 'feeding the world,' contrary to what many animal breeders would like to believe. We all know very well that when the industrial chains push our children by means of advertising to have sausage for their four o'clock snack . . . their interest in doing so has nothing to do with the 900 million undernour-

ished people in the world. Obviously the thing that interests the
industrial chains is their bottom line."[20]

The richer populations become, the more meat they eat.[21] A Frenchman eats 85 kilograms (187 pounds) of meat per year and an American
eats 120 kilograms (265 pounds), while an Indian eats only 2.5 kilograms (5.5 pounds) of meat per year. On average, rich countries eat *ten
times more* meat than poor countries.[22] The world consumption of meat
increased by a factor of five between 1950 and 2006, which is a rate of
increase twice as great as that of the population. If this current tendency continues, meat consumption will have doubled again by 2050.[23]
Although in the rich countries over the last decade, consumption of red
meat is gradually decreasing as a result of the reputation it has begun
to acquire for harmful health effects, at the same time consumption of
poultry is greatly increasing. In the United States, the number of cows
killed in slaughterhouses every year decreased by 20 percent between
1975 and 2009; during the same time, the number of chickens killed
increased by 200 percent.[24] The same tendency can be observed in
France. On the other hand, the consumption of meat has tripled over
the past forty years in the developing countries and is growing spectacularly in China, especially among middle-class consumers. Now in
China's big cities there are restaurants that serve only meat and young
children who eat meat at every meal. In the course of the past twenty
years in China, the consumption of chicken has increased 500 percent
and that of beef 600 percent.[25]

Every year, a bit more than a third of the world production of grains
is used by the animal breeding industry, and a quarter of the world production of fish is used to feed cows, pigs, and fowl, in the form of "fish
meal."[26] As Éric Lambin, professor at the universities of Louvain and
Stanford, tells us, "This competition between humans and livestock
in the consumption of grain results in an increase in the price of the
latter, which has tragic consequences for the poorest populations."[27]

The fact that a quarter of the 2.8 billion people in the world who
live on less than two dollars a day depend on raising animals for their
subsistence, and the fact that this activity contributes significantly to
economic development, must be taken into account, but this does not
disqualify the ideas we have just expressed. It is not these very small

animal-breeding operations that account for massive diversion of the means of food production toward the production of meat today. Rather the offenders here are the large more-or-less industrial farms whose produce supplies the intensive animal breeding operations as well as the monoculture practiced by these industrial farms.[28] Nonetheless, the small farmers among the poor populations also participate, in a less weighty manner, in the degradation of the land they live on. In the long term, their subsistence would be better served by the development of agro-ecological methods that beneficially manage the quality of their soils and the vegetation they produce.[29]

Impact on Our Reserves of Fresh Water

Fresh water is a rare and precious resource. Only 2.5 percent of the water on the planet is fresh water. Almost three quarters of it is contained in glaciers and eternal snows.[30] In many poor countries, access to water is very limited. The people, a majority of whom are women and children, often have to travel several miles on foot to reach a water source.

It is estimated that half of the earth's potable water is consumed in the production of meat and dairy products. In Europe, more than 50 percent of water pollution results from intensive animal breeding, including fish breeding. In the United States, 80 percent of potable water goes for animal breeding. Production of one pound of meat requires, depending on the case, from five to fifty times the amount of water required to grow one pound of grain.[31] *Newsweek* magazine described this volume of water in an imaginative fashion: "The amount of water used in the production of one pound of beef would be enough to float a destroyer."[32] In his work entitled *No Steak*, journalist Aymeric Caron illustrates this situation by calculating that, to produce one kilo of beef, the average amount of water required is almost as much as that used by a person taking one shower per day for a whole year: 15,000 liters.[33]

Animal production is currently using up vast amounts of the groundwater on which innumerable dry regions of the world are dependent. At the present rate, the amount of fresh water used in industrial breeding will increase another 50 percent by the year 2050.[34] Already today, the scarcity of potable water is a threat on a global scale: 40 percent of the population of the world, in twenty-four countries, are suffering from lack of adequate water, deficient in both quantity and quality.[35] More than three million children of less than five years of age die every year from diarrhea essentially caused by contaminated water and pathogenic substances transmitted in their food. Already at this time, 70 percent of our freshwater resources are tainted or polluted.[36]

Animal Breeding and Climate Change

The environmental impacts of meat production are particularly serious in the case of intensive breeding operations. Production of one pound of beef generates fifty times more greenhouse gas emissions than production of one pound of grain.[37] Let us recall that intensive breeding for the production of meat and other products derived from breeding (such as wool, eggs, and dairy products) is quantitatively the second largest cause of greenhouse gases and represents 14.5 percent of the greenhouse gas emissions resulting from human activity.[38] This figure includes the gases emitted in the course of the various stages of meat production: deforestation to create pasturage, production and transportation of fertilizer, fuel for agricultural machinery, manufacture of growth hormones and dietary supplements, flatulence from the digestive systems of the livestock, transport of livestock to the slaughterhouses, treatment and packaging of meat, and transportation of the meat to points of sale. In total, breeding operations serving the production of meat contribute more to climatic warming than the entirety of the transportation sector (which accounts for 13 percent of greenhouse gas emissions) and is surpassed only by the construction industry and its fuel consumption across the globe.

The greenhouse effect is due mainly to three gases: methane, carbon dioxide, and nitrous oxide. Methane is a particularly significant factor, because a molecule of this gas contributes twenty times more to the greenhouse effect than a molecule of carbon dioxide. And 15 to 20 percent of methane emissions on the planet are connected with animal breeding. Over the past two centuries, the concentration of methane in the atmosphere has more than doubled. Its increase has slowed down in the past few years, but could soon begin a faster increase to double again between now and 2070.

Ruminants—steers, cows, buffalo, sheep, goats, and camels—constitute one of the largest sources of methane production (37 percent of the emissions connected with human activity). The methane is created by microbial fermentation in the digestive systems of ruminants. It is expelled into the atmosphere in the course of respiration, through eructation, or in the form of flatulence. It is also given off by the solid waste produced by these animals, by the decomposition of manure, and by the fermentation of animal excreta held in storage tanks.[39] A dairy cow produces 500 liters (132 gallons) of methane per day![40]

As for carbon dioxide, the expansion of the meat industry has contributed in a major way to the increased concentrations of this gas in the atmosphere. This is because industrial meat production depends on the mechanization of agriculture in order to produce the enormous amounts of animal feed that it requires; it depends on the manufacture and use of petroleum-based chemical fertilizers, on deforestation, and on other processes that are significant sources of carbon dioxide.

Nitrous oxide is the most aggressive of the greenhouse gases. It is 320 times more active than carbon dioxide. It is also a stable compound that has a life span in the atmosphere of 120 years. The main sources of nitrous oxide emissions are treatment of fields with nitrogenous fertilizers, the dissolution of these fertilizers in the soil, and the waste products of animal breeding. Sixty-five percent of nitrous oxide emissions are produced by breeding operations. The contribution of nitrous oxide to the greenhouse gas effect is roughly 6 percent.[41]

Production of beef and lamb is responsible for the highest emissions in relation to the energy provided by these foods. It is estimated that by 2050 beef and lamb will be responsible for half of all greenhouse gases resulting from food production while contributing only 3 percent of the caloric requirements of the human population.

Moreover, researchers from Oxford University have calculated the carbon footprint of 65,000 British citizens, among whom were 2,000 vegans and 15,000 vegetarians. It turns out that for a person who, like most Britons, consumes more than 100 grams (3.5 ounces) of meat per day, his or her daily carbon footprint is 7.19 kilograms (15.9 pounds) of carbon dioxide. It is 5.63 kilograms (12.4 pounds) of carbon dioxide per day for a moderate consumer of meat (50 to 100 grams, or 1.75 to 3.5 ounces), while for a vegetarian and a vegan, it is only 3.18 and 2.89 kilograms (7 and 6.4 pounds), respectively. Thus, a vegan contributes 2.5 times less to global warming than a regular meat eater.[42] From this point of view, the so-called "organic" meat is as damaging to the environment as industrial meat, if not more damaging in terms of carbon footprint and land use.

A United Nations report of 2010 estimates that the passion of developed countries for meat consumption will not be satisfiable beyond the point when the human population approaches 9 billion—around 2050. According to the GIEC report of spring 2014, if the problem of emissions from food production is not ameliorated, emissions of greenhouse gases connected with animal breeding could double between now and 2070. Just this factor alone would make it impossible to maintain current objectives for the climate. According to Fredrik Hedenus, this increase in emissions would probably take us beyond a level compatible with the goal of limiting the increase in global temperature to two degrees centigrade.[43] Hedenus reaches the conclusion that changes in diet—meaning less meat and smaller amounts of dairy products—are crucial if we are to have a chance of keeping global warming below this limit of two degrees centigrade.

Animal Excrement

A cow produces on average 23 tons of excrement per year.[44] In the United States alone, industrial animal breeding produces 130 times more excrement than humans, that is, about 88,000 pounds per second. Animal excrement is responsible for more water pollution than all other industrial sources combined.[45] For example, the Smithfield Foods company, which every year kills 31 million pigs, has entirely polluted the rivers of North Carolina.

Animal excrement generates enormous quantities of ammonia, which pollutes rivers and marine shores and also causes infestations of algae (green algae in particular). Green algae tends to stifle marine life. Vast areas of Western Europe, the northeastern United States, and the coastal regions of Southeast Asia, as well as vast plains regions of China, at the present time are receiving considerable amounts of nitrogen.[46] These agricultural surpluses of nitrogen as well as of phosphorus gradually infiltrate into the soil by means of leaching or seepage, polluting groundwater, aquatic ecosystems, and humid zones.[47]

The Effects of Intensive Fishing

Intensive, commercial fishing today has increasingly sophisticated means at its disposal, such as sonar, untearable nets several miles long, factory boats, and so on. These means are progressively leading to the extinction of numerous species of fish, which is having a tremendous impact on marine biodiversity. Today fishing operations from all countries go after fish in all the seas of the world. After having exhausted the supply of fish living near the surface, commercial factory boats continue to drop their nets to deeper and deeper levels. They are now scraping the ocean bottoms. Trawling of the great ocean deeps has a devastating effect on the fragile balance of biodiversity that has developed over the course of thousands of years.[48] The purpose of all this is to provide cheap fish to the large distribution chains of the world's rich countries. These activities in no way contribute to the nourishment of the world's hungry, nor is any thought given to the irreversible damage that results from them. Numerous nets lost by fishing boats are adrift in the ocean, continuing to trap fish and marine mammals. It is estimated that these nets will take several hundred years to decompose in the water.

Moreoever, the quantity of fish actually caught in the world is much larger than the catch that is declared. To give just one example, according to the estimates of marine biologist Daniel Pauly and his colleagues at the University of British Columbia in Vancouver, China annually catches 4.5 million tons of fish, a major proportion of them along the coasts of Africa, but they declare only 368,000 tons to the FAO.[49] Innumerable pirate fishermen are on the water who ignore the quotas imposed on certified fishermen, and they make their contribution to the increasingly rapid exhaustion of marine populations.

For purely commercial reasons and because of inappropriate regulations, commercial fishing involves a tremendous amount of waste. Every year, 7 million tons of fish are caught that cannot be used. In addition a great number of marine mammals, tortoises, and birds are taken in the nets.[50] As Jonathan Safran Foer remarks in his book *Eating Animals:*

> Take shrimp, for example. The average shrimp-trawling operation throws 80 to 90 percent of the sea animals it captures overboard, dead or dying, as bycatch. (Endangered species amount to much of this bycatch.) Shrimp account for only 2 percent of global seafood by weight, but shrimp trawling accounts for 33 percent of global bycatch. We tend not to think about this because we tend not to know about it. What if there were labeling on our food letting us know how many animals were killed to bring our desired animal to our plate? So, with trawled shrimp from Indonesia, for example, the label might read: 26 POUNDS OF OTHER SEA ANIMALS WERE KILLED AND TOSSED BACK INTO THE OCEAN FOR EVERY 1 POUND OF THIS SHRIMP.
>
> Or take tuna. Among the other 145 species regularly killed—gratuitously—while killing tuna are . . . [51]

And he enumerates many of them.

A friend who was one of the pioneers of Greenpeace and a participant in many of the campaigns undertaken on the *Rainbow Warrior,* told me how off the coasts of California and Mexico the big tuna-fishing operations use helicopters to spot schools of dolphin. When the dolphin are seen leaping from the water, this indicates the presence of the shoals of tuna on which they feed. With the help of a fleet of inflatable rubber boats, the fishers then drop immense nets in the indicated area, which are afterward pulled tight with drawstrings like a purse. In this way they take huge numbers of dolphin in the nets along with the tuna. When the nets are finally pulled aboard by powerful winches, the dolphins, which are usually on top of the tuna, are frequently crushed in the winches.

It clearly seems urgent for us to put an end to this "ecocide" in our oceans. The oceans represent one of the most precious ecosystems of our planet, one of the most useful in maintaining the earth's ecological balance. In spite of this, it has been reduced to the level of an "economic resource" or, worse, a garbage pail.

Meat Eating and Human Health

Many epidemiological studies have established that eating meat, especially red meat and delicatessen meats, increases the risk of colon and stomach cancer as well as of various cardiovascular ailments.

A study conducted by the European Prospective Investigation into Cancer and Nutrition (EPIC), which surveyed 521,000 individuals, showed that the participants who ate the most red meat had a 35 percent greater likelihood of developing colon cancer than participants who ate the least red meat.[52]

According to a United Nations report on human development (2007–2008), the risk of colorectal cancer diminished by about 30 percent with each reduction of 100 grams (3.5 ounces) in daily consumption of red meat. Countries where the national diet is very high in red meat, such as Argentina and Uruguay, are the same countries where the incidence of colon cancer is the highest in the world.[53] Consumption of processed meats, such as deli meats, on the other hand, was associated with an increased risk of stomach cancer.

According to a study published at Harvard University in 2012 by An Pan, Frank Hu, and their colleagues, in a sample of 100,000 individuals followed over many years, daily consumption of meat was associated with an increased risk of death from cardiovascular causes in 18 percent of men and 21 percent of women, while the increased risk of death from cancer was 10 percent and 16 percent, respectively.[54] Among people who ate a great deal of red meat, simply replacing the meat with whole grains or other sources of vegetable protein reduced their risk of early death by 14 percent.

Because of the phenomenon of bioconcentration, meat contains around fourteen times more pesticide residues than vegetables, and dairy products contain five times more.[55] What happens is that persistent organic pollutants accumulate in the fatty tissues of animals and in that way enter into human food. These organic pollutants are also found in the flesh of farmed fish, which are fed on concentrated foodstuffs made with, among other things, animal proteins. These molecules are not only carcinogenic but also have toxic effects on the development of the nervous systems of fetuses and young children.[56]

In the United States, 80 percent of antibiotics are used for the sole purpose of keeping animals alive in industrial breeding systems until the time when they are slaughtered. Since the large commercial animal production enterprises are not able to treat sick animals individually, massive amounts of antibiotics are added to the feed of all the animals. From 25 to 75 percent of these substances end up in rivers, in the soil, and in drinking water, resulting in increased resistance to antibiotics in humans and also other undesirable effects.

The authors of a British study involving 65,000 people, including 17,000 vegetarians or vegans, conclude: "National governments that are considering an update of dietary recommendations in order to define a 'healthy, sustainable diet' must incorporate the recommendation to lower the consumption of animal-based products."[57]

Insurers are not mistaken: in the United States, Kaiser Permanente, a large health insurance company with over 9 million members, encourages doctors to "recommend a plant-based diet to all their patients."[58] In the United Kingdom, a life insurance company even offers 25 percent off for vegetarians and vegans.

The Rise of Vegetarianism

Seven million years ago, our australopithecine ancestors were essentially vegetarian. They fed themselves on nuts, tubers, roots, and fruit. They also ate some insects. Occasionally, but rarely, they ate small mammals. Around 2.5 million years ago, *Homo habilis* began to increase their consumption of meat, especially by scavenging the kills of other animals. Hunting took on importance with the *Homo erectus*—who was also the discoverer of fire—about 450,000 years ago according to some estimates. Hunting was important to the Neanderthals, who were mainly carnivores and ate more meat than *Homo sapiens*, who appeared 200,000 years ago. When the hunter-gatherers became sedentary about 12,000 years ago and began to practice agriculture and raise animals, greater consumption of cultivated grains and dairy products resulted in a decrease in meat eating. Only in the twentieth century did the consumption of meat increase significantly.[59]

Nonetheless, in spite of this global increase in meat eating, a growing attraction to vegetarianism can also be observed. In France there are between one and two million vegetarians, representing from 1.5 to 3 percent of the population (a percentage as big if not slightly bigger than that of hunters).[60] This is one of the lowest percentages in Europe, where the average number of vegetarians is estimated to be 5 percent. Great Britain has the largest number (13 to 14 percent), followed by Germany and Switzerland (10 percent). These numbers are expected to grow, since vegetarianism is much more prevalent among students (20 percent in the United States, as opposed to 4 percent in the general population).[61] With around 450 million individuals, that is, about 35 percent of the population, India, as we have seen, is by far the country with the largest number of vegetarians.[62]

In 2009 the town of Gand in Belgium became the first town in the world to become vegetarian—at least once a week. The local authorities decided to establish "one meatless day a week" during which, according to the UN report, at least the town officials ate vegetarian. Posters were distributed encouraging the population to participate in these meatless days as well as maps of the town showing where the vegetarian restaurants were located. This policy was later extended to the town schools.[63] "A day will come when the idea that for the sake of food the people of the past raised and massacred living beings and with complete equanimity displayed their flesh in bits and pieces in shop windows, will no doubt inspire the same revulsion that the cannibalistic meals of the Americans, Oceanians, or Africans inspired in the travelers of the seventeenth and eighteenth centuries."[64]

Who can say if this prediction of Claude Lévi-Strauss will ever come true?

The Good News

As we pointed out before, methane is twenty times more active than carbon dioxide in creating the greenhouse effect. Nevertheless, there is good news: its life span in the atmosphere is only ten years, as opposed to a century in the case of carbon dioxide. Thus all that would be necessary to bring about a rapid and significant reduction in one factor causing climate warming would be to lower production of meat and dairy products. For example, a Swedish study has shown that, if growing green beans and breeding cows are each carried out to obtain an equal level of nutritive energy, producing the green beans generates 99 percent less greenhouse gas than breeding cows.[65]

Another piece of good news is that the world would be able to feed 1.5 billion undernourished people simply by giving the billion tons of grain used annually to feed cattle headed to the slaughter to them instead. If all the inhabitants of North America abstained from eating meat one day a week, that would make it indirectly possible to feed 25 million deprived persons every day for an entire year! It would also be an effective contribution to the struggle against climate change. That is why, according to Rajendra Kumar Pachauri, winner of the Nobel Peace Prize and director of the GIEC (Groupe d'experts Intergouvernemental sur l'Évolution du Climat,[66] a United Nations organization), a movement toward worldwide adoption of a vegetarian diet is essential for combating hunger in the world, as well as energy shortages and the worst effects of climate change. In his opinion, "in terms of immediate action and the feasibility of obtaining reductions in the short term, this [vegetarianism] is clearly the most attractive option."[67]

These assertions are confirmed by the GIEC report of March 2014: "We have demonstrated that reduction of the consumption of meat and dairy products is a key point in our ability to bring climatic pollution from food production down to dependable levels," Fredrik Hedenus explains. "Major changes in diet take time, so we should begin thinking right now of the ways in which we can make our production of food more respectful of the climate."[68]

According to another coauthor of this report, Stefan Wirsenius, emissions of greenhouse gases "can definitely be reduced by increasing the efficiency of production of meat and dairy products by drawing upon new technologies. But if the consumption [of these products] continues to grow, the reductions these measures can bring about will probably be insufficient to keep climate change within tolerable levels."[69]

At this time the good news is that we can all participate effectively in slowing down global warming and doing away with poverty in an easy, fast, and economical way. To do this, it is not necessary to stop traveling or heating our houses (even though we should certainly exercise moderation in these areas also). We only need to do one thing: to decide here and now to reduce our consumption of meat or, if possible, stop eating it altogether.

4

THE REAL FACE OF INDUSTRIAL ANIMAL BREEDING

So what is so shameful that it must be hidden behind the walls of slaughterhouses and in the hangars where industrial breeding takes place? What we have to reveal in this chapter is shocking. Should we provide a warning, saying that sensitive people should read no further? You might be tempted to pass over the following pages and move on to the next chapter. But if we wish to be concerned for the fate of others and, to the extent possible, take action to alleviate their suffering, don't we at least have to see animal breeding as it is? History has shown that looking in the other direction has always left the way open for the worst atrocities and has delayed taking measures for putting an end to them. What is the point of looking at reality with rose-colored glasses? Isn't it better to look at it and let seeing it clearly become the grounds for the courage of our compassion?[1]

Let us listen to the words of the great primatologist, Jane Goodall:

What shocks me the most is that people seem to become almost schizophrenic the moment you bring up the terrible conditions that prevail in intensive breeding operations, the cruel heaping up of sentient beings in tiny spaces—conditions so horrible that you have to constantly give them antibiotics to keep them alive, otherwise they'll just let themselves die. I often describe the nightmare of transport. If they fall during transport, they are yanked up by one leg, which breaks. And the slaughterhouses, where so many of the animals are not even rendered unconscious before being skinned alive or plunged into boiling water. It's obviously excruciatingly painful. When I start talking to people about all that, they often reply: "Oh please, don't talk to me about that. I'm too sensitive and I adore animals." And I say to myself, "Has this person lost it altogether?"[2]

Some people will say, "Yes, it's horrible, but they've made those places much more humane." Humane? When human beings treat their fellows like that, we do not speak of humanity but of inhumanity and barbarism. Some of the descriptions that follow—particularly those by Upton Sinclair, who was the first to describe the fate of the animals in the Chicago stockyards in his novel *The Jungle*—go back a century. Others are contemporary and show how, a few minor improvements aside, the mass killing continues and increases and gets worse every day, every year—whether we look the other way or not. So for once, let's not look away:

Along one side of the room ran a narrow gallery, a few feet from the floor; into which gallery the cattle were driven by men with goads which gave them electric shocks. Once crowded in here, the creatures were prisoned, each in a separate pen, by gates that shut, leaving them no room to turn around; and while they stood bellowing and plunging, over the top of the pen there leaned one of the "knockers," armed with a sledge hammer, and watching for a chance to deal a blow. The room echoed with the thuds in quick succession, and the stamping and kicking of the steers. The instant the animal had fallen, the "knocker" passed on to another; while a second man raised a lever, and the side of the pen was raised, and the animal, still kicking and struggling, slid out to the "killing bed." Here a man put shackles about one leg, and pressed another lever, and the body was jerked up into the air. . . . The manner in which they did this was something to be seen and never forgotten . . . . First there came the "butcher," to bleed them; this meant one swift stroke, so swift that you could not see it—only the flash of the knife; and before you could realize it, the man had darted on to the next line, and a stream of bright red was pouring out upon the floor. This floor was half an inch deep with blood, in spite of the best efforts of men who kept shoveling it through holes. . . .[3]

In 1906 when *The Jungle* appeared, it caused quite an uproar. But since then the only thing that has really changed is that now we kill a lot more animals: 60 billion land animals per year according to the statistics of the FAO. Other sources estimate as many as 100 billion.[4] Melanie Joy has calculated that if 100 million people, a number that corresponds to the number of land animals slaughtered each year in the United States, were to line up single file, the line would reach around the world eighty times.[5]

When a society takes for granted the pure and simple exploitation of other sentient beings for its own purposes, without giving the least heed to the fate of the creatures it turns into mere utilitarian objects in this fashion, that society's moral principles must come under serious scrutiny.

The devaluation of human beings often leads to viewing them as animals and to treating them with the brutality with which animals are often treated. The exploitation of animals is accompanied by a further level of devaluation: they are reduced to the status of infinitely reproducible objects for consumption—meat-producing machines, living toys whose suffering entertains or fascinates the crowds. Their quality of sentient beings is deliberately ignored so as to reduce them to the status of objects.

This point of view was given blunt expression in the nineteenth century by Émile Baudement, holder of the first chair of zootechnology at the Institut Agronomique of Versailles: "Animals are living machines, not in the figurative sense but in the most rigorous literal sense of the word, such as it is used in the world of mechanics and industry. . . . They provide milk, meat, or power. They are machines that produce a certain yield at a certain cost."[6]

The recent remarks of the director of Wall's, a British meat-products company, were even more cynical. He stated: "The breeding sow should be thought of, and treated as, a valuable piece of machinery whose function is to pump out baby pigs like a sausage machine."[7]

The outlook of the system is summed up by Fred C. Haley, the director of a U.S. egg-producing company with 225,000 laying hens: "The object of producing eggs is to make money. When we forget this objective, we have forgotten what it is all about."[8]

In the systems of industrial breeding, the life span of an animal is a fraction of what it would be in natural conditions: about one-fourth for a bovine and about one-sixtieth for a fowl. In the latter case, it is as if the life span of a Frenchman were only a year and four months.[9] The animals are confined in boxes in which they cannot even turn around. They are castrated. The offspring are separated at birth from their mothers. Conscious animals who have momentarily survived the process that was supposed to have killed them are cut into pieces. Some are crushed alive in an endless screw mechanism (this is the fate that awaits hundreds of millions of male chicks every year).

In other circumstances, animals are made to suffer for our entertainment (bullfights, dog fights, cockfights). They are caught in traps that crush their limbs in steel jaws, or they are skinned alive. In a word, we decide where and how they are going to die without giving the least consideration to what they feel.

The Extent of the Suffering We Inflict on Animals

Humans have always exploited animals, first by hunting them and then by domesticating them. But it was not until the beginning of the twentieth century that animal exploitation began to take on colossal proportions. At the same time, it gradually began to disappear from our daily lives, since it was deliberately carried out in places where it would not be seen. In the rich countries, depending on the species, 80 to 95 percent of the animals we eat are "produced" in industrial breeding operations where their short lives are an uninterrupted continuity of pain. All of that becomes possible the moment we begin to regard other living beings as objects for consumption or reserves of meat that we can deal with however we please. Upton Sinclair continues his account:

> There were groups of cattle being driven to the chutes, which were roadways about fifteen feet wide, raised high above the pens. In these chutes the stream of animals was continuous; it was quite uncanny to watch them, pressing on to their fate, all unsuspicious, a very river of death. Our friends were not poetical, and . . . they thought only of the wonderful efficiency of

it all. . . . "They don't waste anything here," said the guide, and then he laughed and added a witticism, which he was pleased that his unsophisticated friends should take to be his own: "They use everything about the hog except the squeal.". . . It was a long, narrow room. . . . At the head there was a great iron wheel, about twenty feet in circumference, with rings here and there along its edge. Upon both sides of this wheel there was a narrow space, into which came the hogs at the end of their journey. . . . It began slowly to revolve, and then the men upon each side of it sprang to work. They had chains which they fastened about the leg of the nearest hog, and the other end of the chain they hooked into one of the rings upon the wheel. So, as the wheel turned, a hog was suddenly jerked off his feet and borne aloft. . . . Once started upon that journey, the hog never came back; at the top of the wheel he was shunted off upon a trolley, and went sailing down the room. And meantime another was swung up, and then another, and another, until there was a double line of them, each dangling by a foot and kicking in frenzy—and squealing. The uproar was appalling, perilous to the eardrums; . . . there would come a momentary lull, and then a fresh outburst, louder than ever, surging up to a deafening climax. . . . One by one they hooked up the hogs, and one by one with a swift stroke they slit their throats. There was a long line of hogs, with squeals and lifeblood ebbing away together; until at last each started again, and vanished with a splash into a huge vat of boiling water. . . . This slaughtering machine ran on, visitors or no visitors. It was like some horrible crime committed in a dungeon, all unseen and unheeded, buried out of sight and of memory.[10]

Above All, the Bottom Line

At the present time, in the United States alone, more animals are killed in a single day than in a whole year in the slaughterhouses of Upton Sinclair's day. According to David Cantor, founder of a study group dedicated to establishing a responsible policy toward animals, it is "a cruel, expedient system, very tightly run, based entirely on profit, in which animals are scarcely regarded as living beings and their suffering and death does not count."[11]

Slaughterhouses have decreased in number, but they have gotten much bigger, each now having the capacity to kill several million animals per year. In the countries of the European Union, there are new regulations intended to somewhat reduce the level of suffering in industrial breeding operations. In the United States, however, recent testimonies such as that of the writer Jonathan Safran Foer[12] indicate that the difference between earlier and now is that now more animals are killed faster, more efficiently, and more cheaply.

Since it is more trouble to care for or even euthanize weak or sick animals who have collapsed and are unable to get up again to follow the others, in the majority of the U.S. states it is legal to let them die from hunger and thirst over a period of days or to throw them alive into garbage bins. That happens every day.

The workers are under constant pressure to keep the slaughtering process moving at full speed. "They don't stop the chain for anything or anybody," says Gail Eisnitz, a researcher for the Humane Farming Association. "As long as that chain is running, they don't give a shit what you have to do to get that hog on the line. You got to get a hog on each hook or you got a foreman on your ass. . . . All the drivers use pipes to kill hogs that can't go through the chutes. Or if you get a hog that refuses to go in the chutes and is stopping production, you beat him to death. Then push him off to the side and hang him up later."[13]

Economic competition forces each slaughterhouse to do everything it can to kill more animals per hour than their competitors. The speed of the drivers in the slaughterhouses makes it possible to "treat" 1,100 animals per hour, which means that a worker has to kill one animal every three seconds. Mistakes are commonplace.[14]

In England, Dr. Alan Long has described what happens in the slaughterhouses, which he has to visit frequently as a researcher, as "relentless, pitiless, and remorseless" enterprises. Some workers confided to him that the hardest thing they had to do was kill lambs and calves, since "they're just babies." "It's a poignant moment," says Dr. Long, when a little crazed calf that has just been pulled away from its mother begins to suckle on the butcher's fingers in the hope of getting some milk from them—and all it gets is human cruelty."[15]

The Hypocrisy of "Care"

In 2008 a statement of the European Council for Research (CER) recommended "taking into account the wellbeing of animals" and stressed the need to "do the maximum to spare pain, distress, or suffering to animals intended for slaughter." But in spite of a few minor advances, we are still far from that goal. If professionals from time to time advise the breeders to avoid such-and-such cruel practice, it is purely on account of the negative effect of that practice on the ability of the animal to gain weight. If they urge that animals on their way to slaughter be treated less harshly, it is because bruises cause the carcasses to lose value. What is being missed is that mistreatment of animals should be avoided because it is immoral in and of itself. The only precautions that are taken are those that keep the animals from dying before they have yielded a profit. Once they have served this purpose, they are destroyed like cumbersome objects and then thrown away like garbage.

As for veterinarians employed by the industry, their principal role is to contribute to the maximization of profit. Medicines are used not to cure disease but as substitutes for ruined immune systems. The breeders do not attempt to raise healthy animals but just to keep their animals from dying too soon. They must stay alive until they are killed. As we have already mentioned, the animals are filled full of antibiotics and growth hormones. Eighty percent of the antibiotics used in the United States are used in industrial breeding operations. As noted by Élisabeth Fontenay, "The worst is hidden behind the monumental hypocrisy that consists in devising and putting into practice a pretended ethics of wellbeing as though it were a set of limits imposed out of respect for the animals faced with the requirements of industrial breeding, when in fact it is obliged to serve the efficient functioning and profitability of the enterprise."[16]

Do Not Enter

During the 1990s, the painter Sue Coe employed a variety of ingenious means to gain entry to the slaughter facilities of different countries, mainly in the United States. She constantly had to deal with outright hostility, from warnings such as "You have no business being here!" all the way to death threats if she published the name of a particular slaughterhouse she had visited. She was never permitted to use a camera. At best she was allowed to make sketches. "Slaughter facilities, particularly the biggest ones, are guarded like military installations. I was generally able to get into them because I knew somebody who had business dealings with the factory or slaughterhouse."[17] During his fifteen years of investigation of slaughter facilities, Jean-Luc Daub was sometimes treated roughly and even struck: "There were numerous attempts at intimidation, and death threats as well. I only remember that once at an animal market, they threatened to hang me from the rafters if I didn't leave the place."[18]

In her book *Dead Meat*, Sue described her visit to a slaughter facility in Pennsylvania in this way: "The floor was very slippery and the walls and everything else were covered with blood. Dried blood had formed a crust on the chains. I surely didn't want to fall down in all that blood and guts. The workers wore non-slip boots, yellow aprons, and helmets. It was a scene of controlled, mechanized chaos."[19]

As in most slaughter facilities, "the place is dirty—filthy even—with flies swarming everywhere." According to another account, the refrigerator rooms are full of rats, and at night they run all over the meat and gnaw on it."[20]

When lunchtime comes, the workers depart. Sue stays there alone with six decapitated corpses that are oozing blood. The walls are splattered with blood and she has drops of it on her notebook. She feels something moving on her right and goes closer to a slaughter stall to get a better look. Inside is a cow. It is not unconscious; it has slipped in the blood and has fallen. The men went to lunch and left it there. The minutes go by. From time to time, the animal struggles, banging its hooves against the enclosure walls. For a moment, it manages to get to its feet enough to look over them. Then it falls back down. You can hear the blood dripping. Music is playing from the loudspeakers.

Sue starts sketching. . . .

A man, Danny, comes back from lunch. He gives the injured cow three or four violent kicks to make it get up, but it can't. He leans over into the metallic box and tries to knock it out with his air pistol. Then he fires a bullet into its head from a few inches away. Danny fastens a chain around one of the rear legs of the cow and raises it up. But the cow is not dead. It struggles. Its legs flail while it is being lifted, head down. Sue notices that some of the cows are not completely unconscious, and there are others that are not knocked out at all. "They flail about like crazy while he is cutting their throats." Danny talks to the ones that are still conscious: "Come on, girl, be nice!" Sue watches the blood spurting out. "It was as though all living beings were nothing but soft containers, just waiting to be pierced."

Danny goes to the door and makes the next cows move in using his electric goad. The terrified cows resist and kick with their hooves. As he is forcing them into the enclosure where they are going to be knocked out, Danny repeats over and over in a singsong tone, "Come on, girl!"

Sue next visits a slaughter facility for horses in Texas. The horses awaiting slaughter are in terrible condition. One of them has a broken jaw. Whiplashes rain down on them with a cracking sound and there is a smell of burning. The horses try to escape from the kill zone, but the men hit them on the head until they make a half turn. Sue's companion sees a white mare in the midst of giving birth to a foal right in front of the enclosure. Two workers whip her to force her to move faster into the kill zone and throw the foal into a vat used for entrails. On a ramp above them, the boss, wearing a cowboy hat, observes the scene nonchalantly.

Coming out of another factory, which reminded her of one of Dante's hells, Sue Coe sees a cow with a broken leg lying in the hot sun. She approaches it, but the security personnel stop her and make her leave. "The Shoah keeps coming to my mind, which upsets me tremendously," Sue writes.[21]

A Global Enterprise

The fate of other industrially bred animals is hardly better. In the United States each year 150 times more chickens are killed than 80 years ago, thanks to the development of battery breeding. Tyson Foods, the biggest chicken-processing company in the world, slaughters 10 million of them *per week*. Fifty billion fowl are killed annually in the world.

Each chicken, during its short life, occupies a space the size of a sheet of letter paper. The air it breathes is full of ammonia, dust, and bacteria.[22] This crowding is the cause of numerous abnormal behaviors: pulling out feathers, aggressive pecking, and cannibalism. "The battery becomes a madhouse for gallinaceans," remarks the Texan naturalist Roy Bedichek.[23] The artificially accelerated growth of chickens can be compared to a child reaching the weight of more than 330 pounds by the age of ten.

To reduce the aberrant behaviors, which are a considerable expense, the breeders keep the chickens in partial darkness, and to keep them from killing each other, they snip their beaks. In the 1940s, the beaks were burned off with blowtorches. Today the breeders use little guillotines equipped with hot blades. The stumps left over from this efficient form of amputation often form neuromas that are extremely painful.[24]

In a U.S. firm where two million laying hens are crowded into hangars that contain 90,000 hens each, one executive explained to journalists from *National Geographic* that "when the production [of eggs] goes down below the level of profitability, the 90,000 hens are sold in bulk to a processor who makes liver paté or chicken soup from them."[25] And then they start again from zero.

Transport is another source of long suffering. In the United States, it is estimated that 10 to 15 percent of chickens transported die during the trip. Of those who arrive at the slaughter facilities, a third present recent fractures resulting from the way in which they were manipulated and transported.

The slaughter facilities are supposed to render the chickens unconscious in an electrified bath. But in order to save money, they use too weak a voltage (about one-tenth of the dose required to bring about sedation). As a result many chickens arrive at the scalding vats still conscious.[26]

The male chicks of laying hens are destroyed—50 million in France, 250 million in the United States, every year. "Destroyed? That seems like a word worth knowing more about," says Jonathan Safran Foer. He goes on:

> Most male layers are destroyed by being sucked through a series of pipes onto an electrified plate. Other layer chicks are destroyed in other ways, and it's impossible to call those animals more or less fortunate. Some are tossed into large plastic containers. The

weak are trampled to the bottom, where they suffocate slowly. The strong suffocate slowly at the top. Others are sent fully conscious through macerators (picture a wood chipper filled with chicks). . . . Cruel? Depends on your definition of cruelty?[27]

As for pigs, in order to prevent them from biting each others' tails, producers cut the tails off with an instrument that crushes the stump at the same time to minimize bleeding. In France, the ministerial decree of January 16, 2003, authorizes live grinding down of the canine milk teeth of piglets less than a week old. The sows are confined in metal boxes hardly bigger than their bodies, where they are bound for two or three months by a neck strap that keeps them from turning or taking more than one forward or backward step. When the sow is ready to be killed, it is placed in a device called a "steel virgin," a metal frame that prevents any freedom of movement. The males are castrated without anaesthesia. The skin of their scrota are cut open with a knife, the testicles are laid bare, and then a worker yanks them until the cord that holds them is broken.[28] The sows of 300 kilograms (over 600 pounds), which have moved very little in their short lives, are hung up on a hook by a hind leg. They then have their throats slit and die as their blood runs out of them, flailing about desperately. According to Jocelyne Porcher, in charge of research at the INRA, "This whole system is an immense fabric of suffering."[29]

Foer recounts: "Piglets that don't grow fast enough—the runts—are a drain on resources and so have no place on the farm. Picked up by their hind legs, they are swung and then bashed headfirst onto the concrete floor. This common practice is called 'thumping.' 'We've thumped as many as 120 in one day,' said a worker from a Missouri farm."[30]

Calves suffer from being separated from their mothers and then are closed up in boxes that prevent them from taking their natural sleeping position, with the head resting on the flank. The boxes are also too narrow to allow the calf to turn or to lick itself. The calves are deliberately given feed with low iron content, because consumers prefer "pale" meat. In this case the color is due to the fact that the animals have intentionally been kept anemic.[31] This is also the reason their boxes are made from wood—to keep anything with iron in it out of their reach.[32]

Every Day, Every Year

In the case of cattle, most often an air gun fires a steel pin into the animal's skull, which is supposed either to kill it or knock it unconscious. But a good number of the animals remain conscious or wake up when workers begin cutting them into pieces. Here again, Jonathan Safran Foer:

> Let's say what we mean: animals are bled, skinned, and dismembered while conscious. It happens all the time, and the industry and the government know it. Several plants cited for bleeding or skinning or dismembering live animals have defended their actions as common in the industry. . . . When Temple Grandin conducted an industrywide audit in 1996, her studies revealed that the vast majority of cattle slaughterhouses were unable to regularly render cattle unconscious with a single blow. . . . The combination of line speeds that have increased as much as 800 percent in the past hundred years and poorly trained workers laboring under nightmarish conditions guarantees mistakes.

Foer continues:

> Sometimes animals are not knocked out at all. At one plant, a secret video was made by workers (not animal activists) and given to the *Washington Post*. According to the *Post*, "More than twenty workers signed affidavits alleging that the violations shown on the tape are commonplace and that supervisors are aware of them." In one affidavit, a worker explained, "I've seen thousands and thousands of cows go through the slaughter process alive. . . . The cows can get seven minutes down the line and still be alive. I've been in the side puller where they're still alive. All the hide is stripped out down the neck there." And when workers who complain are listened to at all, they often get fired.[33]

One worker recounted:

> A three-year-old heifer was walking up through the kill alley. And she was having a calf right there, it was half in and half out. I knew

she was going to die, so I pulled the calf out. Wow, did my boss get mad. . . . They call these calves "slunks." They use the blood for cancer research. And he wanted that calf. . . . It's nothing to have a cow hanging up in front of you and see the calf inside kicking, trying to get out. . . . See, I'm an ex-Marine. The blood and guts don't bother me. It's the inhumane treatment. There's just so much of it. . . .

After the head-skinner, the carcass (or cow) proceeds to the "leggers," who cut off the lower portions of the animal's legs. "As far as the ones that come back to life," says a line worker, "it looks like they're trying to climb the walls. . . . And when they get to the leggers, well, the leggers don't want to wait to start working on the cow until somebody gets down there to reknock it. So they just cut off the bottom part of the leg with the clippers. When they do that, the cattle go wild, just kicking in every direction."[34]

The case is similar with chicken slaughter. The electric current utilized to kill the chickens in the sedation vats is not always effective and is often set at too low a voltage. The result of this, according to the Compassion in World Farming Trust (CIWF), is that "In the European Union, 39.6 million chickens may have their throats slit without having been suitably sedated."[35] Virgil Butler, a former employee of a "small" slaughter facility belonging to the Tyson Foods chain, which supplied the fast-food chain KFC in 2002, the time referred to in this account, tells us the following:

You see, the killing machine can never slit the throat of every bird that goes by, especially those that the stunner does not stun properly. So, you have what is known as a "killer" whose job it is to catch those birds so that they are not scalded alive in the tank. (Of course he can't catch all of them . . . .)

Picture this: You are told by your supervisor that it is your night in the kill room. You think, "Sh*t, it's gonna be a rough night tonight." No matter what the weather is like outside, this room is hot, between 90–100F. The scalders also keep the humidity at about 100%. You can see the steam in the air as a kind of haze.

You put on your plastic apron to cover your whole body from the sprays of blood and the hot water that keeps the killing machine's blade clean and washes the floor. You put on the steel glove and pick up the knife. . . .

You can hear the squawking from the chickens being hung in the next room as well as the metal shackles rattling. You can hear the motors that drive the chickens down the line. It is so loud you could scream and not hear yourself. (I've done it just to see.) You have to communicate with hand signals to anyone who might come in. Although, no one wants to. They only come in if they have to. . . .

Here come the birds through the stunner into the killing machine. . . . Remember, they come at you 182–186 per minute. There is blood everywhere, . . . on your face, your neck, your arms, all down your apron. You are covered in it. . . .

You can't catch them all, but you try. Every time you miss one you "hear" the awful squawk it's making when you see it flopping around in the scalder, beating itself against the sides. Damn, another "redibird." You know that for every one you see suffer like this, there have been as many as 10 you didn't see. You just know it happens.

The sheer amount of killing and blood can really get to you after awhile, especially if you can't just shut down all emotion completely and turn into a robot zombie of death. You feel like part of a big death machine. Pretty much treated that way as well. . . . You are murdering helpless birds by the thousands (75,000 to 90,000 a night). You are a killer.

You can't really talk to anyone about this. The guys at work will think you are soft. Family and friends don't want to know about this. It makes them uncomfortable and unsure of what to say or how to act. They can even look at you a little weird. Some don't want much else to do with you when they know what you do for a living. You are a killer. . . .

You begin to feel a sense of disgust at yourself at what you have done and continue to do. You are ashamed to tell others what you do at night while they are asleep in their beds. You are a killer. . . .

You shut down all emotions eventually. . . . You have bills to pay. You have to eat. But, you don't want chicken. You have to be really hungry to eat that. You know what goes into every bite. . . .

You feel isolated from society, not a part of it. Alone. You know you are different from most people. They don't have visions of horrible death in their heads. They have not seen what you have seen. And they don't want to. They don't even want to hear about it. If they did, how could they eat that next piece of chicken?

Welcome to the nightmare I escaped. I'm better now. I play well with others, at least most of the time. . . .[36]

Working in a slaughterhouse is one of the most trying occupations there is, physically and emotionally. An elevated rate of work accidents has been observed, as well as of psychological difficulties related to stress and to the effort involved in overcoming the natural aversion to killing that is present in most humans.[37] Considerable numbers of former employees and investigators in killing facilities suffer from post-traumatic stress syndrome.

Whose fault is this? Who can we blame? According to the student veterinarian Christiane M. Haupt, who tells us of her experience as an intern in a slaughter facility, it is the consumers who maintain this system, and thus ultimately they are the ones who are responsible for it all:

It occurs to me that, with a few exceptions, the people who work here are not behaving inhumanely, they have simply become indifferent, as I have myself with time. It's a kind of self-protection. No, the really inhumane ones are the ones who order these daily mass murders, and who because of their fierce appetite for meat, condemn these animals to a miserable life and a very sad end, and force other human beings to carry out this degrading work that turns them into gross beings. Myself, I have gradually become a little cog in this monstrous automaton of death.[38]

One hundred million animals are also killed every year for their fur. In a documentary made with a hidden camera by a Swiss team of investigators,[39] one sees the Chinese breeders who are knocking out minks by spinning them around holding them by the rear legs and then banging their heads against the ground. Then they skin them alive, and once the entire skin with the fur on it has been removed, they throw the animals, whose skin is entirely bare and raw, on a heap along with their already processed fellows. The look in the eyes of the minks, as they die slowly, silent and immobile, is intolerable to any onlooker who has even an ounce of pity. The impression is all the more shocking because of the contrast provided by the casual conversation of the breeders, chatting with each other completely nonchalantly, with cigarettes in their mouths, as they continue to "peel" these animals like zucchinis.

The descriptions we read, and still more the scenes we see in documentaries depicting this sad reality, are perhaps intolerable for many of us, but it would be good to ask ourselves why they disturb us so much. Isn't it because we do tolerate all this in the end? Or is it because we are afraid of being submerged in empathic pain if we allow our emotions to enter too intimately into these sufferings?

Unfortunately, we are not dealing here with just a few horror scenes that have been caught in the spotlight. These figures defy the imagination. Every year, more than a billion land animals are killed in France, 10 billion in the United States, and approximately 60 billion in the world. More recently China, India, and a number of other countries with emerging economies have intensified industrial breeding. In France, 95 percent of pigs consumed are products of industrial breeding. This is also the case for 80 percent of laying hens and cooking chickens and 90 percent of calves. Forty million rabbits are killed each year, and they are almost all raised in cages.[40] In *Ces Bêtes qu'on Abat* (These Animals That We Slaughter), investigator Jean-Luc Daub writes: "To those who don't know it, I want to reveal this fact: most of the animals raised in industrial systems see the light of day for the first time on their way to the slaughterhouse. Even, for many of them, this relocation is the first time they have a chance to take a step. This is what we are supporting when we buy a package of bacon or a chicken at the cheapest available price."[41]

In many countries, notably in the European Union, new laws are being passed that are meant to put an end to the worst of these treatments, but they are still being practiced in many systems of animal production elsewhere in the world.

Jean-Luc Daub found again and again that, although there are some slaughter facilities that follow the rules, there are others that pay no attention to them whatsoever. Thus he is led to doubt the efficacy of the actions of the public authorities in this area (in this particular case, public veterinary services). Reading certain passages in his book, one might well ask oneself, as he does, "if the people who commit the acts I have described have lost their minds, since what they do is really unthinkable."[42]

A Thousand Billion Sea Creatures

As for fish, shellfish, and "seafood," one study using data provided by several international organizations regarding annual catches (a study that divides the tonnage of the catches by an estimated average weight of the individuals of each species caught) has come to the astronomically large figure of about a thousand billion fish and other sea creatures killed per year.[43] The overwhelming majority of the catch is accounted for not by populations who traditionally practice fishing in order to supply their basic needs but rather by industrial fishing operations.

This estimate includes neither the very large number of catches that are not officially registered, which amounts to at least double the official number, nor the immense number of marine species that suffer serious negative effects from industrial fishing. In France, the number of fish and shellfish killed each year is around two billion.

As Foer tells us, "No fish gets a good death. Not a single one. You never have to wonder if the fish on your plate had to suffer. It did."[44]

They sometimes suffer agonies of death for hours at a time, caught on the hooks of fishing lines several miles long. Once out of the water, they die of suffocation or from the bursting of internal organs that results from the rapid decompression they undergo as they are pulled up from the depths in nets. It is not rare for them to be gutted alive. The fins of sharks and the fleshy sides of tuna are cut off, and then the mutilated animals are thrown back in the sea, condemned to mortal sufferings that can last for some time. As part of the vicious cycle of suffering, a quarter of all fish taken in world fishing operations are then used to feed the animals in industrial breeding facilities.

Traditional Breeding versus Organic Breeding—A Lesser Evil?

Farmers who practice breeding in natural surroundings offer animals conditions of life that are incomparably better than what prevails in systems of industrial production, and the animals suffer far less. Nevertheless, the situation is far from rosy. The animals continue to be considered products for consumption, and the quest for profit and financial viability continues on at their expense.

Traditional breeders, as Jocelyne Porcher tells us, maintain much more humane relations with their animals. They know them each individually, and their whole operation is not organized around an obsessive effort to maximize profit. The animal is thus not reduced to a "thing" that is exploited without mercy.[45] But a "lesser evil" is not morally sufficient, since one cannot demonstrate that it is necessary to kill these animals (unless it is the only option for survival). Nevertheless, as the philosopher Thomas Lepeltier points out, "Behind the very idealized image of a relationship of trust based on a kind of unspoken contract, there is often a much harsher reality. . . . Traditional breeding remains an activity that is based on the exploitation of animals, which inevitably brings about cruelty."[46]

In particular, one birth after the other, traditional breeders always forcibly separate from the cows, the goats, and the sheep their little calves, kids, and lambs, so that they (the breeders) can take their milk. The newborns that are not set aside to become future mothers or sires are quickly sent to a slaughter facility. As for the adult animals, they undergo the same fate as soon as it is no longer economical to exploit them. The fact that they temporarily enjoy better conditions does not save the animals from the traumas of transport to the place where they will be killed. During transport they undergo the same painful treatment as their fellow animals in the industrial breeding systems. Thus the assertion that traditional breeders do not practice breeding in order to make money from their animals but so they can live with them is questionable, since one way or the other breeding remains a business based on programmed killing.[47]

Moreover, the labels used to attract well-intentioned consumers are often deceptive. The label "organic" used for chickens does not mean at all that the fowl were raised in nature, but simply that they were *fed* organic grains. Even chickens designated as "raised in the open air" in reality live in sordid hangars where 9 to 12 birds are crowded into every square meter. From time to time they are allowed to move around in a corridor enclosed in wire mesh or are let outside for a short time so they can walk around a little. We are still far away from the "happy chickens" that the ads boast of. As for the "free range" designation, it presumes access to a large and open land area, covered in part by vegetation. However, even in these much more livable conditions, the animals endure all kinds of abuse: castration with or without anaesthesia, separations of mothers and offspring, elimination of male chicks at birth, "reform" (that is, killing) of hens with reduced egg output in order not to have to maintain them any longer, and so on.

During a forum organized by Ecolo-Ethik in the senate at the Luxembourg Palace, I quoted George Bernard Shaw, who said: "Animals are my friends, and I don't eat my friends." An organic breeder who was participating at the roundtable and who had proudly shown me a photo of a calf that had been born that very morning at his farm, made the following statement in his presentation: "I am not my animals' friend. I raise them to kill them."

Such a statement, clear and candid as it is, makes us question directly the value of a breeding operation whose final result is the death of the animals. Would it make any sense to propose instead a nonviolent kind of breeding operation that only keeps cows for their milk, sheep for their wool, and hens for their eggs, while protecting the lives of all of them? Until something better comes along, that kind of a proposal might at least help to reconcile the *welfarists*, who aim through reforms to improve the conditions for animals used by humans without, however, challenging the whole system, and the *abolitionists*, who advocate doing away with all forms of instrumentalization of animals. To give an example from history of the two approaches, welfarists used to talk about making the slave trade more "humane." The abolitionists, who at that time were regarded as extremists or crackpots, did not want to make improvements in the slave trade but purely and simply to abolish it. They were the ones, fortunately, who won out in the end.

Killing Humanely?

It cannot be denied that here and there some improvements have been made. In the United States, where for a long time industrial breeding had been exempt from all animal protection laws, the situation has been improved a little bit thanks to the work of Temple Grandin, who redrew plans of slaughter facilities in such a way that the animals are less thrown into panic on the way to death. The ramp that leads the animals in single file toward the place where the killing occurs is now called "the stairway to paradise." A pity the animals don't know how to read. . . . Though it is undeniably desirable to reduce the sufferings of animals in whatever way possible, the attitude that makes ourselves feel better by saying that, from now on, 100 billion animals will be "killed humanely" every year remains a terrible one.

Jurist and author David Chauvet had this to say on this point: "For most people, killing animals is not a problem as long as they are killed painlessly. This is known as 'killing humanely.' Of course none of us would accept being 'killed humanely' unless it was somehow in our own interest, for example, if it meant cutting our own suffering short. But it is certainly not in the interest of animals to be killed so they can end up in little pieces on the shelves of the supermarkets."[48]

This point has not escaped certain defenders of animal rights, who point out that considering it sufficient merely to make the conditions of life and death of animals more "humane" is no more than a means to salve our consciences while we carry on with massacring animals. What has to be done is just to end it, since killing a sentient being without necessity is no more acceptable in open fields than in meat plants.

Most of the suffering we inflict on others has nothing unavoidable about it. Only the conception we have of others makes it possible. If we identify an ethnic group as vermin, we will have no scruple about trying to exterminate it. From the moment when we consider other sentient beings as inferior beings whose fate doesn't matter, we will not hesitate to use them as instruments to bring about our own well-being.

Some people might say, "But when you come right down to it, that's life. Why such a flood of sentimentality about the way we have always behaved? The animals themselves have always eaten each other. These are the laws of nature. What's the point of trying to change them?" We can answer that right away by pointing out that we are supposed to have evolved since our barbarous days. We are supposed to have become more peaceful and more humane. If that is not the case, how can we justify extolling the advance of civilization? Is it not still the case today that people who systematically exercise brutality and violence are called "barbarians"?

It is probably enough for most of us just to be better informed and to made aware of what goes on every day in industrial breeding operations and slaughter facilities for us to change our opinions quite naturally and even be willing to change our lifestyle. With very few exceptions, the media hardly inform the public; in any case, it is pretty much impossible for them to investigate the slaughterhouses freely. Nonetheless, particularly on the Internet, we do encounter reports that pull no punches in showing us the reality of the places where the meat we eat comes from.[49]

According to a study cofinanced by the French ministry of agriculture based on a representative sample of the population, only 14 percent of French people disagree with the proposition: "It is normal for humans to raise animals for their meat." On the other hand, 65 percent answer yes to the question, "Would you find it unpleasant to watch animals being slaughtered?"[50] The conclusion we can draw seems to be that it's fine for animals to be slaughtered as long as we don't have to see it. Out of sight, out of mind.

Standing up for the right thing might be painful, but that pain can, and should be, transmuted into determination and courage—the courage of compassion. As Elie Wiesel put it in his acceptance speech for the Nobel Peace Prize: "Neutrality helps the oppressor, never the victim. Silence encourages the tormentor, never the tormented."[51]

It's completely up to us.

5

SORRY EXCUSES

In order to justify exploiting animals, we have recourse to religious beliefs on which logic and scientific research have little impact. And in addition we have developed all kinds of reasoning that really does not hold up when confronted with contemporary scientific knowledge or simply with honest reflection. In other words, we provide ourselves with a host of excuses so that we can continue to kill or enslave animals and at the same time keep our consciences clean. Here are some of the standard excuses:

- We have the right to exploit animals any way we like because we are much more intelligent than they are.
- In any case, it is a question of us or them.
- There are so many much more serious problems that humanity has to deal with.
- Animals do not suffer, at least not the way we do.
- Predatory behavior and the struggle for life are part of the laws of nature: we are all rivals, and the strong eat the weak.
- We have to live from something, so the exploitation of animals is a necessity.
- Humans need to eat meat in order to maintain good health.
- Killing and eating animals is part of our ancestral traditions.

We Have the Right to Exploit Animals Any Way We Like Because We Are Much More Intelligent Than They Are

Does the fact that we are more intelligent give us the right to exploit or inflict suffering on those who are less intelligent? Leaving aside the relationship between humans and animals, let us imagine for a moment that intelligence was taken as the essential criterion in determining a person's value, and that as a result humans came to the inescapable conclusion that the most intelligent people had the right to subject the others to their will. Obviously, we would find that unacceptable.

Thanks to our extraordinary intelligence, human beings have the ability to do the greatest good, but also to commit the worst evil. We have at our disposal tremendous potential for creativity, love, and compassion, but also for hatred and cruelty. Does the fact that the human race has produced the cantatas of Bach and the poems of Baudelaire give it the right to inflict suffering on animals? Jean-Jacques Rousseau replies in the negative: "Indeed it seems that if I am obligated to do my fellow human no harm, it is less because he is a reasonable being than because he is a sentient being. This is a quality that is shared by animals and humans alike, and therefore it ought to give the former the right not to be needlessly mistreated by the latter."[1] The philosopher and moralist Henry Sidgwick echoes Rousseau's point: "The difference of rationality between two species of sentient beings does not allow us to establish a fundamental ethical distinction between their respective pains."[2]

Intelligence does indeed constitute an appropriate criterion for choosing a professor of philosophy or an accountant, just as artistic talent is an appropriate criterion for choosing an orchestra conductor or physical strength for employing a stevedore. But it cannot be accepted that intelligence should serve as a criterion to determine whether or not a sentient being should be mistreated, deprived of freedom, or put to death. The only point that should guide our choice is that conscious beings feel a natural desire to live and not to suffer. As the great Indian Buddhist sage Shantideva wrote: "I should combat the pain of others because it is pain like my own. I should work for the good of others because they are like me, living beings."[3]

Moreover, every species possesses "intelligence" and particular abilities that it requires to survive and achieve its ends. Certain animal faculties far surpass human ones. Bats are guided by an extremely sophisticated sonar system. Relying on their sense of smell alone, salmon can find their way back to the river in which they were born after a long migration in the ocean. Migrating birds traverse the planet by orienting themselves by the stars or by polarization of light. All of these are feats of which we are quite incapable. As the American philosopher Tom Regan writes: "As for comprehension: like humans, many nonhuman animals understand the world in which they live and move. Otherwise they could not survive. So beneath the many differences, there is sameness. Like us, these animals embody the mystery and wonder of consciousness. Like us, they are not only in the world, they are aware of it. Like us, they are the psychological centers of a life that is uniquely their own."[4]

In *Animal Liberation,* the work that has doubtless contributed the most toward improving the lot of animals over the past thirty years, Peter Singer also maintains that it is sensibility, the capacity to suffer, that must be taken into consideration when we come to determine how we should treat beings: "If a being suffers there can be no moral justification for refusing to take that suffering into consideration. No matter what the nature of the being, the principle of equality requires that its suffering be counted equally with the like suffering—insofar as rough comparisons can be made—of any other being."[5]

Singer of course recognized that beings are unequal, particularly as far as their intelligence and their ability to act on the world are concerned. He speaks of a principle of "equal consideration of interests," which in no way requires that we treat animals the way we treat humans. A cow has no interest in learning to read and write; rather she has an interest in living in a meadow with her fellow bovines for the rest of her days.

This idea was clearly put forward by the English philosopher, jurist, and economist Jeremy Bentham in his famous declaration:

The day may come when the non-human part of the animal creation will acquire the rights that never could have been withheld from them except by the hand of tyranny. The French have already discovered that the blackness of the skin is no reason why a human being should be abandoned without redress to the whims of a tormentor. Perhaps it will some day be recognised that the number of legs, the hairiness of the skin, or the possession of a tail, are equally insufficient reasons for abandoning to the same fate a creature that can feel. What else could be used to draw the line? Is it the faculty of reason or the possession of language? But a full-grown horse or dog is incomparably more rational and conversable than an infant of a day, or a week, or even a month old. Even if that were not so, what difference would that make? The question is not Can they *reason?* nor, Can they *talk?* but, Can they *suffer?*[6]

The capacity for suffering, rather than intelligence, is thus the main factor that gives all beings the right to be considered as equal. This does not imply that all beings, human or nonhuman, must have the same rights in all matters. Sheep and calves, for example, have no need for the right to vote. However, if people were to open their eyes to the way animals do manifest their feelings, through their cries and their body language, they would understand that the animals are "voting" against the suffering that is inflicted on them. They express their suffering in innumerable ways, and we are the ones *who choose to be deaf and blind* to their messages and who decide that their sufferings do not merit being taken into consideration.

In Any Case, It is a Question of Us or Them

Such a dilemma could certainly present itself, but not very often. If it is a question of choosing between running over a dog crossing the road and driving the family car into a ravine, nobody would have to ask what the right choice is. Human life is clearly more precious. This type of decision also comes up when a person is protecting him- or herself from predators. But in daily life, the choice that confronts most of us is not the welfare of human beings *or* that of animals. We can do both. Being a vegetarian in no way conflicts with trying to help homeless people.

As Henri Lautard, a writer of the end of the nineteenth century, very aptly put it, this argument is generally an excuse not to be bothered about anybody, either animals or humans:

And what about people? we might be asked. What about human beings who are languishing in the working class or in poverty? Are you really going to neglect them so you can think about animals? Shouldn't you be concerned about people instead? This objection is raised most of the time by the kind of person who thinks not a bit more about suffering humanity than about the condition of animals. It is a diversion, it is egotism revealing itself. This is the kind of person who when you ask him for a contribution, says: "I have my own poor people to take care of," and when a poor person does present himself, he gives the poor person . . . advice.[7]

The truth is that in general we humans do not have to choose between "us or them" in order to survive. The fact is that we purely and simply have arrived at the conclusion that the life of animals is not worthy of consideration *per se*. We just take the point of view that insofar as they are useful to us in any way, regardless of how trifling, the work animals do for us, the curtailment of their freedom, their flesh, their skin, their fur, their bones, their horns, and their suffering are all things we have an absolute right to, and there is no appeal.

There Are So Many Much More Serious Problems That Humanity Has to Deal With

One of the reproaches I have most often had to face is that it is indecent to turn our attention to animals in order to improve their lot when so much suffering is being experienced by human beings in Syria, Iraq, the Sudan, and elsewhere. The simple fact of giving consideration to animals is an insult to the human race. Hurled at us with a force of indignation that tries to pass itself off as stemming from a higher sense of virtue, this argument can seem to be right on the mark, but as soon as we look at it more closely, we see that it is entirely without logic.

If devoting a part of our thoughts, words, and actions to the reduction of the unspeakable suffering that we deliberately inflict on animals, our fellow sentient beings, constitutes the sin of taking human suffering too lightly, what does spending time listening to popular music, engaging in sports, or lying on the beach getting a suntan amount to? Do people who give themselves over to these activities or other activities like them suddenly become abominable people just because they do not spend all of their time trying to remedy the famine in Somalia?

Luc Ferry's remarks are quite appropriate:

> I would like to have somebody explain to me what the benefit for human beings of torture is. Is the lot of the Christians in Iraq made better by the fact that in China dogs, while still alive, are cut to pieces by the thousands every year and then allowed to slowly expire for hours in the belief that the more atrocious their pain is, the better their meat will taste? Does the abuse of dogs result in our being more sensitive to the misfortunes of the Kurds? . . . We can all give due attention to the people we are close to, to our families, to our jobs, and even engage in politics and social life without having to massacre animals.[8]

If someone spends 100 percent of the time in humanitarian labors, more power to him or her; that person should continue. Moreover, we could safely bet that anyone endowed with that level of altruism would also be benevolent toward animals. Benevolence is not a commodity that needs to be distributed sparingly like cake or chocolate. It is a way of being, an attitude, an intention to do good for those who enter our sphere of attention and the wish to alleviate their suffering. Loving animals *also* does not mean loving humans *less*. In fact, by also loving animals we love people better, because our benevolence is then vaster and therefore of better quality. Someone who loves only a selection of sentient beings, even of humanity, is the possessor of only fragmentary and impoverished benevolence.

It is interesting to note that a study in which neuroscientists scanned the brains of omnivores, vegetarians, and vegans watching images of suffering humans and suffering animals showed that the areas of the brain associated with empathy were more highly activated in vegetarians and vegans than in omnivores, not only when confronted with the images of animal suffering but also when confronted by images of human suffering.[9]

Other studies based on questionnaires have already shown the existence of this correlation, an indication that the more concern people feel for animals, the more concern they feel for human beings.[10]

For those of us who do not labor day and night to alleviate the sufferings of humanity, what harm is there in alleviating the sufferings of animals rather than playing cards? The sophistic assertion of indecency that asserts that it is immoral to take an interest in the lot of animals as long as there are millions of human beings dying of hunger is, most of the time, an evasion that comes from people who on the whole do not do much for either human beings or animals. To someone who was mocking the usefulness of her charitable activities, Sister Emmanuelle replied, "And you, sir, what have you done for humanity?"

In my own humble case, this false indictment of indecency is rather out of place, since the humanitarian organization called Karuna-Shechen that I founded cares for 120,000 patients per year, and 25,000 children study in the schools our organization has constructed. Working to spare animals the immense suffering they undergo does not diminish by one iota my determination to alleviate human misery. Needless suffering must be done away with wherever it is, in whatever form it takes. This is a war that has to be waged on all fronts, and it can be.

Thus the supposition that the welfare of humans is fundamentally in competition with the welfare of animals is unfounded. It is clear that including in our concerns the lot of other species is in no way incompatible with doing our best to solve human problems. The fight against cruelty to animals is part of the same process as the fight against torturing humans. The philosopher Florence Burgat and the jurist Jean-Pierre Marguénaud make this clear in an opinion piece that appeared in *Le Monde:*

> To those who consider the legislative progress that has been made with regard to the protection of animals, and even the idea of recognizing their rights, as an insult to the misery of humans, we must reply that human misery is the result of exploitation of, or indifference to, the suffering of the weakest humans, and that on the contrary, it is an insult to this suffering—if not a legitimation of it—to advocate ruthless indifference to the suffering of other beings who are weaker still and will never be capable of consenting

. . . . The protection of animals and the protection of the weakest human beings are part of the same fight of the Law to help those to whom it has perhaps done harm.[11]

There are a thousand ways to refrain from harming animals and to be vigilant in their protection without the least negative effect on the human species, without reducing by one minute the time one spends with one's family, and without utilizing even the least fraction of the resources set aside to help those human beings who are in dire circumstances. Jean-Luc Daub, who for years carried out investigations of slaughter facilities, has written:

> You still hear comments such as: "And what are you doing about children? about handicapped people? about the prisoners in Guantanamo? etc. etc." As if the mere fact that we are protecting animals makes us responsible for human suffering, or at least ought to make us feel guilty about it. However, most of the people who come up with this kind of comment accomplish nothing in their lives. . . . As to my profession, I am a technically specialized educator. My work is to accompany mentally handicapped people in their everyday life. But here I am justifying myself when in reality there is no reason why I should, and any reasonably intelligent person would not raise such crude and idiotic questions![12]

The bad faith of people who reproach animal advocates for not spending their time on human problems appears in its true absurdity when we realize that they never make similar reproaches to people who paint pictures, engage in sports, are garden enthusiasts, or collect stamps.

Reducing animal exploitation can even present considerable mutual advantages, as Peter Singer explains in relation to vegetarianism:

> It takes no more time to be a vegetarian than to eat animal flesh. In fact, . . . those who claim to care about the well-being of human beings and the preservation of our environment should become vegetarians for that reason alone. They would thereby increase the amount of grain available to feed people elsewhere, reduce pollu-

tion, save water and energy, and cease contributing to the clearing of forests; moreover, since a vegetarian diet is cheaper than one based on meat dishes, they would have more money available to devote to famine relief, population control, or whatever social or political cause they thought most urgent.[13]

Animals Do Not Suffer, at Least Not the Way We Do

This idea reached its height with Descartes, for whom, as we saw, animals "are no more than simple machines, automata. They feel neither pleasure nor pain, nor anything else at all."[14] According to Nicolas Malebranche, an admirer of Descartes, the cries of animals being cut with a knife or their contortions when touched with a hot iron, are only mechanical reflexes and do not correspond in any way to what we humans call the sensation of pain.[15] In the *The Fable of the Bees* (La Fable des Abeilles, 1714), Bernard de Mandeville answers him as follows:

When a large and gentle bullock, after having resisted a ten times greater force of blows than would have killed his murderer, falls stunned at last . . . , what mortal can, without compassion, hear the painful bellowings intercepted by his blood, the bitter sighs that speak the sharpness of his anguish, and the deep sounding groans, with loud anxiety, fetched from the bottom of his strong palpitating heart; look on the trembling and violent convulsion of his limbs; see, while his reeking gore streams from him, his eyes become dim and languid, and behold his strugglings, gasps and last efforts for life, the certain signs of his approaching fate? When a creature has given such convincing and undeniable proofs of the terrors upon him and the pains and agonies he feels, is there a follower of Descartes so inured to blood as not to refute by his commiseration the philosophy of the vain reasoner?[16]

Anticipating contemporary Darwinian analyses and ethological research, Hippolyte Taine wrote the following concerning the love

Jean La Fontaine felt for animals: "He follows their emotions, he represents their reasonings, he becomes tender, he becomes gay, he participates in their feelings. The fact is, he lived in them. . . . The animals contain all the materials of man—sensations, judgments, images."[17]

We now know that in the course of evolution animals developed different forms of sensibility that were adapted to the conditions surrounding them and necessary to their survival. As we said before, many of them acquired sense faculties that in certain areas are quite superior to those of humans. The experience of pain, in particular, was formed and refined over millions of years, because feeling pain is an ability that is essential to survival. It represents an alarm system that incites an animal to get away as fast as possible from anything that puts its physical integrity in danger. Subjective sufferings, which appeared along with the emotions, are present in a great number of species. Darwin wrote: "We have seen that the senses and intuitions, the various emotions and faculties, such as love, memory, attention, curiosity, imitation, reason, etc., of which man boasts, may be found in an incipient, or even sometimes in a well-developed condition, in the lower animals."[18] In other words, neither pain nor psychological suffering nor the emotions appeared in man ex nihilo.

Darwin contemporary Jean-Henri Fabre also had this to say: "The animal, built as we are, suffering the same way we do, is too often the victim of our brutalities. Anyone who with no motive causes an animal to suffer commits an act of barbarism, I might well say, an act of 'inhumanity,' because he tortures flesh that is sister to our own flesh, he brutalizes a body that shares with us the same mechanism of life, the same susceptibility to pain."[19]

Why would animals possess the same system of physiological mechanisms that we do, the same biochemical substances necessary not only to perception but also to the inhibition of pain, if they did not feel any? Moreover, if all the mechanisms for the detection and control of pain are already present in animals, there is no reason to say that the *experience* of pain and psychological suffering appeared suddenly and exclusively in humans. Voltaire, as noted earlier, had already demanded, "Answer me, mechanist: did nature arrange all the apparatus of sensation in this animal in order that it should feel nothing? Does it have nerves in order to be without sensation? Do not suppose this kind of incongruous contradiction in nature.[20] Bernard Rollin, professor of philosophy and animal sciences at Colorado State University, concluded that "it is extremely improbable that animals are simple machines if we ourselves are not."[21]

The incongruity of this idea can become painfully obvious, as the following anecdote reported by Rollin indicates. At a scientific conference, when he suggested that the reason veterinarians use anaesthesia and pain killers on animals is that animals feel pain, one of the researchers present got up and said, "Anaesthesia and pain killers have nothing to do with pain, they are methods of chemical support." To which an Australian participant responded, "He's off his rocker! Why the devil do the animals have to be restrained if they feel no pain?"[22] Let us not forget, as Boris Cyrulnik reminds us, that as recently as the 1960s, it was thought that newborn children felt no pain, and they were operated on without anaesthesia.[23]

As to the degree of sensitivity to pain, this is determined by the complexity of the nervous system and also by the quantity of neurotransmitters and hormones secreted by the body when it undergoes an external aggression or an internal dysfunction. Apprehension and rejection of pain, along with the anxiety that accompanies them, are already present in animals. All of these feelings are of course amplified in humans when mental constructs are added to them; this renders the experience of suffering in humans much more complex.

Depending on the situation, either intelligence or limitations on intelligence can augment the psychological impact provoked by danger. "Human knowledge," comments J.-B. Jeangène Vilmer, "can itself be the source of suffering, which doubles the impact: persons condemned to death suffer from knowing that they are going to die, for example, in six months; whereas a cow does not possess this knowledge. But animal ignorance can also be the source of suffering, because unlike humans, a wild animal cannot distinguish between an attempt to capture it and keep it alive from an attempt to kill it."[24]

Moreover, many animals are extremely stoic, and their behavior may well not appear to us as a manifestation of suffering. A domestic animal that is suffering stops playing; it has a tendency to sleep a lot and considerably modifies its habits. It might become nervous, aggressive toward animals of the same species as well as its masters or, by contrast, remain downcast, prostrate, or try to hide. A cat that has had a limb broken is more likely to hide than to cry out with pain. A dog that has suffered internal injuries from being struck by a car may not manifest anything other than more resigned and placid behavior. Among cows and horses, grinding the teeth is frequently a sign of general pain. Because of not having the knowledge to interpret these messages properly, until recently veterinary caregivers have not taken the trouble to administer pain killers to animals in pain.[25]

Fish are the ultimate voiceless creatures. They do not screech like the pigs having their throats slit, and they have no facial expressions that might reveal their sensations and move us as we are pulling them out of the water and allowing them to "drown" in the air as we would drown in water. Nonetheless, if we attentively observe a dying fish, its desperate efforts to breathe, its crazed eyes, and its final flopping about will tell us enough about the agonies it is enduring. Caught in nets or hooked on fishing lines (which are sometimes tens of miles long), fish can remain alive for hours, even days.[26] When they are pulled up rapidly from the depths, the decompression causes their swim bladders to burst, their eyes to pop out of their sockets, and their esophagi and stomachs to vomit out of their mouths.

Up until just a few years ago, serious scientists cast doubt on the capacity of fish to feel pain. In the meantime, many studies have shown that fish have nervous systems similar to those of other vertebrates for detecting and perceiving pain, and they produce enkephalins and endorphins like those that play a role in countering pain in humans. In this way, it has been possible to show that they are capable of feeling pain as well as fear and distress.[27]

Furthermore, the level of intelligence of fish is higher than was previously thought. Fish from Tanzania use observation and deductive reasoning to determine the social status of their enemies, and they remember it. Later, if a territorial conflict occurs, the individual that has had the opportunity to observe a clash between two other fish of its species can choose to fight with the loser of that earlier battle in order to improve its chances of winning.[28] It has also been observed that largemouth bass learn quickly to avoid hooks simply by observing how others have been caught by them.[29]

Lobsters, crabs, shrimps, and other crustaceans also possess a sensorial system that is highly developed, although different from that of vertebrates; they respond instantly to painful stimuli. Several research studies have shown that crabs learn lessons from painful experiences (electric shocks, for example) and make lasting changes in their behavior when they come upon the place where the shock was initially received: they remain for shorter periods of time in this spot and feed more rapidly than normal even when offered one of their favorite prey.[30] In the opinion of researchers, a single nociceptive reflex to an external stimulus is not capable of bringing about this kind of behavior change. Other researchers have observed that a certain species of shrimp carefully cleans one antenna (and not the other) on which some acetic acid has been placed, but it does not react if an anesthetic agent has been applied beforehand. This behavior indicates that it is a matter here of a reaction to pain and not simply a reflex triggered by contact with a foreign chemical substance. We should know that when a lobster is plunged into boiling water, it remains alive for nearly a minute afterward.[31] Even in earthworms we find substances associated with processes of pain, endorphins in particular. In his work entitled *Les Animaux Souffrent-ils? (Do Animals Suffer?)*, Philippe Devienne makes the following appeal to common sense:

If we see an injured animal moan and tremble, we know directly that it is in pain. We simply say, "it is suffering" and that is neither a matter of opinion nor a knowledge issue. The structure of reality just appears this way in our expressions. We learn that the idea of suffering applies to human beings and to animals, but we do not use it in the case of pens, computers, or chairs. We might say that a robot that has electronic sensors is malfunctioning or is broken, but we do not say of a dog or a horse that it is broken. It has gone blind, it is sick, it has lost consciousness, it is suffering.[32]

When it comes to the psychological suffering of animals, denying it is absurd. "Though the mooing of the dairy cow separated from its calf may not be an expression of physical pain, it is nonetheless an indication of profound distress," Alexandrine Civard-Racinais tells us.[33] Canadian studies have demonstrated clearly that cows undergo distress and trauma when they are separated from their calves just the day after the birth and led immediately into the milking barn. As Boris Cyrulnik notes, "By proceeding in this manner, you empty the world of both the mother and the very young animal; you provoke extremely intense suffering, true despair. These are not nociceptive pathways that are stimulated here, but mental representations that are affected. Both cow and calf have been deprived of what made sense for them."[34]

The expression of mourning can be found among many species. It is particularly noticeable among elephants. When one of them is about to die, its fellows crowd around it, try to lift it up, sometimes even try to feed it. Then when they see that it is dead, they go and fetch branches, which they pile on its body and all around it; sometimes they even cover it completely. The ethologist Joshua Plotnik reports the case of an old female elephant, sixty-five years old, that had fallen down in a very muddy spot in the jungle in Thailand and was unable to regain its feet. Over a period of hours, mahouts and well wishers tried to get it back on its feet. During that whole time, the old elephant's companion Mae Mai, a younger female who was not related to her, refused to leave her side. The men having failed, Mae Mai, in a state of great agitation, came to the side of her old friend and tried several times to get her onto her feet by pushing with her head. Each time this met with failure, Mai Mae banged her trunk on the ground with frustration. When after several days the old female died, Mae Mai repeatedly urinated and began to trumpet loudly. When the mahouts began trying to use a large wooden frame to lift the old female, Mae Mai stood in their way and systematically pushed the wooden frame away from the corpse. She spent the next two days pacing back and forth in the park trumpeting shrilly and bringing forth answering trumpets from the rest of the herd.[35]

Jane Goodall describes how Flint, a young chimpanzee of eight who was very attached to his mother, fell into a deep depression after her death. Three days after her death he climbed up to the nest of branches where his mother had been in the habit of resting and contemplated it for a long time. Then he climbed back down and lay down in the grass, prostrate, his eyes wide open, gazing into space. He practically stopped eating and died three weeks later.[36]

Predatory Behavior and the Struggle for Life Are Part of the Laws of Nature

Many people think like this: "Many animals eat each other and it has always been this way, since the time life appeared on earth. Thus it is futile to go against the laws of nature, as harsh as they may be." Lord Chesterfield speaks of the "general order of nature, which has instituted universal preying upon the weaker as one of her first principles."[37]

Benjamin Franklin was at one time a vegetarian. Then, one day he noticed that the fish he had caught had eaten other fish. He said to himself, "If you eat one another, I don't see why we may not eat you." He immediately gave up being a vegetarian. All the same, he was not entirely deceived by his weak argument, for he added that one of the advantages of being a reasonable creature is that one can find a reason for whatever one wants to do.[38] Let us content ourselves with the knowledge that if we can justify any behavior at all simply by saying that "others do it," we could without the least compunction rob banks, beat women and children, and reestablish slavery.

Competition and predation are certainly more visible and more spectacular than cooperation and mutual help. Nevertheless, it is reasonable to say that the world of the living is characterized more by cooperation than by competition. In fact, as Martin Nowak, director of the Program for Evolutionary Dynamics at Harvard, explains, evolution requires cooperation in order to be able to construct new levels of organization.[39] Darwin wrote concerning cooperation: "However complex the manner in which this feeling is born, since it is very important for all animals who help and defend each other, it will be developed in the course of natural selection; for those communities which contained the greatest number of more compassionate individuals would be the best able to prosper and raise the greatest number of offspring."[40]

Humans call "bestial" anyone who conducts himself brutally. However, almost all the animals who kill do so in order eat, whereas humans are practically the only ones who kill for hatred, for pleasure, or through cruelty. Plutarch comments as follows: "You call serpents and panthers and lions savage, but you yourselves, by your own foul slaughters, leave them no room to outdo you in cruelty; for their slaughter is their living, yours is a mere appetizer."[41]

Having recourse to the "laws of nature" excuse is part of what Jean-Baptiste Jeangène Vilmer calls "the historical alibi," which "consists in justifying meat eating and hunting with the pretext that human beings were originally meat eaters and hunters." "True," he continues, "but they were also sometimes cannibals, and we do not deduce from that that it is acceptable to be a cannibal today. The behavior of primitive humans was justified by their primitive way of life. Once this way of life has disappeared, certain aspects of that behavior are no longer absolutely necessary."[42] Civilization consists in moving from barbarism to humanity, from slavery to individual liberty, from cannibalism to respect for others, but also from unlimited exploitation of animals to respect for all sentient beings.

In a democracy, the laws protect citizens from the violence of their fellows. Why not also include other beings? Democracy is said to be the guarantor of freedom. But if this does not include the freedom of *all* beings, it becomes freedom of a curious sort, a sort that makes use of might-makes-right to justify feeding ourselves on the deaths of others and making our stomachs their cemeteries.

We Have to Live from Something

The "economic alibi" is also frequently called upon. Jeangène Vilmer illustrates:

> Advocates of seal hunting, and first among them the Canadian government, stress the fact that seal hunting is an important industry with a value of more than twenty million dollars that creates jobs in regions where unemployment is especially high, notably in Newfoundland and Labrador. In France, the producers of pâté de foie gras speak of the thirty thousand jobs that the industry creates, and bullfighting fans recall that the corrida employs tens of thousands of people, etc.[43]

However, the legitimacy of an activity should not be judged by the profits it generates and the jobs it can create; otherwise traffickers of drugs or arms could claim the right to pursue their businesses. Slavery was a profitable industry, and the economic argument was put forward many times to defend against abolition of the African slave trade.

Recently Spanish aficionados have let it be known that, if the corrida were prohibited, they would sue for being deprived of the right to work, a fundamental right provided for in the Spanish constitution. Thus we see that not causing harm to others should be added to the definition of legitimate work. Otherwise, a paid killer, who after all does gain his livelihood from his trade, could cite the right to work as legitimizing his profession. The lobby of the deep-water fishing industry, which trawls the ocean bottoms and thus, as we recall, is brutally destructive to their rich biodiversity, has also claimed that several hundred jobs would be lost if the European Union prohibited this kind of fishing. Claire Nouvian of the BLOOM Association[44] tells us that ten deep-water trawlers can skim an area of sea bottom the equivalent of the area of Paris in two days. So the lobby's reasoning is a bit like destroying Notre Dame and the Chartres Cathedral with bulldozers in a few hours and then replying to the protesters, "But, you see, if we don't do this, the bulldozer operators might be out of a job."

Humans Need to Eat Meat in Order to Maintain Good Health

This argument is often used by people who simply want to continue to eat meat or convince their reluctant children to do so. There are roughly 550 to 600 million vegetarians in the world, and they are in as good health as the meat eaters, if not better.

Aymeric Caron explains as follows: "No meat = no protein. There is an idea we take for granted that needs to be refuted once and for all."[45] The food that provides the most protein is soy. Soy is about 40 percent protein, twice as much as meat (about 15 to 20 percent). Other legumes are also significant sources of protein: dried beans, lentils, and chickpeas are around 20 percent. Peanuts are nearly 30 percent. As far as grains go, we find 10 to 15 percent protein in rice, wheat, barley, millet, rye, buckwheat, oats, quinoa, corn, kamut, and spelt. We find 25 percent protein in wheat germ, 30 percent in seitan, which is made from wheat gluten. Spinach, broccoli, and seaweed are equally rich in protein. Moreover, food made from vegetable protein has the advantage of containing carbohydrates—not found in meat—as well as edible fiber.

The myth of "incomplete proteins" promulgated by meat-industry lobbyists is based on old and outmoded research methods. According to the reliable data provided by the World Health Organization and the Food and Health Organization of the United Nations, which are based on a large number of studies,[46] the essential amino acids are present in sufficient quantity and proportion in the majority of vegetable foods. In fact, with regard to their absolute protein content, comparison of a hundred foods shows that the first thirteen on the list in terms of richness in protein are vegetables (soy being 38.2 percent; vetch peas, 33.1 percent; red beans and lentils, 23.5 percent; and a fungus (brewer's yeast), 48 percent). Only in the fourteenth position do we find ham at 22.5 percent and in the twenty-third position tuna at 21.5 percent. Eggs and milk are respectively in the thirty-third and seventy-fifth positions at 12.5 percent and only 3.3 percent. Thus a normal vegetable dish should provide amply for our protein needs.

Animal proteins have no virtue of their own—quite the contrary. In a research study published in 2014, a group of sixteen researchers followed more than six thousand subjects aged 50 to 65. After having observed in detail and then analyzed their dietary habits, they divided the sample into three groups in accordance with their protein consumption: high, medium, and low. This study showed that over the eighteen years of its duration the group with the highest rate of consumption of animal protein had a 75 percent higher overall mortality rate relative to the other groups, specifically a risk of death by cancer that was four times higher. These higher rates diminished or disappeared in the groups where the proteins consumed were vegetable in origin.[47]

As for vitamin B_{12}, which is essential for the formation of hemoglobin in the blood, it can be found in milk and eggs, but it is practically absent in plants. Vegans, as a result, need to obtain it through food supplements that can be made from bacterial cultures.[48]

And for those who think that being a vegetarian affects physical performance, that it might be a handicap for high-level athletes, the journalist Aymeric Caron offers a list of major champions who were vegetarians or vegan. Carl Lewis, winner of nine Olympic gold medals and eight world championships, continues to promote the benefits of a vegetarian or vegan diet.[49] Among the professional athletes who have adopted a vegetarian or vegan diet are Bode Miller, Olympic medal winner and world champion in alpine skiing; Edwin Moses, unbeaten 122 times in a row in the 400 meter hurdles; and Martina Navratilova, holder of the greatest number of titles in the history of tennis. American ultramarathon runner Scott Jurek, who became a vegetarian in 1997 and then a vegan two years later, set a record in 2010 by running 266 kilometers in twenty-four hours. We should also mention Fauja Singh, an Indian vegetarian who became the first centenarian to complete a marathon (he accomplished this feat in Toronto in 2011).

Over long periods of our history, especially the period of the hunter-gatherers, human survival depended in great part on our ability to hunt or fish. Today, mainly because of the considerable expansion of the human population and the intensive exploitation of natural resources everywhere in the world, using tillable acreage and agricultural products for the production of meat is not only no longer a necessity for the survival of the human species, but it constitutes a suboptimal use of alimentary resources. Therefore it is probable that vegetarianism will expand further in our societies, not because of legal regulations that some people will follow and others will ignore, but because of a raising of awareness based on reason and compassion. As Wulstan Fletcher wrote in his introduction to *Food of Bodhisattvas:*

The aim is not to repress one's desire for meat or to terminate one's use of animal products by a draconian act of will. Instead, our task is to develop a heartfelt compassion and a genuine sensitivity to the suffering of animals, such that the desire to exploit and feed on them naturally dissolves. . . . Above all, it is precisely by cultivating a tender conscience, rather than dulling it with specious casuistry, that moral progress is made possible. Eventually, we may arrive at the point where our bodily needs and our way of living cease to be a source of terror and pain for other living beings.[50]

Killing and Eating Animals Is Part of Our Ancestral Traditions

In Nepal, where I live, hundreds of thousands of animals, indeed some years millions, are sacrificed in a bloody manner to invoke the favor of local deities. In 2010 the appeals of a few NGOs and groups of citizens to abandon these rituals aroused groundswells of indignation, and some of the Nepalese ministers objected that this was an "ancestral tradition" that was beyond challenge. In France, one of the arguments of the manufacturers of pâté de foie gras as well as of the bullfighting aficionados is that these are traditions that must be kept alive.

Traditions? How lovely! The Aztecs sacrificed as many as forty persons a day to the sun god. Human sacrifice persisted for long periods among the Hebrews, the Greeks, in Africa, and in India. The Phoenicians sometimes used to burn their own children alive in order to placate the god Baal. Onlookers have spoken with enthusiasm of this kind of killing, saying that "it was a good thing to do."[51] Is it not the natural property of a civilized society to abandon a tradition when it is the source of this kind of suffering?

The philosopher Martin Gibert points out: "It is thus of little importance whether the human being is related to carnivores or herbivores. The length of our intestines or of our canine teeth is a fact of evolution: it cannot determine what is morally acceptable or reprehensible for us to eat. The question is not: 'Can a cheeseburger be properly digested?' The question is not: 'Would your ancestors have eaten it?' The question is: 'Is it morally proper; should you order it?'"[52] The fact that humans are in the habit of eating meat is not an ethical argument. It is a simple fact that tells us nothing whatever about its moral worth. Tradition can explain things, but it cannot *justify* anything.

For the French, the traditions of the corrida and of foie gras are part of our patrimony: the cultural patrimony in the first case, the gastronomic patrimony in the second. The production of foie gras is an ordeal for the geese and the ducks. After having been raised for a time out in the open, the latter are usually shut up in tiny individual cages. Twice a day a hose is forced down their gullets, and in just a few seconds around a pound of thick mush is injected under pressure into their esophagi. It could be compared to forcing an adult human to ingest fifteen and a half pounds of noodles twice a day.[53] The weight of their livers goes from just over a tenth of a pound to nearly a pound and a half in twelve days. This could not happen without causing a variety of ailments: diarrhea, difficult breathing, lesions of the sternum, fractures—to the point where, according to the breeders themselves, the period of force-feeding brings about eight times more deaths than the breeding period preceding it.[54]

On the occasion of a debate in the French National Assembly in 2006 on a law intended to protect the foie gras industry, one deputy denounced the "infernal animal welfare machine that dismantles traditions that are our traditions, especially in the South of France."[55] Infernal for whom? Doubtless for the stomach of the gourmets and for the wallets of the breeders, but certainly not for the animals that are being abused.[56]

Thus we conclude that most of the reasons put forward to justify our societies' lack of consideration for animals boil down to nothing more than sorry excuses, contrived to efface our scruples and to allow us to continue to exploit and mistreat animals with an untroubled conscience.

6

THE CONTINUUM
OF LIFE

The intelligence, empathy, and altruism present in the human species are the fruits of millions of years of gradual evolution. Consequently, it is very much in line with what we should expect when we observe precursory signs of these human emotions, indeed even equivalents, among animals. That was Darwin's idea when he wrote *The Descent of Man, and Selection in Relation to Sex*: "If no organic being excepting man had possessed any mental power, or if his powers had been of a wholly different nature from those of the lower animals, then we should never have been able to convince ourselves that our high faculties had been gradually developed. But it can be clearly shewn that there is no fundamental difference of this kind."[1]

An overall vision of the evolution of species makes it possible to understand more clearly that the question of emotions is one of diversification and degrees of complexity. Following in the footsteps of Darwin, who devoted an entire work to this subject—*The Expression of Emotions in Man and Animals*[2]—a number of ethologists have highlighted the richness of the mental and emotional life of animals. As Jane Goodall, Frans de Waal, and many others have observed, the elementary signals that we use to express pain, fear, anger, joy, surprise, impatience, boredom, sexual excitement, and many other mental and emotional states are not at all unique to our own species.

The point here is that our discriminatory attitudes toward animals are challenged when we become aware of the continuity among species. When we follow that continuity from the most rudimentary

species all the way up to humans, passing along the way through innumerable other species endowed with complex abilities, *different* from
ours (migrating animals, social animals, and so forth), we must think
twice about seeing human beings as special and apart. The continuity of life is manifested in all areas: genetic, anatomical, physiological,
and psychological. As Julien Offray de La Mettrie wrote in the eighteenth century: "Man is not molded from a finer, more precious stuff;
nature employed just one and the same dough, of which she only varied the leavening."[3]

According to Gilles Boeuf, director of the Natural History Museum
of Paris, biologically we profoundly resemble animals. We have the
same cells, the same type of DNA, and so forth. There are 7.7 million
species of animals on earth, and another million species of plants,
fungi, and protozoa. Around 6.5 millions species are found on land
and 2.2 million dwell in the oceans. Among the 1.3 million species who
have been described, 5,000 are mammals, 10,000 are birds, 35,000
species are fish, and 1.1 million are insects; of the insects 80,000 are
coleopteran (beetles).[4] "If God exists," Boeuf comments, "He loves
coleoptera." We have 24,000 genes, only twice as many as the housefly. "It takes only a second to crush a fly," Boeuf adds, "but it took billions of years for the fly to be able to exist."[5]

On the genetic level, 50 percent of the fly's DNA is identical to ours;
but with the chimpanzee the degree of genetic similarity reaches 98.73
percent. We have certainly accomplished marvels with the 1.27 percent
that is ours alone, but from the point of view of evolution, only a few
steps separate us from the common ancestor we share with the great
apes. According to the data in our possession, the evolutionary lineage of ancestors that we share with the great apes separated from the
lineage of the lesser apes about 10 million years ago. Humans share
ancestors with the contemporary great apes that we have no knowledge of. So the genome of humans differs from that of chimpanzees by
only 1.27 percent and by only 1.65 percent from that of gorillas. These
calculations lead us to estimate that our lineage separated from that of
chimpanzees about 5 million years ago, and from that of gorillas about
7 million years ago.

The principal distinguishing evolutionary characteristic of humans in relation to other primates is the erect standing position, which brought in its train a certain number of morphological modifications. On the basis of the erect position, the hand became capable of manipulating a variety of tools. The skull, balanced on the top of the spinal column, was able to develop in such a way as to allow an increase in cerebral mass. A less cramped larynx made it easier to develop an evolved language. All the same, the definition of the genus *Homo* remains rather vague, the principal criterion being the volume of the cranial cavity. Neanderthal man, moreover, had an average cranial capacity of about 1,500 cubic centimeters, slightly bigger than that of modern man.

The genus *Homo*, which groups together all the species of hominids, appeared in Africa about 2.4 million years ago. The most archaic species of this genus—among which we find *Homo ergaster*, *Homo erectus*, and *Homo antecessor*—were followed by *Homo heidelbergensis*, which appeared in Africa a little less than 1 million years ago. This species is considered to have been the common ancestor of modern man and Neanderthal man.

Among all the species that inhabit the earth at the present time, there is none that could be called the ancestor of one or another of the other species. What we have is simply a number of species all more or less related to each other. The bonobo is simply closer to humans than the shark or the housefly is. From a purely biological point of view, no species can truly be considered "more evolved" than any other. Bacteria and ants, for example, are perfectly adapted to their respective milieus and both have had tremendous success in the biosphere. Speaking in terms of "superiority" is a matter of a value judgment that cannot be empirically observed by science. From the chronological point of view, if you reduce to a single year the 15 billion years that is the estimated age of the universe, then civilized man, *Homo sapiens*, did not appear until a minute before midnight on December 31. Thus the species who considers itself the "center of the universe" is in fact a last-minute arrival.

Therefore, if one does not conceive of human beings as a divine creation and thus does not entirely reject the theory of evolution, one can consider human beings as the current endpoint of millions of years of evolution, in the course of which our faculties were refined little by little until they reached the extraordinary degree of complexity that is now ours.

But there is still more. In the course of its history, evolution has never stopped at a fixed point. Some species disappear while others thrive and continue to evolve, because the ones that are most capable of surviving in new conditions and circumstances are the ones that are selected over the course of time. Therefore we have no reason to assert with certainty that *Homo sapiens* has ceased to evolve. If in a few million years we have not ruined our planet to the point of having brought about our own extinction, it is not far-fetched to imagine the emergence of *Homo sapientissimus,* who would surpass us in its intellectual faculties, in the richness of its emotions, in possessing a fabulous level of creativity, an amazing artistic sense, and other capabilities whose existence we cannot guess at present. If *Homo sapientissimus* does not simply replace us altogether, will it regard *Homo sapiens* condescendingly?

The Variety of Mental Faculties

We encounter the continuity between animals and humans again when we examine the nervous systems of animals and the cellular and biochemical mechanisms that allow them to perceive their external surroundings, to feel emotions, and to express them. The mental faculties, in the same way as anatomical features, developed gradually. They also diversified a great deal, since the "world" of a bee, a migratory bird, or a deepwater fish is obviously quite different from the "world" of our own subjective experience. As the philosopher Thomas Nagel has pointed out, we haven't the slightest idea of what it is like to be a bat.[6]

Even if, as Darwin explains, there is a considerable gap between the intellectual faculties of a lamprey eel and a primate, this gap is filled by innumerable gradations that make it possible to retrace the history of gradual and continuous complexification both on the physiological level and on the level of abilities to interact with the surrounding environment. In the end Darwin comes to this conclusion: "Certain facts prove that the intellectual faculties of animals considered very inferior to us are more elevated than we ordinarily think."[7] Thus we are quite far from the peremptory assertion of Buffon, who told us, "The chicken knows neither the past nor the future and is mistaken about the present."[8]

Furthermore, as the philosopher and ethologist Dominique Lestel points out in his *Les Origines Animales de la Culture (Animal Origins of Culture)*, "We still experience great difficulty in accepting the idea that animal behavior can be extremely complex even if this complexity is not of the same nature as the complexity of human behavior. Animal intelligence is not a human intelligence that is *less evolved* than that of humans, but simply a *different* intelligence."[9]

The fact that consciousness is eminently useful for survival inevitably leads us to think that it must be present in many animal species just as it was in our ancestors. As the animal physiologist Donald R. Griffin explains, "The better an animal understands its physical, biological, and social environment, the better it can adjust its behavior to accomplish whatever goals may be important in its life, including those that contribute to its evolutionary fitness."[10] Griffin also points out that in "accepting the reality of our evolutionary relationship to other species of animals, it is unparsimonious to assume a rigid dichotomy of interpretation which insists that mental experiences have some effect on the experience of one animal species [i.e., us humans] but none on any other."[11] And the ethologist Stephen Stich concludes: "In the light of the evolutionary links and the behavioral similarities between humans and higher animals, it is difficult to believe that psychology could explain human behavior but not animal behavior. If humans have beliefs, then animals do too."[12]

Over the past decades, many studies have shown that not only the great apes but also birds, fish, and other animals are capable of empathy and complex reasoning. The ethologist Francine Patterson cites the case of Michael, an orphan gorilla brought from Africa who had learned sign language. One day he indicated that he was sad. When Patterson asked him why, he answered using signs that meant "mother killed," "forest," and "hunters."[13] The primatologist Roger Fouts taught American sign language to several chimpanzees, including the famous Washoe, who had a vocabulary of 350 signs. He tells us that these great apes were able to communicate *among themselves* using this language, and researchers have recorded several hundred of their conversations. The first words that Washoe communicated with signs to his young adopted son, Loulis, were: "Come hug, quick!" For them, these signs became a way to express their emotions, and for us, to understand them. Another case that has been observed is that of mother orangutans who taught their offspring sign language.[14] "Talk, and I will baptize you!" the very Cartesian eighteenth-century cleric Cardinal Polignac cried out to an orangutan that was being held in a cage in the king's garden.[15]

Alex, a parrot from Gabon, fluently used a hundred words and understood a thousand. It understood ideas such as "bigger than" and "smaller than," "the same as" and "different from." When the ethologist Irene Pepperberg, who worked with Alex for thirty years, showed this parrot an object, it could correctly describe its form, its color, and the material it was made out of.[16] It understood, for example, what a key was, and correctly identified this object, no matter what its size and color were. It identified what differentiated it from another object.[17] One day it asked what color it itself was. This was the way it learned the word "gray," after Pepperburg repeated it six times.[18] The last words of Alex to Pepperburg, when she was leaving it for the night, were: "Be well. See you tomorrow. I love you."

The ethologist Richard J. Herrnstein clearly showed that pigeons were capable of assimilating the general idea "human being."[19] He showed the pigeons a large number of photographs, some of which showed humans, others animals or objects. The pigeons received food if they pushed a button with their beak that was in front of the photo of a human and nothing if they pressed the button in front of a photo showing something else. The humans in the photos were of both sexes, all races, all ages, in different postures, naked or dressed. The pigeons very quickly learned to accurately recognize the presence of humans in the photos. This shows, that even though they had no language, they were capable of forming general concepts, such as "human being." He tells us that the pigeons could also recognize particular human individuals, as well as trees, water, fish under water, and others. This indicates that they had the capacity to distinguish particular as well as general characteristics. Even better, during an experiment by Shigeru Watanabe, pigeons were able to successfully recognize paintings according to their style. For example, they distinguished paintings by Picasso from paintings by Monet. They were even able to make generalizations and to recognize "families" of style, Picasso and Braques on one hand, Monet and Cézanne on the other![20]

The Japanese primatologist Tetsuro Matsuzawa showed that the short-term memory of chimpanzees is better than that of adult humans. Chimpanzees were placed in front of a screen where—in random order and for two-tenths of a second each—numbers from one to nine appeared inside empty squares. The chimpanzees were then able to place the correct numbers in the empty squares with an error rate of only 10 percent, which was an error rate half of that of humans. The chimpanzees knew how to count (they could add and subtract simple numbers), and using a keyboard, they could write complex series of words, such as "three red pencils."[21]

Rainbowfish learn after five tries to find an opening that allows them to escape from a net, and more surprising still, they succeed in the exercise on the first try eleven months later.[22] To this day, more than six hundred scientific studies have already been carried out on the learning capacity of fish.

Stanley Curtis of the University of Pennsylvania taught pigs to play a video game utilizing a joystick modified so they could manipulate it with their snout. Not only did they really learn to play, but they did so significantly faster than a trained dog and as fast as a chimpanzee, thus demonstrating an amazing capacity for abstract representation.[23] Kenneth Kephart, professor emeritus at the same university, reports that pigs are as capable as dogs of lifting a latch in order to get out of their pen, that they often do it two at a time, and that they go so far as to open the pens of other pigs to let them out.[24] Suzanne Held from the University of Bristol in England has also shown that pigs are able to form an idea of what one of their fellow animals can or cannot see and thus adopt the point of view of the other animal when they are competing with each other in trying to find food.[25]

As to proofs of empathy, the examples abound, even between different species. The ethologist Ralph Helfer reports having seen a large elephant that had attempted several times to save a baby rhinoceros that had gotten stuck in thick mud. The pachyderm got down on its knees and slipped its tusks under the baby to lift it up. The mother rhino, having not understood that the elephant wanted to save her little one, flew into a rage and charged the elephant, which backed away. This series of events was repeated over the course of several hours. Every time the mother rhino went back into the forest, the elephant came back to try to pull the little one out of the mud. Finally the elephant gave up in the face of the mother's charges. The herd of elephants at last moved on, and luckily the baby rhinoceros finally succeeded in getting itself out of the mud and rejoining its mother.[26]

A number of similar observations have been made of hippopotamuses coming to the aid of animals being attacked by predators. One gripping scene was filmed in the Kruger National Park in South Africa. In the film you see an impala attacked by a crocodile while drinking at the water's edge. The reptile drags its victim into the water and holds it firmly in its jaws while trying to drown it. The impala tries desperately to hold its head above water. Suddenly a hippopotamus that had been on the riverbank rushes into the water at a gallop and charges the crocodile, which lets go of its prey. Severely wounded, the antelope succeeds in heaving itself onto the shore, but collapses after a couple of steps. The hippo follows it, and far from trying to harm it, nuzzles it gently with its snout, licks its wounds and, several times, takes the head of the dying animal into its gigantic mouth, as though trying to breathe new life into it. But the impala's wounds were too deep, and it finally dies. It is not until then that the hippo finally moves away.[27] For Tom Regan, a great number of animals resemble humans:

Like us, they possess different sensory, cognitive, conative, and volitional capacities. They see and hear, believe and desire, remember and anticipate, plan and intend. Moreover, what happens to them matters to them. Physical pleasure and pain—they share with us. But also fear and contentment, anger and loneliness, frustration and satisfaction, cunning and imprudence. These and a host of other psychological states and dispositions collectively help define the mental life and relative well-being of those (in my terminology) subjects-of-a-life we know better as raccoons and rabbits, beaver and bison, chipmunks, squirrels and chimpanzees, you and me.[28]

To become aware, in the light of these discoveries, that human beings are the result of an extraordinary development that took place over millions of years does not amount to a reduction in the value of being human. Those people, who still in spite of everything, insist on making of the human being a category completely apart and for this purpose point to a fundamental difference in nature between humans and animals—all the while claiming to be proponents of evolution—the burden of proof now lies with them.

Speciesism, Racism, and Sexism

Naturally we attach a great deal of importance to anything that is connected with our own immediate concerns, and we have a tendency to turn a blind eye to those who have the misfortune of not belonging to our particular sphere of interest. Our innate preference for our own family, our own community, our own tradition, our own race, and so on, leads us to feel that it is our duty to protect and defend them and at the same time be willing to let the chips fall where they may for all the rest. To the list of our preferred categories, we must also add our own species, for only humans seem important to us.[29]

Again, in 1970 Richard Ryder, a psychologist at Oxford, introduced the concept of speciesism in a brochure that he circulated on the campus of the university. He explained his thought process as follows: "Since Darwin, scientists have agreed that there is no 'magical' essential difference between human and other animals, biologically-speaking. Why then do we make an almost total distinction morally? If all organisms are on one physical continuum, then we should also be on the same moral continuum."[30]

In a collective essay published the following year, Ryder wrote: "If it is accepted as morally wrong to deliberately inflict suffering upon innocent human creatures, then it is only logical to also find it wrong to deliberately inflict suffering on innocent creatures belonging to other species. The time has come to act in accordance with this logic."[31]

The word *speciesism* was added to the *Oxford English Dictionary* in 1985, and in the 1994 edition it is defined as follows: "By analogy with racism and sexism, the term designates the attitude consisting in unduly witholding respect for the life, dignity, and needs of animals belonging to species other than the human species." Peter Singer characterizes speciesism as "a prejudice or attitude of bias in favor of the interests of members of one's own species and against those of members of other species."[32]

Writer and animal rights advocate Joan Dunayer argues that, if speciesism is our failure—on the basis of species membership or species -typical characteristics—to accord all sentient beings equal consideration and respect, we should not be content to call for rights only for a relatively few nonhumans who seem the most human-like (great apes, in particular). Dunayer holds that it is fair, logical, and empirically justified to give all creatures with nervous systems the benefit of the doubt regarding sentience and accord them basic rights such as the right to life and liberty.[33]

Martin Gibert is of the opinion that "Speciesism is a form of *human supremacism*, which is analogous to white supremacism, for example. It postulates that belonging to the human species in itself confers on humans an intrinsic value and a moral superiority over the other species. There we have the idea that would allow us to give priority to human interests over the interests of other species, even if those interests were such pointless ones as foie gras, fur, or dogfighting."[34]

These explanations of speciesism seem clear enough. However, some people have made use of different interpretations of the term to file unjust suits in court and at the same time to attack the cause of animal liberation. The analogy with racism and sexism ought to clarify the issue. Thus, not being a racist or a sexist does not imply that we deny or ignore the differences between the races and the sexes, which would be absurd. In the absence of these differences, racism and sexism would have never existed. The use of these two terms is justified when differences of any kind are being used to support an *egotistical discrimination* based on belonging to a group—the white race or the masculine sex, for example—as well as *the perpetuation of a hierarchy of power* and the exercise of this power for the purpose of *oppressing* those belonging to the *other* group.

There is no lack of tragic examples. The nineteenth-century poet Oliver Wendell Holmes, who was also a professor of anatomy and physiology at Harvard, for example, found it natural that "the white man hates him [the Indian], and hunts him down like the wild beasts of the forest, and so the red-crayon sketch is rubbed out, and the canvas is ready for a picture of manhood a little more like God's own image." At the time of the Nanking Massacre in 1937, the Japanese generals told their troops: "You should not consider the Chinese to be human beings, but rather things of inferior value like dogs or cats." Considering an animal to be a "sausage-making machine" is the same kind of approach. Regarding animals as objects obviously facilitates the work of those who inflict suffering on them all day long. This kind of rationalization allows them to convince themselves that the beings to whom they are committing their atrocities are not sentient, and this helps to take away their sense of guilt.

The kind of speciesism that consists in attributing values and rights to certain beings on the sole basis of their belonging to a particular species is not limited to discriminating between humans and other sentient species, as J.-B. Jeangène Vilmer tells us:

> Speciesism also consists in discriminating among animals. You are a speciesist if on the one hand you protest against killing and eating dogs and cats in Asia and against the hunting of baby seals and whales, but on the other hand you accept killing and eating cows and pigs as well as hunting pheasant and fishing for carp. You are a speciesist because you favor certain species (cats, dogs, baby seals, and whales) because they are "cute" or "lovable" and do so solely on account of their belonging to a certain species. This is what Gary Francione quite accurately calls moral schizophrenia, which consists of loving dogs and cats while at the same time planting our forks in cows and chickens.[35]

Melanie Joy teaches psychology and sociology at the University of Massachusetts. Each semester, she devotes one of her courses to helping students explore their relationships with animals. She begins by asking her students to make a list of the characteristics of dogs and pigs. For dogs, the most frequently used adjectives are *faithful, friendly, intelligent, fun, protective*, and, occasionally, *dangerous*. The pigs, on the other hand, are characterized as *dirty, stupid, lazy, fat, ugly, disgusting*. After this exercise, the discussion takes a form more or less like this:

What makes pigs stupid?
They just are.
Actually, pigs are considered to be even more intelligent than
   dogs. . . . Are all pigs ugly?
Yes.
What about piglets?
Piglets are cute, but pigs are gross.

Why do you say pigs are dirty?
They roll in the mud.
Why do they roll in the mud?
Because they like dirt. They're dirty.
Actually, they roll in dirt to cool off when it's hot, since they don't
   sweat.

After a certain number of questions and answers of this sort, Melanie Joy gets to the key issues:

So why do we eat pigs and not dogs?
Because bacon tastes good (laughter).
Because dogs have personalities. You can't eat something that has a
   personality. They have names: they're individuals.
Do you think pigs have personalities? Are they individuals, like
   dogs?
Yeah, I guess if you get to know them, they probably do.

Have you ever met a pig?
(Apart from an exceptional student, the majority has not.)
So where did you get your information about pigs from?
Books.
Television.
Ads.
Movies.
I don't know. Society, I guess.
How might you feel about pigs if you thought of them as
   intelligent, sensitive individuals who are perhaps not sweaty,

lazy, and greedy? If you got to know them firsthand, like you know dogs?
I'd feel weird eating them. I'd probably feel kind of guilty.
So why do we eat pigs and not dogs?
Because pigs are bred to be eaten.
Why do we breed pigs to eat them?
I don't know. I never thought about it. I guess, because it's just the way things are.[36]

Let us consider this statement for a moment. We send one species to the slaughterhouse and give our affection to another for the sole reason that "it's just the way things are." The unreasonableness of this jumps out at us. "Many of us," Melanie Joy remarks, "spend long minutes in the aisle of the drugstore mulling over what toothpaste to buy. Yet most of us don't spend any time at all thinking about what species of animal we eat and why. Our choices as consumers drive an industry that kills ten billion animals per year in the United States alone."[37] As Aymeric Caron humorously writes in *No Steak*: "Another bizarre point is that in the family of gastropod mollusks, we of course eat escargots, but not slugs. The fact that they don't have their houses on their backs is apparently suspect. No to homeless gastropods! Is that something that really makes sense? . . . With animals we act like schizophrenics, capable of both the worst and the best."[38]

As ethologist Marc Bekoff argues, the drawing of lines between individuals belonging to different animal species is bad biology in view of the evidence for evolutionary continuity. It results in the establishment of false boundaries that have dire consequences for species deemed to be "lower" than others, such as ants, fish, birds, or rats. Most conservation efforts are directed at "higher" and charismatic animals such a whales, polar bears, elephants, or tigers. Speciesism, conscious and unconscious, is the main culprit in our interactions with other animals. It reinforces the status of nonhuman animals as chattels and undermines our collective efforts to make the world a better place for all beings. Bekoff pleads for a "deep" ethology, studies of animals that take us not only into their minds but also into their hearts, as a beginning of expanding our "compassion footprint."[39]

Does Anti-speciesism Contain a Hidden Inner Contradiction?

The humanist philosopher Francis Wolff is of the opinion that anti-speciesism necessarily enters into a contradiction with its own principles, since only humans *can* be anti-speciesist (animals being unable to formulate such a concept). "It's the same as saying that only such and such a race (the white race, for example) should not be racist."[40] He adds that, if one could show that humans should treat animals as they treat themselves, "all one would have shown is that humans should behave toward other animals in a different manner from that in which the animals treat each other or from the manner in which they treat humans." He says this amounts to "adopting for one's own species other norms than those that you defend for the others. Becoming in that way an exception to the rule, human beings draw their norms and values from the characteristics proper to their own humanity."[41]

It is absolutely true that anti-speciesism is a human phenomenon, just like all other forms of reflective and deliberate categorization. Only humans are capable of making into a dogma that one race is inferior and the world would be better off if it did not exist. But also humans alone are capable of opposing dogmas of this kind and showing the shameful quality of them. Being capable of sustaining complex moral concerns relating to a large number of individuals, including persons who are distant in time and space (future generations, for example), and even extending this to other species is, without a doubt, a human characteristic. Only a human can become a speciesist, and only a human can also understand that he or she ought not to be one, since it is indefensible to instrumentalize other species *for the sole reason* that they are not human, if that is the justification that is advanced for it.

This position does not require that the objects of our moral concerns be capable of manifesting reciprocity toward us. Future human generations are obviously incapable of doing anything for us, but even so, would it be ethical for us to wreck the planet they are going to inherit?

On the very basis of possessing intellectual faculties that enable an individual to become aware of the deleterious effects of speciesism, it is to be expected that he or she will renounce it because of the needless suffering that this attitude brings about. Anti-speciesism does not at all say that all species are equal, that they have the same value and should be treated in the same way, but rather that it is reprehensible to profit from the abilities that we alone possess to deliberately harm other species, excusing ourselves by saying they are not human. The only exception would be if our lives were somehow endangered by them. It is evident that the great majority of the forms of animal exploitation we are perpetrating today are not necessary, or are no longer necessary, for our survival. They are based mainly on a lack of consideration for the lot of other sentient beings. Anti-speciesism is an outgrowth of altruism and does not require any form of quid pro quo. Reciprocity cannot be required of animals, from children, from people who are not in possession of all their mental faculties, or from generations to come, whether human or nonhuman.

Respecting Life and the Respective Abilities and Potentials of Each Species

Many thinkers call for respecting life above all other considerations, that is, letting the lives of other beings follow their own courses until they reach their natural end. David Chauvet, a jurist and cofounder of the Animal Rights Association, uses the following irrefutable argument: "One might be tempted to establish a hierarchy of the noble (living for the sake of living, a project that only humans, conscious of their own temporality, could devise) and the ignoble (living solely for the sake of eating and reproducing, for example). . . . What does the [limited] range of the intentions of animals and their simplicity matter? Great things are not required of human beings merely to deserve being alive."[42]

Some people maintain that it is morally acceptable to kill animals if you do it painlessly, because they really do not have a "life plan" and are not conscious at normal times of their finitude, nor are they preoccupied by their ultimate demise. In one of his novels, J. M. Coetzee, winner of the Nobel Prize for Literature, answers them as follows: "You say that death does not matter to an animal because the animal does not understand death. . . . If this is the best that human philosophy can offer, I said to myself, I would rather go and live among horses.[43]

Others have pushed this argument yet further, asserting that because death is a transition into nothingness, if you kill an animal rapidly and without pain, it will not exist as a "subject" capable of suffering and "losing" something. If this kind of argument were admissible, it would be acceptable to kill in her sleep, in a painless manner, a person who lived alone and unknown to anyone, because nobody in the world would suffer from it. Nevertheless, just the fact of living one's life to the end and being able to actualize the potential of it deserves to be respected fully, unless our view is that life is not worth living at any time.

As Martin Gibert explains, "The first response consists precisely in condemning the premature nature of the death of the animal. By being slaughtered, the animal is deprived of experiences it could have had. We perceive a long life as preferable to a short one: in general we take the view that death deprives us of wellbeing."[44]

To make full use of the potential of existence, an animal must enjoy a certain degree of freedom. Martha Nussbaum, professor of law and ethics at the University of Chicago, has established a list of abilities that, in her view, must be respected in animals. *Life* itself is number one. All animals have the right to continue to live, as well as to preserve their *health* and their *physical integrity*. After this come the abilities animals have to *experience their senses*, their *imagination*, and the exercise of their *capacity for thought*. For that, it is necessary to make sure that animals have access to the sources of their pleasures, that is to say, freedom of movement in an environment that is pleasing to their senses. We must also respect the ability of animals to *feel emotions*. To this end, they must have the freedom to associate with other animals and take care of them. Consequently, it is unacceptable to force them to live in isolation.[45]

A number of these potentials can only be guaranteed by also respecting the environments of the animals. Cetaceans are disturbed by the noise of the motors of the boats that crisscross the seas; pollution is harmful to the eyes and skin of fish; the accumulation of mercury in their flesh poisons them. Everywhere wild animals are suffering from the gradual disappearance of their natural habitats.

Anthropomorphism or Anthropocentrism?

The scientists who have demonstrated the richness of the emotions of animals most clearly have often been accused of anthropomorphism—a capital sin among animal behavior specialists. Jane Goodall has even been reproached for giving names to the chimpanzees she studied. If she were doing her work properly, they say, she would merely have given them numbers. Similarly, Frans de Waal has been criticized for using a vocabulary "reserved" for humans to describe the behavior of chimpanzees and bonobos. "Everybody knows," he replied, "that animals have emotions and feelings, and that they make decisions similar to our own. With the exception, it seems, of a few academics. If you go to a psychology department, you'll hear, 'Hmm . . .' When the dog scratches at the door and barks, you say that he wants to go out, but how do you know that he wants to go out? He has simply learned that barking and scratching makes it possible to get doors opened.'"[46]

In fact, many academics still refuse to apply terms to animals that make reference to mental states like anger, fear, suffering, affection, joy, or other emotions similar to ours. As Bernard Rollin tells us, in their effort not to apply terms to animals that also describe human emotions, many researchers do not speak of fear but rather of "retreat behaviors"; they do not speak of the suffering of a rat placed on a hot burner but count the number of its somersaults and convulsions; they do not speak of moans or cries of pain but of "vocalizations."[47] The obvious vocabulary is replaced by a jargon that is more an expression of denial than scientific objectivity. The psychologist Donald Olding Hebb and his collaborators tried for two years to describe the behavior of the chimpanzees at the Yerkes National Primate Research Center near Atlanta while avoiding any description that could be qualified as anthropomorphic. The result was an interminable series of verbose descriptions from which no meaning could be derived.[48] By contrast, when the researchers allowed themselves to use "anthropomorphic" descriptions for emotions and attitudes, they could rapidly and easily describe the particularities of each animal and come to an unambiguous agreement on the fact that such and such an animal, for example, was angry or affectionate. Darwin followed this approach when he wrote: "Dogs shew what may be fairly called a sense of humour, as distinct from mere play; if a bit of stick or other such object be thrown to one, he will often carry it away for a short distance; and then squatting down with it on the ground close before him, will wait until his master comes quite close to take it away. The dog will then seize it and rush away in triumph, repeating the same manoeuvre, and evidently enjoying the practical joke."[49]

So it is not more anthropomorphic to postulate the existence of mental states in certain animals than it is to compare their anatomy, their nervous system, and their physiology to ours. When an animal is visibly joyous or sad, why not call things by their names?

The biologist Donald Griffin coined the term "mentaphobia" to designate the obsession that certain scientists manifest in denying any form of consciousness to animals. Griffin's opinion was that this was a scientific error and that "the intense fervor with which numerous psychologists and biologists insist on the fact that non-human consciousness is a totally inappropriate subject is so profound and emotional that it borders on irrational aversion or mentaphobia."[50]

In *Contre la Mentaphobie (Against Mentaphobia)*, David Chauvet shows how this denial of consciousness in animals serves as an excuse for exploiting animals without feeling guilty about the serious abuses we commit toward them. As he sees it, "consciousness was very definitely substituted for the soul in attributing to humans an ontological value that distinguishes them from the rest of living beings."[51] Asserting that animals do not have consciousness thus is nothing other than the continuation of the Christian and Cartesian idea according to which animals do not possess a soul.

This kind of stubborn resistance goes against common sense and shows a misunderstanding of the very nature of evolution, which implies that psychology, in the same way as anatomy, developed in a gradual fashion. Frans de Waal describes this stubbornness in reserving for humans the monopoly on certain emotions as "anthropocentric denial":[52]

People willfully suppress knowledge most have had since childhood, which is that animals do have feelings and do care about others. How and why half the world drops this conviction once they grow beards or breasts will always baffle me, but the result is the common fallacy that we are unique in this regard. Human we are, and humane as well, but the idea that the latter may be older than the former, that our kindness is part of a much larger picture, still has to catch on.[53]

In the West, multiple cultural factors have contributed to this anthropocentrism. Among these are the tenacious remainders of the Judeo-Christian idea according to which only humans possess a soul. In this elegy to La Fontaine, Hippolyte Taine denounces the prejudices of Descartes and his contemporaries:

From that point on, all life, all nobility, was referred back to the human soul; nature, empty and degraded, was no more than a heap of pullies and springs, as vulgar as a factory, unworthy of interest unless for its useful products, worthy of curiosity at best for the moralist who might be able to derive some structural ideas out of it and some praise for the builder. A poet had nothing to get into there, and he also had to leave out the animals, caring no more for the carp or the cow than for a wheelbarrow or a mill. . . . A chicken is a reservoir of eggs, a cow is a milk shop, a donkey is good for nothing beyond carrying hay to market.[54]

The contempt of the thinkers of the seventeenth century, for whom the animals were no more than "automatons of flesh," can in a way be seen again today in the anthropocentric pride that refuses to place humans within the continuity of the evolution of animals, thinking that it would represent an insult to human dignity because it would be an attack on the superiority of human being as something beyond reason's measure. Élisabeth de Fontanay deconstructs this pretension with elegance and lucidity:

The philosophical tradition with the help of theology, and even without the help of theology, bears a heavy responsibility for the degradation and mistreatment of animals. . . .

Most philosophers from age to age have built a wall of separation between living creatures. They have opposed the human being who exists, to the animal who merely lives; and they have set up man as the proprietor who enjoys the right to use and abuse everything that is not him. This prevailing tradition invented the uniqueness of man, a sort of metaphysical swelling or blister. This tradition has for the most part made use of the concept of animality as a way of stigmatizing whatever does not belong to the realm of consciousness, that is not free, that does not think, thus creating a kind of negative proof of the uniqueness of man. . . .[55]

Over the course of time, the distinguishing factor proposed has been the erect posture, fire, writing, agriculture, mathematics, philosophy of course, freedom and therefore morality, perfectibility, the ability to imitate, the ability to foresee death, making love face-to-face, the struggle for independence, work, neurosis, the ability to lie, to debate social issues, to share food, the capacity for art, the ability to laugh, burial. . . . The study of genetics, of palaeoanthropology, of primatology, and of zoology will soon have pounded to bits these little islands of certainty, this boastful competitiveness, these proofs of unrivaled competence. The language of the chimpanzee, the ability of the English titmouse to remove the tops of milk bottles, the monogamy of the gibbon, the altruism of the ant, the cruelty of the mantis leave us at a loss. . . .[56]

And if we were to spotlight on the public stage—both philosophical and political—the fragility of all those, human and animal, who are incapable of defending themselves, then we would enlarge the concept of guardianship, which would permit us to assume, in a manner not only compassionate but also respectful, the protection of *all* living beings: homo sapiens no longer being "the master and possessor of nature," to recall the words of Descartes, but rather the one who takes responsibility, the protector. For, if there must be an undeniable uniqueness and singularity of man, it is certainly in responsibility that it must reside: responsibility is the single ethical concept to which I could rally without reserve, because it accepts care for the animals as well.

There is without doubt another reason for which many of us are strongly attached to the idea of an uncrossable frontier between humans and animals: if we were to recognize that the animals are not *fundamentally* different from us, it would force us to forbid treating them like instruments, utensils, purely serving our interests. The proof of this is what a research worker told Bernard Rollin: "It makes my work so much easier if I act as though animals hadn't the least consciousness."[57] Very fortunately, today a growing number of researchers recognize the presence of emotions and complex mental processes in animals.

In 2012, on the occasion of the Francis Crick Memorial Conference on Consciousness in Human and Non-Human Animals—an international group of prominent cognitive neuroscientists, neuropharmacologists, neurophysiologists, neuroanatomists, and computational neuroscientists, including Philip Low, Jaak Panksepp, Diana Reiss, David Edelman, Bruno Van Swinderen, and Christof Koch—issued *The Cambridge Declaration on Consciousness*, in which they stated:

The absence of a neocortex does not appear to preclude an organism from experiencing affective states. Convergent evidence indicates that non-human animals have the neuroanatomical, neurochemical, and neurophysiological substrates of conscious states along with the capacity to exhibit intentional behaviors. Consequently, the weight of evidence indicates that humans are not unique in possessing the neurological substrates that generate consciousness. Non-human animals, including all mammals and birds, and many other creatures, including octopuses, also possess these neurological substrates.

In particular they remarked that:

Birds appear to offer, in their behavior, neurophysiology, and neuroanatomy a striking case of parallel evolution of consciousness. Evidence of near human-like levels of consciousness has been most dramatically observed in African grey parrots. Mammalian and avian emotional networks and cognitive microcircuitries appear to be far more homologous than previously thought. Moreover, certain species of birds have been found to exhibit neural sleep patterns similar to those of mammals, including REM sleep and, as was demonstrated in zebra finches, neurophysiological patterns, previously thought to require a mammalian neocortex. Magpies in particular have been shown to exhibit striking similarities to humans, great apes, dolphins, and elephants in studies of mirror self-recognition.

Different Cultures

For about the past twenty years, ethologists have been talking about "animal cultures." As Dominique Lestel, who teaches cognitive ethology at the École Normale Supérieure in Paris, tells us, we must "think of the cultural phenomenon in an evolutionary and pluralist perspective and once and for all stop being driven by the desire to single out 'the unique quality of man.' We must stop thinking about culture in opposition to nature; instead we should become aware of the plurality of cultures that exists among creatures of very different species."[58]

In the case of human beings, the American anthropologist Alfred Kroeber puts forward six conditions required for speaking of "culture." *New* behaviors have to emerge; they must be *disseminated* in the group, starting with the inventor; they must become *standardized*; they must *last*; and they must be *diffused* by the intermediary of *traditions*.[59] He affirms that the chimpanzees studied by Jane Goodall fulfill all these conditions. A synthesis of studies by several groups of researchers who worked on seven particularly well-studied sites and accumulated 151 years of experience in the field, enumerated 65 categories of behaviors, of which 39 were considered to be cultural.[60]

According to Dominique Lestel, the notion of animal culture rests on three pillars: "Individual innovation, the social transmission of it to the rest of the group, and the imitation or social apprenticeship that makes it possible."[61] The cultural behaviors generally cited by philosophers and anthropologists to distinguish humans from animals—the fact that certain groups adopt customs unknown in other groups and that parents teach certain techniques to their offspring—are much more widespread than previously thought among animals. The examples run from chimpanzees to the crows of New Caledonia, and go on to include whales, bears, wolves, and even fish. Thus there are many animal cultures, even if they are *different* from the cultures acquired by human beings.

In the 1960s the great ethologist Jane Goodall was the first to describe the fabrication and use of tools by chimpanzees.[62] Her incredulous colleagues did not accept the evidence for this until she showed them corroborating film footage. Before starting out to "fish for ants," a chimpanzee fabricated a kind of probe out of a branch by cutting it to an appropriate size and removing the leaves. Then, carrying the tool in its mouth or at times under its armpit, it went to an anthill and began enlarging the entrance to it. Then it inserted the probe in the hole and drew it out covered with ants, which had grabbed onto it spontaneously. Then all the chimp had to do was lick the probe stick in order to eat them. Sometimes it also shook the stick vigorously in the hole and, in other cases, banged on the trunk of the tree in which the ant's nest was located in order to get the ants to come out. Once it had had enough to eat, it yielded its place to another chimp, which patiently awaited its turn, sometimes for quite a while.[63] The young chimpanzees began to catch ants or termites in this manner at around the age of three. However, being still awkward and having not yet gotten the hang of it, they generally choose sticks that are too short or too thick.[64]

It sometimes also happens that the chimpanzee uses several tools in the same task—for example, inserting a sponge made of leaves into a hole in a tree filled with water, then using a stick to pull out the soaked sponge and refresh itself—or also one tool for several different tasks. Observations were made of a female chimp that used four tools in succession to extract honey from a hole in a tree.[65] Moreover, when a chimpanzee discovers a new effective technique, this technique spreads quickly within the group, in this way creating a culture unique to this group.

Jane Goodall enumerated ten different ways in which chimpanzees use tools. By now, forty have been identified. It turns out that more than one hundred animal species use tools.[66] The chaffinch of Galápagos uses a twig to help it expose the larvae that hide under the bark of trees, and the sea otter uses a stone to open oysters.[67] The New Caledonian crow makes two types of tools to capture its prey: a twig that naturally has the form of a hook and a pandanus leaf, which it cuts and then fashions into a fish hook shape. Once these instruments have been prepared, it uses them to rummage around under the bark of trees. Between uses, the crow stows them securely near its roost, then it carries them around in its beak to be reused as it flies from one place to another.[68]

Observations have also been made of mother chimpanzees who facilitate their offsprings' learning process by providing them with good tools for breaking nuts and by showing them how to go about doing it. A mother was seen taking away a nut that her offspring had badly positioned on a big root that was serving as an anvil, cleaning the anvil, then placing the nut back on it in a good position. The young chimp then worked on the nut successfully under its mother's attentive regard.[69] In the Taï Forest in the Ivory Coast, when the *coula* nut season comes, the chimpanzees spend at least two hours a day cracking nuts. Once they have collected enough of them, they transport them to one of the anvils they are in the habit of using and strike them with varying weights of stones according to the hardness of the nut. It takes several years to complete learning this technique perfectly.[70]

Nobuo Masataka and his colleagues observed that the long-tailed macaques that live freely in Thailand use human hairs or an equivalent material as dental floss to clean the spaces between their teeth. It turned out that the mother macaques spent twice as much time using the dental floss when they were being observed by their young. It thus seems that they deliberately prolong and accentuate the use of the floss so as to make it easier to teach the skill to their offspring.[71]

Animals also use means of communication that can be very rich, even if they are not based on language as we understand it. The dance of bees, which was brought to the world's attention by the great entomologist Karl von Frisch, is of great complexity. By means of dancing in different figures in different ways, a bee indicates to its fellows the direction to take to find pollen (indicated by a particular dance) or nectar (indicated by another dance) and the distance that they will have to travel to reach it.[72]

Whales perform chants that last from fifteen to thirty minutes, that contain two to seven themes, and that cover seven octaves in pitch. These chants are entirely renewed over the course of five years.[73] When a whale adopts a new chant and new themes, these are copied by other whales and quickly spread through the whale population over distances of thousands of miles.[74] Even though the meaning of these chants is not fully understood (by us), they certainly play an important role in the communication between individuals and in the maintenance of social relations. In 1957 the German ethologist and evolutionist Bernhard Rensch reported the case of an elephant that was able to distinguish twelve musical tonalities and could remember simple melodies even if they were played on different instruments and at different pitches. It was still able to recognize these melodies a year and a half after having first learned them.[75]

Chimpanzees also know how to send precise messages to other members of their group who are out of sight. The ethologist Christophe Boesch has shown that, by drumming in a fast and varied manner on the trunks of several trees for around ten minutes, one male member of a tribe can indicate to other chimpanzees the place where his group is located, the direction it has decided to go in, and that the group is going to stop at a certain point to take a rest. Boesch, who spent months recording and deciphering these drummed messages, observed groups of chimpanzees suddenly and silently change direction after having heard these sound signals containing spatial and temporal information.[76]

Play, dancing, chanting or singing, and the aesthetic sense are also part of animal cultures. For instance, Rensch has been able to show that fish prefer irregular forms while birds on the other hand are more inclined toward regular, symmetrical forms, toward rhythmic repetition of motifs, and toward brilliant and saturated colors, especially blue and black.[77] The bower bird, to seduce his mate, frequently "repaints" his nest with bright colors using colored barks (with a clear preference for blue). He also brings back all sorts of colored objects to his nest.[78] And of course many kinds of animals like to play. In winter, kea parrots make snowballs, which they push ahead of themselves obviously with the sole purpose of entertainment.[79] Sea mammals also play a great deal with each other. Even play between different species has been observed: for example, between crows and wolves in the great northern regions of Canada where wolves do not eat crows,[80] between a sled dog and a polar bear, as well as among different species of monkey. Jane Goodall has described the playful dance that chimpanzees sometimes engage in for half an hour when a big rain starts to fall.[81]

Some monkeys, and also elephants, like to draw.[82] Two chimps in captivity, Alpha and Congo, made hundreds of drawings, which they afterward colored in. They held the brush correctly and did not try at all to get rid of it. They concentrated on their work and the appropriate manipulation of the brush. Their sense of composition got better day by day. After having finished a drawing, Congo handed it to ethologist Desmond Morris and asked with a gesture for another piece of paper.[83]

Dominique Lestel rejects two positions concerning human and animal cultures: the view according to which these cultures are different by nature and the view according to which the differences between them are only a matter of degree. He defends a third point of view that he considers more realistic: "Animal and human cultures have a common origin, but they are separated by intrinsic differences of the same nature as those that separate a society of ants from a society of chimpanzees. The differing features of the two cultures participate in the same evolutionary logic, but they have characteristics that are radically foreign to each other."[84]

Thus the continuum of living beings is not organized in the manner of a hierarchy that leads to the absolute superiority of the human species. It simply reflects the thousand pathways that the innumerable species that populate our planet have followed step by step. This continuum reflects the way in which natural selection has favored the emergence of diversity, complexity, and efficiency in life forms that have become increasingly better adapted to their environment. One cannot help but agree with the following remark of Claude Lévi-Strauss:

Never more than at the end of the last four centuries has Western man been in a position to understand that by granting himself the right to radically separate humanity from animality by attributing to the one everything it refused to the other, he created a vicious circle; and that the same boundary, constantly moved back, would serve to divide humans from other humans and claim for the benefit of a constantly more restricted minority the privileges of the corrupted humanism that instantly arose out of having borrowed from vanity and self-love its principle and idea.[85]

From humans to the great apes, passing by way of the birds, the insects, the fish, and the sea mammals, species of all kinds have used their different faculties to form their own appropriate cultures that reflect the best way each of them can survive and be the "subjects" of their lives. It is this diversity that we must recognize and respect, while of course continuing to appreciate fully the particular qualities that are our own.

As the philosopher Patrice Rouget points out, "In the dialogue of Plato called 'The Statesman,' one of the speakers judiciously remarks that if one took the point of view of cranes in deciding which species surpasses all the others and should enjoy a separate status, no doubt one would reply 'cranes.' Now take us, us human cranes—because we possess the faculty of rhetoric and we know how to be hypocritical, we have replied: 'humans.'"[86]

The Human Exception?

Most species have unique abilities that show their remarkable adaptation to their environment. Bats and dolphins and other cetaceans are capable of directing their movements perfectly in the most complete darkness. If we ask ourselves what the main abilities are that especially distinguish humans, we immediately think of the mastery of complex languages: written, spoken, mathematical, symbolic, artistic, and so on. We think, of course, of our extraordinary intelligence and our great emotional refinement. To those things, certain philosophers add that humans are also the only beings capable of scientific knowledge.[87] At this point, however, without in the least belittling the genius of the human mind, I would like to make the point that animals, in a more limited fashion, are also capable of acquiring complex knowledge. Some wild chimpanzees recognize as many as two hundred species of plant. They know the function of each one of them (in the case of medicinal plants), the places in the forest where they grow, and the time when some of them bear fruit.[88] Moreover, humans are not the only ones capable of moral conduct; the foundations of morality and ethics were acquired in the course of evolution and are already present in certain animals.[89] But it is true that humans can in addition reflect on the morality of their behavior, both by thinking about it individually and by communicating about it with others; and they are capable of forming an "ethical community" that might possibly be able to be extended to the whole of humanity.

According to the philosopher Francis Wolff, although some animals have "conscious" perceptions, these perceptions only engender knowledge and thoughts "of the first degree." By this he means perceptions of the type "here, a predator," "there a sexual partner," beliefs that present themselves as "immediate data about the world." One of the unique characteristics of the human, he adds, "is that he can access a second degree of knowledge, a belief about his belief."[90] A human has the ability to question him- or herself about the truth or falsity of his or her beliefs.

Although it may be the case that an animal equipped with an elementary nervous system—an earthworm, for example—perceives only "immediate data" about the external world, data about food or danger, this does not seem to hold true for animals endowed with more complex faculties. A dog might experience fear or aggression in relation to a stuffed animal, but it modifies its first assessment after closer examination. It inspects this strange being from a distance, cautiously comes closer, sniffs it, and finally comes to the conclusion that it is nothing to fear.

In a similar vein, Kant and many other philosophers have expressed the view that only a human being can produce judgments. But knowledge acquired by today's work in ethology tends to invalidate this idea. A study by Shinya Yamamoto and his team has been able to demonstrate that chimpanzees are capable of precise assessments of the needs of other chimpanzees.[91] Two chimpanzees who know each other are placed in contiguous cages. A small window makes it possible to pass objects from one cage to another. The first chimpanzee receives in its cage a box with seven objects in it: a stick, a drinking straw, a lasso, a chain, a string, a big flat brush, and a belt.

Then the second chimpanzee is put in a situation where it needs a specific tool, which, depending on the arrangement of the experiment, could be a stick for getting at a piece of food or a straw to drink some fruit juice with. The second chimpanzee signals to the first, either through gestures or voice, that it needs help. The first chimpanzee looks over, evaluates the situation, and nine times out of ten chooses the right tool out of the seven possible ones, then passes it to its fellow through the window. The first chimp itself receives no reward.

If the field of vision of the first chimpanzee is blocked by an opaque panel, it still wants to help when it hears the other one ask, but unable to see in order to evaluate the precise help needed, it passes through any one of the seven objects it has at its disposal. This experiment was repeated with several different chimps, and in at least one case, the chimp that was asked for help went to look through a small hole that it noticed near the top of the opaque panel in order to evaluate the situation of the other chimp and to pass it the right tool!

Similarly, Thomas Bugnyar observed that, when a big crow approaches one of its own food caches, it attentively looks around at the other crows. If it sees another crow that might have seen it store something there, it rushes to the hiding place to be sure to get there to get the piece of food before the other crow. If it sees only other crows *that it knows do not know* where the cache is, it takes its time.[92] Thus there is surely an evaluative faculty present, and a judgment is surely made about *what another crow knows or does not know*. Recognizing that other animals possess these kinds of abilities in no way makes less of the fact that we humans possess exceptional abilities that confer on the human experience a richness that we would not trade for anything in the world, be it the sonar of bats, the salmon's sense of smell, or the speed of the leopard. Nevertheless, this richness does not raise us above the animal kingdom, not any more than the ability to fly six thousand miles orienting itself by the stars, by the polarization of light, or the earth's magnetic field raises the migrating bird above the animal kingdom.

According to Patrice Rouget, a philosopher who holds a point of view completely opposite to the one that humans are above animals:

The quest for the unique quality of man as a proof of his irreducible ontological distinction has been a constant preoccupation of philosophy since the beginning. More than a preoccupation, it is a kind of obsession, a challenge that has been transmitted from one generation to the next; and each new thinker has been encouraged to take it up and propose his own personal solution.

A hot potato. . . . Regarding this unfortunate question, it seems that we humans have run into greater difficulties than we ever imagined initially. Nevertheless, we should credit ourselves with the merit of perseverance; the quest has never been given up and from time to time it still produces another worthy discovery. . . . But it is to be feared that there is little hope left. Such constant application accompanied by such regular failure, the very prestige of those who have put forth positions (which proves that we have put into the issue the very best that we have in the way of brain power)—these things should put us on alert: isn't this question in danger of leading nowhere? Wouldn't it perhaps be a good idea to consider stowing it away in the storeroom reserved for the accessories of idealism? Biology, ethology, zoology, palaeontology—all the sciences of living things have brought us to a point where the idealist position has become really hard to maintain. It is perhaps time for the followers of metaphysical humanism to take heed.[93]

We often hear that humans have "extracted themselves from nature." But is it possible to extract oneself from a totality of interdependence with which we are intimately enmeshed? Can I extract myself from my own body? Can clouds extract themselves from the atmosphere? To quote again from Rouget: "Metaphysical humanism really ought to go ahead and extract man from nature. Of course, there is every likelihood that the result of this extraction will be catastrophic, both for everything human and everything non-human. Here again, animals demand our attention—their suffering, the hell that they have been living for such a long time and which is only getting worse, should serve as a healthy warning to us."[94]

Even if he is not a believer, the metaphysical humanist and human supremacist succeed neither in dissociating themselves from the religious tradition in which the fate of animals has no intrinsic importance—the sole reason animals to exist being the use that humans can make of them—nor in taking into account the consequences of the theory of evolution.[95] If human beings do enjoy a "special" ontological status, this privileged status could only result from (1) a supernatural cause; (2) a finalistic (teleological) process, activated by an "anthropic" principle—that is, an organizing principle that would determine the initial conditions of the universe with perfect precision in such a way that life and consciousness (human in particular) would arise in it; or (3) a major discontinuity in the process of evolution that would relate only to the human species among 7.7 million other species.

The first hypothesis is purely a matter of faith. The second is no more than a way of invoking a "first cause" endowed with qualities similar to those that religions attribute to the Creator. As to the third hypothesis, there is no known scientific element that could possibly provide a basis for it. Quite to the contrary, the multiplicity of species of hominids that preceded *Homo sapiens* shows the unfailing continuity of a process that nothing suggests has reached its conclusion.

If, on the other hand, we share a common origin with our co-citizens in this world, if we are all infinitely varied products of the evolution of life, following the same principles of causality that produced and continue to produce a variety of species, then, while continuing to marvel at our own excellent qualities, we can only render due appreciation to the other species as well, and make every effort to live in such a way as to do them the least possible harm.

7

THE MASS KILLING
OF ANIMALS

Genocide versus Zoocide

Each genocide is made unique by the specific horrors it perpetrates. To compare the Holocaust, the Cambodian genocide, or that of Rwanda to any other tragedy is in a way unacceptable, simply out of deference to those who were its victims. Nevertheless, the singularity, the uniqueness, of each of these genocides should not in the least prevent us from understanding the causes of genocide and analyzing the circumstances that allow it to occur and even recur.

What about the mass killing of animals? Our proposal is that we speak of zoocide in cases where animals are systematically put to death in large numbers.[1] Zoocide cannot be placed on the same level as genocide of humans—the differences are essential—but there are some qualities in common that we cannot pass over in silence.

It is clear that we must persevere without a break in our concern for all the human beings who are suffering, who are tortured, violated, and deprived of their rights in many countries throughout the world. But that should not hold us back in the least from turning our awareness to the abuses to which we subject animals. The unthinkable tortures that we continue to inflict on them year after year represent a challenge to contemporary ethics. Pretending not to be aware of this only increases our sense of distance from it and perpetuates the indifference that, in the case of human genocide, has led to our failing to intervene except too little too late. Seeing immense value in human life should not bring us to reduce to nothing the value of animal life.

Comparing without Offending

Out of respect for the victims, it is important to point out right at the beginning that the first people who were struck by a certain number of points in common between the Holocaust and the industrial massacre of animals were not fanatical advocates of the animal cause but precisely the victims of this genocide—survivors or people who had lost close relatives. They were the ones who—almost against their will—found themselves describing the bitter memories of the Shoah that came over them when they were confronted by the reality of the slaughterhouses. They were the ones who were struck by the similarities between the functioning of the camps and that of industrial breeding operations: the large-scale, methodical organization of the killing, the stripping of all value from the lives of other beings, the convenient ignorance shown by the surrounding population. Lucy, whose two young sisters were struck down by the Nazis before their father's eyes, tells us: "I have been haunted my whole life by the images of the Shoah, and there is no doubt that I was attracted to animal rights in part because of the similarities I felt between the institutionalized exploitation of animals and the Nazi genocide."[2]

Such people are too numerous for us to cite, or even mention them all, in this chapter. The most well known is without doubt the Yiddish-language writer Isaac Bashevis Singer, winner of the Nobel Prize for Literature, whose mother and several members of his family were exterminated in Poland. In *The Penitent*, he tells us, "The treatment man inflicts upon the creatures of God make a mockery of all his ideals and his so-called humanism."[3] A character in one of his stories talks in his head to a dead animal: "What do they know—all those scholars, all those philosophers, all the leaders of the world—about such as you? They have convinced themselves that man, the worst transgressor of all the species, is the crown of creation. All other creatures were created merely to provide him with food, pelts, to be tormented, exterminated. In relation to them, all people are Nazis; for the animals it is an eternal Treblinka. . . ."[4]

At Treblinka, 875,000 people were exterminated and only 67 survived. There was only one survivor as of this writing, but also remaining is a terrible scar on the soul of humanity.[5] With the exception of those 67 people, at Treblinka the "final solution" that Hitler had wanted took place. It was the most successful of his exterminations. In the case of animals, humans do not want a final solution. They want to be able to continue as long as possible with the annual killing of 60 billion land animals and a thousand billion marine animals. This zoocide is an eternal recurrence.

So is it acceptable to compare the two mass killings? No, because there are fundamental differences. And yes, because there are numerous points in common: among others, the fact that in genocide, we are killing human beings precisely as though they were animals. Dodging these common points only makes it possible for the mass killing of animals to go on forever. That is exactly what is expressed in this often-cited passage from Jacques Derrida:

> No one can any longer seriously go on denying that human beings do everything in their power to hide or to hide from themselves this cruelty, everything in their power to organize on a worldwide scale the forgetting or non-recognition of this violence that people might compare to the worse genocides. . . . We should neither abuse this genocide comparison nor drop it too readily. Because it becomes complicated here: certainly the annihilation of a species is in play, but it involves the organization and exploitation of an artificial survival of it, an infernal one, virtually endless, in conditions that men of the past would have considered monstrous, beyond all the norms taken for granted for the life of animals; who are thus exterminated because they survive or because of the very fact that we cause too many of them to survive.[6]

Certain sick minds claim that the Holocaust never happened, or at least not on the scale that we know it did. This "negationism" is now a crime in the eyes of the law in several European countries. In the case of the killing of animals on an industrial scale, we find ourselves in the presence of a negationism of an entirely different order, one that *does not deny the facts but denies that they are of any importance.* The continuation of the carnage does not seem to pose a problem.

The putting to death of millions of cattle at the time of the foot and mouth disease epidemic, for example, required setting up a means of massive destruction, including the burial of thousands of still-living animals in huge common pits.[7] Many breeders who were unable to get away from these procedures, which were organized by the army, suffered anxiety attacks, nightmares, hallucinations, guilt feelings, and depressive ailments, which led in some cases to suicide.[8] As shown by the investigation of veterinarians Gaignard and Charron, without a doubt, the colossal number of animals that were struck down accounts for the frequent allusions made by the breeders to Nazi techniques of "extermination" and to "crematorium fumes."

Paradoxically, some leaders of the mass breeding industry, without being completely explicit, acknowledge the analogy of death camps. In a program televised in the 1970s, a journalist asked Raymond Fevrier, at that time the General Inspector of Agronomic Research at the INRA (French National Institute for Agricultural Research), "When one visits modern cow barns, one has a sensation, which one has to admit is rather amazing, of a society that is more or less like that of a concentration camp." To which the expert candidly replied, "It's true, it's true. . . . We have immense power over bovine society."[9]

According to Jocelyne Porcher, "The analogy with the Nazi camps, which I heard at the beginning of my research especially being expressed by non-industrial breeders, is now being expressed by a growing number of industrial breeders and salaried employees. Most of the time it is not in order to reject it as a misplaced excess, but rather just to face it as a fact." This researcher, who was herself formerly a breeder, regards it as important to distinguish between *comparison* and *analogy*. "Comparison aims to draw out the differences and resemblances among objects. It is a reasonable, accountable activity that looks for the balance in things. Analogy, on the other hand, is an exercise of the imagination whose aim is to compare objects which in the abstract are conceived of as very different." She concludes that it is the analogy of, and not the comparison between, industrial breeding—which "creates charnel grounds of billions of animals"—and the Nazi extermination camps that cannot be set aside with the excuse that it is extremely disturbing. She continues as follows:

> The industrial process of animal production involves a deconstruction. Its approach is to deconstruct the animal, to "de-

animalize" it and make it into a thing. Animal production is a monstrous machine that makes things. The analogy with the camps expressed by workers is based on four main points: the loss of identity and singularity, in other words the mass treatment of individuals; violence; loss of communication; and consent to a labor of death. . . . The consent of a portion of the workers and a great part of the managerial staff to violence, and more broadly to the working procedures of industrial systems, also feed the analogy with Nazi extermination camps. Ideology and obedience to orders are more important than the moral values of individuals, even though the risk is not the same as the one that would be taken by a soldier who refused to obey. Refusing to obey for the soldier would have meant death. This is not the case in the industry of animal production.[10]

If a German opposed the policies of the Nazis he risked his life. In most countries those who speak out against the mass killing of animals only risk being met with derision or facing pressure from the industrial lobbies. But in the U.S.A., under the Animal Enterprise Terrorist Act, signed into law by President George W. Bush, animal rights activists are treated as terrorists and some of them are serving prison terms.

Genocide and Zoocide

In the case of animals, the term "genocide" is inappropriate since it only applies to humans. According to the definition given by the United Nations, genocide involves acts "committed with the intention of destroying all or part of a national, ethnic, racial, or religious group as such."[11] Because of the many interpretations of the word *genocide* and the controversies engendered by this term, Jacques Sémelin, a historian and an eminent specialist in this area, is of the opinion that general notions such as "mass violence" or "extreme violence" are often more to the point. Another suggestion of his is the term *massacre*, which he defines as "a form of action, most often collective, involving the annihilation of non-combatants, men, women, children, or unarmed soldiers.[12] He adds that this notion also applies to the killing of animals that has been practiced since the European medieval period and concludes, "This immediate comparison between the massacre of humans and that of animals, a comparison on both the historical and semantic levels, is moreover not an innocuous one."[13]

First of all, let us consider the definition of acts that, according to the convention of the United Nations, constitute genocide of human beings:

a. Murder of members of a group;
b. Serious attack on the physical or mental integrity of members of the group;
c. Intentional subjection of the group to conditions of existence that are likely to lead to its partial or total physical destruction;
d. Measures intended to impede the birth of children within the group;
e. Forced transfer of children of a group to another group.

How could we define zoocide on the basis of the five points set forth by the United Nations convention on genocide? We see that items a, b, and e are completely applicable to the mass killing of animals and in particular to industrial breeding operations.

As far as line c is concerned, in the case of industrial breeding, the conditions of existence to which the animals are subjected are intended to keep them alive as long as they produce eggs or milk or, in the case of animals raised for their meat, until they have reached the right weight for being killed. In this case, the goal is not the elimination of the species or the group, but rather the goal, indefinitely and deliberately renewed, is to cause the members of a group to continue to thrive so they can be killed in greater numbers.

Only line d of the convention does not apply, since in the case of animals, births, far from being impeded, are encouraged to an extreme point, so that there are always animals available to kill.

We might imagine that a time will come when an international convention on zoocide will be created. It might read like this:

a. Slaughter of members of an animal group;

b. Serious attack on the physical or mental integrity of members of the group;
c. Subjection of the group to painful conditions leading up to their systematic slaughter;
d. Measures intended to encourage a maximal number of births within the group with a view to subsequent slaughter;
e. Forced separation of the offspring of the group from their parents.

The Differences

The differences between the massacre of human beings en masse and that of animals are many. They are connected mainly with the *value* of human existence, with the *motivation* that drives those who carry out the killing, with their *goal*, with the *identity* of the victims, the *image* that prevails of the victims, with the *duration* of the persecutions, with the *number* of the victims, with *nature of the reaction* to the violence being perpetrated, and finally with the *memory* of those who are killed.

Value. It is undeniable that human existence has an incommensurable value that cannot be regarded as on the same level as that of the animal. As we already affirmed in chapter 5, "Sorry Excuses," if it comes to having to choose between saving a human life and that of an animal, there is simply no question. Nevertheless, the unrivaled value of human life can never be used to justify inflicting unnecessary suffering on an animal and putting it to death.

Motivation. Genocide is driven by hate, whereas the killing of animals is mainly motivated by greed or desire for profit or pleasure and is accompanied by indifference to the fate of the animal.

Goal. The goal of genocide is to wipe out the victims. The goal of the exploitation of animals on the other hand, is to increase their numbers as much as possible and as quickly as possible in order to be able to use them and kill them, generation after generation.

Identity of the Victims. The victims of what we call genocide are by definition human beings, while the notion of mass killing can be applied to all living species.

Image of the Victims. The populations that are the victims of genocide are demonized. They are presented as harmful beings whose existence alone is a menace to good citizens. They are often characterized as impure, or even as vermin of which we must rid the planet. As for the animals, they are reduced to the status of things, utilitarian objects, objects of consumption, portable goods. The fact that they are alive tends to be more a bother than an advantage. Our vague sense of bad conscience would be diminished if they were not alive, but they have to be in order to make meat, to provide their skin, fur, and so on.

Duration. Every genocide comes to an end one day, whereas the massacre of the animals continues everywhere, every day, and has no foreseeable end—that is unless our point of view changes radically.

Number of Victims. They are considerable in both cases. Quantitative comparisons are not qualitative comparisons. Nonetheless, the almost unimaginable number of animal victims should naturally bring us to think that such a massacre must come to an end. We are by no means in a situation where we have to choose between us and them. Our choice is rather: "Should we or should we not continue to kill hundreds of billions of animals per year, given that it is not necessary to our survival?" (The roughly 550 to 600 million vegetarians on the planet are there to remind us of that latter fact.)

The Nature of Reaction. The world has often been slow to react to genocides. First people are incredulous, then they think that the facts must be exaggerated, and then finally they reach the point of wondering how they should intervene. Nevertheless, at the end of a certain time, the reality of the genocide becomes clear to everyone, and the necessary measures are taken to bring it to an end. In the case of the killing of animals, no one, or almost no one, tries to put an end to it.

Memory. As Jacques Sémelin says, "The dead, the victims of mass violence are still present, living, there in our memories."[14] In the case of the animals we massacre, they are not the object of any concern while they are still alive, so it goes without saying that once they are struck down, they do not remain present in anybody's memory. All that remains, at best, is the memory of a piece of their body that has contributed to our pleasure, without our having the least thought that it was at one time a part of a being that asked no more than to continue to live.

The Similarities

The common points between genocide and the large-scale killing of animals are the *devaluation* of the victims, the *desensitizing* of the perpetrators and the *mental dissociation* operative within them, the *methods* of extermination, the *concealment* of the facts by the perpetrators, and the *unwillingness to know* on the part of those who are in a position to know the facts.

Devaluation. Humans and animals are both devalued. Humans are dehumanized; they are regarded as, and treated as, animals such as rats or cockroaches. The animals are "de-animalized," relegated to the status of things: sausage machines, industrial products, or consumer goods.

Methods. It is on the level of methods and techniques of extermination that the resemblances are the most striking. When the American writer Judy Chicago paid a visit to Auschwitz and saw a mock-up of a crematory oven, she had a revelation: "They were in fact factories on a giant scale—but instead of processing pigs, it was people defined as pigs who were processed here."[15]

The methods are horrifically similar: innumerable living beings devaluated and reduced to numbers are first heaped together in sordid locales, then transported long distances without either water or food, dragged to their execution site, and struck down without mercy. In the case of animals, almost all of their body parts are transformed into usable products such as meat, clothing, shoes, fertilizers, and even into food for other victims of the system (fish meal fed to cattle, for example). In the case of human victims, their money, their jewels, their gold teeth, and all their other possessions are collected. In the Nazi concentration camps, even their ashes were used to make soap. Their hair was also used. Their living bodies were made to undergo medical experiments, and their skin was used to make lamp shades.

In one of the novels of J. M. Coetzee, another winner of the Nobel Prize for Literature, the heroine, Elizabeth Costello, says to her audience: "Chicago showed us the way; it was from the Chicago stockyards that the Nazis learned how to process bodies."[16] Among the main architects of the "final solution," several came from agricultural backgrounds and had worked in breeding or other occupations linked with handling animals. Heinrich Himmler, the chief of the SS; Richard Darré, the minister for food and farming; and Rudolf Höss, the commandant of Auschwitz, who came from an agricultural background—all were fierce partisans of eugenics, of the "improvement" of the German race, and spoke of it just as one would speak of the improvement of a breed of cattle.[17]

The analogies between the death camps and the slaughter facilities are numerous. In the camps of Belzec, Sobibor, and Treblinka, the "gut," the footpath that led to the gas chambers, was called "the road to heaven." At Sobibor, this gut was a path three or four meters wide and one hundred and fifty meters long, flanked on each side by barbed wire filled in with branches so that the condemned could not see what was going on outside and so that their fate was concealed from the other prisoners. The SS shoved their naked victims all the way up to the entry to the gas chambers.

In the United States, pigs enter the slaughter facility by way of the "corridor of death," which was improved by Temple Grandin of the University of Colorado in order to keep the animals calm for as long as possible. After that, they have to continue up an inclined ramp toward the killing place, a ramp baptized by Grandin, as we saw, "the stairway to paradise." Although the similarity in the names is without doubt an accident, that does not make it any the less sinister.

Concealment and the Presumption of Ignorance. Most of the people who lived in the vicinity of the concentration camps say that they did not know what was going on inside, or at least they were not sure. Some of them admitted that they could not permit themselves to know, for their own safety. One Holocaust survivor explained to the American political scientist Kristen Monroe: "But most people look away. They don't want to see because it's disturbing. . . . I fully believe the people who lived next to the concentration camps and say, 'We never saw anything.' Of course they didn't see anything! They didn't want to see. You don't want to think of your son sitting there getting his jollies out of torturing people or sticking them alive in an oven."[18]

The American historian Dominick LaCapra, a specialist in the Holocaust and the exploitation of animals by humans, said this in a BBC interview:

Within well defined limits, it is useful to establish an analogy with the Holocaust because certain structures are very similar. The first is the structure of the false secret. During the Holocaust, in Germany, in Poland and elsewhere, the people knew up to a point what was going on. They knew enough to know that they didn't want to know more. This is not simply indifference. It is a very active process that consists in reducing your thoughts to silence. It is the same sort of thing as walking in the street at night while being aware that there is someone following you—you would rather not turn around.[19]

The sheer scale of the zoocides that we humans carry out year after year makes it impossible for us to go on making believe that nothing of the kind is going on. "The industrial system," writes Jocelyne Porcher, "is an enterprise involving deconstruction of the animal and construction of the thing. But this enterprise is doomed to failure. The animals resist and persist in being animals and not things. By contrast, *we* lose our sensibility and our humanity."[20] Perpetuation of the mass killing of animals constitutes a major challenge to the integrity and ethical coherence of human societies.

8

A LITTLE SIDE TRIP INTO THE REALM OF MORAL JUDGMENT

We have seen the denial of the suffering of animals reflected in the concept "animal automata" of Descartes and the quasi-pathological lack of sensitivity to animal suffering on the part of the Jansenists of Port-Royal, and by way of contrast we have also seen the sadness of Ovid's elegiac plea for animals and the militant indignation of Voltaire at their mistreatment. These judgments doubtless have complex motivations behind them. How can one reach the conclusion that it is normal to make animals suffer, on the one hand, and on the other, how does one come to be scandalized by this same cruelty?

At the present time, studies carried out by American neuroscientists and psychologists on the processes of ethical judgment and moral decisions are resulting in new and surprising findings regarding these often difficult questions.

When we are confronted by an ethical choice, a number of forces, often conflicting ones, exert influence on our judgment. Immediately, for example, when we learn of a child molested by an adult, we have emotional reactions, sometimes visceral ones. If circumstances then give us the time, to those emotional reactions are added our reasonings regarding the different facets of the situation, helping us make the most just decision. And all of that is influenced by the social, religious, and philosophical norms that prevail in the world around us.

The Three Forms of Ethics

Three main forms of ethics are distinguished: deontological, consequentialist (which includes utilitarianism), and ethics based on virtue.

According to the form of ethics called deontological, which is related to the notion of duty or obligation, certain acts should not be committed under any circumstances, no matter what the consequences might be. Immanuel Kant is the most eminent advocate of this "categorical imperative," which sometimes can have unacceptable implications. For example, Kant affirmed that we should never lie, even to a criminal who is asking us where his intended victim has fled to. By lying, according to Kant, we strike a blow against one of the foundations of society, the belief in the given word, especially within the framework of contracts. Thus by lying, in Kant's view, we commit an injustice against humanity as a whole.[1]

Another vision of ethics consists in deciding whether an act is justified by considering its *consequences*. Main proponents of this utilitarian point of view are John Stuart Mill and Jeremy Bentham. More human than Kant's outlook because closer to reality as we experience it, utilitarianism can nevertheless lead to excesses and deviations. It aims to bring about "the well-being of the greatest number" by aggregating the well-being of individuals, and thus as eminent Greek thinkers of old pointed out, can bring us to conclusions such as that it would be good to enslave a hundred people in order to make a thousand free citizens happier. We see what extremes this attitude can take us to, if it is not tempered by other factors such as justice, wisdom, and compassion.

The ethics of *virtue* is the ethics proposed by Buddhism and some ancient Greek thinkers. It is based on a *way of being* that, confronted by different situations, spontaneously expresses itself either through altruistic or egoistic acts. As the neuroscientist and philosopher Francisco Varela wrote, a truly virtuous person "does not act out ethics, but embodies it like any expert embodies his knowledge; the wise man *is* ethical, or more explicitly, his actions arise from inclinations that his disposition produces in response to specific situations."[2]

A purely abstract ethics that is not based on a manner of being and does not take into account the specific aspects of circumstances is of no use. In real life, we always work within a particular context that requires an appropriate reaction. According to Varela, "the quality of our availability will depend on the quality of our being and not on the correctness of our abstract moral principles."

We may remark along with the Canadian Charles Taylor that a good part of contemporary moral philosophy "has tended to focus on what it is right to do rather than on what it is good to be, on defining the content of obligation rather than the nature of the good life. . . ."[3] Ethics must be concrete, embodied, and integrated into experience as we live it. It must reflect the unique character of each being and each situation. In our time, the movement toward concern and care for others that has recently been on the rise, especially in the English-speaking world, provides us with an example of the ethics of virtue.

According to Buddhism, ethics is part of the general project of seeking to relieve all forms of suffering. This process requires us to renounce whatever kinds of egoistic satisfaction that come at the expense of the suffering of others and to make every effort to bring about the happiness of others. To fulfill its ethical contract, altruism must, from this point of view, free itself from blindness and illuminate itself with a wisdom that is free from malevolence; it must enrich itself with altruistic love and compassion. Here, Buddhism agrees with Plato, who said, "The happiest man, then, is one who does not have evil in his soul."[4]

Ethics and the Light Shed by the Neurosciences

Recent experiments have shed new light on a debate that has preoccupied ethical thinkers for centuries. In his research on moral judgment, Joshua Greene, a philosopher and neuroscientist at Harvard University, has studied the effects of moral choice and behavior on the activity of different areas of the brain. He wanted to come to an understanding of how moral judgments are shaped by a mixture of automatic processes (such as emotional instincts) and cognitive processes that can be controlled (such as reasoning and self-control). In the light of these researches, it appears that moral judgment depends on the functional integration of multiple cognitive and emotional systems of which no single one seems to be specifically assigned to moral judgment.

Concerning the way in which we bring ourselves to resolve moral problems, the "rationalist" philosophers, such as Plato and Kant, conceive of moral judgment as a rational enterprise that takes into account the abstract ideals that engender good motivation and thus indicate the direction to follow. In contrast with these rationalists, the philosophers Greene calls "sentimentalists," such as David Hume and Adam Smith, took the position that the emotions are the main basis for moral judgment. Greene's studies show that the emotions and reason together both play an essential role in moral judgment, and that their respective influences have for the most part been inadequately understood.

He advances the theory of a "double process," according to which deontological moral judgments (those related to questions of rights and duties) are, contrary to what one might think, triggered by *automatic emotional reactions*, whereas moral judgments of the utilitarian and consequentialist type (the ones whose aim is to promote "the good") are shaped by *more controlled cognitive processes*.

In his research Greene made use of the "trolley problem," which was originally thought up by philosophers Philippa Foot and Judith Jarvis Thomson. A runaway trolley on rails is headed at breakneck speed toward five people who do not see it coming and will be killed if no one intervenes. The problem can be presented in two ways:

- The case of the switch. You are in a position to throw a switch that will cause the trolley to be diverted onto another track where only one person will be killed by the speeding trolley. Is it morally acceptable to divert the trolley in order to prevent five deaths at the expense of one? Most people questioned reply yes.
- The case of the footbridge. The situation is the same with the difference that you are now standing next to a man seated on the guardrail of a footbridge that runs over the railroad track. The only way to save the five people is to push this man in such a way that he will fall on a switch that will cause the trolley to be diverted onto a clear track. (The guardrail is too high for you to be able to climb it in time to sacrifice your own life to save the five people.) Is it morally acceptable to push this unknown man to his death to save the lives of the five others? Most people reply no.

So now we find ourselves with the following problem: Why does it seem normal for most of us to sacrifice one person to save five others in the case of the switch, but not in the case of the footbridge? For Joshua Greene these two cases bring into play two different psychological reactions and two different neuronal networks. According to the first network, both dilemmas are approached in the same way—in utilitarian terms: it is best to save as many lives as possible. This system implies great self-control and is accompanied by relative emotional detachment. It seems to depend on the dorsolateral, prefrontal cortex, a part of the brain associated with cognitive control and reasoning.

The second neuronal network responds in a very different way to the two dilemmas: it reacts with a strong negative emotional response to the idea of pushing a person off the bridge, but it does not react emotionally to the idea of throwing the switch, which is an emotionally "neuter" object. This is true even though in both cases the action chosen will bring about the death of one innocent person in order to save the five others. It turns out that, when the emotional system is strongly activated in the case where it is necessary to *physically* push someone, that is what dominates the judgment process. This explains why we tend to react in a utilitarian fashion in the case of the switch and in a deontological fashion in the case of the footbridge.

Greene has put forward the hypothesis that social and emotional responses that we have inherited from our primate ancestors underlie the prohibitions that are at the core of deontological views such as those of Immanuel Kant, which forbid crossing certain moral boundaries, no matter what good might result from crossing them.

By contrast, impartial evaluation of a situation—which is what defines utilitarianism—is made possible by structures of the frontal lobe of the brain that have evolved more recently and allow a greater level of cognitive control.

As Greene points out, "Should this account prove correct, however, it will have the ironic implication that the Kantian 'rationalist' approach to moral philosophy is, psychologically speaking, grounded not in principles of pure practical reason, but in a set of emotional responses that are subsequently rationalized."[5] This is also the point of view of a growing number of researchers, notably psychologist Jonathan Haidt, who puts forward the notion that, in numerous situations, we initially sense instinctively or intuitively whether or not a behavior is acceptable, and then subsequently we justify our choices through reasoning.[6]

We see from the preceding account that ethical choices are quite often complex and sometimes harrowing because of the struggle in our mind between our emotions and our reason, between deontological taboos and utilitarian logic. Therefore we must take great care to see that our ethical choices are biased neither by our empathic distress nor by our prejudices.

In the case of animals, the ethics of virtue should lead us to treat them with kindness. When we look at the facts, however, we cannot fail to note the purely arbitrary quality that makes us adopt a deontological position in some cases and a utilitarian one, biased by human interests, in others. A person who kills his cat or dog by banging its head against the wall faces the disapproval of nearly all of his fellow humans; when workers in a slaughter facility subject chickens or piglets to the same treatment, this behavior is not considered reprehensible, because in any case these animals have lost their status of sentient beings worthy of consideration and are well on their way to being transformed into mere consumer products. It often happens on a farm that a pig or a goat is treated almost like a member of the family until the decision is reached that it is time to cut its throat. The victorious racehorse is paraded triumphantly at the racetrack and afterward treated with adulation until the day comes when, old and useless, it is sent to the slaughterhouse because it would cost too much to feed it until it dies. Thus the value placed on animals undergoes total change, from one extreme to the other, at the mere whim of their owners.

"Farid de Mortelle" is the Facebook pseudonym of a young man from Marseille, twenty-five years old, who in January 2014 had himself videoed while torturing a cat. He then put the record of his exploits online on YouTube. You see him standing in front of his friends and throwing a small white and ginger cat as high and as far as possible and watching it fall heavily on the concrete. Hysterical, Farid repeats his act a few seconds later, throwing the little cat violently against a wall. Then he plays with its unconscious body. France was outraged, and a petition calling for punishment of the young man got more than 130,000 signatures in a few days. The "internauts" went into action together to identify and find the guilty party, who was then arrested and condemned to a year in prison. The little cat, Oscar, miraculously survived, despite a broken paw and many bruises. It was picked up by a kindly person and finally found a good home.

In 2007 we learned that Michael Vick, an American football star, had for a number of years been organizing dogfights on his property. This news angered all of the United States. The dogfights had been organized for gambling, and the bets went as high as $26,000. Vick and his friends bought pit bulls, tested them for fighting ability, then electrocuted, hung, drowned, beat to death, or shot to death the ones who were not combative enough. Vick pleaded guilty and had to serve twenty-three months in jail.

Such acts of cruelty are not rare. In these cases, public opinion reacted purely emotionally and deontologically, proclaiming loud and clear that it is unacceptable to treat animals in this fashion. However, the very day that Farid made a martyr out of the little cat, in France nearly 500,000 animals were struck down at the end of a short life—indescribable suffering occurred accompanied by nearly complete indifference on the part of the public. In a slaughter facility in the western part of the country, undersized piglets were destroyed in the meshes of the machine that is utilized to kill them, and other living animals were thrown into an incinerator.[7] Rationally, nothing can justify such a divergence in attitude. As philosopher Gary Francione, who is an advocate of abolition of the instrumentalization of animals, tells us, we are suffering here from a veritable moral schizophrenia for which it is our duty to find a remedy.[8]

9

THE DILEMMA OF ANIMAL
EXPERIMENTATION

The number of animals used annually to carry out experiments in laboratories is estimated to be between 50 and 60 million, of which 12 million are used in the European Union, 12.5 million in France.[1] Most of them suffer in one way or another (from physical pain, stress, loss of freedom, and so forth) and are put to death as soon as they are no longer useful.

Basic research uses the majority of these animals, followed by biomedical research and testing for toxicity in household products and other consumer articles. Next come genetics experiments, which are multiplying rapidly in connection with production of genetically modified, or transgenic, animals. Commercial enterprises make big profits by raising and selling tens of millions of laboratory animals per year and therefore do not have an interest in finding an alternative to experiments on animals. The question of experiments using living animals and vivisection continues, very justifiably, to provoke passionate debate. These methods are mainly used in basic research in the effort to understand the mechanisms of living things and in applied research to find treatments for human ailments, to test the toxicity of new substances, to produce transgenic animals, as well as in education (for example, the dissection of animals in schools). As noted by Jean-Pierre Marguénaud, professor of law at the University of Limoges:

For a long time the freedom to experiment on animals has been an absolute freedom that has been based on the following syllogism, the ongoing persistence of which is quite remarkable: The happiness of humanity depends on the progress of science; now science can only make progress by increasing its knowledge through experiments on animals; therefore, the freedom to experiment on living animals is a prior condition for the improvement of the human condition, so much so that anyone who would go so far as to risk criticizing animal experimentation would expose himself to the danger of being considered an enemy of the human race, someone who is insensitive to the suffering of sick children and their premature deaths because of his excessive consideration of the sensibility of animals.[2]

Animal experimentation is thus presented as a necessary evil, motivated by the desire to alleviate the sufferings of humanity. As Marguénaud points out, "From gentle experimentation to horrific experimentation, all the permutations are possible, and it is quite unacceptable that they should be mistaken for each other as a result of being targeted by the same critiques."[3] "Gentle" experimentation is the kind that uses animals for scientific research and thus imposes some restrictions on their normal way of life, but does so in a way that does not cause them any physical or psychological suffering. Researchers like Claude Bernard along with the great number of his fellow scientists who did not feel the least concern for animal suffering are becoming more and more rare; such researchers these days suffer the disapproval of their peers and are now even punished by law. Claude Bernard, on the other hand, exemplified the earlier tradition by burning more than eight thousand dogs alive.[4] In 1865, in his *Introduction à l'Étude de la Médicine expérimentale, de l'Expérimentation des Êtres vivants* (Introduction to the Study of Experimental Medicine and to the Study of Experimentation on Living Beings), he explained:

The physiologist is not a man of the world, he is a scholar; he is a man who is gripped and absorbed by a scientific idea that he is pursuing. He does not hear the cries of animals, he no longer sees their flowing blood; he only sees his ideas and only perceives organisms that hide from him the problems he wants to uncover. . . . The scientific principle of vivisection is, moreover, an easy one to grasp. It is in fact always a question of separating or modifying particular parts of the living machine so as to study them and thus be able to make a judgment concerning their use or their usefulness.

Attitudes have without question evolved since this declaration, but in spite of new rules made and new measures taken to avoid animal suffering as much as possible, millions of animals continue to endure terrible torments and to be put to death, mainly in the business of testing toxic products. Even though the number of these "guinea pigs" is considerable, it remains much smaller than the number of animals killed for human consumption, and even much smaller than the number of rats poisoned in our city sewers by the sanitary authorities.

In their efforts to justify animal experimentation, its defenders highlight research that might provide the key for the treatment of cancer, of schizophrenia, and other ailments, and thus save humanity from major scourges. Sometimes the death of a large number of laboratory animals is deplored, but they are at least accorded the noble status of having, however involuntarily, served a great cause. In Japan, there is even a monument dedicated to the animals who have perished on the field of honor of scientific research, which proves that there, at least, some awareness exists of having made them suffer and having killed them, whereas in the West such a monument would seem laughable.

Utilization of hundreds of millions of animals for basic research is justified by recalling that, in addition to the tangible enrichment of knowledge it provides, all kinds of as yet unimagined practical applications might come out of it. More than seventy Nobel Prizes have rewarded research carried out on animals. Among the experiments that brought Nobels were experiments on pigs that led to the invention of the MRI (Cormac and Hounsfield, laureates 1979), research on dogs that led to the development of the techniques for organ transplant (Murray and Thomas, laureates 1990), and research on mice that led to the discovery of prions, infectious proteins that cause transmissible spongiform encephalopathies (Prusiner, laureate 1997).

No one can deny that the considerable progress made in medicine in the twentieth century, along with other factors, made it possible for life expectancy, in France, for example, to go from 45 years in 1900 to 80 years today. A researcher who is an acquaintance of mine, Wolf Singer, has pointed out to me that, if someone were to refuse to take drugs that were tested on animals, it would be impossible for that person to be treated by a doctor or to go to a hospital for care, because the near totality of all approved medicines have been tested on animals. To be a vegetarian or a vegan, it is only necessary to stop eating the animals themselves or the products made by exploiting them. Such a decision only takes a fraction of a second, and it is not difficult to find alternatives to animal products. But quite clearly it would be nearly impossible in the world we live in today to do completely without mainstream medical care.

A number of drugs tested on animals for use in humans are also used by veterinarians in the treatment of animals. That is a wonderful thing, but this use of drugs remains confined to pet animals, and in the case of industrial breeding operations, medicines are used only in such a way as to maximize the profit of the owners. Thus, as we have already pointed out, high doses of antibiotics are administered to cattle in the breeding plants to prevent them from contracting infectious diseases during their short lives. The antibiotics they are given are then found in residual levels in "their" meat when it reaches market. We might also add here that, although there is some research devoted specifically to the treatment of animal ailments, in the near totality of cases, the goal of this research is not the well-being of the animals themselves but rather preservation of their health so they can be used by humans. Many people and NGOs in the world, moved by compassion, are at work helping sick or injured animals, and they take advantage of whatever medical knowledge is available to them, but we are speaking here of isolated individual initiatives. Medical research intended solely for the care of animals regardless of their utility to human beings remains a scarcely developed area.

The goals of science are admirable, but we must always come back to the same question: Is it acceptable to make use of our power to inflict suffering on millions of sentient beings? In answer to this, frequently the most convinced deontologists, those who advocate absolute respect for the rights of the individual when it comes to human beings, become the most ardent utilitarians when it comes to the use of animals for the benefit of human beings. The arguments put forward for or against animal experimentation can be divided into several categories.

The Deontological Point of View

Those among the deontologists who think about the lot of animals simply extend to these other sentient beings their idea that, as a matter of principle, a human being cannot allow oneself to use other nonconsenting individuals as mere means of accomplishing one's own personal ends, certainly not at the expense of those individuals' well-being, not to mention at the price of their lives. For a deontologist, respect for the individual is nonnegotiable and cannot be allowed to get lost in any sort of utilitarian considerations, such as: "It is acceptable to sacrifice the happiness of one innocent person in order to ensure the happiness of ten." The American philosopher Tom Regan, in particular, maintains that, in the case of animal experimentation, we violate the rights of animals by setting aside their intrinsic value as "subjects of a life" and turning them into mere instruments for the increase of human well-being. By renouncing the forcible use of animals, we do not violate the rights of humans, whose sole right is to have their own intrinsic value respected. The only thing that we give up is the project of promoting human well-being by violating the rights of animals to live and not suffer.

The Anthropocentric Utilitarians

The utilitarians maintain that the lives of a million people taken as a whole are worth more than those of ten thousand people. The problem begins when it comes to choosing the victims, since individually, each human life has the same value as every other.

The utilitarian point of view is attractive at first blush, but it leaves the door open to all sorts of excesses. Totalitarian regimes, for example, do not bother about being gentle when seeking to implement their utilitarian views. Mao Zedong had no hesitation in saying that the lives of his citizens were a small sacrifice to make in establishing the golden age of socialism.[5]

In the case of animals, anthropocentric utilitarianism cares little about the colossal number of animals sacrificed to promote the interests of the human species. With regard to animal experimentation, the incontestable virtues and advantages of improving the health and longevity of innumerable human beings cannot be denied, but they are stained by the concomitant devaluation of animals used against their will. This devaluation can reach deplorable extremes. In 1974, during a television show, the American journalist Robert Nozick asked a group of scientists if the fact that a particular series of experiments was going to cause the death of hundreds of animals was sometimes considered as a sufficient reason for not going through with it. One of them replied, "Not to my knowledge." Nozick insisted, "Animals don't count at all?" Dr. Adrian Peracchio of the Yerkes National Primate Research Center replied, "Why should they count?" And Dr. David Baltimore of MIT added that he did not think that experimenting on animals constituted a moral problem of any kind.[6]

From this point of view, human life is "priceless" in the sense that it has an infinite value, and animal life is "priceless" in the sense that it has no value at all. Matters have certainly evolved over the past forty years, but there is much left to be done.

According to Mary Midgley, in current attitudes animals have a very low priority rating. Since it is recognized today that most animals are conscious, feel pain, and undergo the experience of suffering, they are regarded as having the right to *some* consideration, but they have to take their place at the end of the line, after all human needs have been taken into account. Thus the lack of consideration for animals is no longer total, but relative. On the practical level, Midgley notes, a number of measures to improve the lot of animals have been called for, but they do not begin to call into question the priority of human needs; animals are clearly not regarded as being in a comparable category.[7]

Fellow Beings or Something Different

Animal experimentation also suffers from a problem of internal logic, because it attempts to reconcile two contradictory ideas:

- The *resemblance* between humans and animals is considered sufficient to support the idea that the conclusions of experimentation on animals can be applied to the understanding and treatment of human ailments. Our bodies are made of the same cells, our organs are very similar (it is possible to transplant a pig's heart into a human if it is slightly modified genetically so as not to be rejected by the beneficiary); and the chimpanzee genome is 98.7 percent identical to ours.
- The *dissimilarity* between humans and animals is sufficient to justify inflicting on animals torments that we would under no circumstances allow to be inflicted on humans.

Either the animal is not like us, in which case there is no basis for carrying out the experiments; or else it is like us, it is our fellow being, in which case we should not carry out on it an experiment that we would find scandalous to carry out on a human. The fly, the chimpanzee, and the human are part of the same continuum of living things. Biologically, between these three beings, there is only a difference of degree. As we have seen, we share with many animals, called "higher animals," most of our emotions and a not inconsiderable part of our intellectual faculties.

According to Bernard Rollin, certain researchers, fortunately increasingly rare, place themselves in a totally contradictory position when, on the one hand, they deny animal pain and, on the other, they study the effects of painful stimuli on animals in order to gain a better understanding of the mechanisms of pain and extrapolate applications from that understanding to human beings.[8]

The list of treatments that have for a long time been inflicted on animals in laboratories where the effects of chronic pain are studied include stimulation of the nerves or the dental pulp with the help of implanted electrodes; repeated electric shocks delivered through the floor of a metal cage; inflammation provoked by subcutaneous injection of turpentine or other chemical agents; creation of necrosis in tissue through subcutaneous injection of formaldehyde; continuous intravenous administration of substances that cause pain; inducement of arthrosis by injection of toxic substances; deliberate fracturing of bones; creation of lesions in the central nervous system by injection of aluminum oxide gel; induction of convulsions; and so on.[9]

Peter Singer made a visit to the New York City offices of United Action for Animals, where, as he tells us, he found that there were filing cabinets full of photocopies of experiments reported in the scientific journals. Each thick file contained reports on numerous experiments, often fifty or more, and the labels on the files alone were clear enough. They included: "Acceleration," "Aggression," "Asphyxiation," "Blinding," "Burning," "Centrifuge," "Compression," "Concussion," "Crowding," "Crushing," "Decompression," "Drug Tests," "Experimental Neurosis," "Freezing," "Heating," "Hemorrhage," "Hindleg Beating," "Immobilization," "Isolation," "Multiple Injuries," "Prey Killing," "Protein Deprivation," "Punishment," "Radiation," "Starvation," "Shock," "Spinal Cord Injuries," "Stress," "Thirst," and many more.[10]

Only extreme devaluation of animals as sentient beings can possibly explain the imposition of such treatments.

What Is the Scientific Value of Extrapolating to Humans Knowledge Acquired by Experimenting on Animals?

A great number of the treatments that have been devised on the basis of experimentation on animals have turned out to be useful for humans, and as we have pointed out, the near totality of the medicines we use have been tested out on animals. All the same, it is important to make clear that a significant number of treatments that have proven effective on animals do not work on humans. The fact is, different species may react very differently to one and the same chemical substance. Thus the researchers at the University of Missouri in Columbia have shown that the breed of laboratory rats used by certain industries for toxicological assessments of the effects of bisphenol A (BPA) were at least 25,000 times more sensitive to hormonal disturbances than the average of other laboratory animals. In other cases, certain animal species turned out to be 100,000 times *less* sensitive than others to toxic substances.[11]

The point is that, although a good number of scientific experiments on animals lead to results that can be extrapolated to humans, such extrapolation is not always trustworthy, and consequences are unpredictable. The saddest and most famous case of this was that of thalidomide, a drug that was used in the decade or so after 1950 as a sedative and antinausea agent for pregnant women. Before being used on humans, it was tested on dogs, cats, rats, monkeys, hamsters, and chickens without producing undesirable effects. But when the product was commercialized and administered to humans, it caused very serious deformities in more than 10,000 newborns, which resulted in death for thousands of them. It was tested once again on animals, and the researchers found that it did not produce deformities except on the females of one particular breed of rabbit.[12] This is only one tragic example among many other cases of divergence between the effects brought on by various substances in animals and in humans. What is medicine for one can turn out to be poison for the other.

Aspirin, for example, is highly toxic for a number of animals. It brings about congenital deformities in rodents, and cats die if they absorb more than 20 percent (in relation to their weight) of the normal human dose once every three days. Ibuprofen, one of the most used painkillers in the world, brings about renal failure in dogs, even in weak doses. Penicillin, which has saved the lives of billions of humans, was not put into use for a long time because it has no antibacterial effects on the rabbits it was tested on. Alexander Fleming only discovered its power to wipe out infections in humans when he finally tried it out on a human subject.

Among the toxicity tests for chemical substances that are candidates for use in humans, the best known is the LD50, an abbreviation for "median lethal dose." This test determines the quantity of a substance necessary to kill half the animals it is given to. These animals suffer enormously long before the point is reached where half of them die. Moreover, this LD50 test is used to evaluate relatively inoffensive substances. In order to bring about the death of the animals, they must

be forced to ingest massive quantities of these only slightly toxic substances. In this case, their deaths result either from the excessive volume they have been made to take in or from the abnormally elevated
concentration of the substance in their bodies, even though the substance is not in itself toxic. As Dr. Elizabeth Whelan, administrative
director of the American Council on Science and Health, comments:
"It doesn't take a Ph.D. in the sciences to grasp the fact that rodent
exposure to the saccharin equivalent of 1,800 bottles of soda pop a day
doesn't relate well to our daily ingestion of a few glasses of the stuff."[13]

Another doctor, Christopher Smith, tells us that "The results of
these tests cannot be used to predict toxicity or to guide therapy in
human exposure. . . . I have never used results from animal tests to
manage accidental poisoning."[14]

The Abuses: Use of Experimentation on Animals for Trivial and Unjustifiable Reasons

For some years now, any research project that involves the use and
killing of animals must be submitted to an ethics committee and must
respect ever stricter rules. Although this is not enough—only replacement of experimentation on animals by a variety of alternatives (which
we consider later) would be truly satisfactory—in the countries where
they are observed, these rules do make it possible to avoid some of the
intolerable abuses that have been committed in the past.

In 1954 at Yale University, Margaret A. Lennox and her colleagues
placed 32 kittens into an oven, where they were subjected to 49 sessions
of intense heat. The kittens began by fighting with each other, then
were struck by multiple convulsions. The brilliant conclusion of the
researchers was that these results were consistent with those observed
in humans suffering from high fevers and with those observed previously in other kittens subjected to the same treatment.[15]

As for the famous psychologist Harry Harlow, in the 1950s he studied the effects of social isolation by incarcerating monkeys, from the
time of their birth, in a stainless steel chamber. He thus demonstrated
that early, severe, and prolonged isolation had reduced these animals
to a state dominated by fear and aggression.[16] Later on, he had, in his

own words, the "fascinating idea" of inducing depression in young monkeys by "allowing the baby monkeys to become attached to false mothers made of cloth which could be made to transform into monsters." The first of these monsters was a mother monkey made of cloth which at regular intervals, on demand, emitted compressed air at a high pressure level, which nearly ripped off the skin of the baby monkey. What did it do then? It clung even harder to this monstrous maternal decoy, because a frightened baby clings at all costs to its mother.[17]

Harlow devised another decoy mother that shook the baby so violently that one could hear its teeth clacking. The baby continued to hold ever more tightly to the false mother. Finally, Harlow fabricated a "porcupine mother," which would "eject sharp brass spikes over the entire ventral surface of its body. Although the infants were distressed by these 'pointed rebuffs,' they simply waited until the spikes receded and then returned and clung to the mother." As Singer noted, "Since Harlow began his maternal deprivation experiments some thirty years ago, over 250 such experiments have been conducted in the United States. These experiments subjected over seven thousand animals to procedures that induced distress, despair, anxiety, general psychological devastation, and death."[18] The philosopher Vinciane Desprct qualifies this unwholesome persistence as "a repetition without end of a maniacal duplication."[19]

These studies, which are now classics, did illuminate certain points in our knowledge concerning the attachment between mother and child, but clearly it would not be out of place for us to ask if it was legitimate to acquire this knowledge through such torture and to keep reproducing subtle variants of this torture down through the years. Ironically, in a farewell note at the end of the dozen years during which he directed the *Journal of Comparative and Physiological Psychology*, Harlow himself acknowledged that "most experiments are not worth doing and the data attained are not worth publishing." He said this after having reviewed, by his own estimate, some 2,500 manuscripts submitted to the journal for publication, of which the majority involved painful experiments on animals![20]

At the beginning of the 1980s at the University of Pennsylvania, Thomas Gennarelli and his team struck baboons on the head to study the lesions caused in this way in the brain in relation to the force of the blows. The American government financed these studies to the tune of $1 million per year. According to the documents approving this research project, the monkeys were to be anesthetized before receiving the blows and injuries to the head. Two investigators from the Animal Liberation Front (ALF) succeeded in sneaking into the laboratory and stealing the video recordings of these experiments. The videos showed baboons that were still conscious and struggling while being tied down to be struck. Also to be seen were animals writhing with pain as they came out of the anesthesia while the researchers were operating on their bared brains. The experimenters could also be heard mocking and laughing at the terrified animals while they were in throes of intense pain. The videos were put in the hands of the media. As a result of the outraged reaction of the public and following a campaign carried on for more than a year by PETA (People for the Ethical Treatment of Animals), a campaign that was supported by hundreds of citizens, the government cut off the funding being allotted to Gennarelli, and his laboratory was closed.[21] With regard to such excesses, it is enlightening to see *Earthlings,* a documentary that presents a number of film clips taken by hidden cameras in various research laboratories.[22]

There is the case of the irascible researcher who vented his anger fits by catching the first laboratory rat that came under his hand and throwing it against the wall. Steven Pinker, a professor at Harvard, tells of having seen a photo, published in a scientific journal, of a rat that had learned to avoid electric shocks by lying on its back and pushing a lever with its paws. The caption referred to "breakfast in bed."[23] Of course the breakfast in question was the electric shocks that were "served" to the animal.

The Draize test, a test for irritation of the eye that has been in use for half a century, aims to evaluate the irritant or corrosive effect of various substances on the eyes of rabbits. This test has been used for a great number of household and cosmetic products. The head of the animal is immobilized in a vise, and the eyes are kept permanently open using metallic clips. Then at regular intervals drops of the chemical product being studied are dripped into the eye of the rabbit. Since rabbits do not have the ability to secrete tears, the products quickly bring about irritations, burns, infections, and often necroses. "It is inconceivable that to beautify women we should inject toxic products into the eyes of animals," exclaimed the famous ethologist Jane Goodall.[24]

In September 2010 the Organisation for Economic Co-operation and Development (OECD) approved an alternative method intended to progressively replace the Draize test. In the interval before the alternative method comes into general use, the rabbits continue to suffer.[25] The American philosopher James Rachels gives us the following criticism of the human exception:

Of course, there are many impressive differences between humans and rabbits. . . . But are these differences relevant? Suppose they were cited as justification for permitting rabbits, but not humans, to be used in the Draize test. Would they be relevant differences? I suggest that this question can be answered as follows. First, forgetting rabbits for the moment, we ask why it would be objectionable to use humans in this way. The answer would be that the procedure is quite painful, and that people's eyes would be damaged beyond repair. This is bad for them because pain is bad, and because people need their eyes for all sorts of reasons. . . .

With this much in hand, we can then turn to the rabbits, and ask whether they are similar to humans in the relevant respects. Can they suffer pain? And do they need their eyesight to carry on their lives? If so, then we have the same reasons for opposing their use that we have for opposing the use of humans. And if someone objects that humans can do mathematics, or enjoy opera, but rabbits cannot, we can reply that even if these differences are relevant when other forms of treatment are at issue, they are irrelevant to the question about the Draize test.[26]

We could ask the same question as Peter Singer: "How can these things happen? How can people who are not sadists spend their working days driving monkeys into lifelong depression, heating dogs to death, or turning cats into drug addicts? How can they then remove their white coats, wash their hands, and go home to dinner with their families?"[27]

Are we talking here about a few "black sheep" in a scientific community that on the whole is benevolent and kind? We might want to think that those unfortunate monkeys fell into the hands of a mad scientist, a psychopath who took pleasure in torturing them. But the fact that his team also took part in the "game" shows us that it more likely we are dealing here with a general situation.

In 1971 the psychologist Philip Zimbardo conceived of an unusual experiment for evaluating the influence of situations on human behavior. In the basement of a building at Stanford University in California, he had a replica of a prison built and recruited volunteers, some to act as prisoners and some to act as guards. In the beginning, the prisoners, like their jailers, had difficulty taking their roles seriously. But in a few days, the situation evolved into something different. The guards would not tolerate either dissension or infraction of the rules on the part of the prisoners and came up with all sorts of humiliating punishments for them, some of whom adopted a submissive and resigned attitude, while others showed signs of rebellion. Bullying on the part of the guards, sometimes obscene, became more and more frequent. Acts of violence were committed. Some of the prisoners began to crack; one went on a hunger strike. The situation deteriorated to such a point that the scientists were compelled to end the experiment after six days instead of the fifteen originally intended.

For Philip Zimbardo, "Evil consists in intentionally behaving in ways that harm, abuse, demean, dehumanize, or destroy innocent others or in using one's authority and systemic power to encourage or permit others to do so on your behalf."[28]

The Stanford experiment and the notorious case of the Abu Ghraib prison in Iraq, where the American guards humiliated their prisoners in an obscene fashion, show how individuals who are not fundamentally monsters can be led to make others suffer, disregarding their own moral values in doing so. Deviations of this type are quite common in prisons around the world. They occur under the insidious pressure of a general situational framework whose logic imposes itself on everyone to the point where its norms replace the personal values of individuals.[29]

Thus, just as is the case in prisons, the abuses committed in some laboratories cannot be attributed to a few black sheep who have infected the flock. It is the sheepfold itself that is contaminated. What characterizes this sheepfold is a tacit consensus among the experimenters according to which it is acceptable to inflict harmful, often painful, treatments on the animals and then, when the tests are completed, to eliminate them without further ado. Once such treatment becomes the norm, it takes very little for the treatment of the animals to deviate further into all sorts of other abuses.

Speciesism Revisited

Human chauvinism is not content merely with affirming that human existence has a greater value than animal existence—who could reasonably doubt that? But it goes further by distancing itself from all sense of duty and compassion toward animals. The incoherence, however, of this position can be shown just by reversing the roles for a moment. That is what Henri-Joseph Dulaurens, who wrote in the seventeenth century, did:

> But what would we say if a dog who had become a surgeon broke the leg of a man to get a better idea of how to heal another dog? What would we say if a cat pulled out the eye of a child to see how the medullary fibers of the optic nerve are extended onto the retina? And finally, what would we say if a doe, armed with a scalpel, opened up the belly of a young wife in order to uncover the mysteries of generation, or just to satisfy her curiosity? Would we not shout "murder"!? Would we not cry "cruelty"!?[30]

We should also consider here an argument of Peter Singer's, the origin of which is to be found in Jeremy Bentham. This is a demonstration that has often been misinterpreted, violently criticized, and loudly pointed at by those who take a dim view of the animal liberation movement. Singer makes the following *ad absurdum* argument: If the lesser development in animals of certain human abilities—intelligence, a life plan, moral values (or the absence of certain abilities, such as philosophical and scientific genius)—justified our right to use them however it suits us, notably for scientific experimentation, what should prevent us from having recourse for the same purposes to human beings who are in a deep and irreversible vegetative state? Such people are indeed also marked by a total absence of abilities possessed by some animals. Some of the great apes have an IQ of 75, and the human average is 100.

Obviously we are horrified by the idea of instrumentalizing other human beings. Quite fortunately, we feel enough empathy and compassion toward them to be concerned by their condition, even though they might be incapable of even slightly manifesting the faculties that give human existence its unique quality. The fact that we are naturally inclined to feel sympathy toward our fellow human beings doubtless has a certain biological element in it as well as a philosophical one. But we have to acknowledge that this sympathy is partial, subjective, and deformed by our prejudices.

The idea of this argument *ad absurdum* is *not* to animalize humans or to humanize animals, nor is it to suggest that we begin to utilize humans in a vegetative state for scientific and medical experimentation, even in cases where doing so could make possible important discoveries that might be useful to humanity. On the contrary, the force of the argument is that we should cease instrumentalizing animals at our whim and without mercy. In essence, what we are talking about is not extending to humans the abuses that we wreak upon animals, but extending to animals the compassion that we feel toward human beings.

A Few Rays of Hope

A new European Union directive of 2010 states: "Animals have an intrinsic value that must be respected and . . . thus they should always be treated like sentient beings." It adds: "The use of animals for scientific or educational ends should therefore be considered only when there is no alternative method that does not involve the use of animals."[31]

The European directive stipulates in its preamble: "Though it is desirable to replace the use of living animals in procedures with other methods that do not involve their use, the use of living animals remains necessary to protect human and animal health as well as the environment."[32] Nonetheless, this directive stresses the necessity of improving the well-being of animals used in research procedures, taking into account new knowledge concerning animal well-being, including the capacity of animals to feel and express pain, suffering, and anxiety.

Thanks to continuous lobbying on the part of associations for the protection of animals, the directive prohibits the use of animals in testing cosmetics.[33] From now on, scientific procedures using animals are obliged to indicate on a scale the level of suffering involved.

Not only vertebrates but also cephalopods (a class of higher molluscs) are covered by the directive, which proposes respecting the principle of the three "Rs" (replacement, reduction, refinement) that was initially formulated in 1959 by the zoologist William Russell and the microbiologist Rex Burch:

- *Replace* the animal models where possible (in particular, with virtual models *in silico*—that is, with computer models).
- *Reduce* the number of animals used in experiments so as to avoid causing excessive numbers of them to suffer or be sacrificed.
- *Refine* the methodology by using less invasive methods and by defining the boundaries beyond which it is necessary to put an end to an experiment in order to avoid useless suffering.

The directive also takes an interest in the lot of the animals after their use in the laboratories: "In certain cases, it is suitable to release the animals into an appropriate habitat or breeding system, or to authorize the placement of animals like dogs and cats in homes, because public opinion is highly concerned with their fate."

Another European directive notes: "Although some member states have adopted national enforcement measures that guarantee a high level of protection to animals used for scientific purposes, other confine themselves to applying the minimal requirements stipulated." The new directive of 2010 concerning animal experimentation was made French law in February 2013.

According to Jean-Pierre Marguénaud, the European parliament took a big step forward by no longer basing the propositions concerning animal welfare on "ethical assessments," which left great latitude for interpretation to the experimenters, and instead giving priority to legality, an element that had been missing. The new European directive obliges every member state to establish a "national committee for the protection of animals used for scientific purposes."[34] In Marguénaud's opinion, these regulations constitute real progress, because they speak about "protection of animals" in a way that means something quite different from the earlier language that referred to "ethical reflection." In other words, animal experimentation will now come more under the jurisdiction of law and will no longer belong entirely to the private domain of the experimenters. The new authorities will now no longer have to limit themselves to formulating good advice to help the researchers adopt proper professional conduct. They will now actually make decisions granting, refusing, modifying, renewing, or withdrawing authorizations in accordance with very precise conditions established by the European directive.[35]

For some, these advances go against the principle of "freedom of scientific research," which is recognized by the charter of fundamental rights of the European Union and represents a precious value in democratic societies. But this "freedom" must of course be limited by the awareness that has become more prevalent today according to which animals are, to put it in Marguénaud's terms, "living beings, often sensitive and sometimes loved, who can no longer continue to be lumped into the same category of things as rags and towels, wheelbarrows, and computers."[36] This is in fact the same view shown in a poll carried out by Ipsos in 2003 in which 64 percent of the French people declared themselves opposed to animal experimentation. The great majority of French people today are very critical of the situation regarding the treatment of animals. Seventy-six percent of them believe that there is too much abuse in animal experimentation. Seventy-three percent consider that the information made available on the conditions in which animal experimentation is carried out is inadequate. Finally, 85 percent of French people are in favor of a complete prohibition of all animal experimentation when it can be demonstrated that alternative methods are viable.[37]

Alternative Methods

Numerous alternative methods, like culturing cells, tissue, and organs, especially in vitro, are now available. They make it possible to reduce considerably the number of animals required for research and toxicity tests.[38]

Research in vitro consists in studying cells, tissue, and organs isolated from living bodies, animal or human. The cellular lines are taken from animals, which afterward are no longer called upon. Otherwise, normally, the tissue or organs come from animals that are killed for this purpose. Banks of human tissue and cell strains have been set up in some countries, but often in others they face legal and ethical obstacles. Experiments in vitro are very promising in the realm of research on the effects of chemical substances.

Computers also make it possible, by means of simulation and virtual reality, to make advances in numerous sectors. This type of research is called *in silico* (because of the silicon used in computers) as opposed to *in vivo* (with a living organism) and *in vitro* (with cultures of cells and tissue). A gastrointestinal computer model, for example, has been developed that simulates the stomach, the small intestine, and the colon. This model makes it possible, notably, to study the interactions between drugs and foods and to perform virtual tests on the effects of certain substances. Artificial skin can now be substituted for that of animals to determine the corrosive or necrotic effect of a substance.

In the realm of education, today it is possible for students to practice vivisection in virtual reality by using, for example, the V-Frog software.[39] This software makes it possible to repeat all the learning stages in a very realistic manner as many times as necessary, without ever using a living frog. Evaluations have shown that students trained using alternative virtual solutions like this attain a level at least equal to that of students who have taken courses that relied on the use of animals.[40]

In practice, the dilemma of animal experimentation is not close to being resolved. The majority of researchers believe that it is not possible to do without it for solving certain complex problems, such as schizophrenia, epilepsy, or autoimmune diseases. These require experimentation on a functioning brain or on a complete organism. They say that these ailments cannot be understood simply by using cell cultures.

Thus we can only hope that a maximum of effort and funds can be dedicated to the development of alternative techniques, with the aim of abandoning animal experimentation, once and for all, for anything inessential (cosmetic products) or utilitarian (household products). It would also be appropriate to make all possible efforts to minimize the sufferings of animals during and after experimentation.

According to Jean-Pierre Marguénaud, it would not be surprising if the next directive, which is due to be promulgated November 10, 2017, at the latest, were to be revised in light of the progress that has been made and incorporate the only ultimatum that might really achieve the final goal: a deadline (2030–2035?) beyond which only alternative methods, such as in vitro and in silico, will be allowed.[41]

For all that, however, such progress will not help us to solve the fundamental question of the morality of instrumentalizing sentient beings for our profit in other areas. This is an egregious blot upon the human conscience that can only be wiped away by ceasing to blindly exercise the idea of might makes right.

I O

ILLEGAL TRADE
IN WILDLIFE

Trade in wild animal species and products derived from them is one of the most profitable illegal activities in the world. It brings in more than $16 billion per year for its perpetrators and ranks in the third position behind trafficking in arms and trafficking in drugs.[1]

Although deforestation, urbanization, and pollution are the primary causes of the disappearance of animal and plant species, traffic in animals also has a significant impact on endangered species. Traffic in wildlife specimens both alive and dead—in their organs, their skin, their fur, their feathers, or their bones—can bring about such a reduction in the population of a species that a critical threshold of survival versus extinction is reached.[2] This kind of illicit trade brings on a vicious cycle: the rarer a species is, the more expensive it becomes; the more expensive it is, the more it is targeted by traffickers and runs the risk of being wiped out.

Endangered species are protected by the Convention on International Trade in Endangered Species (CITES). This intergovernmental accord, also called the Washington Convention, was signed in 1973 by 170 countries.[3] The organization that developed out of this treaty either surveils, regulates, or prohibits international traffic in specific animals whose survival situation is critical.

Bleeding the Ecology and Martyring Animals

According to a 2006 report of the WWF and estimates by CITES, annual illicit trade in wild animals numbers 50,000 monkeys, between 640,000 and 2 million reptiles, 1.5 million birds, 3 million tortoises, and 350 million aquarium fish. This can mean living animals: grey red-tailed parrots, a protected species, as well as boa constrictors, gorillas, tortoises, and leopards. Each year the illegal traffic also includes "derivative products": 1.6 million lizard skins, 2 million snakeskins, 300,000 crocodile skins, 1.1 million furs, 1 million blocks of coral, and 21,000 hunting trophies.[4] These products are used in Chinese medicine and in other traditional medicines. They are also used for decoration, in luxury products, and as good luck charms.

The eggs of the blue parrot of Brazil, also a protected species, sell for up to $4,500 apiece in Europe. But the Amazonian hunter who collects them in the forest gets only $3.50 per egg.[5] The wool of the Tibetan antelope (*Pantholops hodgsonii*, or *chiru* in Tibetan), considered to be the finest in the world, is used to make the shawls known as "shatoosh" ("wool of wools"), which are sold on the black market for up to $3,300 apiece. Only the very fine hairs on the throat of the animal are taken. This antelope, which has become very rare, has become the object of intensive poaching by Chinese traffickers, who do not hesitate to hunt it by jeep using machine guns. This, despite the fact that the animal has been protected since 1979.

For its part, the organization TRAFFIC estimates that the trade in wild animals each year numbers 500 to 600 million tropical fish, 15 million fur-bearing animals, 5 million birds, 2 million reptiles, and 30,000 primates. This includes several tens of thousands of species. The growing demand for new kinds of pets, such as lizards, chameleons, and other geckos is a catastrophe for those species. According to CITES, in France the illegal trade in protected species of reptiles grew by 250 percent between 2004 and 2009.

In China, bear bile is used in traditional medicine, which attributes all kinds of therapeutic qualities to it. More than ten thousand Asian black bears (also known as moon bears or white-chested bears) are imprisoned for life in cages so that they can be tapped twice a day. Twenty-four hundred of them face the same lot in Vietnam, and an undetermined number in Mongolia. The bear is immobilized day and night in a lying position, and the cages are so small the animals cannot even turn over. The tapping of the bile can begin as early as one year of age: a catheter or a large probe is inserted at the level of the waist into an iron corset that helps to keep the catheter in place. The technicians also use more potent pumps, which are very painful: during the extraction, the animals moan and bang their heads against the bars. Some of them go so far as to chew their own paws.

For the most part injured and emaciated, the bears do not live very long. When they die, they are sent to the butcher, their meat being an expensive and sought-after dish. Some of them survive and endure this torture for ten to twenty years. The preparations using their bile sell for up to $450 for four ounces. After the death of the animal, its gall bladder can be sold for as much as $16,500 on markets in China, Honk Kong, Japan, Macao, South Korea, or Taiwan.[6]

Jill Robinson, an Englishwoman who has devoted her life to animal protection, visited a bear bile farm for the first time in China in 1993, posing as a tourist. She felt as though she were suddenly in the middle of a horror film. After seven years of research and negotiation, in 2000 she succeeded in obtaining from the China Wildlife Conservation Association and the Sichuan Forestry Department an agreement to free 500 bears.[7] This was the first agreement signed by the Chinese government and a foreign organization for the protection of animals. Since then, Robinson has founded the Animals Asia Foundation and created a rescue center for moon bears in Chengdu, the capital of the province of Sichuan. This foundation has already saved 260 bears in China and has recently opened a reserve for them in Vietnam, where bile harvesting is still practiced, although it is illegal.[8] According to official figures, 68 bear bile farms are still functioning in China. The Guizhentang Pharmaceutical Company, started in 2000, has in its possession 470 bears, and in view of its success, hopes to bring that number up to 1,200.[9] So there still remains a lot for us to do.

Wild animals are not the only victims of illegal trade. In Europe, traffickers do not wait for cats and dogs to reach the legal age before exporting them from one country to another. Puppies and kittens sell much better than the adult animals. Many of them die during transport, which often occurs in very bad conditions. Belgium is the hub of this trade, because it is easy to obtain the European passports there that are now obligatory for the movement of pet animals.

The Twilight of the Tiger

In the course of ten years, the wild tiger population diminished by half due to loss of habitat and poaching. The worldwide population, estimated at 100,000 individuals at the beginning of the twentieth century, has been devastated. Today, there are only roughly 3,200 tigers left in the wild. Tigers have disappeared in 11 of the 24 countries where they once flourished. Three subspecies have already become extinct. Indonesia allowed the tigers of Bali to disappear in the 1930s, and those of Java went in the 1980s. The last of the most Western sub-species of tiger, the Caspian tiger, had died out by 1972.

Keshav Varma, director of the program of the World Bank to save the tiger (the Global Tiger Initiative), estimated that in 2008, when the program was started, there were ten years left in which to save the tiger in the wild. At that time, he lamented: "The means presently in place to prevent this tragedy are clearly insufficient when it comes to fighting the great international mafias that nowadays operate the illegal trade."[10] If the present trend is not reversed, the wild tiger is doomed to disappear.

To that concern we must add the cruelty that prevails in the numerous "tiger farms" that have been set up in China. These are described by Louis Bériot in his *Ces Animaux qu'on Assassine* (*The Animals We Murder*): "China holds in captivity in its parks, zoos, and farms—in more than 200 locations—two or three times more tigers than roam free in the world. The operators of the farms and many zoos raise them with the intention of killing them and re-selling them in pieces—the skin, the meat, and the bones—in order to supply the Chinese, Korean, Taiwanese, Japanese, and American markets. Because tigers reproduce easily in captivity, they have become an animal that is raised 'in bulk.'"[11]

One of the places Louis Bériot visited was the Xiongsen Bear and Tiger Mountain Village, where 1,400 tigers from Bengal, Siberia, the south of China, and surrounding countries are kept, as well as 400 black bears from China, 300 lions from Africa, and 500 monkeys. In addition, 200 to 300 frozen tiger cadavers are kept in their freezers.[12] This is without a doubt the largest "wild" animal breeding operations in the world. In addition to carrying on this commercial breeding, this vast complex puts on circus performances that attract many visitors.

This enterprise was created in 1993 with the blessings of the government and the regional authorities and benefited from a public grant of more than 350 million yuans (about $39 million). However, the same year, China announced a prohibition of commercial products derived from tigers. Every part of the tiger is sold: its skin, its bones, its penis, its whiskers, its claws, its teeth . . . A tiger skin costs $16,400; its skeleton sells for $219,000. Its bones are used to fabricate a "tonic" wine that is supposed to heal all ills and stimulate all kinds of vital functions. The bones are also used to produce an ointment and other remedies. Once the tigers have attained their full adult size and their bones have ceased to grow, during the weeks preceding their being put to death, they are inadequately fed, even starved. At the Shenyang Forest Wild Animal Zoo, also in China, 40 Siberian tigers died of starvation between December 2009 and February 2010.

Regarding the totality of products derived from the bodies of tigers that are used in Chinese traditional medicine, Andy Fisher of the Wildlife Crime Unit in London says: "Thousands of tests have been carried out on these products and have demonstrated that they bring no more benefit than the ingredients found in cow's milk."[13] This illegal traffic continues to thrive, in spite of laws that are supposed to prohibit it but which are hardly enforced by the Asian governments concerned.

The Craze for Elephant Tusks, Rhinoceros Horns, and Shark Fins

Twenty-five thousand elephants are killed every year for their ivory. As a result of the report put out by the Environmental Investigation Agency (EIA) on the ruinous poaching that prevailed during the 1980s, an international prohibition of commerce in ivory was promulgated and entered into effect in 1989. For several years, a spectacular reduction in the level of poaching was observed in large parts of Africa. Unfortunately, the demand for ivory remains very strong, and elephant populations are again being decimated. Ivory is highly prized in Asia for jewelry, ornaments, and religious sculptures. The amount of ivory reaching East Asia (especially China) from Africa is estimated to be around 72 tons per year (corresponding to an annual kill of 7,000 elephants), having a value of $300 million.

According to Amanda Gent of the IFAW (International Fund for Animal Welfare), "At present, a hundred elephants disappear per day in the 36 African countries that still have them. The poachers are directed and paid by Chinese traffickers, who having established themselves in Africa around fifteen years ago, have significantly developed the trade in ivory, a luxury product that is quite sought after in China and in all of Southeast Asia."[14]

The recent wave of rhinoceros massacres is in great part due to the widespread claims in the Far East, which are completely without foundation, that rhinoceros horn is a remedy for cancer, impotence, and other ailments. Use of rhinoceros horn powder and possession of sculptures made of rhinoceros horn are also regarded as symbols of wealth. Businessmen do not hesitate to pay $98,000 for a rhinoceros horn, which they go on to sell in powdered form for between $1,000 and $2,000 per dose, which is more expensive than cocaine. All that for a product that has no effect whatsoever.[15] In the East, the Chinese Triads of Hong Kong have succeeded in cornering the major part of this traffic. The demand is such that rhinoceros poaching in South Africa (where there are more rhinos than anywhere else in the world) increased 5,000 percent between 2007 and 2012. In 2013 alone, 900 rhinos were killed. One of the animals is killed every ten hours. Today there remain no more than around 25,000 rhinos in the world, compared with 600,000 in the middle of the twentieth century.[16]

More than 200 million sharks are killed every year, of which 75 million are killed for their fins alone. The fishermen cut off the fins and throw the wounded sharks back into the sea, where they suffer from blood loss and are incapable of determining their direction in the water. Thus they are doomed to certain death. Shark fins are principally sold in de luxe restaurants in Hong Kong, Thailand, and China.

The Links between Corruption, Organized Crime, and Terrorist Groups

A study by Leo Douglas of the multidisciplinary Center for Biodiversity and Conservation and the American Museum of Natural History[17] and Kelvin Alie of the IFAW[18] have shown that poachers are often associated with the heads of local military groups or with rebel groups that regularly resort to wildlife trafficking to finance their activities.[19] This is notably the case of the Janjawid of Chad and the Sudan, the Democratic Liberation Force of Rwanda, and the Somalian Islamic group Al Shabab, who cross the border with Kenya to poach elephants in the Arawale Preserve. The revenue from the poaching ends up financing the purchase of arms and ammunition and thus exacerbates regional conflicts.

According to Kelvin Alie, "The corruption spreads like wildfire and affects the military, border guards, the police, the judiciary system, the customs service, the personnel of the embassies, and even the diplomats of many countries. All of them profit from the illegal trade in wild species and actively support the traffickers."[20] In addition, criminologists have observed that valuable wild animals also serve as currency for criminal and terrorist organizations, because the wildlife trade has become an effective means of laundering money.

The fact is, it is easier, less burdensome, and less dangerous to carry on trade in animals than to risk trafficking rare minerals or other natural resources of value, such as oil, gas, minerals, rare arboreal extracts, and so on. The authorities have a harder time surveilling and wiping out the wildlife trade than trade in these other commodities. Forest rangers and anti-poaching squads are often inadequately equipped and paid. In their small numbers, they are not up to confronting poachers armed with AK–47s and grenade launchers, and they are unable to choke off the networks of traffickers who have considerable means at their disposal for corrupting local officials and crossing borders unmolested.

Tourists also play a role in these malpractices by buying handmade objects made of ivory, tortoiseshell, and other by-products of the exploitation of protected species. Thus they are complicit in the ongoing poaching. The same goes for collectors of rare species. Taking a great number of animals out of their natural habitat can upset the balance of an ecosystem and break the chain of interdependence that links all the species that are part of it. The impact of this is felt by the local flora and fauna throughout the ecosystem.[21]

The Hot Spots

The hot spots and pivotal points in the wildlife trade include the Chinese borders and certain parts of Indonesia, Malaysia, New Guinea, the Caribbean, Mexico, the Salomon Islands, Suvarnabhumi Airport in Bangkok, as well as the eastern borders of the European Union.

The Chatuchak Weekend Market in Bangkok, for example, is a known center for illegal trade in animals; here they sell lizards, primates, and other species that are nearing extinction. Similarly, in the Amazon, in the markets of Iquitos and Manaus, a large variety of animals from the tropical forest—agoutis, peccaries, and tortoises—are sold for their meat. Numerous other protected species, notably parrots and monkeys, are marketed there as pets. In March 2009, 450 Brazilian policemen arrested seventy-eight persons belonging to a network that was trafficking 500,000 animals per year, including boas, capuchin monkeys, brockets, hyacinth macaws, Lear's macaws, and other protected species.[22]

The poachers prefer to take young animals. To do this, they often kill the mother who is trying to protect her young. In the case of tamarins, marmosets, spider monkeys, saki monkeys, and many others, they fire on the mother as she is carrying her offspring into the higher branches of the trees. Many of the babies do not survive the fall.

Mass Losses during Capture and Transport

The stress and violence involved in capturing live animals, their conditions of life when incarcerated, and their clandestine transport result in a very high level of mortality. On average, for every ten animals captured in their natural environment, one survives. In the case of the chameleons of Madagascar, the rate of survival is thought to be only 1 percent.[23] Therefore, foreseeing these losses, the traffickers capture a large number of individuals in the wild. The United States is a main destination for tropical-forest animals of the Amazon, which are transported across the borders in the same way as drugs: in the trunks of cars, in suitcases, and in shipping containers. A trafficker was arrested at the Los Angeles airport with fourteen rare birds concealed in his clothing. In 1999 at the Frankfurt airport, 1,300 tarantulas (with a value estimated at about $133,000 today) were discovered in the baggage of a Frenchman returning from Mexico.[24] Examples of this sort abound.

Charitable organizations with limited funds take into their care a small proportion of the animals confiscated by the customs services. In the majority of cases, however, the authorities have no choice but to euthanize the confiscated animals by the thousands, since they are unable either to shelter and feed them or to send them back to their countries of origin.

An Attempt That Backfired

In 2005 the Dalai Lama unequivocally condemned the custom that had become fashionable among well-to-do Tibetans of strutting about on holidays wearing clothing trimmed with tiger skins, leopard skins, and otter skins. He declared that this custom did not at all reflect the ancestral traditions of Tibet and was in flagrant contradiction with the teachings of Buddhism. He added, "The fact that my countrymen are taking up such customs makes me not want to live very much longer." This statement spread like wildfire in Tibet. Nearly all Tibetans tore the animal skins off their garments and made huge heaps of them, which they burned in public places.

In December 2007 in Kashmir, the Wildlife Trust of India (WTI) publicly burned an accumulation of eight truckloads of skins and furs taken from protected species (tigers, leopards, snow leopards, white-chested bears, otters, wolves, etc.), without a doubt one of the biggest accumulations of wild animal skins ever destroyed in this manner.

Unfortunately, these interventions, which were attempts to set an example and create better intentions, had the unexpected and perni-cious effect of considerably increasing the prices of these skins, and at the end of the day, they increased the trafficking. In Tibet, Debbie Banks, one of the main investigators of the Environmental Investiga-tion Agency (EIA), and her colleagues encountered traffickers who had just made deals for some tens of large tiger skins, headed for China, South Korea, Taiwan, and Malaysia. They also easily found stashes of tiger bones ready to be sold to Chinese pharmaceutical companies.

The traffickers in Lhasa took pride in being able to continue their activities without fear because they had connections in high places in both Nepal and China that guaranteed their impunity. Several of them let it be known that they were selling up to 25 leopard skins per month in spite of the significant reduction in demand among Tibetans inspired by the wishes of the Dalai Lama. In the face of these wishes, in order to thwart the Dalai Lama, the Chinese officials were forcing the Tibetans to resume wearing tiger skins, even though this practice was against the laws of the country.

The main routes taken by these traffickers are, in India, the scarcely surveilled passes from Uttar Pradesh, Himachal Pradesh, and Ladakh to Kashmir, as well as via the borders of Nepal and Bhutan.[25]

Inadequate or Barely Enforced Laws

Confiscations and spectacular destructions of ivory, skins of protected species, and other products derived from them can momentarily impede the wildlife trade, but they do not represent a long-term solu-tion. It is essential to beef up the existing laws and especially *to enforce them*, which is far from the usual case. As the organization One Voice points out, "In spite of protective laws on a worldwide scale, we are forced to acknowledge that the poaching and capture of wild animals in their natural habitat, including protected species, is continuing."[26]

White-chested bears and honey bears, for example, although they are protected by the Washington Convention because they are among the most endangered species on the planet, continue to be pursued in India or in China for their bile, their meat, or just for the entertain-ment of tourists enthusiastic about "dancing bears." In Africa, lions are set loose for the pleasure of safari participants or to serve as targets for big-game hunters.

According to Leo Douglas, wildlife trafficking is particularly profitable "because it is not the object of any real social stigma, because the chances of being arrested are quite small, and because those few criminals who do face trial unfortunately often receive only the most ludicrous of penalties." In 2014 in Ireland, two traffickers in rhino horns were arrested. The potential market value of their merchandise was $547,000; the fine they received: $547.[27]

I I

ANIMALS AS OBJECTS
OF ENTERTAINMENT
The Will to Power

As we saw in chapter I, "A Brief History of the Relations between Humans and Animals," James Serpell, professor of animal ethics at the University of Pennsylvania, has shown that the relationship that humans created with animals when they began to domesticate them, a relationship based on contradictory forces of intimacy and slavery, engendered painful feelings of guilt. To get away from this uncomfortable feeling, humans created ideologies that allowed them to continue in their enslavement of animals without experiencing a guilty conscience.[1]

Later on, the ability to subjugate animals and dominate nature began to appear as a measure of the success of human civilization. It even became a means of demonstrating personal, cultural, or national prestige. The kings of Babylon and Assyria had wild animals penned in fortified enclosures where they hunted them from chariots with the assistance of dog packs. They then had their feats immortalized in the bas-reliefs that adorned the walls of their palaces.[2]

The Greeks of antiquity were less inclined toward gratuitous cruelty to animals, but they were great lovers of spectacular parades that featured a large number of exotic animals. In the third century B.C.E, in Alexandria—which was then the cultural center of the Hellenic empire—every year a great multitude of people and animals paraded for a whole day past the stands of the city stadium. The spectacle included elephants, ostriches, and wild asses yoked to chariots, more than two thousand dogs of various exotic species, and 150 men carrying trees to which were bound various birds and arboreal mammals, followed by two dozen exotic animals including lions, leopards, cheetahs, lynxes, a giraffe, a rhinoceros, and sometimes a polar bear.[3]

While the *ludi* (state-sponsored games) of Roman antiquity consisted mainly of chariot races and athletic contests, the *munera* (games sponsored by wealthy individuals) featured fights between gladiators, usually prisoners of war reduced to slavery. But the Romans were also known for their barbarity toward animals. The emperors and the crowds at the games took delight in seeing countless animals put to death by the *bestiari*, gladiators specially trained to combat wild beasts. Hunting spectacles were also put on, in which the *venatores* (wild animal hunters) chased down game and killed it in reconstituted natural settings—groves, thickets, little cliffs—planted in the circus arena. Animals were also incited to fight each other in the Circus Maximus, the largest sports arena the world had ever known (it could hold 250,000 spectators),[4] the Colosseum of Rome, and many other stadiums. Bears and bulls were chained to each other in order to get them to tear each other apart. Elephants, rhinos, hippopotamuses, lions, and leopards were given stimulants to work them up into a rage. The animals that survived were struck down from the seats by spectators transformed into archers who paid for the privilege.

During the inauguration of the Roman Colosseum, which lasted one hundred days in the year 81 C.E., 9,000 wild animals were exterminated. In the course of one festival in the year 240 C.E., not less than 2,000 gladiators, 70 lions, 40 wild horses, 30 elephants, 30 leopards, 20 wild asses, 19 giraffes, 10 antelopes, 10 hyenas, 10 tigers, as well as a rhinoceros and a hippopotamus were put to death. Nero authorized his bodyguards to massacre 400 bears and 300 lions with javelins. But it is the emperor Trajan who holds the record. To celebrate his victories in Dacia, he ordered the public butchery of 11,000 wild animals. As for the emperor Commodius, he shot ostriches with crescent-shaped arrows that decapitated them. Their headless bodies continued to run for a few moments, which was amusing to the public.[5] The multiplication of these games—to up to a hundred per year—and the lucrative trade in wild animals needed to supply the circus brought about the disappearance of several species in the most plundered areas.

This was the case, for example, for the hippopotamus in the valley of the Nile. The collective madness of the mobs hungry for these bloody spectacles finally came to an end in the sixth century after the closure of the Circus Maximus, which gradually fell into ruin. But the violence toward animals continued to be an aspect of human entertainment down through the centuries. The historian Barbara Tuchman described two popular sports of fourteenth-century Europe: "Players with hands tied behind them competed to kill a cat nailed to a post by battering it to death with their heads, at the risk of cheeks ripped open or eyes scratched out by the frantic animal's claws. . . . Or a pig enclosed in a wide pen was chased by men with clubs to the laughter of spectators as he ran squealing from the blows until beaten lifeless."[6]

In our own day, the corrida, the trained-animal acts (wild animals or elephants) that are still presented in many circuses (and which in the view of the trainers themselves are far from as harmless as they appear), the shows put on in many zoos with animals that are resigned to their fate or half mad—all these are no more than the relics of the massacres and parades of antiquity. Nonetheless, these entertainments preserve their dose of palpable cruelty, perhaps hidden or disguised by pleasant features. They consist in fact of exploiting animals or causing them to suffer or even, in the case of the corrida, killing them. These are animals that have done nothing to bring this on themselves, that have asked for nothing, that were doing much better in their natural circumstances. "It has been said that the Roman people were disgusted with the whole thing. But that is a mistake. The Romans always kept their taste for blood. And how many Romans there are in our Gaul of today!" exclaimed Georges Clemenceau speaking of the corrida.[7]

My purpose in this chapter is to raise awareness on this subject. Real changes can only be voluntary ones. Only putting ourselves in the place of another and ascribing intrinsic value to that other will make it possible for us to develop sufficient respect and consideration for it, him, or her. Altruism is what gradually leads to cultural transformations; when they have already happened, the only role of laws is to rubber-stamp them and give them a more formal status.

The Corrida, Festival of Death

The reason I have decided to give a place of priority to the problem of the corrida, despite the fact that the number of victims (12,000 bulls killed per year) is very small in comparison to the mass killing perpetrated by industrial breeding operations (60 billion animals per year) is first of all because the corrida constitutes the very archetype of morbid entertainment for humans that is deadly to animals. In addition, the corrida is the object of an energetic, even "erudite" defense. Eminent philosophers, such as Francis Wolff, as well as famous writers and artists have defended it in the past and still do now. Finally, the debate as to whether to perpetuate it or abolish it unleashes real passions—verbally at least as violent as the spectacle itself. The practice of the corrida thus becomes the very symbol of the anthropocentric prejudices that we harbor toward animals, and for this reason in particular, it deserves to be analyzed. Before getting into this debate, let us imagine for a moment the mental, subjective universe of our impassioned participants.

First let us put ourselves in the place of the aficionado. From his or her point of view, the corrida is a festival, an occasion to be shared with the local community. The setting is ideal; the twists and turns of the fight are exhilarating; the blare of the trumpets is uplifting. The spectators are human beings like you and me, who live normal lives like our own, punctuated with joy and suffering. Many of them are electrified by the high points of the confrontation between the man in his "garb of light" and the bull; others find that it is an art form that transports them. Thus the whole affair is a matter of point of view, subjective perception, of customs and traditions that cause some people to appreciate what horrifies others. The way in which the aficionado perceives the bullfight can be taken for granted.

If we have only a little respect—or perhaps none at all—for the other, the bull in this case, for its fate and its aspirations, then our one-way vision of things will remain our one and only point of view. If it is the case that the aficionado feels empathy for the bull, which many of them say they do, he still takes the position that the "beauty" of the spectacle is worth the suffering of the animal.

In the corrida, even though it is not in the least necessary for his personal survival, the human actor decides to inflict intense suffering on a being that has done him no wrong and to take its life. The philosopher Francis Wolff, a fervent defender of the corrida, has come up with fifty main points to justify its existence. We have chosen to bring to the reader's attention only the most important of these and to examine them. "The corrida is not only a magnificent spectacle. It is not merely pardonable. It can be defended because it is morally good."[8] This is the main thesis defended by this philosopher, professor at the elite École Normale Supérieure of Paris and author of numerous works and articles on this subject.

But killing an innocent has never been considered to be a moral act. Forcing a being, human or animal, to fight without any necessary reason and undergo a death programmed for the pleasure of a number of actors and spectators cannot be considered morally good. Is not morality precisely a knowledge of good and evil that makes it possible to distinguish what is beneficial from what is harmful to others? It requires one being to attribute intrinsic value to other beings, to have respect for them, and to take into consideration the legitimate aspirations that are unique to them—of which the first and most fundamental must be to live.

The Corrida Is a Way to Cultivate Noble Virtues?

It has sometimes been maintained that the corrida is a school of virtue. That is what Pliny said with regard to the circus games. In his panegyric for the emperor Trajan,[9] he put forward the view that violent entertainments help to forge moral values, which include courage (*fortitudo*), discipline (*disciplina*), firmness (*constantia*), endurance (*patientia*), disdain toward death (*contemptus mortis*), love of glory (*amor laudis*), and the will to win (*cupido victoriae*).[10] In this way he dresses up mass massacres in a cloak of virtue.

We find the same justifications among the passionate advocates of the corrida. For Francis Wolff, to fight in the bullring "is to illustrate five or six non-temporal virtues that are today perhaps less glorified than some others, like compassion, which has tended progressively to replace justice." To be a torero, this philosopher explains, requires courage and composure, panache and dignity, self-mastery, loyalty, and solidarity. He concludes: "It is also required that one kill this enemy, which is only justified if, in doing it, one places one's own life in jeopardy. This presupposes complete loyalty toward this adversary and total sincerity in one's own physical and moral commitment. . . . Is this not an example of what we would like to be able to do, a model of what we would like to be able to be?"[11] Hearing such a declaration, we can only ask ourselves where it is that justice resides in an act that consists of putting to death an animal that has not harmed us in the least. Cultivating a virtue that consists in harming another is an ethical contradiction, unless wounding and killing the animal amounts to doing it good in some way. Moreover, these values like panache, dignity, self-mastery—do they not lose their entire sense if they are practiced at the expense of the life of another being who is not guilty of any crime? Doesn't real courage or real panache consist instead in risking one's own life to save another's? Where is the dignity of the combatant if his "adversary" is an innocent who is not able to fight with equal arms?

The "Art" of Killing

"Esthetically, the thrust of the sword is the gesture that completes the act and gives birth to the work of art; the successful thrust of the sword, perfect, immediate, seems to give unity to the work that preceded it, to give totality and perfection to the entire opus."[12] Certainly a spontaneous and perfect movement is what characterizes a masterwork of calligraphy, but killing is not an art, and death is not a work of art or a spectacle, especially if it is imposed upon a living creature that has absolutely no wish to die. As a reader of *Philosophie Magazine* wrote in reacting to this type of argument: "What a flimsy justification for killing!"[13] One thing we can say is for sure: the bull would certainly appreciate a less grisly form of art.

Nobody would think of sticking lances, banderillas, and a sword into the body of a human being and holding the event up as a work of art. The only way one can inflict such a fate on an animal is to devalue it to the level of an object, to the level of a plaything of our will. The bull is forced against any will of its own to be a player in a theatrical combat—a "ceremony" or a "ritual," as the aficionados tell us it is. But the "ending is known in advance: the animal must die, the man must not die."[14] The whole design and setup of this drama is conceived of, evaluated, and philosophized about from a strictly antropocentric point of view.

The Fighting Bull Exists Only to Be Killed

The corrida is also sometimes justified by saying that the "bravo" bulls, the bulls bred for combat, have been especially created with this end in mind, and thus the fight is their only reason for being. "It is not immoral to kill them," writes Wolff, "because this is the purpose they live for—as long as we properly respect the conditions of their life."[15] Our sole duty with regard to the bulls is to "preserve their 'brava' nature, to raise them with respect for this nature, and to kill them (since they live for that alone) with respect for this nature, and with all the regard that is due a respected animal."[16]

But who is it who decided to select the most bellicose bulls with the purpose of fighting them and then finally killing them? Here again, we find ourselves firmly planted in the point of view that presumes the right of the holder of greater intelligence and power to dispose of the life of others. Taking into account all its aspects, this is just like the point of view behind forcing humans who have been reduced to slavery to procreate and then declaring, once they have, that it is the normal thing for their children also to be slaves, since they were brought into the world for this reason alone. Obviously, this comparison is not intended to dehumanize humans but to expose the mental processes that go into the bullfighting case.

On top of all this, the very existence of a distinct race of "bravo" bulls is doubtful, as the historian Éric Baratay explains:

The normal bovine nature of the bulls of the corrida is confirmed by the fact that their proportion among their peers, even though they are specially favored, is small and becoming smaller and smaller; and the bulls that are not selected for combat are sent off to the butchery just like ordinary meat cattle; and the feed is the same for all, there having been a partial replacement of grass with grain in the twentieth century; and for all the bulls the pastures have little by little been reduced to closed fields. The toreros have known for a long time that the bull of the corrida is just an ordinary bovine, just a herbivore, and that it is not aggressive by nature. The celebrated torero Belmonte acknowledged that it is very difficult to provoke a bull in the field. It must be fairly tired out in order to give up fleeing and become convinced that attack is the only alternative; and this result is almost impossible for one man alone to bring about. One can at most speak of a greater reactivity in these bulls that has been brought about through selection. But one can in no way defend the notion that the bullfighting bull is a creature that has left behind the camp of the herbivores, by nature timorous, and entered that of the predators, by nature carnivorous![17]

The Dice Are Loaded

The writer Jean-Pierre Darracq tells us: "Even odds between man and beast . . . are the sole justification for the drama of the bullfight."[18] But this author would do well to review his arithmetic. In Europe between 1950 and 2003, just one single matador died, whereas 41,500 bulls were killed.[19] There is little doubt that the very rare death of a torero has a greater chance of making page one of the newspapers than the deaths of tens of thousands of bulls.[20] Yet even the famous torero Luis Miguel Dominguin clearly stated that fighting in the bullring presents no greater risk of death than many other occupations.[21]

Francis Wolff does not speak of even odds between the torero and the bull, since for him, the corrida is "a fight with equal arms but with uneven odds." We might suspect that if the respective chances of survival were really fifty-fifty, the toreros would have abandoned the arena long since. Nonetheless, Wolff develops his argument as follows:

It is a contest with equal arms, cunning versus force, like David versus Goliath. It is also a fight with unequal odds, since it illustrates the superiority of human intelligence over the brute force of the bull. But how would you have it? Would you want the odds for the man and beast to be even as in the games of the [Roman] arena? Sometimes one dies, sometimes the other dies—would that be more just? In any case it would be more barbarous! The corrida is not an athletic contest of which the outcome should remain uncertain. It is a ceremony, the result of which is known in advance. The animal must die, the man must not die (even though it can happen sometimes that a man dies accidentally and an exceptionally brave bull is pardoned). That is the moral framework of this combat. But uneven does not mean disloyal. That is just the point. The demonstration of the superiority of the man's armament over that of the animal has no sense unless the animal's weapons (body mass and horns) are powerful and have not been artificially reduced. That is the ethics of tauromachy. It is an uneven but loyal combat.[22]

So the bullfights are set up in such a way that one of the protagonists, the human, wins every time, and this is supposed to not be disloyal? How should we define "equal arms"? The man against the bull? The sword against the horns? If we were talking about the man with all his intelligence and cunning, just as he stands there, with his bare hands, against the bull, just as it stands there, with its own form of intelligence and its natural assets, the man would always be the loser.

If the man's superiority is based on the sword, it is not the man who wins, but the man plus an implement to which he owes his nearly certain victory. So if all depends on the addition of this weapon, why the archaic sword? If it is the superiority of his weaponry and his technology that the man wishes to demonstrate, he could make use of a still more powerful arsenal. The fact is, this archaic sword lends this "unequal combat" false airs of nobility it would never have had if the torero used a bazooka instead, and the sword seems to do the job, because with that sword, the man is superior and wins, and without it, he is inferior and is the loser.

Approximately 12,000 bulls die every year in the arena.[23] It must be that the superiority of the man over the beast is a very fragile one, if he seems to feel the need to prove it twelve thousand times a year? As Michel Onfray writes, "The taste for the spectacle of death always reveals the desire for power by the impotent."[24]

Why the Bull?

Why, among all the animals encountered by humans in their history, should the bull be the chosen adversary? Once again, let us hear Francis Wolff: "The bull is the sole adversary that man considers worthy of him. It is the animal against which he can measure himself with pride, and which he consequently treats with the loyalty that an enemy of his measure deserves. Would one demonstrate one's power against an enemy that one scorns and mistreats? Throughout the world of bull-fighting, the animal is fought with respect and never eliminated like vermin or dispatched in a hidden place like a mere meat-producing machine."[25]

So it seems that the bull is indeed one of the only adversaries spectacular enough for the man to fight, the animal against which he can give the impression of being in danger without really running much of a risk. Nowadays, it is no longer good show business to display wild beasts devouring slaves or to make valiant warriors who have been captured in wars fight each other to the death. For a matador to confront a lion would be far too dangerous (unless the sword were replaced by a rifle).

Thus the bull has become the animal of choice, one that is combative enough to guarantee a good show, but not really too dangerous, for the torero has at least 9,999 chances out of 10,000 to be the one of the two adversaries who comes out of the contest alive. Imagine what would become of the "superiority" of the man, even armed with a sword, if the beast he was confronting was a tiger. So the bull is aggressive enough—with a sheep the aficionados wouldn't get their money's worth—but the victory of the man is pretty well assured.

Fight or Flight?

Francis Wolff tells us: "When you cause a mammal to suffer, it flees instinctively. But the 'fighting bull,' far from fleeing, redoubles its attacks. That is the proof that it feels its wounds, not as suffering, but as incitement to combat."[26] In the first place, if the bull's wounds did not cause it to suffer, why would it react at all? Then, we may ask, if a bull were burned by the flames of a prairie fire or injured by stones falling from a mountain slope, would it flee from the danger or would it attack? If it charges in the arena, it is because an individual is attacking and injuring it continuously. In this situation, attacking is the best strategy for survival, especially because all the exits are blocked.

What happens in nature when an animal perceives danger? It all depends on the immediacy of the danger or how far away it is. When there is enough time and room, animals, even the most powerful ones like elephants and lions, would rather put distance between themselves and the danger, since their best chance of surviving a threat is to get away from it. It is, therefore, the avoidance behavior that has been selected as the best guarantee of survival over millions of years of evolution.

If the danger is a little closer, most animals freeze on the spot and observe the threat attentively, remaining as inobtrusive as possible, particularly if they are potential prey. Then they decide what tack to take. If the danger is close and immediate, and still more if the animal is cornered, the dominant type—the big cat, the bull, or the mastiff—will decide to attack, because attack represents its best chance of coming out of the encounter whole. We know also that a wounded bear or tiger is much more aggressive or dangerous than an untouched animal. Some animals play dead, and others try to hide or flee, but quite often even an animal weaker than the predator it faces will put up a desperate fight at the last moment. Depending on the species involved and especially depending on the circumstances, we may observe flight, immobility, or attack.

The Aficionados Say They Have No Wish to See Harm Done

The aficionados are shocked and regard themselves as having been insulted if you suggest that they get sadistic pleasure out of watching the sufferings of the bull. Georges Courteline writes regarding them: "My abhorrence toward the bullfights has gradually been extended to those who frequent them. The idea that people can derive entertainment, some from attempting to render more ferocious an animal that was not ferocious to begin with, and others from seeing horses being disemboweled, then sewed up, then disemboweled a second time, causes me to pour upon the latter the same disgust that the latter arouse in me."[27]

And Michel Onfray raises the language still another notch:

It takes a significant sadistic tendency to pay for a ticket into an arena where the show consists of torturing an animal, making it suffer, wounding it cruelly, seeking ever greater refinement in the acts of barbarity committed against it, having them codified (just the way an inquisitor or torture specialist knows just how far to go to keep the victim alive as long as possible even though they are going to kill it anyway); and to rejoice madly when the bull collapses because there is no other possible way out for him.[28]

"Absurd!" replies Francis Wolff: "It is difficult to believe and yet it is true: the aficionado gets no pleasure from the suffering of the animal. None of them could bear to cause to suffer, or even to see suffer, a cat, a dog, a horse, or any other animal."[29] He adds, "I don't know any of them who would be capable of beating his dog or even of voluntarily harming a cat or a rabbit." They are so sweet to some, so pitiless to others, mental dissociation sadly being a common phenomenon these days. This psychological process is one of devaluing, dehumanizing— or in this case "de-animalizing"—the sentient being that a particular ideology has designated "the enemy," the human or animal that is to be tortured and slain. No doubt the toreros and the aficionados do indeed pamper their pets. But once inside the arena, the torero and his audience have set up in themselves the mental dissociation necessary to no longer consider the bull a sentient being but to regard it now as the enemy to be destroyed. It is only by means of this kind of a psychological compartmentalization that the torero succeeds in desensitizing himself to the pain of the animal and the public succeeds in supporting his actions.

According to Francis Wolff, there is only one argument against bullfighting, and it is not a good one:

> It is that which we call sensibility. One cannot bear seeing (or even imagining) an animal injured or dying. This feeling is more than merely respectable. . . . The feeling of compassion is one of the hallmarks of humanity and one of the sources of morality. But those who are against the corrida should know that the aficionados share this feeling with them. . . .[30]

The aficionado should respect the sensibilities of all and not impose his tastes or his own sensibilities on others. Nevertheless, those who are against bullfighting should also acknowledge in their turn that the aficionado is as human, as lacking in cruelty, as

capable of pity as they are themselves. . . . Should the sensibilities
of some be enough to condemn the sensibilities of others?[31]

If the aficionados are full of compassion and "as human, as lacking
in cruelty," as anyone else, why don't they express this compassion by
protecting the animal rather than in tormenting it and then killing
it? In the literary tradition, compassion is defined as "the feeling that
tends to lament and share the misfortunes of others (*Grand Robert Dictionary*), but at the present time, psychologists and neuroscientists, as
well as Buddhists, speak more precisely of the desire to remedy the suffering of others and to eliminate the causes of this suffering. From this
point of view, compassion is the form that altruistic love takes when it
is confronted with the suffering of others.[32]

Can we compare the sensibility of someone who feels empathy
toward an innocent animal that some people have decided to kill after
having wounded it again and again, with the sensibility of someone
who, while apparently feeling the same pity as the first person toward
the animal, yet celebrates its demise as a great and grandiose spectacle,
a festival, and an art? Where, in such a case, does the sensibility and
empathy of the aficionado reside? It seems that, in contrast to the bull
that is receiving the blows, the aficionado has been anesthetized. But
it is not appropriate for us to focus our attention purely on the human
spectators of the event. The question ultimately is not about the nature
of their sensibility. Their actions are relatively minor to say the least,
and their attitude possibly somewhat ambiguous. Instead of thinking
about them, our main focus should be on the fate of the bull, the bull
being the one who actually loses his life. Is it not the bull the main one
concerned here?

"Nobody watches a bullfight to see an animal tortured, and still less
to see it die," stresses a blogger named Aliocha in the periodical *Marianne*.[33] So, if it is only for the pleasure of the festival atmosphere and
the show, then the problem of suffering can be dropped: stop wounding the bull and killing it, and let the toreros perform their flourishes
with the cape as much as they want. (This is, moreover, the way bullfights are done in the United States—no banderillas, no wounds, no
kill. Just a recreational confrontation between the torero and the bull,
purely for the show.) Aliocha continues: "We praise the torero if he has

killed his adversary without causing suffering." The kill is made, but oh-so considerately. . . . As for the bull, who can honestly maintain that he dies of his dreadful wounds without having felt a thing?

If the spectators do not like to see the animals suffer, how can we explain the reactions to the decree enacted by Miguel Primo de Rivera in 1928 that made it mandatory for the picadors' horses to wear protective padding (these horses were hitherto regularly disemboweled by the bulls)? This measure was not at all appreciated by the hard-core aficionados, who lamented that it brought about the disappearance of the "true corrida." As Élisabeth Hardouin-Fugier reported in her *Histoire de la Corrida en Europe du xviiie au xxie Siècle (History of the Corrida in Europe from the Eighteenth to the Twenty-First Centuries)*, one of those hard-core fans, Laurent Tailhade, said: "It is always satisfying for me to see five or six horses thoroughly eviscerated."[34] The historian of the corrida Auguste Laffont adds that, with the advent of the *peto*, which protects the horse from disembowelment, "the sacred emotion disappeared." Picasso declared himself to be inconsolable, and others averred that the protection of the horses "denatured the most beautiful third of the combat." In France, certain arenas, like the one at Dax, refused to protect the horses, thinking in this way to attract more spectators. Isn't the only thing gained in this way, since the combat itself is not altered in any way, the opportunity to enjoy, in addition to the fate of the bull, the disembowelment and suffering of the horses?

The Bull Does Not Really Suffer

In any case, the aficionados say, the problem of suffering does not actually come up, because the bull feels no pain during the combat. They cite the studies carried out in the laboratory of Juan Carlos Illera del Portal, director of the Department of Animal Physiology in the veterinary college of the University of Madrid, according to which the bull, thanks to his "hormonal shield," feels only very little pain, because his organism produces ten times more beta-endorphins (indogenous opiates that mitigate the effects of pain) than that of a human.[35] But Georges Chapouthier, director of Research Emeritus at the CNRS (Centre National de Recherche Scientifique) in Paris points out that the study by Juan Carlos Illera del Portal does not provide any indication of the methodology it used and makes no reference to scientific publications. Chapouthier calls "absurd" the idea that the secretion of endorphines signifies that the bull does not suffer. Other published studies indicate, to the contrary, that massive secretions of endorphines by the brain is the very sign that the animal is being subjected to intense pain and that its body is attempting to minimize the effects of it.[36]

José Enrique Zaldívar Laguía, a member of the Veterinary College of Madrid, also refutes the hypothesis that a heightened presence of beta-endorphins in the blood necessarily diminishes pain. The very high level of beta-endorphins found in the bull's blood proves that it has undergone very intense physical and psychological attack and not the fact that it does not suffer.[37]

According to the testimony of Zaldívar Laguía before the deputies of the Catalan Assembly on March 4, 2010, most of the studies carried out by the veterinarians affiliated with the arenas report that the thrusts of the picadors, whose weapons are the first used against the bull, provoke lesions in more than twenty of its muscles. This weapon, the *puya*, is "a sharp and cutting metallic weapon with a six centimeter shaft and a pyramidal point of 2.5 centimeters, each edge of which is as sharp as a scalpel. . . . Not only does it sever muscles, tendons, and ligaments, but also veins, arteries, and important nerves. The findings indicate that the average depth of these wounds is 20 centimeters, and wounds to the depth of 30 centimeters have been observed." These thrusts bring about "fractures of spinal apophyses and perforations of the vertebrae, fractures of ribs and of linking cartilege. . . . Inevitable are lesions of the spinal marrow, hemorrhaging of the medullary ducts and very significant neural lesions. . . . The bull also loses between three and seven liters of blood.[38]

Next come the banderillas, which are sharp as razor blades and have barbed ends. They are planted in the bull's back to bleed him and prevent him from dying too quickly from an internal hemorrhage caused by the lances of the picadors. At the end the matador plunges a curved sword of eighty centimeters' length into the withers of the exhausted animal. It is intended to hit the inferior vena cava and the posterior aorta, located in the thoracic cavity of the animal. But in point of fact, the weapon most often cuts into the nerve cords close to the spinal marrow, causing the bull to suffer intense respiratory difficulties. Often the blade causes an internal hemorrhage or tears a lung. In the latter case, the bull vomits blood and dies of asphyxia.[39] If the bull does not die, the matador repeats the operation with a smaller sword, which he plants between the bull's horns so as to cut into its brain. If that still fails to do the job, a *peon* delivers the coup de grâce with a *puntilla*, a short, double-edged, stabbing knife. But according to Zaldívar, the puntilla does not cause instant death but rather a death by a process of asphyxia resulting from a paralysis of the bull's respiratory action that ends in hypoxia of the brain.[40]

In brief, according to the deposition of Jean-François Courreau of the National Veterinary School of Alfort before the French parliament: "If the fighting bull possesses this kind of supernatural adaptation allowing it to bear pain, mistreatment, and suffering, I think this hypothesis would deserve considerable space in a scientific publication, but nothing of the sort has appeared so far."[41]

So Many Great Thinkers and Artists Have Understood and Admired the Corrida

For those who imagine the aficionados to be a race of humans who lack humanity, we can only recall the names of all those artists and writers—like Mérimée, Lorca, Cocteau, Hemingway, Montherlant, Bataille, Leiris, Manet, or Picasso. Is it possible that they were no more than so many bloodthirsty perverts? Could it be that an uninitiate knows more than they do about what the corrida really is and about what they feel at the core of their sensibility and with all their art?[42]

How could they all be mistaken on this point? asks Francis Wolff, author of the sentences above. But in what way could the literary or artistic talent that they all doubtless possessed possibly justify this or that opinion for or against the corrida? In the world of science, mistaking simple correlations for causal links is enough to invalidate the interpretation of the results of a study or a research project. But this is just the mistake that is made by people who use the idea of being in good company as an argument, and in this case, it is the mistake of those who say that if great writers and artists are in favor of the corrida, the corrida can only be legitimate. But truly, there is no causal link there. The fact that somebody excels in one area of expertise is no guarantee that they are a good human being. Céline, who is celebrated as one of the great writers of the twentieth century, was violently anti-Semitic. The great Austrian ethologist Konrad Lorenz was a Nazi sympathizer. Hitler prided himself on being a painter, Mao prided himself on being a poet, and Stalin was a good singer. If they had had the genius of a Rembrandt, a Baudelaire, or a Mozart, would that have lessened the horror of their crimes? Elegance of style does not make human kindness, and a bad writer might have a heart of gold.

Francis Wolff defends his use of the "fallacy of good company":

Nobody is pretending that the tastes of respectable people are themselves also automatically respectable. What is in question here is if we can accept cataloging the corrida as a cruel and barbarous spectacle without heeding what has been transmitted to us concerning its sublime power by all these artists and poets who are at least as sensitive to suffering as any other human beings, including even jurists and philosophers.[43]

Okay. Let us hear what has been transmitted to us by these eminent personnages in question who are connoisseurs of the corrida. Ernest Hemingway in Death in the Afternoon, a novel devoted to the corrida, proclaims: "When a man is still in rebellion against death he has pleasure in taking to himself one of the Godlike attributes; that of giving it. This is one of the most profound feelings in those men who enjoy killing. These things are done in pride. . . . But it is pride which makes the bullfight and true enjoyment of killing which makes the great matador."[44] Joy in killing . . . Can we admire and hold up as a model somebody who considers killing to be one of the great satisfactions of being human?

Hemingway added as well that, when compared to the tragedy of the death of the bull, that of the horse in the arena has a quality of comedy about it. Another author, Michel Leiris, expressed the view that the "the ignoble blood of the horses" symbolizes the female menses.[45] At this moment, I have before my eyes two photographs. In one of them, you see a bull vigorously goring the belly of a big white horse, which seconds before had been ridden by a picador who had wounded the bull with his lance. In the next picture, you see the horse, which has risen again to its feet, ready to gallop away with its intestines hanging out of its belly and dragging on the ground. A harmless horse and a bull enraged to the point of madness by being lanced—both of them going to their deaths for the pleasure of human beings.

Let us examine in addition what has been transmitted to us by other writers, jurists, and philosophers who also felt they knew enough about the corrida to allow themselves to write about it. For example, Émile Zola wrote: "I am absolutely against bullfights, spectacles whose imbecilic cruelty is an education in blood and mud for the masses." Does this make Zola an imbecile or a bad writer?

We could also make a list—of course without its having any greater validity than our opponents' list, because it also makes use of the fallacy of good company—an equally impressive list of great writers, artists, and thinkers who have considered these spectacles in the arena deplorable. This, not at all exhaustive, list includes Jose Maria de Heredia, Georges Clemenceau, Georges Courteline, Léon Bloy, Jules Lemaître, Théodore Monod, Jacques Derrida, Jacques Brel (who sang "Mais l'épée a plongé et la foule est debout, c'est l'instant de triomphe où les épiciers se prennent pour Néron" [But the sword has plunged in and the crowd's on its feet; it's the moment of triumph when grocers take themselves for Nero]), Élisabeth Badinter, Jean-François Kahn, Hubert Montagner, and many others.

People are free to think what they want about the corrida. The bull, for his part, would certainly prefer not to be cut up by a whole arsenal of sharp weapons; he would surely rather end his days peacefully in the field where he was raised. He does not get a choice. We decide for him. This is where the abuse of power lies.

As for the "fallacy of bad company," which consists in taking the example of tyrants and genocides who have defended the animal cause, it is also without foundation. The attempt has sometimes been made to blacken the name of defenders of animals by recalling that Hitler and the Nazis were infatuated with this cause at the same time as they were pursuing their monstrous behavior against humans. If such an argument had any validity, the facts that the commander of the Bergen-Belsen concentration camp, Josef Kramer, was a great music lover and that other notorious torturers, once they returned home, were attentive family fathers would have the effect of denigrating classical music, on the one hand, and blackening the name of kindness toward children on the other. As the historian Élisabeth Hardouin-Fugier has shown, such sophistic arguments have been used to justify the instrumentalization of one the greatest atrocities in our history in order to cast scorn on animal protection.[46] We must also remember that most animal advocates were and are fervent advocates of the rights of men and women, and have also fought against racism, torture, and all forms of injustice.

Outlawing Traditions Only Where They Don't Exist

Francis Wolff denies that he is justifying the practice of bullfighting just because it is traditional and celebrates the fact that "most of the major progress in morality has been made by going against entrenched practices that are supposed to have been legitimized by tradition: slavery, the suicide of widows in India, or the circumcision of young girls." But in his view the situation is different with regard to the corrida: "It is not because it is traditional that the corrida is authorized, but it is authorized only in those places where it is a tradition." He adds: "That does not make the corrida 'universally good,' but rather locally legitimate. What may be seen as an act of cruelty in Stockholm or Strasbourg can be perceived in Dax or Nîmes as an act of loyal defiance and an act of ritual that is integral to the regional identity."[47]

A line of the French penal code does indeed authorize the corrida as well as cockfighting in those places where an "uninterrupted local tradition" can be attested.[48] Thus they are prohibited throughout French territory *except where they take place*. What sort of a meaningless law is that?! What is the point of prohibiting a tradition in a place where it does not exist? What need would there be of outlawing fights between dogs and bears in Nîmes, the corrida in Lapland, or human sacrifice in Belgium? How can we go about getting rid of a cruel tradition if we forbid it everywhere except where it is practiced? It is within the very domain of "cultural" tradition in question that we must wage the war against this practice. We must do away with the mystical aura that the corrida enjoys and remind its followers again and again of the level of cruelty involved in it.

Moreover, this "regional identity" of the corrida seems to concern only a minority of people. According to an Ipsos poll of July 2010, 71 percent of the inhabitants of Gard, a kind of capital of tauromachy, say that they are not attached to the corrida. On the national scale, 66 percent of the French people say they are in favor of abolishing the practice.[49] Catalonia, where the culture of tauromachy has long been taken for granted, decided in 2010, in conformity with the wish of the majority of its citizens, to abolish it.[50]

The Freedom to Kill

According to Alain Renaut, another philosopher and a professor at the Sorbonne, the corrida represents "the submission of brute nature (that is to say, violence) to human free will, a victory of freedom over nature."[51] But what "freedom" are we talking about here? The freedom to kill without need? Because the corrida in no way represents a situation of legitimate self-defense against animal aggression. In a democracy and in a law-abiding state, every citizen has the right to do what he or she wishes to the extent that his or her actions do not harm fellow citizens. The aim of the laws is to protect citizens against the violence of others. The laws are in a certain way "imposed," because everyone is supposed to respect them, whether they like it or not. Transgression of the laws (such as those against murder, rape, or intentionally causing injury) has been judged unacceptable by society.

The establishment of a social contract is one of the characteristics of civilizations. So it is not a matter of "imposing" measures that outlaw the massacre of innocents, but a matter of protecting them from any such massacre. In fact, the first corrida, which took place in Bayonne, France, in 1853, was a direct infraction of the Grammont law, which punished mistreatment of animals. But the corrida benefited from the support of Empress Eugénie, and the prefects did not apply the law.

The corrida thus continues to be an exception under the existing laws of France for the protection of animals, and an even greater exception under the laws of the European Union.

It Would Be a Good Thing to Teach Children to Appreciate the Ritual of the Kill

The corrida allows free entry for children under the age of ten. In the bullfighting schools of several countries (notably Spain, France, and Portugal), children and adolescents train with calves using a bladed weapon. For Francis Wolff, this is no problem:

> The child can learn and come to understand in the same way as an adult. He or she can quickly learn to distinguish the human from the animal, and especially the admired and feared bull from loved and cherished animals, such as a pet cats or dogs. And the corrida can provide an occasion for parents to explain the key points of ritual (to which children are particularly sensitive), to talk with their children about life and death, or to offer commentary on the behavior of the animal and the art of the human.[52]

The United Nations Convention on the Rights of the Child does not seem to share this opinion. It recently made a ruling that "participation of children and adolescents (male and female) in activities connected with tauromachy constitutes a serious violation of the articles of the Convention regarding the rights of the child."[53] During the committee's deliberations, Sergio Caetano, a representative of the Franz Weber Foundation of Portugal, made the following statement: "In the course of lessons or actual events of tauromachy in which they participate, children must violently wound bulls using sharp and cutting instruments; they must also hold onto the animal without any protection in order to gain control over it and are regularly subject to accidents. Moreover, children who witness such happenings are witnesses of major violence."

The Committee therefore recommended to member states to take legislative measures to definitively prohibit the participation of children in tauromachy.

It Is Better to Live the Life of a Fighting Bull and Die in the Arena Than to Live in an Industrial Breeding Facility and Die in the Slaughterhouse

Some people think it is better to die nobly and quickly in the arena than in a miserable way in an abattoir. In truth, as much in one case as the other, it is better to remain alive.

Francis Wolff asks animal advocates to "choose the more desirable fate: that of a work ox, of a bull or calf headed for the slaughterhouse (bred and raised en masse for the most part), or that of the fighting bull. The last enjoys four years of free life and then faces a quarter of an hour of death in the ring."[54]

But it is not a question of choosing between bad and worse, because in two of the cases we are imposing death on an animal that surely has no wish to die. Ideally, a bull should not be sent either to the ring or to the slaughterhouse. The logical alternative to the bullring is not the slaughterhouse but a peaceful life in a meadow where the animal can die a good death.

When there is a forced choice among a limited number of possibilities, any reasonable person will choose the one that involves the least suffering. But neither the corrida nor the slaughterhouse is a forced choice. The best choice is to spare the animal both.

This argument has recourse to both the "fallacy of the worst" and the "fallacy of consolation." Should we say to someone we are torturing for an hour before executing him or her: "Be happy, we could have tortured you for six months without stopping"? We could excuse ourselves for regularly raping a child by saying: "But it is suffering less than if it were in a concentration camp." Claiming that one bad treatment is better than another that would be even worse does not confer legitimacy on the first. So the question is not if there is something worse than the corrida but whether the corrida itself is acceptable.

It is obvious that the number of victims of the corrida is nowhere near the order of the billions of land animals slaughtered every year so their flesh can be eaten. Still, suffering is an experience felt by each individual who undergoes it, and the cruelty is always the same. What changes are the sphere in which it occurs, the number of its victims, and the different disguises it is dressed up in, which range from the art of gastronomy to sport (in the case of hunting for sport, where the kill is not necessary for the survival of the hunter). As the Spanish writer Antonio Zozaya tells us, there is only one cruelty, no matter what its object is: "Making an animal suffer is causing suffering. Whoever or whatever is the victim of this useless cruelty, it is still cruelty. . . . The important thing is not knowing who one is tormenting; the essential point is not to torment. . . . There is only one cruelty in the world, the same one for humans and for animals, for ideas and for things, for gods and for earthworms. So let us shun this barbarity that so demeans us."[55]

Circus Animals—The Pain behind the Glitter

Isn't it entertaining to watch the elephants make the round of the ring, each one holding in its trunk the tail of the one in front of it? Don't we admire the lion tamer who has the courage to put his head in the gaping maw of the roaring beast? But these feats are only the end point of a long accumulation of brutalities inflicted on the trained animals. The wand prettily decorated with flowers with which the trainer seems to caress the ear of the elephant to guide it through its movements hides a sharp iron hook that will quickly come jabbing into the pachyderm's ear at the least sign of disobedience. Let us listen to the remarks of an American elephant trainer caught live by a hidden camera as he was training an apprentice:

Hurt him! Make him scream! If you're afraid of hurting him . . . don't set foot in this hall. If I tell you "crack his head," "crush his damned foot," what does that mean, huh? Because it's very important to do it, eh? When he starts to fidget, bam! Right under the chin! . . . Stick that hook in, as far as it goes . . . and when it's all the way in, keep pushing, yeah, yeah, yeah. He'll start screaming. When you hear him screaming, you'll know that you've succeeded in getting his damned attention a little bit. . . . Okay, let's go.[56]

"That's the way it is in all the circuses in the world," Vladimir Deriabkine, a famous bear tamer, tells us. He got his bears to play the roles of bartender, car mechanic, sailor, astronaut, and lover. During the show, they became almost human. For ten years, Deriabkine has not entered a circus ring. He gave up animal training. Why? "Because," he says, "it's a barbaric activity. Trainers have always hidden the underbelly of their work from the spectators. But I'm going to tell you what none of them will ever say. If they knew the truth about the training, it would only turn the spectators away from the circus acts." He told his story at length to the journalist Vladimir Kojemiakine:

I loved my work. . . . My only regret for a long time in those days was not being recognized as a great circus performer. But today I realize that you can never get an award for animal-training work. A medal for cruelty is out of the question. The cruelty does not happen in the ring, but behind the scenes. I put on, among others, an act that always brought the house down: one of the bears fell on its knees in front of Liouda, my partner, squeezing in its paws a heart made of papier-mâché. Seen from the stands, the effect was spectacular and very touching. But during the rehearsals, it was a different matter altogether!

I saw a bear killed for refusing to perform its number. The trainer's nerves snapped, he blew up, and he struck. That is an image I will never forget—the image of the trainer's boots dripping with the bear's blood, he had gone after the poor animal that hard.

A bear tamer from St. Petersburg told me that his bears, they were his kids. He felt for them and he educated them. His children, my ass! You just make money on the backs of those children. You eat well, you dress fancy, you sleep in clean sheets while they sleep in cages. And still today in Russia, bears are treated like criminals. They still have to travel in these tiny cages—it's disgusting. Because for a trainer, the animals are nothing but living accessories.

I remember a number that was called "Joined Hands." An elephant held out its paw, a tiger put its paw on top of that, and at the end, the trainer added his hand on top of both. It presented a kind of symbolic vision of the friendship between the animals and the trainer. In fact, behind this poetic image, there is nothing but violence. Go ahead and try shaking hands with a sworn enemy:

they won't do it unless you threaten them with death. They will refuse. And the moment you remove the threat, they will go for your throat.

When I decided to quit the profession, I had six bears left. Now bears—circuses always have a surplus of them. There's no solution for it. One morning, early, my assistants took them away. The following day, my bears were dead. And they were artists, they were applauded, they gave the audience a lot of pleasure! They're all doomed to end up like that.[57]

To the question, "Are there any nice trainers?" Deriabkine replied, "Nice executioners—do you know any of those? Let's be clear: cruelty is part of being a trainer. The moment you take a bear cub and put it in a cage so you get it to perform in the ring, it's a catastrophe for the animal. And for the man also, if he has a heart."

Dick Gregory, a comedian and civil rights activist who was close to Martin Luther King, said: "When I look at animals held captive in circuses, that makes me think of slavery. Animals in circuses represent the domination and oppression we have fought for so long. They wear the same chains and the same fetters."

According to the French League for the Defense of the Rights of Animals (LFDA), two hundred traveling circuses still crisscross France and put on shows that include wild animals. In Finland and Denmark, such shows are already prohibited, except in the case of seals in Finland, and Asian elephants, camels, and llamas in Denmark. We can gauge the evolution of our sensibilities over the time from the Roman circuses to the time of the Cirque du Soleil, which is doubtless the most popular one in the world today. It does not have a single trained-animal act in its program.[58]

Zoos: Show Prisons or Noah's Arks?

In colonial times, not only rare animals but also "exotic" humans were exhibited in zoos and at the famous World Fairs and Colonial Fairs. They were an amusement for children and a curiosity for their parents. Behind the animal exhibits, which attracted sizable crowds, lay the completely illegal animal trade that operated between the European capitals and their respective colonies. In *Belles Captives: Une Histoire des Zoos du Côté des Bêtes (Splendid Prisoners: A History of Zoos from the Point of View of the Animals)*, Éric Baratay presents an exposé of the cruel methods used in these animal captures and their cost in animal lives. These hunts were still going on as late as the period between the World Wars. "Repentant animal traders," he tells us, "estimated the losses [animals that died in the course of the take] between 15 and 30 percent in general, but the percentages could in some cases be quite a bit higher—80 percent for the gibbons of Laos."[59] The historian has tracked the losses during transport and those connected with the difficult period of adaptation, and altogether they come to 50 percent on average. You have to count ten deaths for every animal that is finally exhibited.

In his day, Philippe Diolé, who worked with Jacques-Yves Cousteau and was a cofounder of the LFDA, decried the miserable conditions in zoos in a series of op-ed pieces in the *Le Figaro*. According to him, "70 percent of the zoological parks should be closed down."[60] Although they appeared in 1974, these articles remain sadly accurate for most of the countries of the world today. In Kathmandu, where I live, the zoo is no more than a bleak location where the animals wait to die. In an article entitled "Prisons dans un Jardin" (Prisons in a Garden), Philippe Diolé calls for the closing of the menagerie in the Jardin des Plantes in Paris. For him it was no more than a scene of animal degradation, a leftover from a former age:

> The humiliation of animals is no more bearable than that of people. As has been the case for a century and longer, the servals, pumas and tigers exhibited there are like the walking dead.
>
> They suffer from despair, but more than anything else, they are dispossessed. They have lost the green richness of leaves and grasses and even the earth where they flourished. The big paws of the cats, with their sensitive pads, are injured by the tough cement. Raptors hop about on their own droppings. The pink flamingos move about in sewer water. . . . In prison, a man loses his liberty, but in a cage, an animal loses the space where his complex life was organized: its behavior is thrown off, its state of mind is shaken. There is no other outcome for it than madness, which is

sometimes a mercy. That is why the bear goes on and on with its dizzy back-and-forth along the wall that its muzzle just brushes. The elephant rocks from side to side without a break. A young wolf pulls out its claws. The zoo captives, with few exceptions are mentally ill, obsessed by their incarceration, frustrated, full of anxiety and aggression.

This psychiatric hospital that exploits animal suffering is not worthy either of our time or especially of the eminent personalities affiliated with the museum. The menagerie of the Jardin des Plantes, right in the middle of Paris, is an anachronistic and scandalous enclave, where for three francs one can see miserable animals, shaky buildings, and broken tiles.

So let's get rid of all that and plant some flowers.[61]

By now, according to Norin Chai, researcher and head of the veterinary service of the menagerie of the Jardin des Plantes, significant progress has been made: "The zoos are ultimately only the reflection of those who administer them. Some remain just places for the animals to die, while others have evolved in the direction of more humanity, either as a result of public opinion or because of genuine conviction."[62] Starting in the 2000s, many legislatures have brought about a change in the conditions of life in the zoos of the developed countries.[63] The well-being of animals, their preservation, and relevant scientific research have now become mandatory activities. In Europe the Balai Directive governs all the zoological parks worthy of the name and obliges institutions to provide a high level of veterinary care.[64]

In 1992 the conference of the United Nations in Rio recognized the preservative function of zoos. Thus these establishments will continue to prosper—let us not forget that they are commercial enterprises—and can henceforth take on an ecological legitimacy that brings them the sympathy as well as the visits of large numbers of the public. The zoo is often no longer purely a place of mortal captivity but a place for the reproduction and safeguarding of endangered species. In certain cases the animals are eventually released into their original habitat. Nowadays, lots of scientists working in zoos see them functioning as a kind of Noah's Ark that preserves numerous species that are on the verge of disappearing. We must acknowledge that there have been successes. The Arabian oryx (*Oryx leucoryx*), a species that had pretty well disappeared a few decades ago, is once again seen on the sands and in the oases of Oman and Israel. The celebrated Przewalski's horse (*Equus przewalskii*) gallops once more across the Mongolian steppes. The Micronesian kingfisher (*Todiramphus cinnamominus*), the condor of California (*Gymnogyps californianus*), and the scimitar oryx (*Oryx dammah*) have been saved as a result of having been bred in captivity; soon that might well be the case for the addax (*Addax nasomaculatus*) also.

Certain associations, like the Zoological Society of Frankfurt and the Zoological Society of London, which work for the preservation of wildlife, carry on preservation projects in situ. At these sites zoo veterinarians join wildlife veterinarians in working for the protection of endangered species.[65] They do research work on the diseases that endanger the survival of various species and have notably played an essential role in aviary medicine in the Galápagos Islands.[66] Some of the avian diseases are the result of pollution. Vultures, for example, are on the verge of extinction in South Asia because they eat the corpses of domestically bred animals to which farmers have administered the drug diclofenac. This anti-inflammatory, which was frequently used by veterinarians until it was recently banned, turned out to be a virulent poison for scavengers, in which even in weak doses it brings on terminal renal failure.[67]

Professor Jean-Claude Nouët, cofounder of the LFDA, tempers the enthusiasm of the zoo directors: "The successful re-introductions [of animals into the wild] can be counted on the fingers of one hand." Éric Baratay has a more optimistic view: "The fingers of both hands, at the most." Indeed, since the 1990s, it has become obvious that the number of species approaching extinction has gone far beyond the resources that zoos can offer to preserve them in captivity.

Creating Genuine Reserves and Teaching Animals to Live in the Wild Again

Jean-Claude Nouët, while recognizing the undeniable successes there have been in reintroducing species into their original habitats, remains cautious: "The zoos don't preserve species, they conserve them, which is not the same thing." Élisabeth Hardouin-Fugier expresses the following opinion: "Rather than salvaging a Noah's Ark that is as expensive and cramped as a spacecraft, the thing to do is curb the flood."[68] In other words, it is better to protect the natural habitat of animals in situ (with the benefit of preserving the habitats themselves) than to establish and maintain institutions intended to save the animals from extinction at the risk of serious physical and mental damage to species whose members are, at the end of the day, no more than involuntary exiles from their savannah, forest, or native jungle. The creation of reserves and national parks is a much better solution.[69]

If zoos were not primarily commercial enterprises, there would be no reason for this scenario of caging lions and giraffes and then killing them when they are no longer needed. As for the project of preserving species on the brink of extinction, this could be carried out in a scientific manner in protected reserves in the heart of the species's natural habitat.

Another worthy project is saving young animals that have been captured by traffickers and whose mothers have been killed. On the Internet, there is a video that shows an orphan chimpanzee regaining its health after having been taken in by Jane Goodall and her team when it was close to death. When the moment came for it to be liberated into the wild by those who had saved it and cared for it, it took the time to give Jane Goodall a long hug before disappearing into the forest.[70]

Similarly, in China and Vietnam, Jill Robinson frees bears from farms where they are kept in extremely painful conditions so their bile can be milked.[71] (See chapter 10, "Illegal Trade in Wildlife.") The organization One Voice does as much for bears that were mistreated by trainers of hunting dogs. You see, in Russia, in order to assess the ferocity of their dogs, their trainers let them loose on young bears that are tied up. Wounded in many places, very few of these bears survive this torture.

Reintroducing an animal into its wild habitat is a very delicate enterprise that takes a lot of time, resources, and care, especially when the animal comes to the point of relearning to hunt or integrating into a group that it did not grow up with. So after having taken care of the animals, it is necessary to accompany them into the wild during their apprenticeship in a life of freedom.

At this point we come to the fundamental question: Is it moral to capture an animal and imprison it? The claim is made that zoos make it possible for children to have a "living" relationship with wild animals and thus develop a sense of empathy for them. But is putting wild animals on show for them as though captivity was their normal situation a good way to teach children empathy for them? We might well doubt it when we look at these haggard big cats that pace back and forth all day long along the bars of their enclosures in perpetual search of a way out. And if children do feel empathy for these animals, won't they find themselves wishing they could be set free? Nowadays, they can get to know animals much better by watching the extraordinary documentaries being shown on television and also available over the Internet. These documentaries take them into the real world of the wild species. They can also study the natural behavior of the animals in their natural environment. As an amateur ornithologist in my teenage years, I spent much of my leisure time observing birds in nature, while I found the spectacle of zoos very upsetting.

Some zoological parks and zoos allow their inmates to live in larger spaces where the public can enter into contact with life in the wild. The Thoiry Park in the Yvelines district of the Île-de-France occupies 445 acres. The Vincennes Zoo reopened its doors on April 12, 2014, after six years of renewal work that allowed them to considerably improve the life of the animals. Gone are the cages and narrow enclosures, the glass showcases, the ditches and the bars. They have been replaced by open spaces, open air, and plants. Is that enough to justify the captivity of the animals? According to the writer Armand Farrachi, zoos are by definition artificial places, devised for the captivity of exotic animals. "So much the better if the zoological park of Paris, like other "bio-parks," prioritize "bio-conservation" through the "management" of animals living their lives in "semi-freedom." But the principal remains: Giving your slaves a longer chain is not setting them free."[72]

As Farrachi reminds us, the notion of "good treatment" obliterates all connotations of freedom and reinforces the human in the position of master and possessor of nature, "doing whatever he likes with inferior species, if possible as an enlightened master rather than an executioner. His indulgence will go no further than that."

And When We Don't Need You Anymore . . .

When the animals are no longer needed or there are too many of them, what do we do? We kill them. The Copenhagen Zoo has recently distinguished itself by "euthanizing" a baby giraffe that it did not know what to do with, then four lions, then two lion cubs—at the very moment that giraffes are disappearing from West Africa and the number of lions is in freefall all over Africa.

As was reported widely in the media,[73] Marius, a giraffe one and a half years old, in perfect health, was "euthanized" on February 10, 2014, at the Copenhagen Zoo. The term "euthanize" is the one the zoo used, even though this act has nothing whatever in common with the killing of an animal suffering from intolerable pain. The zoo management had no idea what to do with the animal and had concluded that Marius did not have "a genetically interesting heritage." So the animal, in perfect health, was executed in public with a slaughtering pistol and was cut into pieces in front of the television cameras. The pieces of its body were then thrown out into a field to feed the big cats. All of this was done in front of an audience of stunned children. This execution was supported by the European Association of Zoos and Aquariums (AEZA), despite having what they call a "conservation committee" and boasting of possessing an "ethical charter."[74]

Solutions other than "euthanasia" were ruled out. The zoo defended itself by saying that castration is more cruel and would have "undesirable effects." As to reintroducing no longer needed animals into nature, according to the zoo, that is a process that "has little chance of success and which, in the case of giraffes, is not desired by the African countries."

The Copenhagen Zoo recidivated in March 2014 by killing four lions, of which two were cubs less than ten months old. It justified itself as follows: "They would have been killed by the new male the first chance he got."[75] And "in any case, the two lion cubs were not big enough to get along on their own."[76] The zoo would not have had enough room to house them separately and would not have succeeded in placing them elsewhere. The world shrinks cruelly when nobody wants to spend a penny to save some surplus lions!

One consolation: "All our animals are not cut to pieces in front of visitors," the zoo director declared, adding that "this establishment is recognized throughout the world for its work with lions." And he concluded, "I am proud that one of them [the so-called 'new male'] will be the progenitor of a new genetic line." Really good work. . . .

Amusement Parks That Massacre Dolphins

Every year dozens of dolphins are captured and then sold to trainers on the payroll of aquatic parks. Taken out of their natural habitat, they are doomed to survive in environments to which they are not suited, where the rate of mortality is high and births are rare. It is in these terms that the association One Voice describes dolphinariums, lucrative enterprises that put on shows of trained dolphins and, sometimes in luxury settings, offer sessions publicized as "dolphin therapy."

A dolphin in its element swims up to sixty miles per day to hunt, for pleasure, and to cultivate social relations with its peers. Thus the conditions in which they are held do not allow them to pursue their normal behavior. They are deprived not only of their freedom but also of the richness of their social relations and their normal modes of communication. The water of the pools in which they are kept, often chlorinated, causes many ailments.

Orcas, another species that is a victim of these aquatic parks, survive no longer than seven years in them. In their natural habitat, the females live about 50 years (with a maximum of 80 to 90 years) and the males 30 years (with a maximum of 50 to 60 years). As has been revealed in the documentary *Blackfish*,[77] as well as in other investigative pieces, the owners of these amusement parks, such as Seaworld in San Diego, California, carefully conceal from the public and from newly hired trainers the dangers that trainers face, which range from serious injury to death. The facts are that orcas taken from different schools are confined in small basins, despite the fact that in the sea they usually swim ninety miles per day. They are separated from their young and forced to execute a variety of acrobatic feats. This treatment causes them to suffer from stress and despair, which they sometimes take out on their trainers.

Every year, during the six months of the fishing season, the villages of Taiji and Futo in Japan are the scene of a mass dolphin kill. The fishermen intercept the cetaceans on their migratory route, then chase them until they are exhausted or else drive them using a wall of sound created by striking metallic rods immersed beneath the surface of the water. Next they bunch them together in the shallow waters of a cove whose entry they block afterward with nets in order to prevent the dolphins from escaping. At that point the fishermen only have to harpoon the dolphins, which are swimming in a sea of blood, then hoist them aboard their boats or pull them up on the shore. Sometimes they even drag them alive along the asphalt with their little trucks. Every season, around 23,000 dolphins and other small cetaceans are massacred in this fashion in the name of a 400-year-old tradition.

The best specimens are captured alive so they can be sold to dolphinariums for prices as high as $150,000. The others are sold for $600 to $800 apiece to restaurants. Without the trade with the dolphinariums, the market in dolphin meat would no longer be viable, since the demand for the meat is decreasing constantly.

Richard O'Barry was a dolphin trainer in the 1960s. One day, one of his dolphins apparently committed suicide in front of him by ceasing breathing (in dolphins, breathing is not automatic as in humans, but results from a voluntary effort). O'Barry was so upset that he gave up the training profession to devote himself to the protection of this species. In particular, he served as a consultant for the One Voice organization, whose team filmed a poignant series of documentaries at Taiji. These images of a bloody sea full of dolphins in their death agony were shown around the world and shocked public opinion. In addition to showing the dolphin massacre, this footage proved for the first time the connection between the fishermen and the amusement parks, which until then had been denied. It showed the trainers rejecting animals that were too small or had been injured in favor of the most "beautiful" specimens—the ones that conformed to the criteria of the dolphinariums from all over the world that order their animals from there.[78]

O'Barry also served as a consultant for the film entitled *The Cove*, which won the Oscar for best documentary in 2010. This film confirmed the existence of the business connection between the trade in dolphins to be kept in captivity and the fishermen who massacre the rest of them, especially at Taiji.[79] Produced in 2007 by Louie Psihoyos, a former photographer at *National Geographic*, this film was made in secret, using underwater microphones and cameras hidden in rocks. Although water parks and dolphinariums are starting to have a bad reputation in North America and Europe, unfortunately their number is increasing significantly in China, continuing to fuel demand for dolphins and other such creatures.

In order to put an end to this traffic, it is important, for one thing, to oppose the creation of new dolphinariums, and then to demand the release of all cetaceans utilized as objects of entertainment in the aquatic parks. One Voice suggests that the fishermen, who are highly qualified by their ancestral experience, should from now on be employed as eco-guards or guides for eco-tourists to help them enjoy one of the greatest spectacles that exists: the sight of dolphins at liberty.

Hunting and Fishing for Pleasure: Killing for Sport or for Entertainment

Hunting and fishing are practiced by many peoples for their survival. When this is not the case, these pursuits are classified under the rubric of "recreational sports." Europeans who hunt for pleasure are certainly not in the same position as Eskimos who kill to ensure their survival or to prevent a polar bear from devouring them. The hunters of wealthy nations may eat most of what they kill, but they rarely need this dietary element in order to survive. Moreover, the motivations put forward by the hunters themselves do not mention the need for food, but rather cite contact with nature (99 percent), companionship (93 percent), and the maintenance of property (89 percent).[80] These are all laudable goals in themselves, but not ones that in any way necessitate the use of a rifle.

Regarding fishing, Théophile Gautier wrote with refined insight, "Nothing calms the passions like this philosophical diversion that fools reduce to a mockery like all the other things they don't understand."[81] Such a pity that the fish can't really grasp the extent to which this philosophy can be entertaining. . . .

Winston Churchill declared very high-mindedly: "You come back from fishing washed clean, purified . . . completely filled with a great happiness." The fish are surely charmed to hear about it. The famous aviator Pierre Clostermann had the kindness to release the fish he caught "so they could grow up to be more prudent in the future." A form of tough-love education, to be sure. I share with this war pilot the feeling that "nothing compares to the beatific solitude of a pond awakening in a windless dawn or the happiness of gently rowing through the faint mist of daybreak." But why associate this serenity with an activity that draws its pleasure from inflicting death on other beings?

Some go the extent of depicting hunting as an act of love, as does shotgun writer a Michael McIntosh: "In hunting, man fulfills the demands of his own nature. It is a restorative act by which he demonstrates his elemental bond with the universe. And, it is prompted by love."[82]

Human beings often exhibit the kind of lopsided vision elegantly summed up by George Bernard Shaw: "When a man kills a tiger, he's a hero; when a tiger kills a man, it's a ferocious beast." The rare cases of bathers attacked by sharks make headlines in the media, which come up with titles like "Killer Sharks on the Loose!" On the average, annually, around thirty people perish in the world as a result of having inopportunely found themselves in the path of these sharks. (Mosquitoes are incomparably more dangerous, for they kill between 1.5 million and 2 million people in the world every year by transmitting malaria, dengue fever, or yellow fever.) As for the humans, they kill an average of 100 million sharks per year.

Hunters as Protectors of Nature?

Hunting organizations claim to be fervent protectors of nature and pride themselves on playing a more informed and effective role in regulating wildlife than the ecologists. In the United States, the NRA claims that "Hunters and other gun owners are among the foremost supporters of sound wildlife management and conservation practices in the United States."[83] In the same vein, Benoît Petit, president of the St. Hubert Club of Belgium, an association for defense and promotion of hunting (St. Hubert is the patron saint of hunting) states: "The hunter, the person who is the steward of a hunting domain, observes his animals, and manages and husbands his territory all through the year. The act of culling an animal only represents a few seconds in the ongoing effort that he is continually making."[84]

According to this view, hunting is "a necessity for the ecology." However, as the association One Voice points out, the impact of hunters on the environment and their way of managing the wildlife is more than questionable.[85] They claim that their mission is to make sure, by means of their "culling" (once again a term that deliberately gives an impression of harmlessness but masks a predatory human reality), that stable and healthy animal populations are maintained. In this way, they replace the effect of natural predators such as wolves, bears, and lynx. They make much of the point, for example, that over the past thirty years the populations of wild boars have spread geographically and multiplied in numbers by a factor of five. The deer population has also increased. Therefore, they say, it is crucial to regulate this growth by means of the hunt. However, many other, less violent means of intervention can be envisaged, such as sterilization of the dominant males, who account for the greatest proportion of reproduction. Moreover, in a truly natural environment, rich in biodiversity, the balance between prey and predators would stabilize at optimal levels of density, and intervention would not be necessary.

Natural predation limits the populations and eliminates the weakest individuals, but that is far from the privileged choice of the hunters, who prefer to kill the "most beautiful" beasts. In view of the complexity of biological balances, it is somewhat pretentious to try to play the role of substitute for nature. In Yellowstone National Park in the United States, a significant diminution in the number of trees was observed. The ecologists who took on this problem showed that authorization of the hunting of wolves—which the hunters asserted had become too numerous—had resulted in an increase in the number of deer, and the deer were the ones who had eaten the shoots of the trees. Since wolf hunting was prohibited again, the number of deer has decreased, and the trees are growing again.

In other cases, as the American philosopher Brian Luke tells us, "the population of deer is elevated *because* men like to kill deer. Wildlife managers manipulate plant life, exterminate natural predators, regulate hunting licenses, and sometimes even raise deer and release them in nature."[86] In other words, hunting is not done because it is necessary to regulate overly numerous populations of animals; rather, the size of these populations is artificially increased in order to provide a reason to hunt. On top of this, hunters, far from being content with shooting wild animals or trapping animals who have been declared "nuisances," increase certain wild populations by introducing domestically raised animals (rabbits and pheasants) for the pleasure of killing them. For the most part, these animals have grown used to the hitherto harmless company of humans; they do not fear them and do not run from their guns.

Questioned one day about his view of hunting, the naturalist and explorer Théodore Monod replied as follows: "It is obvious that prehistoric humans needed to kill animals. Currently, Eskimos kill seals and Bushmen kill giraffes—it is necessary for them. They don't have a choice. But apart from cases like these, it's a total anachronism. We do not hunt here either in self-defense or for food. We hunt for entertainment."[87] Théodore Monod spent his life fighting against poverty, racism, torture, and all sorts of other injustices, as well as against destruction of the environment. He was inspired in his commitment to the cause of humans and animals by Albert Schweitzer and by his own father, the Protestant pastor Wilfred Monod.

Hunting with Hounds, a Bloody Amusement for the Elite

Even though it is done only by a very small part of the population in the countries where it still goes on, this kind of hunting is a deeply cruel leftover from the past. It "consists of pursuit on horseback and with dogs of a wild animal, usually a stag, to the point of exhaustion, then stabbing it, drowning it, or breaking its legs (if it has not been torn apart by the hounds) before 'serving' it, that is, cutting its throat," as writer Armand Farrachi explains.[88]

As Alexandrine Civard-Racinais tells us in her *Dictionnaire horrifié de la Souffrance animale (Horrified Dictionary of Animal Suffering)*: "We'll have to believe that Armand Farrachi and the numerous opponents of hunting (73 percent of the French people according to a poll carried out by Sofres in March 2005) have understood nothing about this 'school of refinement, perseverance, and well-informed respect for nature,' as the Société de la Vénerie (Society of the Hunt) would have it."[89] As a fine example of this perseverance and respect, on

November 2, 2007, in the township of Larroque in the Tarn, a stag pursued by forty dogs smashed to bits the bay window of the living room of the Family B. The stag was stabbed to death with a dagger in the family kitchen by one of the members of the Grésigny Hunt, the organizers of this particular hunt.[90]

This kind of hunting is thousands of years old, according to the historians of this particular style of the sport. It only acquired real importance in France during the reign of Francis I, when it became an "art de vivre" that attracted the nobility. This king himself was known as "the great hunter of France." In fact, hunting with hounds remained until the twentieth century the prerogative of a nobility clad in red- or black-tailed riding coats and boots, with caps in the colors of their particular hunt club.

Just as in the case of ordinary hunting with a rifle, the advocates of this sport boast of contributing to the balance of the ecosystem. They base their legitimacy on ancestral aristocratic traditions and tout the virtues of this "amusement" as one that increases endurance and the skill of the hunter and his packs of dogs. Today, its proponents minimize its elitist aspect and present it in more democratic terms as a "sport." They create nonprofit associations where each member pays dues, just as in other sports clubs.[91]

Let us imagine a forest in springtime, serene and fresh, where you might expect to hear only the twittering of birds, the breeze in the trees, the furtive sound of a rodent or a deer rustling in the soft litter of dried leaves from the previous autumn. All at once, you hear the clamor of riders in red jerseys on galloping horses, the furious belling of hounds (which are sometimes deliberately kept hungry), and the blast of horns marking the high points of the hunt. For a brief moment, the stag stands immobile, trying to decide in which direction to flee. It darts forward and leaps over some brush, desperately seeking a stream where it can drown its scent and scatter the dog pack at its heels. If it is lucky, it will find water. If the dogs catch it, it will be pitilessly torn to pieces, disemboweled, and then stabbed—excuse me, "served." The hunters will be able to rejoice in a great day of hunting as they stand before the cadaver of the magnificent stag that has just lost its life . . .

In a similar vein, the nineteenth-century English hunter Roualeyn Gordon-Cumming tells us in his memoirs of his pride in killing an African elephant. After the beaters had driven the pachyderm into shooting range, Gordon-Cumming decides to "devote a little time to contemplating this noble elephant before shooting it down." He has a coffee made for himself and, while sipping it, contemplates "one of the finest of African elephants which stands awaiting my pleasure next to a tree. . . . I was master of these immense forests that now provided me with this highly noble and uplifting sport." After having admired his victim for a good while, he decides to fire. Not without having "made several attempts trying to find the vulnerable points," he finally succeeds in mortally wounding the elephant and watches its death throes. "Great tears rolled from its eyes, which slowly closed, then re-opened. Its colossal body trembled convulsively. It fell down onto its side and expired. Its tusks, beautifully curved, were the heaviest ones I had ever seen."[92]

To come back to hunting with hounds, the decorum, the special vocabulary, and the introduction of music seem to have as their goal to make everyone forget the macabre ending of this diversion.

In France there was a legislative proposal to outlaw this anachronistic custom of hunting with hounds in May 2013. It was outlawed in 2004 in England (where the practice was particularly prized), abolished in Germany in 1952, and in Belgium in 1995. It survives, however, in the United States (where it was exported by British colonials who introduced hunting the red fox with hounds), in Canada, and in other countries. We cannot but identify with the words of Albert Schweitzer, winner of the Nobel Peace Prize: "The time will come when public opinion will no longer tolerate amusements in which animals are mistreated or killed. When will we reach the moment when the hunt, the pleasure of killing animals for 'sport,' will be considered a mental aberration?"[93]

The Golden Rule Applies to All Beings

Consider the golden rule, which is common to almost all religions and cultures: "Do not do to others what you would not wish them to do to you." If we extend that to all sentient beings, how could we imagine that an animal would choose to be incarcerated in a zoo, to undergo the torments inflicted on it by a neurotic circus trainer, or be stabbed in the back by sharp banderillas and, shortly after, executed with a sword? Without even going so far as to imagine what we humans might feel in those situations, we can at least recognize that animals themselves are completely capable of making their own choices: a wild sow chooses carefully the lair in which she will give birth to her litter; if you open the cage of a wild animal, it will immediately dash away into the forest. Any animal in good health will choose life over death.

Those who nevertheless persist in justifying the torments we inflict on animals should begin by explaining why the golden rule applies only to human beings and by what right they consider themselves authorized in so limiting it.

12

ANIMAL RIGHTS, HUMAN OBLIGATIONS

If you are exasperated by your computer not working and you can't succeed in fixing it, you are free to throw it out the window. Such a gesture will certainly not do anything to repair it, but it is your right. On the other hand, if you are irritated by the yowling of a cat and you catch it and try to smash its skull against a wall, it will try to fight you off and escape. In this case, your behavior is much more serious, because you are attacking a living being. It is not a right you are exercising here; it is an abuse of power.

As the philosopher Florence Burgat puts it: "The resistance that animals put up to being caught is fully a part of their struggle to have their most fundamental right recognized: the right to pursue their own life. The animal that resists being captured is manifesting its will to live—not to be captured, tormented, injured, shut up, tied up, or killed. Every being that undertakes this struggle by whatever means it has at its disposal is concretely expressing its wish to have its right to live recognized."[1]

If we were to write a single article of a hypothetical Universal Declaration of the Rights of Living Beings, it could be formulated as follows: "Every living being has the right to live and not be the victim of suffering imposed on it by others." Henry Stephens Salt, an English reformer and a friend of Mahatma Gandhi, said: "Pain is pain . . . whether it be inflicted on man or on beast; . . . and the creature that suffers it, whether man or beast suffers evil; and the sufferance of evil, unmeritedly, unprovokedly . . . is Cruelty and Injustice in him that occasions it."[2]

If the question of the rights of humans is already sufficiently complex, that of animals is even more so. A number of philosophers are of the opinion that rights and obligations only concern existing persons, conscious of their rights and capable of respecting them in relation to others.[3] Thus they deny all rights to animals as well as to human beings of future generations (the latter, since they are nothing more than a multitude of potential and indeterminate individuals).

Another side of the problem is expressed by the English philosopher Mary Midgley, for whom the concept of rights is at once too broad and too ambiguous: "It can be used in a wide sense to draw attention to problems, but not to solve them. In its moral sense, it oscillates uncontrollably between applications which are too wide to resolve conflicts ('the right to life, liberty and the pursuit of happiness') and ones which are too narrow to be plausible ('the basic human right to stay at home on Bank Holiday'). As many people have already suggested, its various uses have diverged too far to be usefully reunited."[4]

Instead of arguing about the notion of rights, one way to resolve this impasse is to speak the language of consideration, respect for others, and the duty or obligation of the goodwill we have toward all sentient beings. If making altruism and compassion extend to all human beings without any discrimination is a special quality of being human, extending the same to animals only follows logically. Having said that, even if the question of rights is complex philosophically, as a practical matter it is essential to protect animals by ascribing to them certain legal rights that it is our duty to defend in their name.

Equal Consideration or Equal Rights?

Contrary to what is often stated sarcastically by those who want to make a mockery of the question of animal protection, none of the eminent advocates of animal liberation, such as Peter Singer, nor any of the champions of animal rights, like the philosopher and deontologist Tom Regan, have ever asserted or even implied that the life of a mouse was equal in value to that of a human. They never claimed that mouse and man had identical rights or that they had to be treated in exactly the same way. While recognizing the many differences that exist between humans and animal species, Peter Singer nevertheless defends the principle of equal consideration of their interests. As for Tom Regan, he maintains that animals share with human beings the fundamental right to be treated with respect on the basis of their inherent value.

Peter Singer puts forward the argument that, except in cases of absolute necessity, it is unjustifiable to inflict suffering on another living being, whether or not it is of the same species as us. In spite of the undeniable inequalities between human beings and animals (with respect to their physical and intellectual capabilities), we should grant to both equal *consideration*. We must of course understand, Singer tells us, that equal consideration for different beings can also mean different treatments and different rights.[5]

It is clear that human and nonhuman beings do not need to have the same rights in all matters. It would be absurd to call for the right of abortion for men and access to higher education for mice. On the other hand, Singer writes: "If a being suffers there can be no moral justification for refusing to take that suffering into consideration. No matter what the nature of the being, the principle of equality requires that its suffering be counted equally with the like suffering."[6]

The needs of beings are very different. Put a million dollars in front of a sheep: it won't have much of a reaction, and if you take it away, that won't bother it at all. A man will react in an entirely different fashion. The cow delights in fresh grass, which leaves the tiger indifferent. On the other hand, if you stab them with a knife, the man and the sheep will feel the same pain and will each struggle with equal desperation to escape death.

Peter Singer considers it unacceptable to dehumanize human beings as well as to treat animals like things, to mistreat certain humans because of their race or sex or to mistreat animals for the sole reason that they belong to a species different from our own. According to him, the capacity to suffer and feel pleasure is a sufficient condition for asserting that a being has interests. At the bare minimum, its interest is not to suffer.[7]

Tom Regan tells us that the potential flaws and aberrations of the utilitarian approach in actual practice make it impossible for that

philosophy to come up with a coherent vision of animal protection.[8]
Therefore he defends the rights of animals to be respected because
they possess intrinsic value:

> We do not say that humans and other animals are equal with
> regard to all their characteristics. For example, we do not say
> that dogs and cats can do algebra or that pigs and cows appreciate
> poetry. What we do say is that the many non-human animals are,
> just like humans, psychological beings who have their own expe-
> rience of well-being. In that sense, they and we are alike. . . .
>   We do not say that humans and other animals always have the
> same rights. Already all humans do not have the same rights. For
> example, those who are affected by significant mental retardation
> do not have the right to attend university. What we do say is that
> these humans, like other humans, have in common with other
> animals a fundamental moral right: the right to be treated with
> respect. . . .
>   It is true that certain animals, like shrimps or mussels, are
> perhaps capable of feeling pain, but they do not have most of the
> other psychological capacities. If that is true, then they do not
> have some of the rights that other animals have. Nevertheless,
> there can be no moral justification for inflicting pain on anyone if
> it is not necessary. And since it is not necessary for humans to eat
> shrimps, mussels, and other similar animals, nor to make use of
> them in other ways, there can be no moral justification to inflict
> the pain on them that invariably accompanies these uses.[9]

More precisely, Regan is of the opinion that injuries intentionally
inflicted on a sentient being cannot be justified by adding up the
advantages that others can derive from causing them.[10]

Just as does Peter Singer, Regan acknowledges without ambiguity
that the death of a human being represents a greater loss than that
of a dog. That is the reason why, when circumstances demand such a
choice, it is the dog that must be sacrificed. Moreover, for Regan, the
number makes no difference, since the death of any particular human
being represents a more significant loss than the death of any particular dog, that is, any one of ten, of a hundred or a million dogs, *considered individually*. He adds that a group of ten dogs does not constitute

an entity in itself that would have more moral weight than a human being. However reasonable this may be, this point of view becomes problematic when the numbers become astronomical, as was the case at the time of the mad cow and SARS epidemics of recent decades. But how is it possible to set a limit that is anything but arbitrary? That is certainly one of the most difficult questions to settle. Peter Singer and Tom Regan, in all reasonability, simply advocate the abolition of massive exploitation of animals as well as the adoption of a vegan diet.

Moral Agents and Moral Patients

Moral philosophy makes the distinction between moral agents and moral patients. Moral agents are those who are capable of distinguishing good from evil and of deciding to do or not do what morality, as they conceive it, dictates. Therefore we consider them responsible for their actions. Taking into account the fact that they can also become the object of good or bad acts on the part of other moral agents, they participate in a relationship of reciprocity.

Moral patients are those who are only passively affected by the good or bad actions carried out by moral agents but are themselves incapable of formulating moral principles and deliberating on whether or not their actions have a moral basis before carrying them out.

Adult human beings who are in possession of all their intellectual faculties are both moral agents and moral patients. On the other hand, children, heavily handicapped persons, and the mentally ill are not moral agents and are not considered morally responsible for their actions. Nevertheless, they remain moral patients who, as such, benefit from a certain number of rights.

Animals are generally considered moral patients.[11] If a snake eats a frog, its intention is not to do something bad but only to feed itself. Similarly, if it bites a human being who is passing nearby, it is because it is trying to defend itself. When an animal attacks another moral patient (the frog) or a moral agent (the passing human), its action cannot be judged in moral terms.

This does not prevent us from frequently developing illogical attitudes toward animals. Because of the self-proclaimed privileges of human domination, Jean-Baptiste Jeangène Vilmer explains, "humans can mistreat an animal without that being considered 'evil'" (the animal is not then considered to be a moral patient) and at the same time hold it against that animal if it defends itself and injures its tormenter (the animal then is considered a moral agent)."[12]

If animals are indeed moral patients, as the philosophers of the animal liberation movement assert, then we have a responsibility toward them. The way in which we treat them becomes the object of a moral evaluation and can be considered more or less good. That, according to Jeangène Vilmer, is the area of concern of animal ethics.

This distinction makes it possible for moral agents to recognize the duties they have toward moral patients. Thus it becomes incumbent upon them to show concern for those who do not have the capacity to formulate and stand up for their own rights, notably their right to live and not suffer. It is equally important that our laws should translate this responsibility and these duties into concrete terms. We could say that, the more a moral patient is helpless and defenseless, the more moral agents have the duty to protect and care for them. The degree of vulnerability of a moral patient should be proportional to the requirement to protect it.

For Tom Regan, the principle of respect requires us to relate to all individuals possessing an intrinsic value by adopting a mode of conduct that respects this value, whether the value possessors are moral agents or moral patients. Even beyond that, we have the duty to not cause harm to moral patients. Finally, the right to being treated with respect cannot be adjudged to be either stronger or weaker in the case of moral patients than it is in the case of moral agents.[13]

Morality: An Ability That Comes from Evolution

That being said, the distinction between moral agents and patients should not be allowed to fall into the kind of caricatured dualism that makes absolute distinctions between humans and animals or between humanism and animalism. The dogmatic and arbitrary quality of such dichotomies becomes evident the moment we take into account the continuity of evolution and the process of gradual transformation that link all animal species. The manifestations of empathy, gratitude, consolation, mourning, mutual help, protection, sense of fairness, and so on that have been observed in animals are not the product of chance. The same is true of the ability to distinguish between actions that are good for or harmful to others. All the abilities that exist in humans have been selected for over the course of millions of years of evolution because they were useful for survival. Therefore they are also useful for other species, and we should expect to find in animals emotions and mental states that approach those of human beings, including a moral sense.

So it is not surprising that research carried out over the past few decades has shown that the great part of our moral sense is innate.

We have seen that, according to Jonathan Haidt, we first sense instinctively whether a behavior is morally good or bad, and then we justify our judgments with reasoning after the fact. Following the same line of thought, in his book entitled *The Bonobo and the Atheist: In Search of Humanism among the Primates*, the ethologist Frans de Waal makes clear on the basis of a body of observations and research studies that morality is not an innovation on the part of humans, as many people have hitherto believed. Far from having developed morality solely through our power of rational reflection, we have benefited from capacities already developed by the social animals who have preceded us.[14]

Observations of behavior in animals that can be described as moral abound. In his *Expression of the Emotions in Man and Animals*, Darwin tells the story of a dog who, each time he passed near the basket in which his friend, a sick female cat, was lying, never failed to lick her a few times. It also happens that chimpanzees mediate in an impartial manner among peers of theirs who are quarreling, trying to separate them and calm them down, thus showing not only an individual moral sense but also concern for the harmony of their community.[15]

Sarah Brosnan and Frans de Waal have shown that capuchin monkeys have a sense of fairness.[16] Two capuchins were placed in adjacent cages and are able to observe one another. The experimenter gave a token to each monkey alternately, then held out her hand for the monkey to give the token back. In exchange for doing so, the monkey got a slice of cucumber. The monkeys quickly learned the meaning of the exchange and appreciated it greatly. At the end of twenty-five exchanges, the experimenter continued to give a piece of cucumber to one of the monkeys, but she gave raisins, a fruit the capuchins are very fond of, to the other. The first one noticed this injustice, as it saw it, and not only refused the piece of cucumber most of the time, but from time to time went so far as to throw it out of its cage. This sense of fairness has also been observed in dogs, who consent several times to do a certain trick without getting an immediate reward, but refuse to continue doing so as soon as they see another dog receive a piece of sausage as a reward for doing the same trick.[17]

Frans de Waal recounts the story of Lody, a bonobo in the Milwaukee Zoo. Lody was a very protective dominant male who in particular took care of Kitty, an old female who was deaf and blind. Since Kitty was in danger of getting lost in an area with many doors and tunnels, every morning Lody took her by the hand and guided her to the sunny spot on the grass that Kitty was especially fond of. At the end of the day, he guided her back inside her shelter with the same care. When Kitty had one of her frequent fits of epilepsy, Lody stayed at her side and refused to leave her.[18]

One day, Lody bit the finger of the veterinarian, Barbara Bell, who was giving him vitamins through the bars of his cage. He heard the cracking noise, raised his eyes apparently in surprise, and let go. But he had bitten too hard. Barbara was missing a finger from her hand, and the doctors were not able to graft it back on. A few days later, the unfortunate injured party came back to the zoo and, seeing Lody, raised her bandaged had as if to say, "Look what you did!" Lody came over and examined the hand attentively, then went to the farthest corner of his enclosure and sat down there with his head lowered and his arms wrapped around himself.

In the next years, Barbara left to work in another city. Fifteen years after the accident, she made an impromptu visit to the Milwaukee Zoo and, mingling with the rest of the crowd, went to have a look at the enclosure where Lody was living. As soon as Lody saw Barbara, he ran over and tried to look at her left hand, which was hidden behind the railing. He kept on looking toward her left side, as though insisting on seeing the hand he had bitten, until finally the victim raised her hand. Lody stared at the mutilated hand, then looked Barbara in the eyes, then looked back at the hand. "He knew," the veterinarian concluded, an opinion that Frans de Waal, with his extensive experience of bonobos, agreed with entirely. If it is true that bonobos are conscious of the consequences of their actions, that shows to what degree they are capable of feeling the types of concerns that underlie the moral sense in humans.

Frans de Waal reaches this conclusion:

> This brings me back to my bottom-up view of morality. The moral law is not imposed from above or derived from well-reasoned principles; rather, it arises from ingrained values that have been there since the beginning of time. The most fundamental one derives from the survival value of group life. The desire to belong, to get along, to love and be loved, prompts us to do everything in our power to stay on good terms with those on whom we depend. Other social primates share this value and rely on the same filter between emotion and action to reach a mutually agreeable modus vivendi. . . . Morality has much more humble beginnings, which are recognizable in the behavior of other animals. . . . Our evolutionary background lends a massive helping hand without which we would never have gotten this far.[19]

Do We Have to Be Conscious of Our Rights in Order to Have Them?

The argument according to which only those beings can have rights who are conscious of them and are capable of defending them is a fallacious one. It is "as though the omnipotence of one being or the weakness of another could have an influence on the existence of the rights of the latter. . . . After all, we do grant rights to idiots, to the totally senile, and to the incurably insane." So argues Louis Lépine, a French lawyer who was the president of the European International Committee for the Protection of Animals.[20] Similarly, the fact that a person is deeply asleep and therefore not conscious of his or her rights does not divest that person of the rights that we accord to all human beings.

Moreover, there are different ways of being conscious of a natural right. That animals are not capable of being conscious of the "concept" of rights does not alter the facts that, like us, they aspire not to suffer and they try to the best of their ability to achieve the most favorable conditions for their survival. Jean-Jacques Rousseau made the point that just being sentient guarantees the "participation of animals in natural rights."[21] Saying this, he swept aside the perennial notion, reiterated by Hobbes, according to which "for the weak of mind, for children, and for the insane, there is no law, not any more than there is for animals." This idea was also advocated by Hugo Grotius, a Dutch jurist of the seventeenth century, who in his work *De jure belli ac pacis (Concerning the Laws of War and Peace)* stipulates: "No being, other than those who are capable of formulating general principles [i.e., who are capable of reason] are qualified to have rights."[22]

Louis Lépine takes it to be obvious that "animals possess the consciousness of their right to life in the form, perhaps obscure but still very real, that we commonly call the instinct of self-preservation, and that they also possess a conscious sense that their life ought to unfold normally in conditions that are appropriate to their nature and to the particular unique character of their species."[23] Thus his view is that it is essential to attribute to animals the right to life and to not having to endure inescapable suffering at the hands of human beings.

When we see that another being has a need, the fulfillment of which would permit that being to experience well-being and to avoid suffering, empathy immediately and spontaneously makes us also feel this need. Then our care for the other generates a desire to help fulfill that need. Conversely, if we place little value on the other, we won't care. The other's needs will not matter to us, and perhaps we will not even notice them.

However, experience has taught us that we cannot really count on the compassion of our fellow humans. It is essential to *protect* animals from the abuses and sufferings inflicted upon them by those who, in point of fact, lack compassion toward them. We do not protect human beings from torture, loss of liberty, and from other people who might seek to kill them just because human beings are conscious of their rights, but because it is unacceptable to inflict these wrongs upon them.

In places where human rights are given little respect, the rights of animals are given even less. The Chinese government, for example, which contests the Western concept of the rights of man, totally disdains the rights of animals. As we have seen, cruelty toward animals is common practice at facilities that breed fur-bearing animals, extract bile from bears, deal in tiger parts, and in many other commercial enterprises of that sort.

Duties toward Animals according to "Humanist" Philosophy

In *Notre Humanité (Our Humanity)*, humanist philosopher Francis Wolff writes: "Even though our obligations are first directed toward humanity, they can also have as their object—in a relative and derivative way—certain other beings such as animals."[24] He distinguishes three types of duties, which relate, respectively, to pets, domestic animals, and wild animals. According to the distinction he makes here, "With pets, we have emotional relationships, often reciprocal, which explain the concern, care, and devotion that we can feel toward them and they also sometimes can feel for us, their masters." For the case of animals that are useful to us, domestic animals and bred animals (called "profit-bringing" animals), Francis Wolff has the following to say: "We owe them conditions of life proportional to their significance for us. Thus we owe them protection and food, because in exchange they give us their help, their meat, and their skin. Thus it is moral to kill those animals who live only for that."[25] But the animals do not "give" us their meat and their skin: it is we who decide to take it from them by force. Moreover, it is difficult to conclude that these animals "live only for that," because it is we who decide unilaterally to raise them in order to kill them. As we pointed out earlier, arbitrarily deciding that a child is destined to become a slave does not make slavery moral.

Regarding wild species, Francis Wolff is of the opinion that we have "no duty to assist, protect, or respect them, thus no moral obligation toward them properly speaking." Nevertheless he thinks we have a general sort of obligation toward animals, that we ought to respect the balance of ecosystems, and we ought to respect biodiversity to the extent that it meets human needs and necessities. For example, this means fighting against species considered "harmful" and protecting certain endangered species. Francis Wolff decries cruelty, by which he means inflicting suffering deliberately and needlessly on any being. Such cruelty is "always wrong—it must be condemned as despicable, abject behavior unworthy of a human being, and it must sometimes be halted." But the philosopher adds that the absence of any obligation toward wild animals means that hunting or fishing for sport "have nothing morally reprehensible about them, not any more than eating lobster, even if it entails the 'pain' of the fish taken on the hook, of the rabbit shot, or the lobster in boiling water, as long as, to the extent possible, these practices respect ecological balances, biodiversity, and the natural conditions necessary for the life and reproduction of the animals."[26] However, speaking of hunting or fishing "for sport" implies that neither one nor the other is necessary for our survival but that they are carried on for our "pleasure," whether it is gastronomic or lies in sport or play. If that is so, do we not have a case here of suffering inflicted "deliberately and needlessly"?

So as their name implies, "humanist" duties toward animals are entirely conceived of in terms of the interests of human beings. By contrast, Francis Wolff defines "animalism" as "any doctrine that makes of *the animal as such*, whether it is human or non-human, the privileged, indeed sole, object of our moral attention, whether that takes the form of the ethics of compassion, of utilitarian philosophy, or of a theory of rights."[27] The ethical system that we are defending here does not make the animal a "privileged" object of our morality; it simply regards it as necessary to include animals along with the rest of us sentient beings.

Martin Gibert distinguishes two forms of humanism:

On the one hand, "inclusive humanism" designates a group of values, norms, and moral virtues that form the basis for a constant extension of the circle of morality. It advocates equality, freedom, and solidarity and shows concern for the most vulnerable. It is inclusive in the sense that it does not set out any a priori limits on the sphere of application of these values. This is the humanism of Voltaire and Rousseau, of Jeremy Bentham and John Stuart Mill, of Martin Luther King and Gandhi.

On the other hand, "exclusive humanism" consists in limiting moral consideration solely to members of the human species. Justice, equality, and benevolence—yes, but only those who possess the VIP card. Thus exclusive humanism is fundamentally speciesist and is indistinguishable from human supremacism."[28]

Does Enjoying a Right Require Reciprocity?

A number of thinkers, principally among those of the humanist tendency, deny all rights to animals, invoking the fact that animals are incapable of reciprocity. This is also the opinion of Francis Wolff, who declares:

Reducing a man or a woman to slavery, not recognizing others as persons, treating them as a means to satisfy our needs, refusing the principles of reciprocity or justice, violating the principles of the liberty, equality, and dignity of human beings—none of these things can be sheltered under the idea of cultural diversity or even under the highly seductive notion of "moral relativity"—it is all simply barbarism. And these universal principles cannot apply to animals by definition, because they presuppose the recognition of others as equals; they presuppose the reciprocity without which there would be no such thing as justice.[29]

Such a point of view raises the crucial question of whether we should refuse to respect the rights of the most vulnerable. Should we condemn nursing babies, very young children, or people suffering from mental pathologies for not respecting the rights of sane human beings? Should parents punish their babies for crying at night and not respecting their right to sleep? Shouldn't a schizophrenic who in mid-hallucination throws himself on a caregiver and tries to hit her be the object of care and not aggressive reaction? Should we say that beings like these are failing to respect our rights? The very fact of temporary immaturity in some cases or of confirmed pathology in others automatically renders inapplicable any notion of the reciprocity of rights. Tenderness, care, and empathy are the responses these people ought to get from us, rather than the imposition of the unrealistic requirement of some kind of reciprocity. In *The Case for Animal Rights*, Tom Regan concludes: "These animals do not have the duty to respect our rights; but that does not eliminate or diminish our obligation to respect theirs."[30]

We should also note that it seems a bit contradictory to speak of "universal" principles as Francis Wolff does, adding that these principles do not apply to animals. Can the notion of rights really be restricted to the human species when there exist at least 7.7 million species of animals? Even though it may be true that we are especially intelligent and endowed with many marvelous faculties, a little humility is still in order.

Aren't the Duties We Have toward Animals Really "Indirect Duties" to Humans?

It is the view of some thinkers that, if we have duties toward animals, it is not because we ought to be concerned with their fate but rather because by habituating ourselves to being cruel toward them, we risk losing our sensitivity and becoming cruel to our fellow humans. This point of view, which is call the "indirect duty" view, was held most notably by Immanuel Kant:

> Someone who kills his dog because his dog is no longer of any use to him . . . does not in truth infringe upon the duty he has toward his dog, because the latter is incapable of judgment; but he is committing an act that clashes with the feeling within himself of humanity and benevolence, which he ought to heed on account of the duties he has towards humanity. If he does not wish to stifle these qualities, he should exercise kindness of heart toward animals, for the man who is cruel toward them also becomes hardened toward men, whereas this gentleness toward animals goes on afterward to be applied to men themselves.[31]

Paul Janet, a French philosopher of the nineteenth century, contests the validity of this anthropocentric view: "We say that we ought not be cruel to animals so as not to become so to men. But if we were assured of not being cruel to men, would it follow from that that it would be permissible to be so toward animals? . . . We would rather say quite simply that kindness toward an animal is a duty to this animal."[32] The point is, we should stop referring the whole matter back to human beings and grant "direct rights" to animals, rights which they possess intrinsically.

The American philosopher Joel Feinberg also thinks that we have "direct duties" toward animals, based on the fact that they have their own interests linked to their cognitive faculties and the ability to establish a distinction between what is beneficial to them and what is harmful.[33] According to him, if we should hold the idea that it is not only our *duty* to treat animals with humanity but, in addition, we should behave that way toward them directly *on their own account* (and not indirectly because of the effect it has on humans). If we believe that such treatment is their due, then it can be demanded on their part by a third party, and to deprive them of such treatment constitutes injustice and legal damage (and is not just a form of violence). And if all that is the case, then we are indeed saying that they have *rights*.

As Tom Regan has shown,[34] three criticisms of Kant's position can be put forward. First, Kant is mistaken when he states that "animals do not have consciousness of themselves." A great number of reasoned arguments and research studies come together to confirm that many species of animals possess self-consciousness. As we saw in chapter 6, "The Continuum of Life," the fact that consciousness is eminently useful for our survival leads us to think that it must be present in numerous species, as it was in our own ancestors.

Second, if we take the position that animals in general are "incapable of judgment," then we must come to an agreement on the implications of this phrase. A dog is certainly capable of making the judgment that a situation is a source of suffering and that a certain object is indeed a bone and therefore desirable. Or if we understand the trait of "judgment" to mean the ability to form *moral* judgments,[35] then it is true that certain species of animals, molluscs and insects, for example, are not capable of such conceptions. However, it has now turned out to be the case that other species of animals, in particular the great apes and dogs, do possess this ability (notably, a sense of fairness).

Moreover, as the English philosopher Mary Midgley believes,[36] even if animals were incapable of "judging," as Kant says, then that would only reinforce our obligations toward them. The point here is that we have a moral obligation to protect and care for all those who are too ignorant, fragile, disoriented, incompetent, or indecisive to be capable of judging whether or not they are being wronged. We are in fact responsible for our own conduct toward those who either benefit from or are hurt by it. Kant cannot deny animals all rights without at the same time depriving all human moral patients of them. Now, it is clear that the latter certainly possess rights.

Third, Regan shows that Kant is not making a valid point when he asserts that animals only exist "as means to an end"—the end in this case being the benefit of humans. Says Regan: "The plausibility of the idea that animals only have a value if they serve human ends diminishes as soon as we begin to recognize that, like the human beings they resemble in this respect, animals have a life of their own that is susceptible of becoming better or worse for them independently of their usefulness for others."

So the value of animals cannot be reduced to their usefulness for the human species. That was already the point of view of the early twentieth-century American zoologist and philosopher John Howard Moore, who stated in no uncertain terms:

> *Every being* is an *end*. In other words, every being is to be taken into account in determining the ends of conduct. This is the only consistent outcome of the ethical process which is in course of evolution on the earth. This world was not made and presented to any particular clique for its exclusive use or enjoyment. The earth belongs, if it belongs to anybody, to the beings who inhabit it—to *all* of them. And when one being or set of beings sets itself up as the sole end for which the universe exists, and looks upon and acts toward others as mere means to this end, it is usurpation, nothing else and never can be anything else, it matters not by whom or upon whom the usurpation is practiced.[37]

The instrumentalization of animals is part of the more general instrumentalization of the world as a whole, which, according to

French philosopher Patrice Rouget, "thus acquires a new status, that of a resource, a storehouse of available materials, entirely and exclusively set aside for whatever use human beings want to make of it. There is not one sector of the world that escapes utilitarian scrutiny."[38]

For Rouget, this instrumentalization results in "a degraded and disenchanted relationship to a world considered as a mere quantitative resource, as a source of profit exclusively dedicated to the use of humans. . . . This relationship presumes a radical dismissal of the existence per se of the whole of the non-human world, an existence that long antedates the attention brought to bear on it by the practical reason of human beings and which will happily continue to stand outside it."[39]

Since 2007, a lawyer named Antoine Goetschel has been assigned by the government of the Swiss canton of Zurich to plead the cause of animals. He has devoted himself to defending the rights of mistreated animals, pleading more than two hundred cases per year and making sure that laws protecting animals are applied. One such law is the one prohibiting impaling a live fish on a hook to serve as bait in trawling.[40] In 1973 the Swiss modified their constitution to make protection of animals a duty of the state. The mass breeding of chickens has progressively been replaced by a system that permits the birds to circulate freely, scratch the soil, roll in the dust, fly to a perch, and to lay their eggs in protected boxes lined with a suitable material.

An Integral Vision of the Rights of Animals

A number of authors who actively support the animal cause say, in effect: "All the animals need is for us to leave them in peace."[41] All right, fine, but in point of fact it is unthinkable to confine ourselves to merely leaving the animals in peace, as though they lived in a world that is detached from ours. The biosphere is fundamentally interdependent, and our life is inextricably bound up with the life of animals due to the simple fact that we are all active members of the world that we live in and continually modify through our activities. For the most part, animals are our victims, but in some cases we are theirs (tigers, mosquitoes). Sometimes they are our companions (dogs and cats), sometimes they help us (seeing-eye dogs), sometimes they invade us (locusts, termites). Even though we have been ignorant of each other for a long time (the animals of the deep sea or of impenetrable jungles), with the advent of the anthropocene era and the pervasive impact that we have today on our environment, conditions are such that no life form remains beyond the reach of our activities. Thus it is essential to rethink our relationship with animals in a more coherent and equitable fashion and in a spirit that sees humans and animals as fellow citizens of the planet.

This is exactly what has been done in a brilliant manner by Sue Donaldson and Will Kymlicka, who in 2011 published their book *Zoopolis: A Political Theory of Animal Rights*,[42] an innovative work on the rights of animals to life and liberty, which received the biannual award of the Canadian Association of Philosophy. Will Kymlicka is a Canadian academic known for his work in political philosophy who has devoted numerous writings to issues related to national, ethnic, or cultural minorities. Sue Donaldson, his partner, is an independent researcher. They envisage three principal types of rights for animals, depending on their way of life. In the case of wild animals, they propose to treat them as sovereign political communities, disposing of their own territory. The principle of sovereignty aims at protecting peoples from the paternalistic or profit-oriented encroachments of more powerful peoples. As far as wild animals are concerned, the International Covenant on Economic, Social, and Cultural Rights (United Nations, 1966) can serve as a basis for reflection. Article 1 of this Covenant postulates that "all peoples have the right of self-determination." Article 2 stipulates that "all peoples may . . . freely dispose of their natural wealth and resources," and "In no case may a people be deprived of its own means of subsistence."

Wild animals have the ability to feed themselves, move from place to place, avoid dangers, manage the risks they take, play, choose a sexual partner, and raise a family. For the most part, they do not seek contact with humans. It is therefore desirable to preserve their way of life, protect their territory, respect their wish to govern themselves, and to avoid actions directly harmful to them (e.g., hunting and destruction of biotopes) or indirectly harmful (e.g., pollution and general degradation of the environment due to human activity). According to these authors, there is no reason to intervene to prevent predatory activity among wild animals—to save the gazelle from the fangs of the lion.

With regard to domestic animals that live with us and are dependent on us, Donaldson and Kymlicka propose to make them citizens of our political communities: "Why should concepts such as community, sociability, friendship, and love be hedged by species?"[43] They argue that, in many situations, domestic animals are capable of expressing their preferences by coming toward us or by taking flight, for example. Moreover, co-citizenship is not limited to the right to vote; it also confers the right to inhabit a territory under decent conditions and be represented in our institutions. Just as young children and mentally handicapped people have the right to be represented when decisions are taken that concern them, domestic animals can be represented by spokespersons who perceive them as individuals with preferences.

Donaldson and Kymlicka distance themselves from abolitionist positions that imply the disappearance of domestic animals, since doing away with the exploitation of domesticated animals does not necessarily require putting an end to centuries of shared existence. Generally speaking, the first domesticated animals were wild species that approached humans with whom they had learned to communicate in various ways. The abolition of slavery led to integration into society of former slaves, not to their extinction. Only the disappearance of the monsters created by zootechnology would be a welcome thing—turkeys whose bodies have been deformed (in order to develop the breast part, favored for eating) to the point where they are no longer able to mate naturally, or immense sows that have large litters of 28 piglets that they are then not capable of feeding, to cite only two examples.

With intelligent management, humans can profit from the normal and spontaneous activities of animals living in environments that suit their preferences and needs. For example, we can gather horse dung or the excrement of other animals to be used as fertilizer. We can leave it to sheep herds to keep the grass mown in our large public parks. Goats can clear the undergrowth of forests and thus mitigate the risk of fire. The olfactory acuity of dogs can save lives and be a precious tool in many situations. It is also possible to envisage the use of animal labor in exchange for food and care, but then the specific personality of each kind of animal must be taken into account, the animals must take to the work voluntarily, and the workload must not become so great that it prevents the animals from engaging in other activities and relationships that are important to them.

The third category includes animals neither domesticated nor wild who live in areas inhabited or cultivated by humans but maintain an autonomous lifestyle—pigeons, sparrows, gulls, crows, mice, bats, squirrels, raccoons, and so on—but whose livelihood is bound up with human activity. Donaldson and Kymlicka suggest treating them as "de facto residents." They have the right to live where they are (they are not regarded as intruders), we must respect their fundamental rights, but we have no active obligations in their regard: for example, protecting them from predators or providing them with health care.

In essence, Donaldson and Kymlicka take the view that we must acknowledge that animals have inviolable rights that vary according to their way of life:

> What are the implications of recognizing animals as persons or selves with inviolable rights? In the simplest terms, it means recognizing that they are not means to our ends. They were not put on earth to serve us, or feed us, or comfort us. Rather, they have their own subjective existence, and hence their own equal and inviolable rights to life and liberty, which prohibits harming them, killing them, confining them, owning them, and enslaving them. Respect for these rights rules out virtually all existing practices of the animal-use industries, where animals are owned and exploited for human profit, pleasure, education, convenience, or comfort.[44]

The Rights of Animals in the Sight of the Law

For a long time, as Dean Carbonnier, a celebrated jurist, tells us, "one of the essential traits . . . of our civilization consisted in pitilessly keeping animals outside the law."[45] However, in the meantime, things have slowly improved, even if there is still a lot to do.

In France, on April 14, 2014, the jurisprudence committee of the National Assembly recognized animals as having the status of "living beings endowed with sensibility" and did this in conformity with the opinion of the majority of the French people (89 percent, according to a poll carried out by the IFOP in 2013). Before that, according to the civil code, which relates to society as a whole and constitutes the basis of French law, animals that were someone's property were considered "by their nature" as "movable goods" and "by their use" as "immovable goods," that is, goods allocated to service (of humans) and to being exploited for their usefulness (by humans).[46] The civil code has now been brought into accord with the penal code and the rural code, which recognize already, explicitly or implicitly, that animals are living and sentient beings.

To that may be added the regulations in the penal and rural codes whose purpose is to protect animals. Two articles deal with deliberate and accidental attacks on the life of an animal or its physical integrity, a third condemns bad treatment of animals, and a fourth punishes seriously the tormenting of animals and acts of cruelty toward them.[47]

As for the rural code, it explicitly recognizes animals as sentient beings, with article L214 of the law of July 10, 1976, specifying: "Any animal, being a sentient being, should be kept by its owner in conditions compatible with the biological imperatives of its species."

As for wild animals at large, they do not belong to anyone. They are called "res nullius," that is, "no one's thing."

The contradictions existing up until now in these three codes have hindered the development of a coherent policy. And now there still remains an immense distance between the existing legal texts (notably article L214) and their application.

On the European level, the Treaty of Rome (1957) saw in animals only "merchandise and agricultural products." As for the Treaty on the Functioning of the European Union, it stipulates that "The Union and its member states fully recognize the requirements for the wellbeing of animals understood as sentient beings." A directive of 2010 relating to the use of animals for scientific research stipulates: "The wellbeing of animals is one of the values of the European Union," adding that "animals have an intrinsic value that must be respected . . . and thus should always be treated as sentient beings." The application of this legislation is based on the criterion of *suffering*, and the European Union directive recognizes that the suffering of animals has been proved scientifically.

In 2002 Germany became the first country in the European Union to include the rights of animals in its constitution, and several other countries have gone on to do the same, explicitly writing protection of animals into their founding documents. In this way, they have recognized it as a duty of the state. In Germany, legislators approved by a two-thirds majority the resolution that the words "and animals" be added to the phrase in their constitution obliging the state to "respect and protect the dignity of human beings." In their respective constitutions, Switzerland, Luxembourg, India, and Brazil protect all animals without distinction. The United Kingdom adopted an Animal Welfare Act in 2006 that confers legal status on all animals kept by human beings and introduces an obligation of "good treatment." The Finnish legislative house went even further by recognizing that animals have intellectual abilities. In Switzerland, beginning in 2003, the civil code has clearly stated that "animals are not things."

The laws of Austria are the most advanced in this area. The Law of Animals, for example, stipulates that "the state protects the life and wellbeing of animals in their status as cohabitants with human beings." According to this law, it is forbidden to kill an animal without a valid reason, to keep an animal with the intention of producing fur, to keep or use animals in a circus (except for domestic animals), even if it is not with the intention of making money. This same law stipulates that each province must retain lawyers who specialize in animal rights and who are empowered to intervene in any case involving the protection of animals. The Austrian law on animal experimentation prohibits carrying out experiments on any of the great apes, except if the experiment is carried out for the express benefit of the apes being used in the experiment.[48]

According to the Swiss lawyer Antoine Goetschel, once animals are mentioned in the constitution of a state, it becomes easy to bring all the provisions of that state's legal codes regarding animals into agreement, since the validity of all the codes derives from the constitution. Moreover, if the state becomes concerned with the fate of animals, when an abuse occurs, it is enough to apply to the state for redress, and it is no longer necessary in each case to arouse public opinion to counteract cases of the mistreatment of animals.[49] In addition, along with the governmental legal systems, companies can also establish charters in which they voluntarily commit themselves to the proper treatment of animals.

In spite of all these improvements in the legal situation, in many countries the situation remains far from brilliant. For example, the U.S. meat and dairy industries have succeeded in getting enough elected officials on their side to obtain exemptions from the laws protecting animals.

In Jean-Pierre Marguénaud's opinion, "granting animals the status of a legal subject only results in putting in place a juridically technical means capable, in a given case, of providing the protection adjudged necessary for the interests of certain animals." He adds that this does not in the least amount to generalizing the rights of human beings to include animals, since a "legal subject" is not equivalent in status to a "legal person," and so does not suffice to do away with the legal separation between humans and animals.[50] Commenting on this point, Élisabeth de Fontenay writes: "Like the moral person, the animal is therefore a legal person without, however, being a legal subject; and this juridical reality must be brought clearly to the fore so that our debates on the subject can stop being absurd."[51]

The Disparity between Law and Practice

In the opinion of many jurists and ecologists, the constitutional amendment (recognizing animals as sentient beings) is only a symbolic step. Laurence Abeille, a deputy of the French National Assembly, introduced a number of subamendments challenging practices that deny "animal sentience," such as mass breeding, bullfighting, and cockfighting. All these were rejected on the pretext of being "irrelevant." When Jean-Marc Neumann, jurist and vice president of the French Foundation for Animal Rights, Ethics, and Science, was asked what this amendment would really change, he replied: "A few sentences in the civil code, but fundamentally nothing. In the end, with this amendment, animals will still be subjected to the rules governing physical goods. . . . So that will not change our behavior toward animals, which will still be able to be sold, rented, exploited. . . . The most cruel practices, such as the corrida, hunting with dog packs, cock fighting, ritual slaughter, or certain forms of fishing and breeding have not at all been challenged."[52]

What can we do, then, for animals to be really protected, under the law, from the different forms of cruelty of which they are still victims? Neumann has in view a general animal protection law that would harmonize all the different codes that are in force (the penal, rural, and environmental codes). The disparities that exist between the different codes regarding the status of animals basically prevent a systematic application of this amendment. Thus the civil code excludes wild animals from its domain. Wild animals fall under the legislation of the environmental code, which does not recognize their sentience. Moreover, explains Neumann, "the penal code does not officially recognize animals as sentient, but does so only 'implicitly.'" The consequence of this is that a crime committed against an animal is less punished than a simple theft of goods, if it is punished at all. As for bred animals, they are governed by the rural code, which, although it recognized them in 1976 as "sentient animals," considers the fact of their suffering, "as useful because necessary for the nourishment of the population," this jurist explains.[53]

The real question seems to be of a personal and civil nature: "Do we want to continue with the exploitation and suffering of animals, or are we ready to make certain efforts and sacrifices to avoid it?" This is the question that Neumann asks. Legislation is the end product of a raising of consciousness that leads to a spirit of reform, but only rarely to a radical change. This being the case, the legislative development has to be understood in the framework of the slow process of the evolution of collective mentalities. Since it is impossible to upset our lifestyles and our eating habits by decree from one day to the next, we can only proceed in stages by putting in place measures that prevent the most cruel practices against animals. Each one of us is a responsible, and integral, part of this evolutionary societal process that can lead to the protection of animals. Each of us can begin by asking ourselves: "Should I eat my friends or not? Should I continue to be entertained by their pain? Do I want to continue to find relaxation in pulling them out of the water and letting them suffocate to death?"

CONCLUSION

An Appeal to Reason and Human Kindness

In the spring of 2014, I had the opportunity to meet with Ólafur Ragnar Grímsson, the president of Iceland, on the occasion of the Spirit of Humanity forum. He told me that there had not been a single soldier on the island since the closing of the American base in 2006. He also said that the annual death rate due to firearms was only 0.6 per 100,000 inhabitants. Iceland, he told us, is "a country where people trust each other and where you are welcome." And in truth, there was no security control at the entrance to the presidential residence, which you enter just as though it were an ordinary house. There is a lesson here for those who advocate the unregulated sale of firearms and who insist in no uncertain terms, as do many in the United States, that the more the population is armed, the more the conditions of security will prevail.[1]

In exchanging a few words with the president, I went so far as to say that Iceland surely set a good example for the rest of the world, but that the image of a haven of peace presented by the island would certainly be improved if the Icelanders gave up killing hundreds of whales every year. And it is indeed a curious paradox: On the plane that took me to Iceland I watched a documentary that presented Iceland as one of the best places in the world for whale watching, a place that encourages ecological tourism. At the same time, not far from one of the whale-watching zones, the employees of the Hvalur whaling company each summer carry out a large-scale massacre of these same whales.[2] The president made a polite remark, averted his eyes, and turned to talk another guest.

A week later, I was in Chile, where I visited Francisco Varela School, a school named in honor of a great Chilean neuroscientist, a late lamented friend of mine, who founded the Mind and Life Institute, of which I am a member. After touring the classes, I spoke to the three hundred pupils of the school, gathered in a large hall. One of them asked me, "Do you eat meat?" After having told him no, I asked the pupils:

"Are cows your friends?"

"Yes!"

"Are fish your friends?"

"Yes!"

"Are birds your friends?"

"Yes!"

They all demonstrated the same enthusiasm. Then I asked them: "Do you want to eat your friends?"

The answer was a resounding "no" in unison. For the pupils of this institution, which is supposed to be a progressive school, respect for animal life should be taken for granted. However, most of the pupils were not vegetarians, especially because Chile, being a neighbor of Argentina, is one of the countries in the world where meat figures most prominently in the diet.

These two anecdotes demonstrate the inconsistency that exists between our thoughts and deeper feelings, on the one hand, and our behavior on the other. Most of us are fond of animals, but our compassion stops at the edge of our plate. And our egoistic conduct without a doubt backfires on us: as we have seen, industrial mass breeding is one of the major causes of climate change, and regular consumption of meat is harmful to human health. This activity of ours is not only morally debatable, it unreasonable from any point of view.

This unreasonable approach is based on a lack of respect for other life forms, a lack of respect resulting from ignorance, pride, egoism, or ideology. As far as animals are concerned, a lack of respect caused by ignorance consists, in particular, in not recognizing that they feel emotions and are sensitive to pain. It is also a matter of ignoring the continuum that binds all species of animals into one whole. When, as is now the case, there is adequate scientific data on hand to substantiate this, then it becomes a denial of reality if we choose to ignore it.

Lack of respect resulting from pride is imagining that our superiority in certain areas gives us the right of life and death over animals. Lack of respect based on egoism consists in using animals as though they were mere instruments for satisfying our desires or for promoting our financial interests. Finally, lack of respect through ideology is justifying our instrumentalization of animals on the basis of religious dogmas, philosophical theories, or cultural traditions.

Our attitude toward animals calls into question our entire ethical outlook and is evidence of how fragile it is. This ethical outlook of ours is what governs how we behave toward each other. That is why it is essential for us to accord animals an intrinsic value, to have consideration for them and to take account of their legitimate aspirations. If we exclude all nonhuman beings from our ethical system, that system becomes shaky. This is what Milan Kundera clearly tells us: "Mankind's true moral test, its fundamental test (which lies deeply buried from view), consists of its attitude towards those who are at its mercy: animals. And in this respect mankind has suffered a fundamental debacle, a debacle so fundamental that all others stem from it."[3]

As we pointed out in the introduction, we are not at all speaking here about animalizing humans or humanizing animals, but instead about showing respect to both and according to each its own proper value, whatever that may be. It seems that, if we were merely to reach out and extend to animals the golden rule that we usually reserve for humans—do not do to others what you would not have them do to you[4]—both humans and animals would benefit. It is clear, however, that being concerned with the fate of animals does not in the least diminish the need to be concerned with the destiny of humans—quite the contrary: both of these concerns are derived from a sense of altruism and are not, with the exception of a few cases, in direct competition with each other.

So we can do a lot better than we have been doing. Real altruism and compassion should know no bounds. They are not merely tit-for-tat paybacks carried out under the heading of good behavior or because of an idea we have about wanting to value other beings. Compassion relates to all suffering and is directed toward all who suffer. Someone who is moved by genuine compassion is not capable of inflicting suffering on other sentient beings, as Schopenhauer points out in his *On the Basis of Morality:* "Boundless compassion for all living beings is the surest and most certain guarantee of pure moral conduct, and needs no casuistry. Whoever is filled with it will assuredly injure no one, do harm to no one, encroach on no man's rights; he will rather have regard for every one, forgive every one, help every one as far as he can, and all his actions will bear the stamp of justice and loving-kindness."[5]

However, to the extent that there remains a significant number of us who do not feel enough compassion toward animals to give up mistreating them, it is essential for there to be recourse to the legal system, to put in place laws that protect animals. The right to live and not suffer cannot be the exclusive privilege of human beings. When humans attempt to justify their exploitation of animals, all they do is try to perpetuate the law of "might makes right," a right which is morally contestable. As Bertrand Russell put it, "There is no objective reason to believe that the interests of human beings are more important than those of animals. We could destroy animals more easily than they could destroy us: that is the sole firm basis for our claim of superiority."[6]

The enemies of animal advocates take malicious pleasure in presenting them as utopian idealists, animal idolaters who would do better to concern themselves with the innumerable sufferings of humans, as overly sensitive souls who never stop feeling sorry for their cats and dogs, even as fanatics, as stupid as they are dangerous, who do not shrink from flirting with terrorism.[7]

Omnivores do their best to make vegans and vegetarians look ridiculous, especially those who have adopted their diets for moral reasons (they are not subjected to reproach if they do it on their doctor's orders). Two English sociologists made a study of how the British media portrays vegans: 5 percent of media portrayed them positively, 20 percent were neutral, and 75 percent were negative. According to the two sociologists, this negative portrayal "makes it possible to reassure omnivore readers concerning the normality of their ethical choice, and by association, the normality of their personality in contrast to the abnormality of the vegans."[8] This point is confirmed by a U.S. study according to which nearly half of omnivores associated vegetarians with a variety of negative terms: crazy, weird, uptight, strict, opinionated, radical, preachy, self-righteous.[9] The study suggests that this negative approach is explained in large part by "the threat of an anticipated moral reproach" coming from the vegetarians. According to Martin Gibert, "The 'vegephobic' is not afraid of vegetarianism—he is afraid of being judged. If he holds a grudge against vegetarians, it is because they represent a stinging reminder to him of his own cognitive inconsistencies. Without so much as opening his mouth, the vegetarian forces the omnivore to admit that eating animals is a choice."[10]

Most of us would find it revolting to have to slit the throat of an animal every day with our own hands, but we are ready to condone the killing of animals, the abusive treatment they are subject to, as well as the ecological disaster caused by industrial breeding and fishing just because "everybody does it." Renan Larue points out:

> The unanimity of violence somehow reduces the sense of individual responsibility. It helps us to avoid thinking about it too much. The mere presence of a vegetarian tends to disrupt this tacit, unconscious consensus. . . . Up to that point it was neither good nor evil to eat meat—meat-eating stood outside the sphere of morality. But in the presence of a vegetarian or vegan, the carnivore is forced to see that an alternative exists and that thenceforth he can choose between killing or sparing animals, between destroying or preserving nature.[11]

In the face of such prejudices, how is it possible to adopt a realistic attitude that has some chance of changing things? This is what James Serpell, a professor of animal ethics, thinks about the matter:

> It would also, in my view, be unrealistic to imagine that we can hope to achieve global vegetarianism, or a complete end to the economic utilization of animals or the natural environment. Paradise, in this sense, cannot be regained because it never really existed. Nevertheless, it is clear that we cannot go on treating the world and its contents like some gigantic supermarket. Economic, political, or religious ideologies that promote unrestrained exploitation are dangerous. They threaten our survival not only by the irreparable damage they cause, but also by denying, suppressing or corrupting feelings and morality. Fortunately, and thanks largely to our past excesses, ethical arguments based on the principles of empathy and altruism, and economic objectives based on long-term human interests, are, at long last, beginning to converge. We can but hope that out of this union a sane and responsible compromise will emerge.[12]

How have major changes in attitude come about in society, even when those changes at first appeared improbable and unrealistic? How has it happened that things that were completely taken for granted came to be seen as unacceptable? The way it works is that, right at the beginning, a few individuals become aware of a particular situation that is morally indefensible. They come to the conclusion that the status quo cannot be maintained without compromising the ethical values that they respect. At first isolated and ignored, these pioneers end up pooling their efforts and becoming activists who upset habitual outlooks and bring about a revolution in ideas. At that point they tend to be mocked and reviled. But little by little, other people who were shy at first come to believe that the pioneers are right in what they are doing, and they begin to sympathize with their cause. When the number of those in favor of the new approach reaches a critical mass, public opinion begins to swing in their direction. Gandhi summarized this process as follows: "At first they ignore you, then they laugh at you, then they fight you, and then you win." Let us think of the abolition of slavery, of the defense of human rights, of female suffrage, and any number of other breakthroughs.

There are several factors that can facilitate such changes and contribute to cultural evolution. The first of these is the power of ideas. *Satyagraha*, the principle of nonviolent resistance put forward by Gandhi, means "the power of truth" or "insistence on the truth." The second factor is the imitative instinct. The fact is, most human beings are inclined to conform to dominant attitudes, customs, beliefs, and values. Conformity to moral norms is encouraged by the community, and nonconformity draws disapproval. The third is the embarrassment and the feeling of shame that we feel when we persist in defending a moral position that is disavowed by the majority of society. Cultures evolve. In the course of generations, individuals and cultures never cease to influence each other. Individuals who grow up in a new social environment become different just by acquiring new habit patterns that transform their way of being. They then contribute in their turn to the further evolution of their society, and so it goes on.

The abolition of slavery in England is a striking example of this type of turnaround. As the historian and writer Adam Hochschild tells us: "If, early in that year [1787], you had stood on a London street corner and insisted that slavery was morally wrong and should be stopped, nine out of ten listeners would have laughed you off as a crackpot. The tenth might have agreed with you in principle, but assured you that ending slavery was wildly impractical. . . . It was a country in which the great majority of people, from farmhands to bishops, accepted slavery as completely normal."[13] Important economic interests were also in play. However, a minority of abolitionists succeeded in just a few years in winning over to the abolition of slavery a public opinion that had at first been indifferent or often hostile to that idea.

According to Olivier Grenouilleau, author of a number of works on slavery,[14] four principal elements define this practice: (1) the slave is "other"; (2) the slave is a human being possessed by another; (3) the slave is always "useful" to his master; and (4) the slave is a human being whose own life has been suspended. Replace the word "human" with the phrase "mass-bred animal" and it is not difficult to see the comparison—no offense to human beings intended. The fact is, the animals we instrumentalize for their labor, their flesh, their skin, their bones, and other parts of their bodies belong to another species; they are "other." They are also kept by an owner (the owner today being nothing but an industrial system with multiple anonymous faces); they must remain "useful," or they are "reformed" (the euphemism for slaughter); and their own life has been suspended, not with the hope of possible liberation but just until a premature and programmed death.

According to the philosopher of science Thomas Lepeltier, the first task of the abolitionists was to make the British people aware of what lay behind the sugar they were eating, the tobacco they smoked, and the coffee they drank. Ultimately, however, before the general population came to the point of actively opposing slavery, they had to begin to see that this system was a taint on the image they had of themselves. It was not until the moment they recognized that they were implicitly complicit in a system that they saw as shameful that the British people actually opposed it.

Today, at least in the West, not only slavery but also racism, sexism, and homophobia—even though they remain endemic in our societies—are theoretically disapproved by the majority of people. Soon the same could happen, let us hope, to our attitude toward animals. "The idea that it is odious," writes Lepeltier in *La révolution végétarienne* (*The Vegetarian Revolution*), "to see in a sow not a person but a mere mass of pâté has not yet infiltrated all minds, and it has still less begun to influence the eating behavior of the majority of the population. Many people still have difficulty making the connection 'between the nearby and the far away,' that is, between the pleasures of the table and the suffering of the animal, even if, in principle, no one or nearly no one any longer accepts the idea that we ought to make animals suffer for the sake of our culinary pleasures alone. So there is still a way to go before we reach the moment of abolishing the slaughterhouses."

We are all in favor of morality, justice, and kindness. Therefore, there is not one of us who could not tread the path that leads to greater ethical consistency and put an end to the psychological acrobatics and contortions that we put ourselves through constantly in an attempt to reconcile our moral principles with our behavior. It is entirely up to us, as the words of philosopher Martin Gibert make clear: "I like meat. . . . I also like the feel of leather and fur. Nevertheless, I no longer put animal products on my plate or on my shoulders. I no longer condone animal suffering. I am a vegan. It's not that I particularly like animals. . . . I'm a normal type in my relationship to animals. But I am also sensitive to moral arguments. And today these arguments—with regard to animal and environmental ethics—have become too serious for me to set aside veganism with a shrug of the shoulders and a wave of the hand. . . . Veganism is not a dietary program. . . . It is a movement of resistance to the oppression of which the animals we exploit for their meat, their milk, or their fur are the victims. . . . The basic argument is simple. If it is possible to live without inflicting unnecessary suffering on animals, then that's what we ought to do."[15]

According to a study conducted in Australia, the reasons given for continuing to eat meat, in spite of all the arguments, are eating pleasure (78 percent—"I like it, period!"), reluctance to change habitual patterns (58 percent), the idea that humans were made to eat meat (44 percent), the fact that one's family eats it (43 percent), and a lack of information on vegetarian and vegan diets (42 percent).[16]

Excepting populations that cannot survive except through hunting and fishing, it seems to me impossible to put forward a valid reason—based on morality, justice, and kindness or on necessity as opposed to appetite, habit, dogma, ideology, conformism, profit, or lack of information—that justifies eating, clothing oneself with, or seeking entertainment at the price of the suffering and death of other sentient beings.

It is clear that the way we eat and our use of products derived through animal suffering go against the values that are upheld by a society that never ceases to boast of the progress it has made in the realm of human rights, women's rights, the rights of children, and the rights of minorities and the oppressed. How can we see ourselves as manifesting equality, fraternity, and liberty when we subject, exploit, imprison, and massacre our neighbor, whether this neighbor is a person of a different skin color, walks on four legs, is covered with hair, has to live in the water, or has other characteristics we do not have?

Clearly it is time to extend the notion of "neighbor" to other life forms. If we were to understand and feel thoroughly and fully that in truth we and animals are fellow citizens of the world, rather than seeing animals as some subcategory of living beings, we could no longer permit ourselves to treat them as we do. At the dawn of the twentieth century, Émile Zola was already writing: "Could we not begin by coming to an agreement on the love we owe to animals? . . . And that simply in the name of suffering, to kill suffering, the abominable suffering by which nature lives and which humanity should exert itself to reduce as much as possible by means of a continuous struggle, the only struggle in which it would be wise to remain obstinate?"[17]

But certainly there is good news as well. For the past three decades, mobilization in favor of animals has not ceased to increase. This is not the work of a few fanatical "animalists," but the work of sensible people whose empathy and compassion have turned toward animals. It is becoming more and more difficult to pretend to be ignorant of the relationship between the sufferings of the calf and the cutlet on the table. Sympathy for the protection of animals is continuously growing in public opinion.

The number of vegetarians in the world (half a billion today) also continues to grow, especially among young people. At the present time in France there are as many vegetarians (between 1 and 2 million) as there are hunters (around 1.2 million), and the number of the latter on a global scale diminishes each year. The percentage of hunters in the French population has gone from 4.5 percent to 1.5 percent from 1970 to 2014.[18] This percentage is diminishing especially among the young.

The same thing is happening in the United States, where the number of households containing a hunter has gone from 32 percent to 19 percent between 1977 and 2006.[19]

In April of 2014, an amendment to the French civil code was passed that recognized animals as sentient beings, and in this way this recognition was extended to the entire French legal system. The logical march of history seems to favor progressive discrediting of the mass killing of animals. One day, let us hope, an international convention prohibiting zoocide will be promulgated and the vision of H. G. Wells will become a reality: "No meat on the round planet of Utopia. There was a time when there was. But today we no longer tolerate the idea of a slaughterhouse. . . . I still remember my joy when I was a child at the closing of the last slaughterhouse."[20]

A growing number of us no longer are content with a conservative ethic regarding the behavior of humans toward their fellow beings. Many of us now feel that benevolence toward all beings is no longer an optional addendum to our ethics but an essential part of it. It is incumbent upon us to continue to promote the achievement of impartial justice and compassion toward all sentient beings.[21] Kindness is not an obligation, it is the most noble expression of human nature.

Thegchog Chöling
Paro, Bhutan
May 21, 2014

ACKNOWLEDGMENTS

My boundless gratitude goes first of all to my spiritual masters, who have given a direction, a meaning, and a sense of joy to every moment of my existence, and in particular to those who inspired in me the wish to become a vegetarian: Kyabje Kangyur Rinpoche and his sons Pema Wangyal Rinpoche and Jigme Khyentse Rinpoche; as well as to those spiritual masters who opened my heart to altruistic love and compassion, Kyabje Dilgo Khyentse Rinpoche and His Holiness the Fourteenth Dalai Lama.

I am very grateful to the Shining Hope Foundation, which is dedicated to humanitarian, animal, and environmental causes, for the support they provide to a mobile clinic project that cares for forty thousand patients per year in Bihar, India, under the aegis of our humanitarian association Karuna-Shechen. This support has allowed me to devote to the preparation of this book the time that I would otherwise have had to spend in finding the financial resources necessary for the accomplishment of that project.

I thank with all my heart Carisse Busquet and Christian Bruyat for their patient and expert proofreading of the French manuscript and also Raphaële Demandre, Martine Fournier, Caroline Lesire, and Ilios Kotsou, who carefully read through particular chapters and provided me with valuable suggestions. The errors and imperfections that remain are due to my own limitations alone.

I am very thankful to Jacques Sémelin, a prominent specialist in mass violence and a professor at the Institut d'Études Politiques in Paris for having twice read through the chapter called "The Mass Killing of Animals—Genocide versus Zoocide" and having taken the time for a long and impassioned conversation about it; to Norin Chai, head of the veterinary service of the Jardin des Plantes Zoo in Paris, for reading over the pages concerned with zoos and for the information she generously provided me with; to Gérard Busquet for his valuable suggestions and information about India, Hinduism, and Islam; as well as to Francis Wolff, professor at the École Normale Supérieure in

Paris, for having received me and engaged in discussion with me in a spirit of openness and cordiality, in spite of our very different views, on the question of our relationship with animals and about the corrida in particular.

Thanks to Jane Goodall for her inspiration and for the understanding we share, and to Jean-Baptiste Jeangène Vilmer for our exchange of letters and for our common commitment.

Finally, I cannot adequately express my gratitude to my editors Nicole Lattès, my longtime friend and editor, and Guillaume Allary. They attentively read and reread many versions of the manuscript and provided me with kind guidance every step of the way, as well as to the entire team at Allary Éditions, which worked hard to create and promote this book.

Finally, I am deeply grateful to Nikko Odiseos and the entire team at Shambhala Publications for bringing out this English edition of *Plea*. My heartiest thanks go to the editors Dave O'Neal and Breanna Locke for their careful work, and to Sherab Chödzin Kohn for his eloquent translation.

May this *Plea for the Animals* help to lessen the suffering of all sentient beings!

NOTES

INTRODUCTION

1. M. Ricard, *Altruism: The Power of Compassion to Change Yourself and the World* (New York: Little, Brown, 2015).
2. G. Mace et al., "Biodiversity," in *Ecosystems and Human Well-Being: Current State and Trends*, ed. H. Hassan, R. Scholes, and N. Ash (Washington, DC: Island Press, 2005), 79–115; S. Diaz et al., ibid., pp. 297–329.

CHAPTER 1. A BRIEF HISTORY OF THE RELATIONS BETWEEN HUMANS AND ANIMALS

1. D. P. Fry, *Beyond War: The Human Potential for Peace* (New York: Oxford University Press, 2007); L. E. Sponsel, "The Natural History of Peace: A Positive View of Human Nature and Its Potential," in *A Natural History of Peace*, ed. T. A. Gregor (Nashville, TN: Vanderbilt University Press, 1996), 908–12.
2. Alfred Lord Tennyson (1809–1892), *In Memoriam A.H.H.*, 1850.
3. S. C. Strum, *Almost Human: A Journey into the World of Baboons* (Chicago: University of Chicago Press, 2001).
4. J. Clutton-Brock, *Domesticated Animals from Early Times* (London: Heinemann/British Museum [National History], 1981), 34ff; S. Davis, "The Taming of the Few," *New Scientist* 95, no. 1322 (1982), 697–700. Cited by J. Serpell, *In the Company of Animals: A Study of Human-Animal Relationships* (Oxford and New York: B. Blackwell, 1986), 4.
5. Fry, *Beyond War*; D. P. Fry and P. Söderberg, "Lethal Aggression in Mobile Forager Bands and Implications for the Origins of War," *Science* 341, no. 6143 (2013): 270–73. According to anthropologist Jonathan Haas, "Archaeological proof for any form of war on the planet before ten thousand years ago is negligible," J. Haas, "The Origins of War and Ethnic Violence," in *Ancient Warfare: Archaeological Perspectives*, ed. J. Carman and A. Harding (Stroud, UK: Sutton, 1999), 11–24.
6. According to data compiled by the United States Census Bureau, www.census.gov/population/international/data/worldpop/table_history.php.
7. By 2011, half of the forests of the earth had been destroyed, the majority of them during the prior fifty years, and since 1990, half of our tropical forests have disappeared (it is possible that they will have disappeared entirely by forty years from now). E. C. Elli, K. Klein Goldewijk, S. Siebert, D. Lightman, and N. Ramankutty, "Anthropogenic Transformation

of the Biomes, 1700 to 2000," *Global Ecology and Biogeography* 19, no. 5 (2010): 589–606.

8. J. Rockström, W. Steffen, K. Noone, Å. Persson, F. S. Chapin, E. F. Lambin, and H. J. Schellnhuber, "A Safe Operating Space for Humanity," *Nature* 461, no. 7263 (2009): 472–75.

9. Serpell, *In the Company of Animals*, 186.

10. R. Corbey and A. Lanjouw, eds., *The Politics of Species: Reshaping Our Relationships with Other Animals* (Cambridge: Cambridge University Press, 2013).

11. Serpell, *In the Company of Animals*, 142, citing M. Levine, "Prehistoric Art and Ideology," in *Man in Adaptation: The Institutional Framework*, ed. Y. A. Cohen (Chicago: Aldine Transaction, 1971), 3: 426–27.

12. Following D. Lestel, *L'animal est l'avenir de l'homme* [The animal is the future of man] (Paris: Fayard, 2010), Kindle edition, 1111.

13. J. Campbell, *Historical Atlas of World Mythology*, vol. 1, *The Way of Animal Powers* (New York: Times Books Limited, 1984), 81–122.

14. T. Ingold, *Hunters, Pastoralists, and Ranchers: Reindeer Economies and Their Transformations* (Cambridge: Cambridge University Press, 1980), 282. Cited in Serpell, *In the Company of Animals*, 144.

15. M. Fortes, "Totem and Taboo," *Proceedings of the Royal Anthropological Institute of Great Britain and Ireland* (1966): 5–22. Cited in Serpell, *In the Company of Animals*, 144.

16. K. Thomas, *Man and the Natural World: A History of the Modern Sensibility* (New York: Pantheon Books, 1983), 25–30. Cited in Serpell, *In the Company of Animals*, 137.

17. C. Darwin, *Notebook B* [1838], ed. J. van Wyhe, in *Contre la mentaphobie* [Against mentaphobia], trans. D. Chauvet (Lausanne, Switzerland: L'Âge d'Homme, 2014), 13.

18. Serpell, *In the Company of Animals*, 138.

19. A. M. Beck and A. H. Katcher, *Between Pets and People: The Importance of Animal Companionship* (New York: Putnam, 1983), 60; J. C. Berryman, K. Howells, and M. Lloyd-Evans, "Pet Owner Attitudes to Pets and People: A Psychological Study," *Veterinary Record* 117, no. 25–26 (1985): 659–61. Cited in Serpell, *In the Company of Animals*, 63.

20. J. Porcher, *Vivre avec les animaux: Une utopie pour le xxie siècle* [Living with animals: A utopia for the twenty-first century] (Paris: La Découverte, 2011), 99.

21. V. Butler, "Inside the Mind of a Killer," *The Cyberactivist*, August 31, 2003, www.cyberactivist.blogspot.com.

22. E. Fisher, *Women's Creation: Sexual Evolution and the Shaping of Society* (New York: Doubleday, 1979), 190 and 197. Cited in C. Patterson, *Un éternel Treblinka* [Eternal Treblinka] (Paris: Calmann-Lévy, 2008), 32–33.

23. Patterson, *Un éternel Treblinka*, 33.

24. Genesis 1:25–26.

25. Patterson, *Un éternel Treblinka*, 36.

26. *Sefer Hassidim.* Cited in R. Schwartz, "Tza'ar Ba'alei Chayim: Judaism and Compassion for Animals," in *Judaism and Animal Rights: Classical and Contemporary Responses,* ed. Roberta Kalechofsky (Marblehead, MA: Micah Publications, 1992), 61.

27. *Avodah Zorah* 18b.

28. Like Rabbi Bonnie Koppel, who said, "There can be no doubt that the ideal according to the Torah is vegetarianism." This position is also shared by Rami Shapiro and Yitzhak Halevi Herzog, former Chief Rabbi of Israel. See *The Vegetarian Mitzvah* at www.brook.com/jveg. See also É. de Fontenay, *Le silence des bêtes, la philosophie à l'épreuve de l'animalité* [The silence of the beasts: Philosophy facing the challenge of animality] (Paris: Fayard, 1998).

29. Aristotle, *La Politique* [The politics] (Paris: J. Vrin, 1970), 16.

30. Cicero, *Traité des lois* [Treatise on the laws], trans. G. de Plinval (Paris: Les Belles Lettres, 1968), I, 25.

31. Porphyry was the author of "Against the Christians" and "On Abstinence from Animal Food," a long and erudite apology for vegetarianism. This was translated into French by the abbot of Burigny in 1747. In 1761, the abbot sent a copy of it to Voltaire, who in the latter part of his life became an ardent advocate of the animal cause. See Voltaire, *Pensées végétariennes* [Thoughts on vegetarianism], var. ed., notes and postface by Renan Larue (Paris: Fayard/Mille et une nuits, 2014).

32. M. Kundera, *The Unbearable Lightness of Being,* trans. M. H. Heim (New York: Harper Perennial, 1991), 286.

33. Leviticus 19:18.

34. R. Larue, *Le végétarisme et ses ennemis* [Vegetarianism and its enemies] (Paris: Presses Universitaires de France [PUF], 2015), chap. 2.

35. See Mark 5:11–13. The same story is recounted in Matthew and Luke.

36. John 21:1–13.

37. Saint Augustine, *De moribus ecclesiae catholicae. Œuvres,* "La morale chrétienne" (Paris: Desclée de Brouwer, 1949), II, XVII, 59.

38. Patterson, *Un éternel Treblinka,* 43.

39. Aquinas, *Summa Theologica,* ll-ll, q. 25, a.3., quoted by Larue, *Le végétarisme et ses ennemis,* 104–5.

40. A. Bondolfi, *L'homme et l'animal: Dimensions éthiques de leur relation* [Humans and animals: Ethical dimensions of their relationship] (Luxembourg: Éditions Saint-Paul, 1995), 94.

41. According to Boris Cyrulnik in B. Cyrulnik, É. de Fontenay, P. Singer, K. L. Matignon, and D. Rosane, *Les animaux aussi ont des droits* [Animals have rights too] (Paris: Le Seuil, 2013), Kindle edition, 3315.

42. Following the presentation of Michel Baussier, president of the French Order of Veterinarians, in his talk "Le droit de l'animal" [The rights of animals], in a program organized by Ecolo-Ethik in the French senate, February 7, 2014.

43. I am grateful for this information supplied by Renan Larue.

44. R. Descartes, *Discours de la méthode*, V^e partie [Discourse on method, part V] (Paris: J. Vrin, 1987).

45. N. Fontaine, *Mémoires pour servir à l'histoire de Port-Royal*, vol. 2, "Aux dépens de la Compagnie" [Memoirs in service of the history of Port-Royal, vol. 2, "At the expense of the company"] [1736], 52–53. Re-edited by Slatkine, 1970. Original in French, taken here from the English translation cited in L. C. Rosenfield, *From Beast-Machine to Man-Machine: The Theme of Animal Soul in French Letters from Descartes to La Mettrie* (Oxford: Oxford University Press, 1940). Also cited in P. Singer, *La libération animale* [Animal liberation] (Paris: Grasset, 1993), 306.

46. Voltaire, *Dictionnaire philosophique*, article "Bêtes" [Animals] in *Œuvres complètes* (Paris: Arvensa Éditions, 2014), Kindle edition, 74852–74861.

47. Í. Kant, *Leçons d'éthique* [Lecture on ethics] (Paris: Le Livre de poche, 1997), 391.

48. J.-P. Sartre, *Cahiers pour une morale* [Notes for an ethics] (Paris: Gallimard, 1983). Cited in P. Rouget, *La violence de l'humanisme: pourquoi nous faut-il persécuter les animaux?* [The violence of humanism: Why must we persecute animals?] (Paris: Calmann-Lévy, 2014), Kindle edition, 493–94.

49. J. M. Meyer, *Nous sommes des animaux mais on n'est pas des bêtes*, interviews with Patrice de Plunkett (Paris: Presses de la Renaissance, 2007).

50. B. Spinoza, *Éthique* [Ethics] (Éditions Vassade, 2013), Kindle edition, 3991.

51. Serpell, *In the Company of Animals*, 134–35.

52. Philostrate, *Apollonius de Tyane. Sa vie, ses voyages, ses prodiges* (Paris: Les Belles Lettres, 1972), II, 9.

53. Larue, *Le végétarisme et ses ennemis*, chap. 1, "La querelle des anciens."

54. Ibid., 23–24.

55. Ovid, *Métamorphoses*, Book XV, trans. A. S. Kline, http://tikaboo.com/library/Ovid-Metamorphosis.pdf, 735–36.

56. Plutarch, *Sur l'usage des viandes* [On the eating of flesh], in *Traités de morale de Plutarque* [Moral treatises of Plutarch], translated from the Greek by Dominique Ricard (Paris: Lefèvre Éditeur, 1844), t. IV, 563.

57. Ibid., 566.

58. Plutarch, *De esu carnium*, part I, ed. H. Cherniss and W. C. Helmbold, 552–53.

59. J. Meslier, *Mémoire des pensées et sentiments de Jean Meslier* [1719–1729] [Memoir of the thoughts and feelings of Jean Meslier], in *Œuvres complètes* (Paris: Éditions Anthropos, 1970–1972), t. I, 210–18. Cited by J.-B. Jeangène Vilmer, *Anthologie d'éthique animale: apologies des bêtes* [Anthology of animal ethics: In praise of animals] (Paris: PUF, 2011), 51.

60. I thank Renan Larue for this clarification.

61. A. Linzey and D. Cohn-Sherbok, *After Noah: Animals and the Liberation of Theology* (London: Mowbray, 1997), 10. Cited in J. Nakos, *Les Cahiers antispécistes* [Antispecieist Journal], nos. 30–31 (December 2008).

62. H. Primatt, *The Duty of Mercy and Sin of Cruelty to Brute Animals* [1776], ed. R.

Ryder (Fontwell, Sussex: Centaur, 1992). Cited in R. Ryder, p. 66 of the edition of 1989, in J.-B. Jeangène Vilmer, *L'éthique animale* [Animal ethics] (Paris: PUF, 2011), 32.

63. Primatt, *The Duty of Mercy and Sin of Cruelty to Brute Animals*, 8–12, trans. E. Utria. Cited in Jeangène Vilmer, *L'éthique animale*, 88.

64. P. B. Clarke and A. Linzey, eds., "Animal Rights," in *Dictionary of Ethics, Theology and Society* (London and New York: Routledge, 1996). Cited in Jeangène Vilmer, *L'éthique animale*, 110.

65. A. Linzey, *Animal Gospel: Christian Faith as though Animals Mattered* (London: Hodder and Stoughton, 1998). The translation by Estiva Reus appeared in *Les Cahiers antispécistes* [Antispecieist Journal], no. 28 (May 2007).

66. Linzey, *Animal Gospel*, chap. 3.

67. R. Runcie, "Address at the Global Forum of Spiritual and Parliamentary Leaders on Human Survival," April 11, 1988, pp. 13–14.

68. Pope Francis, encyclical *Laudato si*, chap. 2, part V, "A Universal Communion," 27, no. 92.

69. Ibid., chap. 3, part III, "The Crisis and Effects of Modern Anthropocentrism," 130.

70. See Larue, *Le végétarisme et ses ennemis*, 89.

71. Rabbi David Rosen in the *London Gazette*, December 2009 Suppl., 23–31. David Rosen is also the president of the World Conference of Religions for Peace.

72. S. Dresner and S. Siegel, *Jewish Dietary Laws* (New York: United Synagogue Book Service, 1980).

73. *Earthlings* [documentary film], directed by S. Monson (Burbank, CA: Nation Earth, 2006), available at www.earthlings.com.

74. A.-H. B. A. Masri, *Les animaux en Islam* [Animal Welfare in Islam], trans. Sébastien Sarméjeanne, preface and science proofreading by Malek Chebel (Paris: Éditions Droits des Animaux, 2015).

75. A.-H. B. A. Masri, *Animals in Islam* (Petersfield, England: Athene Trust, 1989), 17.

76. Ibid., 21–22.

77. I am indebted to Carisse and Gérard Busquet for informing me of these tales. See R. C. Foltz, *Animals in Islamic Tradition and Cultures* (Oxford, England: Oneworld Publications, 2006), 50–51.

78. Quoted by Malek Chebel in his preface to A.-H. B. A. Masri, *Les animaux en Islam*, 8.

79. Report of the CGAAER, no. 11167, ordered by minister Bruno Lemaire of the Conseil général de l'alimentation, de l'agriculture et des espaces ruraux [General Council for Food, Agriculture and Rural Areas]. Cited by Franz-Olivier Giesbert in F.-O. Giesbert, *L'animal est une personne: Pour nos soeurs et frères les bêtes* [The animal is a person: For our sisters and brothers, the animals] (Paris: Fayard, 2014), 139.

80. K. M. Ganguli, *The Mahâbhârata of Krishna-Dwaipayana Vyasa*, 12 vols. (New Delhi: Munshiram Manohar Lal, 1970).
81. The Laws of Manu, 5.33. Cited in W. Doniger, *The Hindus: An Alternative History* (New York: Penguin/Viking, 2009).
82. Ibid., 48–50.
83. Extracts from the *Tirukkural*, a didactic poem composed about 2,200 years ago in Tamil Nadu in the south of India by the Hindu sage Thiruvalluvar. Following Carisse and Gérard Busquet and the French Wikipedia article "Tirukkural."
84. A. Caron, *No Steak* (Paris: Fayard, 2013), Kindle edition, 4524–4554.
85. M. K. Gandhi, *Autobiographie ou mes expériences de vérité* [The story of my experiments with truth] (Stock, 1982), 230.
86. G. Busquet, *À l'écoute de l'Inde: des mangroves du Bengale aux oasis du Karakoram* [Listening to India: From the mangroves of Bengal to the oases of the Karakoram] (Paris: Transboréal, 2013), 243–50.
87. Drawn from Shabkar, *Les larmes du bodhisattva: Enseignements bouddhistes sur la consommation de chair animale* (Paris: Éditions Padmakara, 2005), 68. English version: Shabkar Tsogdruk Rangdrol, *Food of Bodhisattvas: Buddhist Teachings on Abstaining from Meat*, trans. Padmakara Translation Group (New Delhi: Shechen Publications, 2008).
88. For a detailed account of this subject, see Wulstan Fletcher's introduction to Shabkar, *Food of Bodhisattvas*.
89. Shantideva, *The Way of the Bodhisattva*, trans. Padmakara Translation Group (Boston: Shambhala Publications, 2003), verses 95 and 96, 123.
90. T. Gyatso Dalaï-Lama, *Comme un éclair déchire la nuit* [A flash of lightning in the dark of night] (Paris: Albin Michel, 1992).
91. The plant's growth hormone, auxin, is concentrated on the side of its stem that is in shadow. This side grows faster than the sun-illuminated side, with the result that the stem bends. This phenomenon is accentuated by the weight of the flower. By contrast, as the philosopher Hans Jonas has pointed out, the animal is not only capable of moving but also of perceiving at a distance. In addition, it can react differently in external situations that are the same. See H. Jonas, *The Phenomenon of Life: Toward a Philosophical Biology* (Evanston, IL: Northwestern University Press, 2000). Following Dominique Lestel, in D. Lestel, *Les origines animales de la culture* [The animal origins of culture] (Paris: Flammarion, collection "Champs essais," 2001), 275.
92. Cited in Shabkar, *Food of Bodhisattvas*, 68.
93. Among spiritual masters known for having become vegetarians, there are many masters of the Kadampa order of Tibetan Buddhism, beginning with Atisha, and also masters from all the other schools of Tibetan Buddhism. Examples are Milarepa, Drigung Kyobpa, Taklung Thangpa, Phagmo Drupa, Thogme Zangpo, and Drukpa Kunleg. Masters of more recent periods who have become vegetarians include Jigme Lingpa, Nyagla Pema Dudul, and

Patrul Rinpoche. In our own time, we have Kangyur Rinpoche and his sons Pema Wangyal Rinpoche and Jigme Khyentse Rinpoche, as well as Chatral Rinpoche, who at the present time is 102 years old. In eastern Tibet, there is Khenpo Tsultrim Lodrö, who every year liberates several million animals that have been marked for human consumption.

94. Ashoka's edict number 5 against the killing of animals is engraved on one of the nineteen surviving Ashokan pillars that is now located at Feroze Shah Kotla in Delhi. This pillar was transported from outside the city in the fourteenth century by Firoz Shah Tughlaq to his new capital, Firozabad, of which only a few remnants are found in Old Delhi. Thanks to Gérard Busquet for these precisions.

95. In the present day in Tibet, it is much easier to obtain grains, vegetables, and fruits than formerly. These are now transported by road from China.

96. Flavius, *Vita Apollonii*, éd. G. Olearius (Lipsiae: Fritsch, 1709). Cited in T. Stuart, *The Bloodless Revolution: Radical Vegetarians and the Discovery of India* (London: HarperPress, 2012), Kindle edition, 1133–1139.

97. Stuart, *The Bloodless Revolution*, Kindle edition, 1176.

98. G. Busquet, *Vaches sacrées et chiens maudits* [Sacred cows and cursed dogs], unfinished manuscript.

99. T. Tryon, *Philotheos Physiologus: A Dialogue between an East-Indian Brackmanny or Heathen-Philosopher, and a French Gentleman, in The Way to Health, Long Life and Happiness* Andrew Sowle, Kindle edition, 1683.

100. T. Tryon, *The Knowledge of a Man's Self: Or the Second Part of the Way to Long Life* (London: T. Bennet, 1703), 36. Cited in Stuart, *The Bloodless Revolution*, Kindle edition, 1706–1707.

101. G. P. Marana, *L'espion dans les cours des princes chrétiens, ou, Lettres and mémoires d'un envoyé secret de la porte dans les cours de l'Europe où l'on voit les découvertes qu'il a faites dans toutes les cours où il s'est trouvé, avec une dissertation curieuse de leurs forces, politique et religieuse* [The spy in the courts of the Christian princes, or, Letters and memoirs of a secret emissary of the Turkish court in the courts of Europe, in which it can be seen what discoveries he made in all the courts to which he went, with a dissertation investigating their military forces, politics and religion], ordinarily called *L'espion turc* (Paris: Coda, 2009) or *Letters Writ by a Turkish Spy* (26th ed., vols. 1–7, published 1770), https://archive.org. Cited in Stuart, *The Bloodless Revolution*, Kindle edition, 2725. This novel was the inspiration for the *Lettres persanes* [Persian letters] of Montesquieu.

102. G.-L. Buffon, *Histoire naturelle, IV* (1766), 164–94. Cited in T. Stuart, *The Bloodless Revolution*, Kindle edition, 4267.

103. Stuart, *The Bloodless Revolution*, Kindle edition, 2311.

104. Voltaire, "Il faut prendre un parti" [One must take sides], in *Œuvres complètes* (Paris: Garnier, 1877), t. 28, 534–35.

105. A. Schopenhauer, *Le Fondement de la morale* [On the basis of morality], trans. A. Burdeau (Paris: Aubier Montaigne, 1978), 153–54 and 158.

106. P. B. Shelley, *The Complete Works of Percy Bysshe Shelley*, ed. R. Ingpen and W. E. Peck (*New York:* Gordian Press, 1965). Cited in Stuart, *The Bloodless Revolution*, Kindle edition, 8342.

107. Following Élisabeth de Fontenay in Cyrulnik et al., *Les animaux aussi ont des droits*, Kindle edition, 1849.

108. C. Tudge, *So Shall We Reap: What's Gone Wrong with the World's Food and How to Fix It* (London: Penguin UK, 2004).

109. C. Darwin, *The Descent of Man, and Selection in Relation to Sex* (London: John Murray, 1871), 193.

110. Darwin's notebooks on transmutation of species, Part II, Second notebook [C] (February to July 1838). Edited by G. de Beer. *Bulletin of the British Museum (Natural History), Historical Series* 2, no. 3 (May 1960): 75–118. Beer, Gavin ed. 1960, 196.

111. Darwin, *The Descent of Man, and Selection in Relation to Sex*, 101. French edition: C. Darwin, *La descendance de l'homme et la sélection sexuelle* (Paris: Reinwald, Libraire-éditeur, 1891).

112. For a more detailed presentation of these positions, see Jeangène Vilmer, *Éthique animale*, 35.

113. R. Ryder, "Speciesism Again: The Original Leaflet," *Critical Society* 2 (2010): 1–2.

114. P. Singer, *Animal Liberation: The Definitive Classic of the Animal Movement* (New York: Harper Perennial Modern Classics, 2009). The first edition is dated 1975.

115. The WWF is the World Wildlife Fund; the EIA is the Environmental Investigation Agency.

116. Personal communication.

CHAPTER 2. OUT OF SIGHT, OUT OF MIND

1. A study of middle-class American families done by Alina Pavlakos, in W. Crain, "Animal Suffering: Learning Not to Care and Not to Know," *Encounter* 22, no. 2 (Summer 2009): 2.

2. Following Élisabeth de Fontenay, in B. Cyrulnik, É. de Fontenay, P. Singer, K. L. Matignon, and D. Rosane, *Les animaux aussi ont des droits* [Animals have rights too] (Paris: Le Seuil, 2013), Kindle edition, 2009.

3. M. Ricard, *Plaidoyer pour l'altruisme* [A plea for altruism], *op. cit.*, chap. 29.

4. *Le Bestiaire spirituel de Paul Claudel* [The spiritual bestiary of Paul Claudel] (Lausanne, Switzerland: Mermod, 1949), 16–131; and *Figures et paraboles* [Figures and Parabolas] (Paris: Gallimard, 1936). Cited in Jeangène Vilmer, *op. cit.*, 275.

5. Among those exceptions, let us note, in France, a documentary by Yann Arthus-Bertrand, which was telecast on France 2, and a few other documentaries like *L'adieu au steak* [Goodbye to steak] telecast by Arte, March 27, 2012.

NOTES 283

6. *Earthlings* [documentary film], directed by S. Monson (Burbank, CA: Nation Earth, 2006), available at www.earthlings.com; *Food, Inc.*, directed by R. Kenner (Los Angeles, CA: Magnolia Pictures, 2010); and *LoveMEATender*, directed by M. Coeman (Brussels, Belgium: RTBF, 2011), http://festivalali menterre.be/love-meat-tender/.

7. The advertisement NBC refused to show can be seen on the PETA web site, at http://www.peta.org/blog/nbc-nixes-familyfriendly-thanksgiving-day-parade-ad/. People for the Ethical Treatment of Animals (PETA) is a nonprofit organization that defends the rights of animals. PETA has more than two million followers and sympathizers. It concentrates its efforts on four principal themes: industrial animal breeding, breeding of animals for their fur, animal experimentation, and the use of animals for entertainment. PETA also critically addresses issues such as fishing, the massacring of animals considered as pests, the abusive chaining of dogs, cockfighting, bullfighting, and the eating of meat.

8. A. Caron, *No Steak* (Paris: Fayard, 2013), Kindle edition, 1753.

9. É. de Fontenay, *Sans offenser le genre humain: Réflexions sur la cause animale* [No offense to the human species: Reflections on the animal cause] (Paris: Albin Michel, 2008), 205.

10. Following P. Singer, *Animal Liberation: The Definitive Classic of the Animal Movement* (New York: Harper Perennial Modern Classics, 2009), 328.

11. J. Porcher, "Élevage industriel: penser l'impensable?" [Industrial breeding: Thinking the unthinkable?], *Travailler*, no. 14 (2005): 9–20; J. Porcher, *Vivre avec les animaux: une utopie pour le xxie siècle* [Living with animals: A utopia for the twenty-first century] (Paris: La Découverte, 2011), chap. 3.

12. Cf. J. S. Foer, *Eating Animals* (New York: Little, Brown, 2009), EPUB 54, 133.

13. The *Washington Times*, October 22, 1987. Cited in Singer, *Animal Liberation*, 173.

14. "Frank, are you telling the truth about your chickens?" The *New York Times*, October 20, 1989.

15. J.-F. Nordmann, "Des limites et des illusions des éthiques animales" [Limits and illusions of animal ethics], in Jeangène Vilmer, *op. cit.*, pp. 399–404.

16. S. Coe *Dead Meat.* (New York: Four Walls Eight Windows, 1996).

17. M. Joy, *Why We Love Dogs, Eat Pigs and Wear Cows: An Introduction to Carnism* (San Francisco: Conari Press, 2010), 11.

18. One Voice, "Le commerce de la viande de chien en Chine: une vérité choquante qui n'honore pas les hôtes des prochains Jeux olympiques" [The dog meat business in China: A shocking truth that is no credit to the hosts of the next Olympic games], January 2008. Cited in Caron, *No steak*.

19. A. Bandura, C. Barbaranelli, G. V. Caprara, and C. Pastorelli, "Mechanisms of Moral Disengagement in the Exercise of Moral Agency," *Journal of Personality and Social Psychology* 71, no. 2: 1996.

20. M. Gibert, *Voir son steak comme un animal mort: Véganisme et psychologie morale.* (Montreal, Canada: Lux Éditeur, 2015), 13–14.

21. Cyrulnik et al., *Les animaux aussi ont des droits,* Kindle edition, 1641.

22. Porcher, *Vivre avec les animaux,* 82.

23. Following A. Heim, *Intelligence and Personality* (Harmondsworth, England: Pelican, 1971), 150. Cited in Singer, *Animal Liberation,* 94.

24. M. Midgley, *Animals and Why They Matter* (Athens: University of Georgia Press, 1984), 4.

25. Joan Dunayer, author of *Speciesism* (Derwood, MD: Ryce, 2004), in an interview broadcast on the BBC as part of a program directed by Victor Schonfeld: *One Planet,* "Animals and Us," December 31, 2009.

26. G. Chapouthier, *Les droits de l'animal* [Animal rights] (Paris: Presses Universitaires Francaise, 1992), 68–71.

27. B. Luke, "Justice, Caring and Animal Liberation," *The Feminist Care Tradition in Animal Ethics: A Reader,* 125–52, in J. Donovan and C. J. Adams, *Beyond Animal Rights: A Feminist Caring Ethic for the Treatment of Animals* (New York: Continuum, 1996). Cited in Jeangène Vilmer, *op. cit.,* 95.

28. J.-C. Bailly, *Le versant animal* [The animal side] (Paris: Bayard, 2007).

29. Two months after having been put online, this video had been viewed more than three million times in its original Portuguese version. In Brazil, where only a very small percentage of the population has adopted a vegetarian diet, this video aroused vigorous debates on the subject of vegetarianism and the way we treat animals generally.

30. M. Yourcenar, *The Abyss,* 9th ed., trans. Grace Frick (New York: Farrar, Straus, and Giroux, 1997), 190.

CHAPTER 3. EVERYBODY LOSES

1. This chapter is an expanded and updated version of chapter 34, "Un retour de flamme" [A backlash] from my book, *Plaidoyer pour l'altruisme* [A Plea for Altruism], *op. cit.*

2. According to a study of seventy countries published by the ILO (International Labor Organization) under the auspices of the United Nations, since the beginning of the 1990s, the inequality gap with regard to revenue has continued to increase in most regions of the world.

3. GIEC is the Groupe d'experts intergouvernemental sur l'évolution du climat des Nations unies (International Panel on Climate Change, or IPCC); FAO is the Food and Agriculture Organization.

4. The reference here is to emissions connected with construction (i.e., utilization of natural resources and the energy output required for that) as well as emissions from using electricity and operating heating systems, and so forth, in public, industrial, and private buildings.

5. M. E. Ensminger, *Animal Science* (Saddle River, NJ:Prentice Hall, 1990).

NOTES 285

6. J. Diamond, *Collapse: How Societies Choose to Fail or Succeed* (New York: Viking, 2005).
7. J. Rockström, W. Steffen, K. Noone, Å. Persson, F. S. Chapin, E. F. Lambin, H. J. Schellnhuber et al., "A Safe Operating Space for Humanity," *Nature* 461, no. 7263 (2009), 472–75. These researchers identified nine principal planetary "limits" that are related to climate change: the level of reduction of the ozone layer, the extent of land use (for agriculture, animal breeding, forest industries), use of fresh water, the level of loss of biodiversity, acidification of the oceans, entry of nitrogen and phosphorus into the biosphere and the oceans, the level of aerosols in the atmosphere, and levels of chemical pollution.
8. According to the report of the Millennium Ecosystem Assessment (MEA), published under the auspices of the United Nations.
9. P. Sukhdev, preface to the work of A. Wijkman and J. Rockström, *Bankrupting Nature: Denying Our Planetary Boundaries* (New York: Routledge, 2012). Sukhdev is the founder of the 2020 Corporation, an organization dedicated to environmentally responsible economic practices.
10. According to the Worldwatch Institute.
11. *Amazon Cattle Footprint*, Greenpeace, 2009. More than 200 million hectares of these forests have been destroyed since 1950 mainly to make space for cow pastures or cattle ranches. D. Kaimowitz, *Livestock and Deforestation: Central America in the 1980s and 1990s: A Policy Perspective* (Jakarta, Indonesia: Center for International Forest Research [CIFOR], 1996); D. Kaimowitz, B. Mertens, S. Wunder, and P. Pacheco, *Hamburger Connection Fuels Amazon Destruction* (Bogor, Indonesia: CIFOR, 2004).
12. J. Rifkin, *La troisième révolution industrielle* [The third industrial revolution] (Paris: Éditions Les Liens qui Libèrent, 2012). In F. M. Lappé, *Diet for a Small Planet* (New York: Ballantine Books, 1971), 4–11, Frances Moore Lappé points out that an acre of grain provides five times more protein than the same acre used to produce meat; an acre of legumes provides ten times more; and an acre of leafy vegetables fifteen times more. See also J. Doyle, *Altered Harvest: Agriculture, Genetics and the Fate of the World's Food Supply* (New York: Viking Press, 1985); and M.-M. Robin, *Les moissons du futur: Comment l'agroécologie peut nourrir le monde* [Future harvests: How agro-ecology can feed the world] (Paris: La Découverte, 2012).
13. B. Parmentier, *Nourrir l'humanité: les grands problèmes de l'agriculture mondiale au xxie siècle* [Feeding humanity: The great problems of world agriculture in the twenty-first century] (Paris: La Découverte, 2009), 38. Cited in A. Caron, *No steak* (Paris: Fayard, 2013), Kindle edition, 5168. The yield would be even smaller if this same acre were used to produce red meat.
14. J. S. Foer, *Faut-il manger les animaux?* [Eating animals], trans. G. Berton and R. Clarinard (Paris: Le Seuil, collection "Points," 2012), 265 and note 105. This calculation is from governmental and American university sources. According to figures provided by Aymeric Caron, it takes between 3 and 4 vegetable-

based calories to produce 1 calorie of chicken, between 5 and 7 vegetable calories to produce 1 calorie of pork, and between 9 and 11 vegetable calories to produce 1 calorie of beef or lamb. Caron, *No Steak*, Kindle edition, 558.

15. Lappé, *Diet for a Small Planet*, 4–11.

16. According to Worldwatch Institute, an organization for basic research established in the United States. One of their current projects is comparative analysis of various ecologically sustainable agricultural innovations intended to reduce poverty and hunger. For example, more than 90 percent of the 225 million tons of soy harvested in the world serves as feed for animal breeding operations. If all the grain earmarked to feed American livestock was consumed directly, it could feed 800 million humans. D. Pimentel, S. Williamson, C. E. Alexander, O. Gonzalez-Pagan, C. Kontak, and S. E. Mulkey, "Reducing Energy Inputs in the U.S. Food System," *Human Ecology* 36, no. 4 (2008): 459–71.

17. "Compassion in World Farming." Cited in M. Jolicoeur, AHIMSA, 2004.

18. According to the U. S. Department of Agriculture, Foreign Agricultural Service (USDA-FAS), 1991.

19. Action contre la Faim [Action Against Hunger]. According to the FAO, the number of undernourished people in the world reached 925 million in 2010. This was a nearly 9 percent increase over the average for 2006–2008. The Programme alimentaire mondial (PAM, World Food Program) gives the same figure. Cited in Caron, *No Steak*, 494, and Kindle edition, 5151–5153.

20. J. Porcher, www.agrobiosciences.org/article.php3?id_article=1096, September 2004. Cited in Caron, *No Steak*, Kindle edition, 543.

21. Relationship between the consumption of meat (in kilograms per person) and wealth has been demonstrated and graphed by PNB, Partners for a New Beginning.

22. A. J. McMichael, J. W. Powles, C. D. Butler, and R. Uauy, "Food, Livestock Production, Energy, Climate Change, and Health," *The Lancet* 370, no. 9594 (2007): 1253–63.

23. FAO, *L'ombre portée de l'élevage: Impacts environnementaux et options pour atténuation* [The shadow cast by animal breeding: Environmental impacts and options for attenuation] (Rome: FAO, 2006); FAO, *Comment nourrir le monde en 2050* [How to feed the world in 2050], 2009.

24. H. Herzog, *Some We Love, Some We Hate, Some We Eat: Why It's So Hard to Think Straight about Animals* (New York: Harper Collins, 2010), 192. Cited in Caron, *No Steak*, Kindle edition, 5140.

25. Ray, "Tendances de la Chine en matière de production et de consommation de viande" [Chinese tendencies regarding the production and consumption of meat], on the website of La Gestion agricole du Canada [Farm Management Canada]. Cited in A. Caron, *No Steak*, Kindle edition, 5144.

26. FAO, *L'ombre portée de l'élevage*, and "World Agriculture: Towards 2015–2030" (Rome: FAO, 2002).

27. É. Lambin, *Une écologie du bonheur* [An ecology of happiness] (Paris: Le Pommier, 2009), 70.

28. Lappé, *Diet for a Small Planet*, 11–12, 21.

29. FAO, *L'ombre portée de l'élevage*.

30. M.V. Dompka, K. M. Krchnak, and N.Thorne, "Summary of Experts' Meeting on Human Population and Freshwater Resources," in *Human Population and Freshwater Resources: U.S. Cases and International Perspective*, ed. Karen Krchnak (New Haven, CT: Yale University, 2002).

31. G. Borgström, *Harvesting the Earth* (New York: Abelard-Schuman, 1973), 64–65. According to other estimates provided by the CNRS (Centre national de la Recherche Scientifique), it takes approximately 1 ton of water to grow a kilogram of grain. If you take into account the amount of water necessary to grow the grain fed to animals, the water that they drink, and the water it takes to maintain them, in a kilo of chicken there are 4 tons of virtual water; in a kilo of pork, 6 tons; in a kilo of lamb, 9 tons; and in a kilo of beef, 15.5 tons. CNRS, www.cnrs.fr/cw/dossiers/doseau/decouv/usages/consoDom.html. Cited in A. Caron, *No Steak*, Kindle edition, 5178–5180.

32. "The Browning of America," *Newsweek*, February 22, 1981, 26. Cited in J. Robbins, *Se nourrir sans faire souffrir* [Eating without causing suffering] (Montréal, Canada: Alain Stanke, 1991), 420. For scientific publications on this subject, see A. Y. Hoekstra and P. Q. Hung, "Virtual Water Trade: A Quantification of Virtual Water Flows between Nations in Relation to International Crop Trade," in *Virtual Water Trade: Proceedings of the International Expert Meeting on Virtual Water Trade [Value of Water Research Report Series 11]* (Delft, The Netherlands: UNESCO-IHE, 2002), 166; A. K. Chapagain and A. Y. Hoekstra, *Virtual Water Flows between Nations in Relation to Trade in Livestock and Livestock Products* (Delft, The Netherlands: UNESCO-IHE, 2003); D. Zimmer and D. Renault, "Virtual Water in Food Production and Global Trade: Review of Methodological Issues and Preliminary Results," in *Virtual Water Trade: Proceedings of the International Expert Meeting on Virtual Water Trade [Value of Water-Research Rapport Series]* (Delft, The Netherlands: UNESCO-IHE, 2003), 93–109; T. Oki, M. Sato, A. Kawamura, M. Miyake, S. Kanae, and K. Musiake, "Virtual Water Trade to Japan and in the World" in A.Y. Hoekstra, *Virtual Water Trade: Proceedings of the International Expert Meeting on Virtual Water Trade [Value of Water Research Report Series]* (Delft, The Netherlands: UNESCO-IHE, 2003).

33. Caron, *No Steak*, Kindle edition, 633.

34. M. W. Rosegrant and S. Meijer, "Appropriate Food Policies and Investments Could Reduce Child Malnutrition by 43% in 2020," *The Journal of Nutrition* 132, no. 11 (2002): 3437S–3440S.

35. According to the World Bank and the McKinsey Global Institute (2011), *Natural Resources*, www.mckinsey.com/mgi/our-research/natural_resources.

36. International Food Policy Research Institute and the United Nations Committee on the Environment.

37. J.-M. Jancovici, *L'avenir climatique: Quel temps ferons-nous?* [The future of the climate: What kind of weather will we create?] (Paris: Le Seuil, 2005).

38. This is the figure given in the last estimate produced by the FAO in *Tackling Climate Change through Livestock* (Rome: FAO, October 2013). This is the most complete report that has been produced thus far on greenhouse gas emissions in connection with animal breeding. The breeding of cows accounts for two-thirds of these emissions. The figure of 14.5 percent is the result of an analysis that includes the complete life cycle of this process; that is, it includes carbon dioxide emissions resulting from deforestation undertaken in support of breeding operations, production and conditioning of feed products for animal breeding, and so forth. However, the same method was not applied to transport. Another study carried out by researchers from Cambridge University, the National University of Australia, and other institutions states that the figure should be in the area of 17 percent (McMichael et al., "Food, Livestock Production, Energy, Climate Change, and Health"). Those who reject this figure put forward the level of 4 percent given by the IPCC (Intergovernmental Panel on Climate Change), but in this case only direct emissions were measured, and the entire life cycle of breeding operations was not taken into account. It is important to consider this entire life cycle, because indirect emissions produced by livestock constitute a significant proportion of overall emissions.

39. www.conservation-nature.fr/article2.php?id=105.

40. R. Desjardins, D. Worth, X. Vergé, D. Maxime, J. Dyer, and D. Cerkowniak, "Carbon Footprint of Beef Cattle," *Sustainability* 4, no. 12 (2012): 3279–301.

41. FAO, *L'ombre portée de l'élevage*, 125.

42. P. Scarborough et al., "Dietary Greenhouse Gas Emissions of Meat-Eaters, Fish-Eaters, Vegetarians and Vegans in the UK," *Climatic Change* 125, no. 2 (2014): 179–92. Cited in M. Gibert, *Voir son steak comme un animal mort: Véganisme et psychologie morale* (Montreal, Canada: Lux Éditeur, 2015), 85.

43. F. Hedenus, S. Wirsenius, and D. J. A. Johansson, "The Importance of Reduced Meat and Dairy Consumption for Meeting Stringent Climate Change Targets," *Climatic Change* 124 (2014): 79–91.

44. According to the Worldwatch Institute.

45. U.S. Secretary for the Environment and General Accounting Office (GAO). Cited in Foer, *Faut-il manger les animaux?*

46. These amounts can reach 200 to 1,000 kilograms of nitrogen per hectare per year. H. Steinfeld, C. De Haan, and H. Blackburn, *Livestock-Environment Interactions: Issues and Options [Report of the Commission Directorate General for Development]* (Fressingfield, UK: WREN Media, 1997).

47. C. A. Narrod, R. D. Reynnells, and H. Wells, *Potential Options for Poultry Waste Utilization: A Focus on the Delmarva Peninsula* (Washington, D.C.: U.S. Environmental Protection Agency [EPA], 1993).

48. See the data and reports supplied by the Bloom Association, www.bloomas sociation.org.

49. D. Pauly, D. Belhabib, R. Blomeyer, W. W. W. L. Cheung, A. M. Cisneros-Montemayor, D. Copeland, and D. Zeller, "China's Distant-Water Fisheries in the 21st Century," *Fish and Fisheries* 15, no. 3 (2014): 474–88.

50. According to the FAO.

51. Foer, *Eating Animals, op. cit.*, p. 66. Environmental Justice Foundation Charitable Trust, *Squandering the Seas: How Shrimp Trawling Is Threatening Ecological Integrity and Food Security around the World* (London: Environmental Justice Foundation, 2003).

52. EPIC (European Prospective Investigation into Cancer and Nutrition). Report prepared under the supervision of Elio Riboli (2005). Another study that appeared in the *Archives of Internal Medicine* based on a sample of 500,000 individuals shows 11 percent of (premature) deaths among men and 16 percent among women can be prevented by reduction of consumption of red meat. R. Sinha, A. J. Cross, B. I. Graubard, M. F. Leitzmann, and A. Schatzkin, "Meat Intake and Mortality: A Prospective Study of Over Half a Million People," *Archives of Internal Medicine* 169, no. 6 (2009): 562.

53. Lambin, *Une écologie du bonheur*, 78.

54. A. Pan, Q. Sun, A. M. Bernstein, M. B. Schulze, J. E. Manson, M. J. Stampfer, and F. B. Hu, "Red Meat Consumption and Mortality: Results from 2 Prospective Cohort Studies," *Archives of Internal Medicine* 172, no. 7 (2012): 555. These analyses take into account risk factors due to chronic ailments, age, body mass indices, physical activity, family history of cardiac disease, and major cancers.

55. R. Haque, P. C. Kearney, and V. H. Freed, "Dynamics of Pesticides in Aquatic Environments," in *Pesticides in Aquatic Environments*, ed. M. A. Q. Khan (Plenum Press, 1977), 39–52. H. Ellgehausen, J. A. Guth, and H. O. Esser, "Factors Determining the Bioaccumulation Potential of Pesticides in the Individual Compartments of Aquatic Food Chains," *Ecotoxicology and Environmental Safety* 4, no. 2 (1980): 134–57.

56. Lambin, *Une écologie du bonheur*, 80.

57. P. Scarborough, P. N. Appleby, A. Mizdrak, A. D. Briggs, R. C. Travis, K. E. Bradbury, and T. J. Key, "Dietary Greenhouse Gas Emissions of Meat-Eaters, Fish-Eaters, Vegetarians and Vegans in the UK," *Climatic Change* 125, no. 2 (2014): 179–92.

58. www.ncbi.nlm.nih.gov/pmc/articles/PMC3662288. Cited in Gibert, *Voir son steak comme un animal mort*, 126.

59. Following Caron, *No Steak*, Kindle edition.

60. Estimate of the Association végétarienne de France [Vegetarian Association of France] dated October 2011.

61. FAO, www.fao.org/docrep/004/y1669f/y1669f09.htm. Cited in Caron, *No Steak*, 205.

62. The Hindu-CNN-IBN State of Nation Survey, 2006.

63. According to the BBC report, "Belgian City Plans *Veggie* Days," May 12, 2009.

64. C. Lévi-Strauss, "La leçon de sagesse des vaches folles" [The wise lesson of mad cows], *Études rurales* (2001), http://etudesrurales.revues.org/27.

65. http://phys.org/news/2011-01-climate-tax-meat-results-greenhouse.html. Cited in Caron, *No Steak*, Kindle edition, 5180.

66. Also called the IPCC, Intergovernmental Panel on Climate Change.

67. Interview in the *Telegraph*, September 7, 2008.

68. See Hedenus et al., "The Importance of Reduced Meat and Dairy Consumption for Meeting Stringent Climate Change Targets."

69. Ibid.

CHAPTER 4. THE REAL FACE OF
INDUSTRIAL ANIMAL BREEDING

1. This chapter is an augmented and updated version of Chapter 23, "L'industrialisation des animaux, une aberration morale" [Industrialization of animals, a moral aberration] from my book *Plaidoyer pour l'altruisme* [A plea for altruism], *op. cit.*

2. Jane Goodall in a conversation with the author in Brisbane, Australia, June 2011.

3. U. Sinclair, *The Jungle* (San Diego, CA: Icon Classics, 2005), 42.

4. According to the statistical division of the FAO; see http://faostat.fao.org.

5. M. Joy, *Why We Love Dogs, Eat Pigs, and Wear Cows: An Introduction to Carnism* (San Francisco: Conari Press, 2010), 27. Joy speaks of going back and forth between the earth and the moon four times, which is the equivalent of going around the earth eighty times.

6. R. Jussiau, L. Montméas, and J.-C. Parot, *L'Élevage en France: 10000 ans d'histoire* [Animal breeding in France: Ten thousand years of history] (Dijon, France: Éducagri Éditions, 1999). Cited in F. Nicolino, *Bidoche: l'industrie de la viande menace le monde* [The meat industry is a threat to the world] (Paris: Les Liens qui Libèrent, 2009).

7. *National Hog Farmer*, March 1978, 27. Cited in P. Singer, *Animal Liberation: The Definitive Classic of the Animal Movement* (New York: Harper Perennial Modern Classics, 2009), 126.

8. *Poultry Tribune*, November 1986. Cited in Singer, *Animal Liberation*, 174.

9. The life expectancy of a cow and of a pig is twenty years. Calves are slaughtered at the age of three years, dairy cows are "reformed" (i.e., slaughtered) at around six years, and the pigs at six months. The life expectancy of a chicken is about seven years in normal life conditions, but it is slaughtered at six weeks. This applies in France to about one billion animals.

10. Sinclair, *The Jungle*, 36–38.

11. D. Cantor, Responsible Policies for Animals, Inc. (RPA), www.rpaforall.org.

Cited in C. Patterson, *Un éternel Treblinka* [Eternal Treblinka] (Paris: Calmann-Lévy, 2008), 114.

12. J.-S. Foer, *Faut-il manger les animaux?* [Eating animals] (Paris: Le Seuil, collection "Points," 2012).

13. G. A. Eisnitz, *Slaughterhouse: The Shocking Story of Greed, Neglect, and Inhumane Treatment inside the U.S. Meat Industry* (Amherst, NY: Prometheus, 1997), 181. Cited in Patterson, *Un éternel Treblinka*, 166.

14. Following Singer, *Animal Liberation*, 163.

15. Foer, *Faut-il manger les animaux?*, 240.

16. de Fontenay, *Sans offenser le genre humain*, 206. See also F. Burgat, *L'animal dans les pratiques de consommation* [The animal and our eating habits] (Paris: PUF, 1998).

17. S. Coe, *Dead Meat* (New York: Four Walls Eight Windows, 1996).

18. J.-L. Daub, *Ces bêtes qu'on abat: Journal d'un enquêteur dans les abattoirs français* [The animals that we slaughter: Journal of an investigator in the French slaughterhouses] (Paris: l'Harmattan, 2009), 28.

19. Coe, *Dead Meat*. The descriptions from Coe's book are a synopsis of the original text, pp. 111–33, made with the help of extracts given in Patterson, *Un éternel Treblinka*, 106–8.

20. Eisnitz, *Slaughterhouse*, 182.

21. Coe, *Dead Meat*, 120.

22. G. Carpenter et al., "Effect of Internal Air Filtration on the Performance of Broilers and the Aerial Concentrations of Dust and Bacteria," *British Poultry Journal* 27 (1986): 471–80. Cited in Singer, *Animal Liberation*, 172.

23. R. Bedichek, *Adventures with a Texas Naturalist* (Austin: University of Texas Press, 1961). Cited in R. Harrison, *Animal Machines: The New Factory Farming Industry* [1st edition, 1964] (Boston: CABI Publishing, 2013), 154.

24. J. Breward and M. Gentle, "Neuroma Formation and Abnormal Afferent Nerve Discharges after Partial Beak Amputation (Beak Trimming) in Poultry," *Experienta* 41, no. 9 (1985): 1132–34.

25. *National Geographic Magazine*, February 1970. Cited in Singer, *Animal Liberation*, 177.

26. Foer, *Faut-il manger les animaux?*, 176.

27. J. S. Foer, *Eating Animals* (New York: Little, Brown, 2009), EPUB 39.

28. "Dehorning, Castrating, Branding, Vaccinating Cattle," publication no. 384 of the Mississippi State University Extension Service, in collaboration with the USDA. See also USDA, "Beef Cattle: Dehorning, Castrating, Branding and Marking," *Farmers' Bulletin* no. 2141, September 1972, in Singer, *Animal Liberation*, 225.

29. J. Porcher, "Histoire contemporaine d'un cochon sans histoire" [Contemporary history of a pig with no history], *Revue du M.A.U.S.S.*, no. 1 (2004): 397–407.

30. Foer, *Eating Animals*, EPUB 142.
31. *Stall Street Journal*, November 1973.
32. Ibid., April 1973.
33. Foer, *Eating Animals*, EPUB 170.
34. Ibid, EPUB 174.
35. Cited in A. Civard-Racinais, *Dictionnaire horrifié de la souffrance animale* [The horrified dictionary of animal suffering] (Paris: Fayard, 2010), Kindle edition, 1230.
36. V. Butler, "Inside the Mind of a Killer," *The Cyberactivist*, August 31, 2003, www.cyberactivist.blogspot.com.
37. See M. Ricard, "The Natural Repugnance to Kill," chap. 29 in *Altruism: The Power of Compassion to Change Yourself and the World* (New York: Little, Brown, 2015).
38. *Les Cahiers antispécistes* [Antispeciesist notebooks], no. 21 (February 2002). Cited in B. Cyrulnik, É. de Fontenay, P. Singer, K. L. Matignon, and D. Rosane, *Les animaux aussi ont des droits* [Animals have rights too] (Paris: Le Seuil, 2013), Kindle edition, 3135–39.
39. *A Shocking Look Inside Chinese Fur Farms*, a documentary made by Mark Rissi for Swiss Animals Protection/EAST International, which can be seen on the PETA website, www.peta.org/issues/animals-used-for-clothing /chinese-fur-industry.aspx.
40. Figures cited in A. Caron, *No steak* (Paris: Fayard, 2013), Kindle edition, 1392.
41. Daub, *Ces bêtes qu'on abat*, 27.
42. Ibid., 23.
43. A. Mood and P. Brooke, *Estimating the Number of Fish Caught in Global Fishing Each Year* (fishcount.org.uk/published/std/fishcountstudy.pdf), July 2010. These authors made use of statistics published by the FAO regarding the tonnage of annual catches for each species and calculated the number of fish by estimating the respective average weight of fish of the various species included in the study.
44. Foer, *Eating Animals*, EPUB 2366–2367.
45. This is one of Porcher's themes in *Vivre avec les animaux: une utopie pour le xxie siècle* [Living with animals: A utopia for the twenty-first century] (Paris: La Découverte, 2011).
46. T. Lepeltier, *La révolution végétarienne* [The vegetarian revolution] (Auxerre, France: Éditions Sciences Humaines, 2013), 74–75.
47. Porcher, *Vivre avec les animaux*, 116.
48. D. Chauvet, *La volonté des animaux* [The will of animals] (Gagny, France: Droits des animaux, 2008), version revised and annotated by the author, reprinted in *Les Cahiers antispécistes* [Antispeciesist notebooks], nos. 30–31 (December 2008).
49. See the websites of PETA, One Voice, L214, and many others, as well as the documentary *Earthlings*, available at www.earthlings.com.

50. G. Cazes-Valette, *Le rapport à la viande chez le mangeur français contemporain* [Relationship of the contemporary French eater to meat] (Groupe ESC-Toulouse/CCIT, October 2003–November 2004), 345. Available at www.esc -toulouse.fr. Cited by E. Reus and A. Comiti, *Les Cahiers antispécistes*, no. 29 (February 2008).

51. E. Wiesel, acceptance speech for the Nobel Peace Prize, December 10, 1986.

CHAPTER 5. SORRY EXCUSES

1. J.-J. Rousseau, *Discours sur l'origine et les fondements de l'inégalité parmi les hommes* [Discourse on the origin and foundations of inequality among men] (Paris: Aubier Montaigne, 1973), 59.
2. H. Sidgwick, "The Establishment of Ethical First Principles" [1879], *Mind*, no. 13: 106–11.
3. Shantideva, *Bodhicaryâvatâra: La marche vers l'éveil* [The way of the bodhisattva] (Padmakara, 2008).
4. T. Regan, "The Burden of Complicity," preface to S. Coe, *Dead Meat* (New York: Four Walls Eight Windows, 1996). Tom Regan is a professor of moral philosophy at North Carolina State University at Raleigh.
5. P. Singer, *Animal Liberation* (New York: Ecco, 2002), 8.
6. J. Bentham, *An Introduction to the Principles of Morals and Legislation* (Clarendon Press, 1879), XVII, § I, IV, note 1, 311.
7. H. Lautard, *Zoophilie ou sympathie envers les animaux: Psychologie du chien, du chat, du cheval* [Zoophilia or sympathy for animals: The psychology of the dog, the cat, the horse] (Paris: Société française d'imprimerie et de librairie, 1909), 7–10. Cited in J.-B. Jeangène Vilmer, *Anthologie d'éthique animale: apologies des bêtes* [Anthology of animal ethics: In praise of animals] (Paris: PUF, 2011), 234.
8. Luc Ferry, *Le Figaro*, November 6, 2014.
9. Massimo Filippi et al., "The Brain Functional Networks Associated to Human and Animal Suffering Differ among Omnivores, Vegetarians and Vegans," *PLoS ONE* 5, no. 5 (2010). Cited in M. Gibert, *Voir son steak comme un animal mort: Véganisme et psychologie morale* (Montreal, Canada: Lux Éditeur, 2015), 181–82.
10. B. Preylo et H. Arikawa, "Comparison of Vegetarians and Non-Vegetarians on Pet Attitude and Empathy," *Anthrozoos* 21, no. 4 (2008): 387–95; T. Signal and N. Taylor, "Empathy and Attitudes to Animals," *Anthrozoos* 18, no. 1 (2005): 18–27. Cited in Gibert, *Voir son steak comme un animal mort*, 181–82.
11. F. Burgat and J.-P. Marguénaud, "Les animaux ont-ils des droits?" [Do animals have rights?], *Le Monde*, July 15, 2010.
12. J.-L. Daub, *Ces bêtes qu'on abat: Journal d'un enquêteur dans les abattoirs français* [The animals that we slaughter: Journal of an investigator in the French slaughterhouses] (Paris: l'Harmattan, 2009), 30–31.
13. Singer, *Animal Liberation*, 220–21.

14. R. Descartes, *Discours de la méthode*, V^e partie [Discourse on method, part V] (Paris: J. Vrin, 1987).

15. T. Lepeltier, *La révolution végétarienne* [The vegetarian revolution] (Auxerre, France: Éditions Sciences Humaines, 2013), 156.

16. B. de Mandeville, *The Fable of the Bees: or, Private Vices, Public Benefits* (1714), https://archive.org/details/fableofthebeesor027890mbp, 118–19.

17. H. Taine, *La Fontaine et ses fables* [La Fontaine and his fables] (Paris: Hachette, 1911), 166 and 107.

18. C. Darwin, *The Descent of Man* [1874], Wiley Online Library, chap. 3, 193.

19. J.-H. Fabre, cited in A. Géraud, *Déclaration des droits de l'animal* [Declaration of the Rights of Animals] (Paris: Bibliothèque A. Géraud, 1939), 29; in Jeangène Vilmer, *Anthologie d'éthique animale*, 244.

20. Voltaire, *Œuvres complètes* [Complete works] (Paris: Arvensa Éditions, 2014), Kindle edition, 74852–74861.

21. B. E. Rollin, *The Unheeded Cry: Animal Consciousness, Animal Pain and Science* (Oxford: Oxford University Press, 1989), 154–56.

22. Ibid, 118.

23. B. Cyrulnik, É. de Fontenay, P. Singer, K. L. Matignon, and D. Rosane, *Les animaux aussi ont des droits* [Animals have rights too] (Paris: Le Seuil, 2013), Kindle edition, 3243–3245.

24. J.-B. Jeangène Vilmer, "Le critère de la souffrance dans l'éthique animale anglo-saxonne [The criterion of suffering in the animal ethics of the English-speaking countries]," in J.-L. Guichet, *Douleur animale, douleur humaine: Données scientifiques, perspectives anthropologiques, questions éthiques* [Animal Pain, Human Pain: Scientific Data, Anthropological Perspectives, Ethical Questions] (Versailles, France: Quae, 2010), 191–99.

25. D. B. Morton and P. H. Griffiths, "Guidelines on the Recognition of Pain, Distress and Discomfort in Experimental Animals and an Hypothesis for Assessment," *Veterinary Record* 116, no. 16 (1985): 431–36. Cited in Rollin, *The Unheeded Cry*, 194.

26. The Organisation for Animal Health (OIE) has therefore laid emphasis on ethical responsibility in their efforts to improve how fish are treated. OIE, *Aquatic Animal Health Code*, Appendix 3.4.1., "Introduction to Guidelines for the Welfare of Farmed Fish" (2008); available at www.oie.int/Eng/normes/fcode/en_chapitre_3.4.1.htm.

27. K. P. Chandroo, I. J. Duncan, and R. D. Moccia, "Can Fish Suffer? Perspectives on Sentience, Pain, Fear, and Stress," *Applied Animal Behaviour Science* 86, no. 3 (2004): 225–50. See also L. U. Sneddon, V. A. Braithwaite, and M. J. Gentle, "Do Fishes Have Nociceptors? Evidence for the Evolution of a Vertebrate Sensory System," *Proceedings of the Royal Society of London*, Series B: *Biological Sciences* 270, no. 1520 (2003): 1115–21. L. U. Sneddon, "Ethics and Welfare: Pain Perception in Fish," *Bulletin-European Association of Fish Pathologists* 26, no. 1 (2006): 6. AHAW, "Scientific Opinion of the Panel on Animal

Health and Welfare on a Request from European Commission on General Approach to Fish Welfare and to the Concept of Sentience in Fish," *The EFSA Journal* 954 (2009): 1–26. J. Nordgreen, J. P. Garner, A. M. Janczak, B. Ranheim, W. M. Muir, and T. E. Horsberg, "Thermonociception in Fish: Effects of Two Different Doses of Morphine on Thermal Threshold and Post-Test Behaviour in Goldfish (*Carassius auratus*)," *Applied Animal Behaviour Science* 119, no. 1 (2009): 101–7.

28. Observations of the species *Astatotilapia burtoni* of Lake Tanganyika in Tanzania; see L. Grosenick, T. S. Clement, and R. D. Fernald, "Fish Can Infer Social Rank by Observation Alone," *Nature* 445, no. 7126 (2007): 429–32. Rainbowfish trained to find holes in nets in order to escape from them take five tries to learn how to do this and succeed at doing it again, on the first try, eleven months later. See C. Brown, "Familiarity with the Test Environment Improves Escape Responses in the Crimson Spotted Rainbowfish (*Melanotaenia duboulayi*)," *Animal Cognition* 4, no. 2 (2001): 109–13.

29. R. O. Anderson and M. LeRoy Heman, "Angling as a Factor Influencing Catchability of Largemouth Bass," *Transactions of the American Fisheries Society* 98, no. 2 (1969): 317–20.

30. R. W. Elwood and M. Appel, "Pain Experience in Hermit Crabs?" in *Animal Behaviour* 77, no. 5 (2009): 1243–46.

31. J. R. Baker, "Experiments on the Humane Killing of Crabs," *Journal of the Marine Biological Association of the United Kingdom* 34, no. 1 (1955): 15–24.

32. P. Devienne, *Les animaux souffrent-ils?* [Do animals suffer?] (Paris: Le Pommier, 2008).

33. A. Civard-Racinais, *Dictionnaire horrifié de la souffrance animale* [The horrified dictionary of animal suffering] (Paris: Fayard, 2010).

34. Following Cyrulnik et al., *Les animaux aussi ont des droits*, Kindle edition, 3534.

35. Cited in F. de Waal, *L'âge de l'empathie: Leçons de nature pour une société plus apaisée* [The age of empathy: Lessons from nature for a more peaceful society] (Paris: Les Liens qui Libèrent, 2010), 198–99.

36. J. Goodall, *Through a Window: My Thirty Years with the Chimpanzees of Gombe* (Phoenix, 2011), 190. (Photo of Flint prostrate, p. 213.)

37. Cited in Singer, *Animal Liberation*, 315, note 43.

38. Ibid., 315, note 44.

39. We know, for example, that more than five hundred species of bacteria form colonies on the teeth and oral mucus membranes of humans, providing the obvious potential for cooperation as well as competition. In fact it has been shown that it is cooperation between these species that allows them to survive in an environment where a single species would be incapable of proliferating. See P. E. Kolenbrander, "Mutualism versus Independence: Strategies of Mixed-Species Oral Biofilms in Vitro Using Saliva as the Sole Nutrient Source," *Infection and Immunity* 69 (2001). Regarding bacteria, see also J. H. Koschwanez, K. R. Foster, and A. W. Murray, "Sucrose Utilization in

Budding Yeast as a Model for the Origin of Undifferentiated Multicellularity," *PLoS Biology* 9, no. 8 (2011).

40. C. Darwin, *The Descent of Man, and Selection in Relation to Sex*, ed. J. Moore and A. Desmond (London: Penguin, 2004), 130.

41. Plutarch, *Sur l'usage des viandes* [On the eating of flesh], in *Traités de morale de Plutarque* [Moral treatises of Plutarch], translated from the Greek by Dominique Ricard (Paris: Lefèvre Éditeur, 1844), t. IV, 565.

42. Jeangène Vilmer, *Anthologie d'éthique animale*, 126.

43. Ibid., 130.

44. www.bloomassociation.org.

45. A. Caron, *No Steak* (Paris: Fayard, 2013), Kindle edition, 2936.

46. *Protein and Amino Acid Requirements in Human Nutrition*, report of a joint WHO/FAO/UNU expert consultation, WHO technical report series no. 935. See http://apps.who.int/iris/bitstream/10665/43411/1/WHO_TRS_935_eng.pdf.

47. M. E. Levine, J. A. Suarez, S. Brandhorst, P. Balasubramanian, C.-W. Cheng, F. Madia, and V. D. Longo, "Low Protein Intake Is Associated with a Major Reduction in IGF-1, Cancer, and Overall Mortality in the 65 and Younger but Not Older Population," *Cell Metabolism* 19, no. 3 (2014): 407–17. On the other hand, an elevated level of protein consumption is associated with a slight reduction in cancer and overall mortality rates after the age of 65; however, it is associated with a quintupling of mortality due to diabetes in all age groups. Thus minimal consumption of animal protein in middle age followed by moderate consumption in old age seems to bring improvement in health and longevity.

48. Summarizing Caron, *No Steak*, Kindle edition, 2939–2964.

49. See Carl Lewis's preface to J. Bennett and C. Lewis, *Very Vegetarian* (Nashville, TN: Thomas Nelson, 2001).

50. Shabkar Tsogdruk Rangdrol, *Food of Bodhisattvas: Buddhist Teachings on Abstaining from Meat*, trans. Padmakara Translation Group (New Delhi: Shechen Publications, 2008), 42, 44.

51. J. F. Burns, "Stoning of Afghan Adulterers: Some Go to Take Part, Others Just to Watch," *International Herald Tribune*, November 3, 1996.

52. Gibert, *Voir son steak comme un animal mort*, 27.

53. See L214's publicity campaign at http://stop-foie-gras.com.

54. According to the data published by CIFOG, which is the public relations arm of the foie gras industry in France. Economic report from the year 2002, cited in Civard-Racinais, *Dictionnaire horrifié de la souffrance animale*, Kindle edition, 873.

55. Cited in Nicolino, *Bidoche*, 299.

56. As Civard-Racinais reminds us: "In the world every year, 43 million web-footed creatures are force fed, 36 million of them in France, mainly in the Southwest and in Alsatia, and this in spite of a European directive dated

July 20, 1989, relating to the protection of animals in breeding operations. This directive stipulates: 'No animal may be fed or made to drink in a way that causes suffering or needless injury.' In accordance with this directive, many countries in the European Union have prohibited the practice of force-feeding." A. Civard-Racinais, *Dictionnaire horrifié de la souffrance animale*, Kindle edition, 871.

CHAPTER 6. THE CONTINUUM OF LIFE

1. C. Darwin, *The Descent of Man, and Selection in Relation to Sex*, vol. 1 [digital version] (Cambridge: Cambridge University Press, 2009), 34–35.

2. C. Darwin, *The Expression of the Emotions in Man and Animals* (New York: D. Appleton, 1899).

3. J. Offray de La Mettrie, *L'homme machine* [The human machine] (Paris: Frédéric Henry, 1747), 159.

4. C. Mora, D. P. Tittensor, S. Adl, A. G. Simpson, and B. Worm (2011) "How Many Species Are There on Earth and in the Ocean?" *PLoS Biol*, 9 (8), e1001127.

5. From a speech given at the conference Le Droit de l'Animal (Rights of Animals), organized by Ecolo-Ethik in the French senate, February 7, 2014.

6. T. Nagel, *The View from Nowhere* (New York: Oxford University Press, 1989).

7. Darwin, *The Descent of Man and Selection in Relation to Sex*.

8. G.-L. Buffon, *Œuvres complètes* [Complete works], t. 1, p. 34, 1828. Cited in Chauvet, *La volonté des animaux* [The will of animals], *op. cit.*, 19.

9. D. Lestel, *Les origines animales de la culture* [The animal origins of culture] (Paris: Flammarion, collection "Champs essais," 2001), 19.

10. D. R. Griffin, *The Question of Animal Awareness: Evolutionary Continuity of Mental Experience* (New York: Rockefeller University Press, 1976), 85.

11. Ibid., 74.

12. S. P. Stich, "Do Animals Have Beliefs?" *Australian Journal of Philosophy* 57, no. 1 (1979): 18.

13. Cited by Élisabeth de Fontenay in B. Cyrulnik, É. de Fontenay, P. Singer, K. L. Matignon, and D. Rosane, *Les animaux aussi ont des droits* [Animals have rights too] (Paris: Le Seuil, 2013), Kindle edition, 1567.

14. According to Cyrulnik et al., *Les animaux aussi ont des droits*, Kindle edition, 3273.

15. D. Diderot, *Le Rêve de D'Alembert* [D'Alembert's dream] [1769] (Youscribe Publica, 2012), Kindle edition, 1361.

16. S. M. Wise, *Drawing the Line: Science and the Case for Animal Rights* (Cambridge, MA: Perseus Books, 2002), 104.

17. "An Interview with Alex, the African Grey Parrot," *Scientific American* (www.scientificamerican.com), September 12, 2007.

18. "Science's Best Known Parrot Died on September 6th, aged 31," *The Economist*, September 20, 2007.

19. R. J. Herrnstein and D. H. Loveland, "Complex Visual Concept in the

Pigeon," *Science* 146, no. 3643 (1964): 549; and R. J. Herrnstein, D. H. Loveland, and C. Cable, "Natural Concepts in Pigeons," *Journal of Experimental Psychology: Animal Behavior Processes* 2, no. 4 (1976): 285.

20. S. Watanabe, J. Sakamoto, and M. Wakita, "Pigeons' Discrimination of Paintings by Monet and Picasso," *Journal of the Experimental Analysis of Behavior* 63, no. 2 (1995): 165; S. Watanabe, "Visual Discrimination of Real Objects and Pictures in Pigeons," *Learning and Behavior* 25, no. 2 (1997): 185–92.

21. T. Matsuzawa, "Use of Numbers by a Chimpanzee," *Nature* 315, no. 6014 (1985): 57–59.

22. C. Brown, "Familiarity with the Test Environment Improves Escape Responses in the Crimson Spotted Rainbowfish (*Melanotaenia duboulayi*)," *Animal Cognition* 4 (2001).

23. M. Helft, "Pig Video Arcades Critique Life in the Pen," *Wired*, June 1997.

24. L. Duchene, "Are Pigs Smarter than Dogs?" Penn State University, Probing Question (2006). Posted online temporarily on the Pennsylvania State University website at http://news.psu.edu/tag/probing-question.

25. S. Held, M. Mendl, C. Devereux, and R. W. Byrne, "Behaviour of Domestic Pigs in a Visual Perspective Taking Task," *Behaviour* 138, no. 11–12 (2001): 1337–54.

26. R. Helfer, *The Beauty of the Beasts* (Los Angeles: Jeremy P. Tarcher, 1990), 82–83.

27. This footage can be viewed at www.dailymotion.com/video/x4xukx_hippo potame-sauve-impala-du-crocodi_animals.

28. T. Regan, *The Case for Animal Rights* (Berkeley: University of California Press, 2004), xvi.

29. For a presentation of Buddhist views on these questions, see Wulstan Fletcher's preface to Shabkar Tsogdruk Rangdrol, *Food of Bodhisattvas: Buddhist Teachings on Abstaining from Meat*, trans. Padmakara Translation Group (New Delhi: Shechen Publications, 2008).

30. R. Ryder, "Speciesism Again: The Original Leaflet," *Critical Society* 2 (2010).

31. R. Ryder, "Experiments on Animals," in *Animals, Men and Morals*, ed. S. Godlovitch (New York: Grove Press, 1974), 81.

32. P. Singer, *Animal Liberation* (New York: Ecco, 2002), 6.

33. J. Dunayer, "The rights of sentient beings. Moving beyond old and new speciesism," in *The Politics of Species: Reshaping Our Relationships with Other Animals*, ed. R. Corbey and A. Lanjouw (Cambridge: Cambridge University Press, 2013), 27–39.

34. M. Gibert, *Voir son steak comme un animal mort: Véganisme et psychologie morale.* (Montreal, Canada: Lux Éditeur, 2015), 168.

35. J.-B. Jeangène Vilmer, *Éthique animale* [Animal ethics] (Paris: PUF, 2008), 47.

36. M. Joy, *Why We Love Dogs, Eat Pigs, and Wear Cows: An Introduction to Carnism* (San Francisco: Conari Press, 2010), 24–28.

37. Ibid.

38. A. Caron, *No Steak* (Paris: Fayard, 2013), Kindle edition, 879 and 927.
39. M. Bekoff, "Who Lives, Who Dies and Why," in *The Politics of Species*, ed. R. Corbey and A. Lanjouw, 15–26.
40. F. Wolff, *Notre humanité: d'Aristote aux neurosciences* [Our humanity: From Aristotle to the neurosciences] (Paris: Fayard, 2010), 337.
41. Ibid., 336.
42. Chauvet, *La volonté des animaux*.
43. J. M. Coetzee, *Elizabeth Costello* (New York: Viking, 2003), EPUB 79.
44. Gibert, *Voir son steak comme un animal mort*, 42. See also Tatjana Višak, *Killing Happy Animals: Explorations in Utilitarian Ethics* (New York: Palgrave MacMillan, 2013).
45. According to Martha Nussbaum, the potential for animals to accomplish the various goals that they pursue in their natural environments must also be respected, along with the possibility of maintaining relationships with other species, and finally the possibility of engaging in play. M. Nussbaum, *Frontiers of Justice: Disability, Nationality, Species Membership* (Cambridge, MA: Harvard University Press, 2006), 351 and 392–400. For a detailed presentation of these points, see Jeangène Vilmer, *Éthique animale*, 97–98.
46. Frans de Waal in discussion with Martha Nussbaum, www.youtube.com.
47. Until the contrary is proved, if the behaviors of animals can be described "as if" the animals were consciously experiencing suffering, had access to abstraction, and so forth, the most simple hypothesis is that they are suffering. They do definitely have access to abstraction and other faculties that we human beings possess, who share with them the same evolutionary lineage, possess the same sensory organs, and present in most cases comparable neurological and (in some cases) cerebral responses. See the detailed arguments presented on these points by B. E. Rollin, *The Unheeded Cry: Animal Consciousness, Animal Pain and Science* (Oxford: Oxford University Press, 1989), chap. 6.
48. D. O. Hebb, "Emotion in Man and Animal," *Psychological Review* 53, no. 2 (1946): 88. Cited in G. B. Matthews, "Animals and the Unity of Psychology," *Philosophy* 53, no. 206 (October 1978): 440.
49. C. Darwin, *The Descent of Man* (Amazon Digital Services, March 24, 2011), Kindle edition, 1383–1386.
50. D. R. Griffin, *Animal Minds: Beyond Cognition to Consciousness* (Chicago: University of Chicago Press, 1992), 34. Cited in D. Chauvet, *Contre la mentaphobie* [Against mentaphobia] (Lausanne, Switzerland: L'Âge d'Homme, 2014), 55.
51. Chauvet, *Contre la mentaphobie*, 50.
52. Frans de Waal coined the term "anthropodenial," which designates the denial, commonly observed in the scientific community and in the general public, of any similarity between the mental and emotional states of humans and animals.
53. F. de Waal, *The Age of Empathy* (New York: Three Rivers Press, 2009), 131.

54. H. Taine, *La Fontaine et ses fables* [La Fontaine and his fables] (Paris: Hachette, 1911), 163.
55. Élisabeth de Fontenay, speech on the occasion of the conference "Le droit de l'animal" [The rights of animals] organized in the French senate by Ecolo-Ethik, February 7, 2014.
56. de Fontenay, *op. cit.*, 33.
57. Rollin, *The Unheeded Cry*, 23.
58. Lestel, *Les origines animales de la culture*, 8.
59. A. L. Kroeber, "Sub-Human Culture Beginnings," *The Quarterly Review of Biology* 3, no. 3 (1928): 325–42. A. L. Kroeber and C. Kluckhohn, "Culture: A Critical Review of Concepts and Definitions," in *Papers of the Peabody Museum of Archaeology and Ethnology, Harvard University, vol. 47, no.1* (Cambridge, MA: The Museum, 1952). Cited in Lestel, *Les origines animales de la culture*, 108–10.
60. A. Whiten, J. Goodall, W. C. McGrew, T. Nishida, V. Reynolds, Y. Sugiyama, and C. Boesch, "Cultures in Chimpanzees," *Nature* 399, no. 6737 (1999): 682–685. Cited in Lestel, *Les origines animales de la culture*, 118.
61. D. Lestel, "Des cultures animales," *Sciences et Avenir*, special no. 152 (October/November 2007): 26–29. See also Lestel, *Les origines animales de la culture*, and the reference work, W. C. McGrew, *The Cultured Chimpanzee: Reflections on Cultural Primatology* (Cambridge: Cambridge University Press, 2004).
62. J. Goodall, "Tool-Using and Aimed Throwing in a Community of Free-Living Chimpanzees," *Nature* 201 (1964): 1264.
63. C. Boesch and H. Boesch, "Mental Map in Wild Chimpanzees: An Analysis of Hammer Transports for Nut Cracking," *Primates* 25, no. 2 (1984): 160–70. T. Matsuzawa, "Field Experiments on Use of Stone Tools by Chimpanzees in the Wild," *Chimpanzee Cultures* (1994). 351–70. Cited in Lestel, *Les origines animales de la culture*,130–31.
64. Lestel, *Les origines animales de la culture*, 69.
65. This chimp first attempted to get at the honey with a stick, but the booty turned out to be out of reach. Next she attacked the side of the beehive with a big chisel she had picked up, then continued her work with a finer chisel. She finally pierced the nest with a fine, pointed chisel and went on to feast on the honey that oozed out along its outer walls. W. C. McGrew, "The Intelligent Use of Tools: Twenty Propositions," in K. R. Gibson and T. Ingold, *Tools, Language and Cognition in Human Evolution* (Cambridge University Press, 1994), 151–70. Cited in Lestel, *Les origines animales de la culture*, 86.
66. R. W. Shumaker, K. R. Walkup, and B. B. Beck, *Animal Tool Behavior: The Use and Manufacture of Tools by Animals* (Baltimore, MD: Johns Hopkins University Press, 2011).
67. Lestel, *Les origines animales de la culture*, 62.
68. G. R. Hunt, "Manufacture and Use of Hook-Tools by New Caledonian Crows," *Nature* 379, no. 6562 (1996): 249–51. Cited in Lestel, *Les origines animales de la culture*, 130.

69. K. Sumita, J. Kitahara-Frisch, and K. Norikoshi, "The Acquisition of Stone-Tool Use in Captive Chimpanzees," *Primates* 26, no. 2 (1985): 168–81. Learning behaviors have also been observed among cetaceans and other species. See Lestel, *Les origines animales de la culture*, 155.

70. J. Goodall, *The Chimpanzees of Gombe: Patterns of Behavior* (Cambridge, MA: Harvard University Press, 1996).

71. N. Masataka, H. Koda, N. Urasopon, and K. Watanabe, "Free-Ranging Macaque Mothers Exaggerate Tool-Using Behavior When Observed by Offspring," *PLOS ONE* 4, no. 3 (2009).

72. K. von Frisch, *Vie et mœurs des abeilles* [The dancing bees: An account of the life and senses of the honey bee] (Paris: Albin Michel, 2011).

73. R. S. Payne and S. McVay, "Songs of Humpback Whales," *Science* 173, no. 3997 (1971): 585–97.

74. R. S. Payne, *Communication and Behavior of Whales* (Boulder, CO: Westview Press, 1983). C. W. Clark, "Acoustic Behavior of Mysticete Whales," in J. A. Thomas and R. A. Kastelein, *Sensory Abilities of Cetaceans: Laboratory and Field Evidence*, vol. 196 (New York: Springer, 1990), 571–83. Cited in Lestel, *Les origines animales de la culture*, 134.

75. B. Rensch, "The Intelligence of Elephants," *Scientific American* 196 (1957): 44–49.

76. C. Boesch, "Symbolic Communication in Wild Chimpanzees?" *Human Evolution* 6, no. 1 (1991): 81–89. Cited in Lestel, *Les origines animales de la culture*, 182.

77. B. Rensch, "Play and Art in Apes and Monkeys," in E. W. Menzel, *Precultural Primate Behavior* (New York: Karger, 1973). Cited in Lestel, *Les origines animales de la culture*, 228.

78. A. J. Marshall, *Bower-Birds: Their Displays and Breeding Cycles: A Preliminary Statement* (Oxford: Clarendon Press, 1954). See also www.scienceshumaines.com/l-art-de-seduire-des-oiseaux-aux-humains_fr_25706.html.

79. J. Diamond and A. B. Bond, *Kea, Bird of Paradox: The Evolution and Behavior of a New Zealand Parrot* (Berkeley: University of California Press, 1998). Cited in Lestel, *Les origines animales de la culture*, 200.

80. L. D. Mech and L. Boitani, *Wolves: Behavior, Ecology, and Conservation* (Chicago: University of Chicago Press, 2003), 388. Cited in Lestel, *Les origines animales de la culture*, 202.

81. J. Goodall, *Les chimpanzés et moi* [Chimpanzees and me] (Paris: Stock, 1971), 65–66.

82. G. Flores, "When I See an Elephant . . . Paint?" *The Scientist*, June 1, 2007.

83. D. Morris, *The Biology of Art: A Study of the Picture-Making Behaviour of the Great Apes and Its Relationship to Human Art* (London: Methuen, 1962). Cited in Lestel, *Les origines animales de la culture*, 229.

84. Lestel, *Les origines animales de la culture*, 162.

85. C. Lévi-Strauss, *Anthropologie structurale* [Structural anthropology] (Paris: Pocket, 2003).

86. P. Rouget, *La violence de l'humanisme: pourquoi nous faut-il persécuter les animaux?* [The violence of humanism: Why must we persecute animals?] (Paris: Calmann-Lévy, 2014), Kindle edition, 348.

87. Wolff, *Notre humanité*, 357.

88. T. Matsuzawa, "Sociocognitive Development in Chimpanzees: A Synthesis of Laboratory Work and Fieldwork," in T. Matsuzawa, M. Tomonaga, and M. M. Tanaka, *Cognitive Development in Chimpanzees* (Tokyo Springer: 2006), 3–33. See also L. Spinney, "When Chimps Outsmart Humans," *New Scientist* 190 (2006): 48–49.

89. See in particular F. de Waal, *Le bonobo, Dieu et nous* [The bonobo, God, and us] (Paris: Les Liens qui Libèrent, 2013).

90. Wolff, *Notre humanité*, 358.

91. S. Yamamoto, T. Humle, and M. Tanaka, "Chimpanzees' Flexible Targeted Helping Based on an Understanding of Conspecifics' Goals," *Proceedings of the National Academy of Sciences of the United States of America*, 2012.

92. T. Bugnyar and B. Heinrich, "Ravens, Corvus Corax, Differentiate between Knowledgeable and Ignorant Competitors," *Proceedings of the Royal Society: Biological Sciences* 272, no. 1573 (2005).

93. Rouget, *La violence de l'humanisme: pourquoi nous faut-il persécuter les animaux?*, Kindle edition, 575–78. Among others, according to Rouget, and referring here only to the modern era: Descartes, Spinoza, Leibniz, Kant, Fichte, Hegel, Heidegger, Sartre, Levinas. For the details of their diverse and varied propositions—sometimes ingenious, sometimes inane, sometimes outright upsetting—which have appeared over the course of the development of modern philosophical thought, the reader may profitably refer to the work of É. de Fontenay, *Le silence des bêtes, la philosophie à l'épreuve de l'animalité* [The silence of the beasts: Philosophy faces the test of animality]. (Paris: Fayard, 1998).

94. Ibid., 949.

95. For an exposé detailing this point, see Gibert, *Voir son steak comme un animal mort*, 170.

CHAPTER 7. THE MASS KILLING OF ANIMALS

1. I am grateful to Jacques Sémelin for suggesting that I use—in fact, create—a specific word for the mass killing of animals. I have thus proposed the word "zoocide" in order to avoid confusion with "genocide," which by definition refers to human beings. The Greek word *zoon*, "living being," originally designated all living species with the exception of plants. Thus it included humans. However, in the current and accepted usage, it specifically refers to animals. "Zoology," for example, is defined by the Grand Robert Dictionary as being a "branch of the natural sciences which has as its object the study of animals"; and "zoolatry" is defined as "the worship of deified animals and, by

extension, an excessive taste for animals." Thus it seems to us that "zoocide" is appropriate to specifically designate the massive and deliberate killing of animals.

2. C. Patterson, *Un éternel Treblinka* [Eternal Treblinka] (Paris: Calmann-Lévy, 2008), 214.

3. I. B. Singer, *Le pénitent* [The Penitent] (Paris: Stock, 1984).

4. I. B. Singer, *Collected Stories: Gimpel the Fool to the Letter Writer* (New York: Library of America, 2004).

5. The sixty-seven survivors were part of a group that rebelled and managed to escape from the camp. Most of that group were caught and killed, but a few succeeded in getting away. The last remaining survivor, Samuel Willenberg, born in 1923, passed away on February 19, 2016.

6. J. Derrida, *L'animal que donc je suis* [The animal that therefore I am] (Paris: Galilée, 2006), 46.

7. As *La France agricole* [Agricultural France] of February 8, 2011, notes: "The animals are supposed to be killed and then buried in holes four to five meters deep covered by two layers of vinyl. But this regulation is sometimes ignored because of the large number of corpses to be interred."

8. See J. Porcher, *Vivre avec les animaux: Une utopie pour le xxie siècle* [Living with animals: A utopia for the twenty-first century] (Paris: La Découverte, 2011), 90, citing L. Gaignard and A. Charon, "Gestion de crise et traumatisme: les effets collatéraux de la 'vache folle.' De l'angoisse singulière à l'embarras collectif " [Managing crisis and trauma: The collateral effects of "Mad Cow." From Individual Anxiety to Collective Embarassment], *Travailler* [Working] 14, no. 2 (2005): 57–71, specifically 66.

9. Program televised by Eurêka on December 2, 1970, entitled "Sauver le boeuf . . . ," [Save the cattle] with commentary by Guy Seligman and Paul Ceuzin. See the archives of the INA (Institut national de l'audiovisuel), a repository of all French radio and television audiovisual archives, www.ina.fr/video /CPF06020231/sauver-le-boeuf.fr.html.

10. Porcher, *Vivre avec les animaux*, 92.

11. Convention on the Prevention and Suppression of the Crime of Genocide, Resolution 230 of the United Nations, December 9, 1948, Article 2.

12. J. Sémelin, *Purifier et détruire: Usages politiques des massacres et génocides* [Cleanse and destroy: Political uses of massacres and genocides] (Paris: Le Seuil, 2005), 391.

13. J. Sémelin, "Du massacre au processus génocidaire" [From massacre to the process of genocide], *Revue internationale des sciences sociales* (2002): 4.

14. Jacques Sémelin, speech on the occasion of the launching of the site www .massviolence.org, April 3, 2008, at the Institut de Sciences Politiques in Paris.

15. J. Chicago and D. Woodman, *Holocaust Project: From Darkness into Light* (New York: Viking, 1993), 58.

16. J. M. Coetzee, *Elizabeth Costello* (New York: Viking, 2003), EPUB 69.
17. See in particular R. Breitman, *The Architect of Genocide: Himmler and the Final Solution* (London: Grafton, 1992), 249–50. J. Weiss, *Ideology of Death: Why the Holocaust Happened in Germany* (Chicago: Ivan R. Dee, 1996), 272. R. Höss, *Commandant of Auschwitz: Autobiography* (Cleveland, OH: World Publishing Company, 1960). Cited in Patterson, *Un éternel Treblinka*, 180–81.
18. K. R. Monroe, *The Heart of Altruism: Perceptions of a Common Humanity* (Cambridge University Press, 1996), 101–2.
19. Dominick LaCapra in an interview broadcast on the BBC during a program produced by Victor Schonfeld: *One Planet*, "Animals and Us," December 31, 2009, and January 3, 2010.
20. Porcher, *Vivre avec les animaux*, 93.

CHAPTER 8. A LITTLE SIDE TRIP INTO THE REALM OF MORAL JUDGMENT

1. Í. Kant, *Sur un prétendu droit de mentir par humanité* [On a supposed right to lie from philanthropy] (Paris: J. Vrin, 2000), 68.
2. F. J. Varela, *Ethical Know-How: Action, Wisdom, and Cognition* (Stanford, CA: Stanford University Press, 1999), 30.
3. C. Taylor, *Sources of the Self: The Making of the Modern Identity* (Cambridge, MA: Harvard University Press, 1989), 3.
4. Plato, *Gorgias*, trans. Donald Zeyl (Indianapolis, IN: Hackett, 1987), 47.
5. J. D. Greene, *Moral Tribes: Emotion, Reason and the Gap between Us and Them* (London: Atlantic Books, 2013). J. Greene and J. Haidt, "How (and Where) Does Moral Judgment Work?" in *Trends in Cognitive Sciences* 6, no. 12 (2002): 517–23. J. D. Greene, L. E. Nystrom, A. D. Engell, J. M. Darley, and J. D. Cohen, "The Neural Bases of Cognitive Conflict and Control in Moral Judgment," *Neuron* 44, no. 2 (2004): 389–400.
6. J. Haidt, *The Righteous Mind: Why Good People Are Divided by Politics and Religion* (London: Allen Lane, 2012).
7. Following Élisabeth de Fontenay, in B. Cyrulnik, É. de Fontenay, P. Singer, K. L. Matignon, and D. Rosane, *Les animaux aussi ont des droits* [Animals have rights too] (Paris: Le Seuil, 2013), Kindle edition, 1674.
8. G. Francione and A. Charlton, *Eat Like You Care: An Examination of the Morality of Eating Animals* (Kentucky: Exempla Press, 2013).

CHAPTER 9. THE DILEMMA OF ANIMAL EXPERIMENTATION

1. www.understandinganimalresearch.org.uk/the-animals/numbers-of-animals.
2. J.-P. Marguénaud, *L'expérimentation animale: entre droit et liberté* [Animal

NOTES 305

experimentation: Between rights and freedom] (Versailles, France: Quae, 2011), Kindle edition, 198–202.

3. Ibid., 156.

4. D. Lestel, *Les origines animales de la culture* [The animal origins of culture] (Paris: Flammarion, collection "Champs essais," 2001), Kindle edition, 311.

5. Mao said, "If you add up all the landowners, the rich peasants, the counter-revolutionaries, the bad elements, and the reactionaries, their number probably does not come to more than thirty million. . . . In our population of 600 million people, these thirty million are only one in twenty. What is there to worry about? We have so many people, we can afford to lose a few of them. So what?" Li Zhuisi and A. F. Thurston, *La vie privée du président Mao* [The private life of President Mao] (Paris: Omnibus, 1994). He also said, "The dead have advantages. They fertilize the soil." J. Chang and J. Halliday, *Mao: The Unknown Story* (London: Vintage, 2007), 457. Directly or indirectly, Mao caused the death of 50 million people.

6. "The Price of Knowledge," a program televised on December 12, 1974, on WNET/13. Cited in Singer, *op. cit.*, 126 and 155, note 2.

7. M. Midgley, *Animals and Why They Matter* (Athens: University of Georgia Press, 1984), 13.

8. B. E. Rollin, *The Unheeded Cry: Animal Consciousness, Animal Pain and Science* (Oxford: Oxford University Press, 1989), 114.

9. List cited by the Committee for Research and Ethical Issues of the International Association for the Study of Pain. "Ethical Guidelines for the Investigation of Experimental Pain in Conscious Animals," *Pain* 16 (1983): 109–10. Rollin, *The Unheeded Cry*, 188.

10. P. Singer, *La libération animale* [Animal liberation] (Paris: Grasset, 1993), 112.

11. F. S. Vom Saal and C. Hughes, "An Extensive New Literature Concerning Low-Dose Effects of Bisphenol A Shows the Need for a New Risk Assessment," *Environmental Health Perspectives* 113, no. 8 (2005): 926.

12. Singer, *La libération animale*, 101 and note 57.

13. Cited in Singer, *La libération animale*, 102.

14. Ibid., 99, and note 56.

15. M. A. Lennox, W. A. Sibley, and H. M. Zimmerman, "Fever and Febrile Convulsions in Kittens: A Clinical, Electroencephalographic, and Histopathologic Study," *The Journal of Pediatrics* 45, no. 2 (1954): 179–90. Cited in Singer, *La libération animale*, 108.

16. H. F. Harlow, R. O. Dodsworth, and M. K. Harlow, "Total Social Isolation in Monkeys," *Proceedings of the National Academy of Sciences of the United States of America* 54, no. 1 (1965): 90.

17. H. F. Harlow, "The Nature of Love," *The American Psychologist* 13 (1958): 673–85. H. F. Harlow, *Love in Infant Monkeys* (San Francisco: W.H. Freeman, 1959). Cited in Singer, *La libération animale*, 71.

18. Singer, *La libération animale*, 74.

19. V. Despret and F. Burgat, *Penser comme un rat* [Thinking like a rat] (Versailles, France: Quae, 2009), Kindle edition, 1553.
20. Singer, *La libération animale*, 120 and note 104.
21. Ibid., 133–34, note 118; and C. Patterson, *Un éternel Treblinka* [Eternal Treblinka] (Paris: Calmann-Lévy, 2008), 208.
22. *Earthlings* [documentary film], directed by S. Monson (Burbank, CA: Nation Earth, 2006), available at www.earthlings.com.
23. S. Pinker, *The Better Angels of Our Nature: Why Violence Has Declined* (New York: Viking Adult, 2011), 455.
24. Jane Goodall, from a speech given at the conference Le Droit de l'Animal (Rights of Animals), organized by Ecolo-Ethik in the French senate, February 7, 2014.
25. See A. Civard-Racinais, *Dictionnaire horrifié de la souffrance animale* [The horrified dictionary of animal suffering] (Paris: Fayard, 2010), Kindle edition, 638.
26. J. Rachels, *Created from Animals: The Moral Implications of Darwinism* (Oxford: Oxford University Press, 1990), 180–81.
27. Singer, *La libération animale*, 117.
28. P. Zimbardo, *The Lucifer Effect: Understanding How Good People Turn Evil* (New York: Random House, 2007), 5.
29. Ibid.
30. H.-J. Dulaurens, *Le compère Mathieu, ou les bigarrures de l'esprit humain* [Jolly Mathieu, or the motley quality of the human mind], vol. III [1766] (Paris: Les marchands de nouveautés [The novelty mongers], 1834), 11–18. Cited in Jeangène Vilmer, *op. cit.*, 78.
31. Concerning the proposed changes, see also A. K. Turner, "Proposed EU Changes in Animal Experimentation Regulations," *Medical Communications* 18, no. 4 (2009): 238.
32. Directive 2010/63/EU of the European Parliament and Council, September 22, 2010, concerning the protection of animals used for scientific purposes.
33. Nevertheless, animals are still being used in the testing of cosmetics and household products in many countries. In addition, in 2003 the European Commission adopted a proposition concerning the regulation of chemical products with the European Union called REACH (Registration, Evaluation, Authorisation and Restriction of Chemicals). This proposition calls for the testing of 30,000 chemical products already in use and would necessitate the use of 4 to 20 million laboratory animals according to estimates. Many animal protection organizations have stepped in to urge the national and European authorities to put in place methods that do not involve the use of animals. The REACH testing program has been criticized by experts who consider it badly planned, expensive, and very unlikely to attain the goals envisaged.
34. 2010/63/EU Article 27 and 29. Cited in Marguénaud, *L'expérimentation animale*, 600.

35. Articles 36, 38, 40 and 44. Cited in Marguénaud, *L'expérimentation animale*, 619.
36. Marguénaud, *L'expérimentation animale*, 659.
37. According to another poll carried out in 2007 under the auspices of GIRCOR —an organization that brings together the biological and medical research institutions in France as well as public research institutions, pharmaceutical companies, and private research institutes—56 percent of the French people are in favor of animal experimentation if it is carried out as part of a project with therapeutic goals. However, some of the questions posed in the poll seem formulated in such a way as to obtain responses favorable to the continuation of animal experimentation. For example, "If animal experimentation were no longer possible in France, the laboratories would relocate their research projects to other countries. Do you find that completely acceptable (5 percent said yes), somewhat acceptable (13 percent), somewhat regrettable (41 percent), altogether regrettable (38 percent), don't know (3 percent)?" We can clearly see that in this questionnaire the issue of animal experimentation is masked behind that of relocation to other countries, which made it possible for 41 percent and 38 percent of people questioned (79 percent in total) to view animal experimentation as legitimate. For a questionnaire to be scientifically valid, it is essential that the questions be formulated in such a way as not to influence or bias the responses. The telephone poll was carried out for GIRCOR by the Beaufixe agency and l'Institut LH2 on December 27 and 28, 2007, with a sample of 1,003 persons representative of the French population over the age of 18.
38. For a detailed report from the European Commission concerning these alternative methods, see T. Seidle and H. Spielmann, "Alternative Testing Strategies Progress Report 2011 and AXLR8-2 Workshop Report on a Roadmap to Innovative Toxicity Testing," *AXLR8 Consortium*, 2011.
39. V-Frog 2.0 is a product of Tractus Technology. See www.tactustech.com /vfrog. See also "Virtual Dissection," *Science*, February 22, 2008.
40. J. P. Lalley, P. S. Piotrowski, B. Battaglia, K. Brophy, and K. Chugh, "A Comparison of V-Frog to Physical Frog Dissection," *International Journal of Environmental and Science Education* 5, no. 2 (2010): 189–200.
41. Marguénaud, *L'expérimentation animale*, 890.

CHAPTER 10. ILLEGAL TRADE IN WILDLIFE

1. Because this is a clandestine activity, exact figures for it are difficult to obtain. L. R. Douglas and K. Alie, "High-Value Natural Resources: Linking Wildlife Conservation to International Conflict, Insecurity, and Development Concerns," *Biological Conservation* 171 (2014): 270–77. The Worldwide Fund for Nature or World Wildlife Fund (WWF) also estimates the traffic in wild animals at 15 billion euros per year. Other sources give higher figures. See also

D. Roe, *Making a Killing or Making a Living: Wildlife Trade, Trade Controls, and Rural Livelihoods* (London: IIED, 2002).

2. This was the case, for example, for Steller's sea cow. See the Wikipedia article "Steller's Sea Cow." See also the reports by the NGO Renctas at www.renctas .org.br/en/trafico-de-animais.

3. CITES is the abbreviation for Convention on International Trade in Endangered Species of Wild Fauna and Flora. Among the other main organizations that are concerned with endangered species and the wildlife trade, let us mention:

   • TRAFFIC, an organization that combats the wildlife trade that is financed by the WWF and the UICN (Union Internationale pour la Conservation de la Nature), an organization founded in 1948 in Switzerland, that represents 83 countries, 114 governmental agencies, 11,000 volunteer scientists in 160 countries, and more than a thousand nongovernmental agencies;
   • FREELAND, which coordinates two groups: the Liberty Alliance, which combats slavery and traffic in humans, and ARREST (Asia's Regional Response to Endangered Species Trafficking), which operates against the wildlife trade;
   • the Environmental Investigation Agency (EIA);
   • Greenpeace, which combats, among other things, the so-called "scientific hunting" of cetaceans;
   • the Species Survival Network, an international coalition of 80 NGOs that works to support the application of the CITES treaty; as well as
   • One Voice, the Elephant Action League (EAL), Wildlife at Risk, Saving Vietnam's Wildlife, and many others.

4. A. Auffret and S. Queré, *La peau de l'ours: le livre noir du trafic d'animaux* [The skin of the bear: The black book of the wildlife trade] (Paris: Nouveau Monde éditions, 2012), Kindle edition, 253–60.

5. Article by J.-J. Fontaine, "Ouvrez la cage aux oiseaux" [Open the Bird Cages], *La Liberté*, May 4, 2009.

6. http://defenseanimale.com/ours-tortures-pour-leur-bile-en-chine; www .animalsasia.org/intl/our-work/end-bear-bile-farming/; www.endangered specieshandbook.org/trade_traditional_bears.php.

7. China Wildlife Conservation Association and the Sichuan Forestry Department.

8. R. Brown, "Sense of Release," *Sydney Morning Herald*, July 19, 2009.

9. A. Auffret and S. Queré, *La peau de l'ours*, Kindle edition, 2696–2703.

10. L. Bériot, *Ces animaux qu'on assassine: Trafics, mafias, massacres* [The animals we murder: Traffic, mafias, massacres] (Paris: Le Cherche Midi, 2013), 15–16.

11. Ibid., 17.

12. Ibid., 88.

13. Ibid., 25.
14. Cited in Bériot, *Ces animaux qu'on assassine*, 24.
15. Ibid., 27. Quoting Andy Fisher.
16. According to the NGO Wildlife Aid and Bériot, *Ces animaux qu'on assassine*, 243.
17. Center for Biodiversity and Conservation, American Museum of Natural History.
18. IFAW, the International Fund for Animal Welfare.
19. A. Richard, "Les États se mobilisent contre le trafic d'animaux sauvages" [Governments mobilize to combat the traffic in wild animals], *La Recherche*, no. 486 (April 1, 2014).
20. Douglas and Alie, "High-Value Natural Resources." See also the review of this publication in *Natura Science*, www.natura-sciences.com/biodiversite/especes-menacees/braconnage654.html.
21. According to Valérie Galarneau and Johanne Gravel of the Biodôme de Montréal, 2014.
22. Auffret and Queré, *La peau de l'ours*, Kindle edition, 1387–1390.
23. According to the documentary by Adam Schmedes, *Madagascar: Land of the Chameleons* (Loke Film, 2012).
24. Auffret and Queré, *La peau de l'ours*, Kindle edition, 97–98.
25. Cited in Bériot, *Ces animaux qu'on assassine*, 55 and 256.
26. www.one-voice.fr/loisirs-et-compagnie-sans-violence/sauvegarder-les-animaux-sauvages-dans-leur-milieu-naturel-o.
27. Richard, "Les États se mobilisent contre le trafic d'animaux sauvages."

CHAPTER 11. ANIMALS AS OBJECTS OF ENTERTAINMENT

1. J. Serpell, *In the Company of Animals: A Study of Human-Animal Relationships* (Oxford and New York: B. Blackwell, 1986), 142.
2. W. Burkert, *Homo Necans* (Berkeley: University of California Press, 1983). Cited in Serpell, *In the Company of Animals*, 175.
3. T. Yi-Fu, *Dominance and Affection: The Making of Pets* (New Haven, CT: Yale University Press, 1984), 74. Cited in Serpell, *In the Company of Animals*, 176.
4. Constructed in the sixth century B.C.E. near Rome under the reign of Tarquin the Elder, it was expanded several times, notably under Julius Caesar. It could accommodate 250,000 spectators. Having been ravaged several times by fire, it was reconstructed in stone in the year 64 C.E. and abandoned in 549 C.E. after a final chariot race. It then fell to ruins.
5. J. M. C. Toynbee, *Animals in Roman Life and Art* (London: Thames and Hudson, 1973), 21–23. S. Goodenough, *Citizens of Rome* (London: Hamlyn, 1979), 108–10. Cited in Serpell, *In the Company of Animals*, 176.
6. B. W. Tuchman, *A Distant Mirror: The Calamitous Fourteenth Century* (New York: Ballantine Books, 1991), 135. Cited in S. Pinker, *The Better Angels of Our Nature: Why Violence Has Declined* (New York: Viking Adult, 2011), 67.

7. G. Clemenceau, *Le grand Pan* [The great Pan] (Paris: Bibliothèque Charpentier, 1896), 148–354. Cited in J.-B. Jeangène Vilmer, *L'éthique animale* [Animal ethics] (Paris: PUF, 2011), 204–5.

8. F. Wolff, *50 raisons de défendre la corrida* [Fifty reasons to defend the corrida] (Paris: Fayard/Mille et une nuits, 2010), Kindle edition, 111. I must here express my thanks to Francis Wolff, who was kind enough to receive me cordially and engage with me in dialogue.

9. Pliny, *Panegyric*, xxxi. Cited in M. Wistrand, *Entertainment and Violence in Ancient Rome: The Attitudes of Roman Writers of the First Century* A.D. (Göteborg, Sweden: Acta Universitatis Gothoburgensis, 1992), 69.

10. Wistrand, *Entertainment and Violence in Ancient Rome*, 15. T. Wiedemann, *Emperors and Gladiators* (New York: Routledge, 1992), 38.

11. Wolff, *50 raisons de défendre la corrida*, Kindle edition, 750.

12. Ibid., 351.

13. Guillaume Billaut, reacting to the dialogue between Francis Wolff and André Viard, "Noces de sang" [Nights of blood] in *Philosophie Magazine*, no. 16 (January 2008).

14. F. Wolff, *Notre humanité: d'Aristote aux neurosciences* [Our humanity: From Aristotle to the neurosciences] (Paris: Fayard, 2010), 313.

15. Ibid., 477.

16. Ibid., 489.

17. É. Baratay, *Point de vue animal: Une autre version de l'histoire* [The animal point of view: Another version of history] (Paris: Le Seuil, collection "L'Univers historique," 2012), Kindle edition, 3784.

18. É. Baratay and É. Hardouin-Fugier, *La corrida* (Paris: PUF, Collection "Que sais-je?" no. 568, 1995), 106.

19. É. Hardouin-Fugier, *Histoire de la corrida en Europe du xviiie au xxie siècle* [History of bullfighting in Europe from the eighteenth to the twenty-first century] (Paris: Connaissances et Savoirs, 2005), 233. Up until 2010, from the death of José Candido Esposito in 1771 to that of Pepe Cáceres in 1987, 57 matadors have been killed by the bulls they faced. Seventy-three picadors and 159 banderillos have met the same fate. These numbers are from the "Nomenclature en hommage aux victimes du toreo" [List in honor of the victims of bullfighting], compiled by André Lopez Torente, published in 2007 by the bullfighting association La Muleta. Cited in Wikipedia.

20. Baratay and Hardouin-Fugier, *La corrida*, 105.

21. Ibid.

22. Wolff, *Notre humanité*, 313.

23. Ibid., 460. According to Hardouin-Fugier, *Histoire de la corrida en Europe du xviiie au xxie siècle*, 233: in 2005, 5,532 bulls were killed in Spain alone.

24. M. Onfray, *Bulletin de l'alliance anticorrida*, no. 26 (April 2007).

25. Wolff, *Notre humanité*, 375.

26. F. Wolff, "Corrida: vers un triomphe des valeurs humanistes?" [The corrida: Toward a triumph of humanist values?] *Le Figaro*, August 16, 2010.

27. G. Courteline, *La philosophie de Georges Courteline* (Lausanne, Switzerland: L'Âge d'Homme, 2000), 24–25. Cited in Jeangène Vilmer, *L'éthique animale,* 242.

28. M. Onfray, "Le cerveau reptilien de l'aficionado" [The reptilian brain of the aficionado] *La chronique mensuelle de Michel Onfray,* no. 89 (October 2012).

29. Wolff, "Corrida: vers un triomphe des valeurs humanistes?," 123.

30. Ibid.

31. Ibid., 133.

32. The neuroscientist Tania Singer, the director of the Department of Cognitive Neurosciences at the Max Planck Institute in Leipzig, defines compassion as the altruistic motivation to intervene on behalf of someone who is suffering or is in need. Thus it is a profound awareness of the suffering of another, coupled with the desire to alleviate it and to do something for the welfare of that other. Thus compassion implies a feeling of caring that is warm and sincere, but one that does not require that we feel the other's suffering, as is the case with empathy. T. Singer and N. Steinbeis, "Differential Roles of Fairness- and Compassion-Based Motivations for Cooperation, Defection, and Punishment," *Annals of the New York Academy of Sciences* 1167, no. 1 (2009): 41–50; T. Singer, "The Past, Present and Future of Social Neuroscience: A European Perspective," *Neuroimage* 61, no. 2 (2012): 437–49.

    Olga Klimecki, who was at the time a researcher working in Tania Singer's laboratory, sums up the view of the researchers as follows: "In the affective dimension, I experience a feeling for you; in the cognitive dimension, I understand you; and in the motivational dimension, I want to help you." See O. Klimecki, M. Ricard, and T. Singer, "Empathy versus Compassion— Lessons from 1st and 3rd person Methods," in T. Singer and M. Bolz, *Compassion: Bridging Practice and Science—A Multimedia Book* [e-book], 2013.

    For a detailed presentation of the various aspects of altruism, compassion, and empathy, see also M. Ricard, *Plaidoyer pour l'altruisme* [A plea for altruism], *op. cit.*

33. Aliocha, "Corrida: les contresens de Michel Onfray" [Corrida: The absurdities of Michel Onfray], *Marianne,* October 9, 2012.

34. Hardouin-Fugier, *Histoire de la corrida en Europe du xviiie au xxie siècle,* 154–55.

35. Marc Roumengou, synopsis of the conclusions of Juan Carlos Illera, at torofstf.com and "Quand la science se penche sur la souffrance des toros" [When science looks at the suffering of the bulls], *Libération.fr,* February 22, 2007. Cited in the Wikipedia article "Opposition à la corrida."

36. T. A. V. der Kemp, J.-C. Nouët et al., *Homme et animal: De la douleur à la cruauté* [Human and animal: From pain to cruelty] (Paris: l'Harmattan, 2008), 40–42.

37. J.-E. Zaldívar, "Rapport technique vétérinaire sur les corridas: Pourquoi il est indéniable que le taureau souffre" [Technical veterinary report on the corrida: Why it is undeniable that the bull suffers], 4–5, at http://flac-anticorrida.org.

38. Cited in A. Civard-Racinais, *Dictionnaire horrifié de la souffrance animale* [The

horrified dictionary of animal suffering] (Paris: Fayard, 2010), Kindle edition, 1097.

39. Wikipedia article "L'estocade" [The stabbing of the bull].

40. Zaldívar, "Rapport technique vétérinaire sur les corridas," 1.

41. Cited in Civard-Racinais, *Dictionnaire horrifié de la souffrance animale*, Kindle edition, 1335.

42. Wolff, "Corrida: vers un triomphe des valeurs humanistes?," *Le Figaro*, August 16, 2010.

43. F. Wolff, "La vaine rhétorique des avocats des taureaux" [The empty rhetoric of the advocates of the bulls], *Libération*, September 7, 2010.

44. E. Hemingway, *Death in the Afternoon* (New York: Charles Scribners Sons, 1932), EPUB 183.

45. M. Leiris, *Miroir de la tauromachie* [Tauromachy as a mirror] (Paris: Éditions GLM, 1938).

46. Hardouin-Fugier cites in particular the eminent jurist Roger Nerson, who in an article entitled "La condition animale au regard du droit" [The animal condition in the sight of the law], declared that "there are monstrous hypocrites among animal advocates given that the Nazis outlawed force-feeding of geese under the Third Reich and prohibited experimentation with animals in the same Auschwitz camp where they were using humans as guinea pigs!" Having said this, Nerson goes on in an abusive manner to postulate the existence of an intrinsic relationship between these two factors that are not in the least causally linked. He also criticizes Luc Ferry for having fallen into the same error in his work, *Le nouvel ordre écologique: l'arbre, l'animal et l'homme* [The new ecological order: Trees, animals and humans] (Paris: Grasset, 1992) in which he writes, "We must look into the disquieting implications of the link between the most sincere zoophilia (which doesn't simply talk the talk, but also really takes action) with the hatred of the most relentlessly brutal men in history" (p. 184). É. Hardouin-Fugier, "La vivisection est supprimée en Allemagne: recyclage et exploitation d'une désinformation récurrente (1933–2009)" [Vivisection has been prohibited in Germany: Recycling and exploitation of a recurrent piece of disinformation (1933–2009)], *Revue semestrielle de droit animalier* 1 (2009), 207–14.

47. Wolff, "La vaine rhétorique des avocats des taureaux." See also Wolff, "Corrida: vers un triomphe des valeurs humanistes?," 655.

48. Penal code, line 3 of article 521-1.

49. IFOP poll, May 2010.

50. See my article "L'interdiction de la corrida: un pas vers la civilisation" [The prohibition of the corrida: A step in the direction of civilization], *Le Figaro*, August 4, 2010.

51. A. Renaut, "L'esprit de la corrida" [The spirit of the corrida], *La Règle du jeu* 7 (1992): 94.

52. Wolff, "Corrida: vers un triomphe des valeurs humanistes?," 546–51.

53. The international Convention on the Rights of the Child—the most ratified human rights convention in the world—guarantees the right of all children less than eighteen years of age (male and female) to conditions of life that are favorable to their physical, psychological, moral, and social development and requires signatory states to adopt measures that protect this right of children.

54. Wolff, "Corrida: vers un triomphe des valeurs humanistes?," 408.

55. A. Zozaya (1859–1943), in Sociedad Protectora de Animales, *Por los seres indefensos (¡Pobres animales!)* [On behalf of defenseless beings: Poor animals!], *Antología Zoofila*, 1910; French translation by the Countess de San Jorge, *En faveur des êtres sans défense: pauvres bêtes! Anthologie zoophile espagnole* [1925] (Bayonne, France: Imprimerie du Courrier, n.d.), 25–31. Cited in Jeangène Vilmer, *L'éthique animale*, 236–37.

56. In the documentary film *Earthlings* directed by S. Monson (Burbank, CA: Nation Earth, 2006), available at www.earthlings.com.

57. Interview of animal trainer Vladimir Deriabkine by Vladimir Kojemiakine, *Courrier International*, no. 641, March 13, 2003.

58. Following Civard-Racinais, *Dictionnaire horrifié de la souffrance animale*, Kindle edition, 1041.

59. É. Baratay, "Belles captives: une histoire des zoos du côté des bêtes," a chapter in *Beauté animale: catalogue de l'exposition*, Galeries nationales du Grand Palais, March 21 to July 16, 2012 (Paris: RMN, 2012). See also É. Baratay and É. Hardouin-Fugier, *Zoos* (Paris: La Découverte, 2013).

60. "Le drame animal" [The animal drama], *Le Figaro*, from August 28 to September 2, 1974.

61. "Prisons dans un jardin" [Prisons in a garden], *Le Figaro*, June 11, 1974.

62. Great thanks to Norin Chai for his pointers and for having reread the pages on zoos.

63. Notably (in France) the law of March 25, 2004, www.legifrance.gouv.fr /affichTexte.do?cidTexte=JORFTEXT000020735788.

64. www.defra.gov.uk/ahvla-en/imports-exports/balai-directive.

65. S. L. Deem, "Role of the Zoo Veterinarian in the Conservation of Captive and Free-Ranging Wildlife," *International Zoo Yearbook* 41, no. 1 (2007), 3–11. The Internet site of the association of world zoos and aquariums (www.waza .org) is a precious source for numerous projects sponsored by zoos throughout the world.

66. We can cite the white-nose syndrome among bats (*Geomyces destructans*) in North America, West Nile among numerous bird species (for example, crows), and chytridiomycosis (*Baqtrachochytrium dendrobatidis*) among amphibians (personal communication from Norin Chai). Regarding the Galápagos Islands, see P. G. Parker, N. K. Whiteman, and R. E. Miller, "Conservation Medicine on the Galápagos Islands: Partnerships among Behavioral, Population, and Veterinary Scientists," *The Auk* 123, no. 3 (2006): 625–38; and P. G. Parker and S. L. Deem, "Wildlife Health Monitoring and Disease

Management: Protecting the Biodiversity of Galápagos," in M. Wolff and M. Gardener, *The Role of Science for Conservation* (London and New York: Routledge, 2012).

67. A multidisciplinary approach (One Health/Conservation Medicine programs) studies the interconnection between the health of wild animals, domestic animals, and humans and their ecosystems. S. L. Deem, "Disease Risk Analysis in Wildlife Health Field Studies," in M. E. Fowler and R. E. Miller, *Zoo and Wild Animal Medicine: Current Therapy* (St. Louis, MO: Elsevier Health Sciences, 2011), 2–7.

68. É. Baratay and É. Hardouin-Fugier, *Zoos: Histoire des jardins zoologiques en occident* [Zoos: The history of zoological gardens in the west] (Paris: La Découverte, 1998).

69. Many NGOs, such as One Voice, contribute to the creation and development of such sanctuaries.

70. The video of the chimpanzee with Jane Goodall can be seen on the site of the Jane Goodall Institute, www.janegoodall.org. In 2006 the Jane Goodall Institute (JGI) created the Chimp Eden sancturary in the magnificent 1,000 hectare natural reserve of Umhloti. It is the first, and for the moment the only, sanctuary for chimps in South Africa. The foundation's team is devoted to rehabilitating young orphan chimpanzees. The Help Congo Association has a similar program in the Congo.

71. Animals Asia Foundation.

72. A. Farrachi, "Le Zoo de Vincennes ouvre: ça ne change rien, c'est toujours une prison pour les animaux" [The Vincennes Zoo is opening: Nothing has changed, it's still a prison for animals], *Le Nouvel Observateur*, April 12, 2014.

73. See "Euthanasié, dépecé et jeté aux fauves: le sort d'un girafon bouleverse le Web" [Killed by euthanasia, cut up and thrown to the big cats: The fate of a baby giraffe upsets the Web], *Le Nouvel Observateur*, February 10, 2014.

74. www.slate.fr/life/83453/girafes-zoos.

75. "Après Marius le girafon, le zoo de Copenhague tue 4 lions" [After Marius the baby giraffe, the Copenhagen Zoo kills 4 lions], *Le Nouvel Observateur*, March 25, 2014.

76. Communication from the Copenhagen Zoo, March 25, 2014.

77. Broadcast in France on *Arte*, June 29, 2014.

78. See the files available on the site one-voice.fr: "Saison en enfer pour les dauphins" [Season in Hell for the dolphins]; "Dauphins captifs en état de choc" [Captive dolphins in a state of shock].

79. *The Cove* is an American documentary that won the Oscar for the best documentary film of 2010. Its subject was the controversial kill of 23,000 dolphins by fishermen in the Bay of Taiji, Wakayama Prefecture, Japan. The film also won the U.S. Audience Award at the Sundance Film Festival in January 2009.

80. According to www.abolition-chasse.org/chasse_chasseurs.htm.

81. Cited in *Le Nouvel Observateur* special coverage, "Le Bonheur" [Happiness], 1988, 35. Also the source of the following citations of W. Churchill and P. Clostermann.

82. Michael McIntosh was a shotgun writer and a regular contributor to the *Missouri Conservationist*, the magazine of the Missouri conservation department. Quoted at http://blog.timesunion.com/animalrights/the-hunting-delusion/4436.

83. www.nraila.org/issues/hunting-and-conservation.

84. "La chasse, nécessité écologique ou simple divertissement" [Hunting: Ecological necessity or just entertainment], *Libre Belgique*, October 13, 2013.

85. See www.one-voice.fr/loisirs-et-compagnie-sans-violence/les-chasseurs-gestionnaires-de-la-faune-ou-comment-l-ecologie-t-elle-ete-detournee.

86. B. Luke, *The Feminist Care Tradition in Animal Ethics*. Cited in Jeangène Vilmer, *L'éthique animale*, 129. See also B. Luke, *Brutal: Manhood and the Exploitation of Animals* (Urbana and Chicago: University of Illinois Press, 2007).

87. J. Nakos, "Théodore Monod et les protestants français défenseurs des animaux" [Théodore Monod and the French Protestant animal advocates], *Les Cahiers antispécistes*, nos. 30–31 (December 2008). Cited in A. Caron, *No Steak* (Paris: Fayard, 2013), Kindle edition, 2510.

88. A. Farrachi, representative of the Collectif pour l'Abolition de la Chasse à Courre [Association for the Abolition of Pack Hunting], *Libération*, November 10, 2008. Cited in Civard-Racinais, *Dictionnaire horrifié de la souffrance animale*.

89. Civard-Racinais, *Dictionnaire horrifié de la souffrance animale*, Kindle edition, 1402.

90. Ibid., 1405.

91. "La chasse a courre dans une société moderne à l'heure d'aujourd'hui: Art suranné ou Antiquité anachronique?" [Hunting with hounds in a modern society in the present day: Outdated art or anachronistic relic?], article by Foulques Jubert, 26 pp., www.thedogmuseum.com/images/TPE/Venerie-final.pdf.

92. R. Gordon-Cumming, *Five Years of a Hunter's Life in the Far Interior of South Africa: With Notices of the Native Tribes, and Anecdotes of the Chase of the Lion, Elephant* [1850] (Charleston, S.C.: Nabu Press, 2013). Cited in M. Midgley, *Animals and Why They Matter* (Athens: University of Georgia Press, 1984), 14–15.

93. C. Patterson, *Un éternel Treblinka* [Eternal Treblinka] (Paris: Calmann-Lévy, 2008), 207.

CHAPTER 12. ANIMAL RIGHTS, HUMAN OBLIGATIONS

1. F. Burgat, *Une autre existence: La condition animale* [Another existence: The animal condition] (Paris: Albin Michel, 2011), Kindle edition, 287.

2. H. S. Salt, *Animals' Rights: Considered in Relation to Social Progress* [1894], ed.

Society for Animal Rights, www.animal-rights-library.com/texts-c/salt01 .htm.

3. R. T. De George, "The Environment, Rights, and Future Generations," in *Responsibilities to Future Generations*, ed. E. Partridge (Buffalo, NY: Prometheus Books, 1981), 157–65. A former professor at Oberlin College in Ohio, Norman Care maintains that one cannot entertain bonds of love with beings of the future, or even properly consider them, and that "their interests are not capable of interesting us." N. S. Care, "Future Generations, Public Policy, and the Motivation Problem," *Environmental Ethics* 4, no. 3 (2008): 195–213.

4. M. Midgley, *Animals and Why They Matter* (Athens: University of Georgia Press, 1984), 63.

5. P. Singer, *Animal Liberation* (New York: Harper Perennial Modern Classics, 2009), passim.

6. Ibid., 8.

7. Ibid.

8. According to Regan, the formal principle of justice requires that each individual be given his or her due. This point is not controversial. The controversy begins when we ask what their due is. The answers to this question offer either normative interpretations or theories of justice. Three of these interpretations have been considered: (1) perfectionism, which maintains that what is due to individuals is a function of the degree to which they possess certain qualities (for example, intellectual capacity); (2) utilitarianism, which maintains that what is due to individuals is equal consideration of their interests (or pleasures, etc.); and (3) the theory of the equality of individuals, which maintains that what is due to individuals is equal respect for their intrinsic value. T. Regan, *La philosophie des droits des animaux* [The philosophy of animal rights], trans. D. Olivier (Lyon, France: Françoise Blanchon Éditeur, 1991), 510. This work is a simplified version of the great classic by the same author, T. Regan: *Les droits des animaux* [Animal rights], trans. E. Utria (Paris: Hermann, 2013), which appeared in 1983 under the title *The Case of Animal Rights*.

9. Regan, *La philosophie des droits des animaux*. Cited in J.-B. Jeangène Vilmer, *Anthologie d'éthique animale: apologies des bêtes* [Anthology of animal ethics: In praise of animals] (Paris: PUF, 2011), 312.

10. Ibid., 23.

11. For a detailed presentation, see Regan, *La philosophie des droits des animaux*, 328ff.

12. Jeangène Vilmer, *Anthologie d'éthique animale*, 19–20.

13. Regan, *La philosophie des droits des animaux*, 487, 497, and 537.

14. F. de Waal, *The Bonobo and the Atheist: In Search of Humanism among the Primates* (New York: W.W. Norton, 2013), 4 and 17.

15. C. R. Von Rohr et al., "Impartial Third-Party Interventions in Captive Chimpanzees: A Reflection of Community Concern," *PLoS ONE* 7 (2012): e32494.

16. S. Brosnan and F. de Waal, "Monkeys Reject Unequal Pay," *Nature* 425 (2003): 297–99.

17. F. de Waal, *The Bonobo and the Atheist*, 17.

18. Ibid., 186. Bonobo stories from the Milwaukee County zoo, told by the ape caretaker Barbara Bell to Jo Sandin and myself. J. Sandin, *Bonobos: Encounters in Empathy* (Milwaukee, WI: Zoological, 2007).

19. de Waal, *The Bonobo and the Atheist*, 311 and 327.

20. L. Lespine, "Les souffrances et les droits des animaux" [Suffering and the rights of animals], a lecture given in Geneva at the Bureau international humanitaire Zoophile (International Bureau of Humanitarian Animal Lovers), September 14, 1928, published by the Animal Defence and Anti-Vivisection Society. Cited in Jeangène Vilmer, *Anthologie d'éthique animale*, 248–49.

21. J.-J. Rousseau, Preface to the *Discours sur l'origine et les fondements de l'inégalité parmi les hommes* [Discourse on the origin and foundations of inequality among human beings] (Amsterdam, The Netherlands: Marc-Michel Rey Éditeur, 1755).

22. H. Grotius, *The Rights of War and Peace including the Law of Nature and of Nations*, trans. A. C. Campbell (New York: M. Walter Dunne, 1901), bk. I, chap. 1, § 11. Cited in Tristam, Kindle edition, 4186–4202.

23. Lespine, "Les souffrances et les droits des animaux."

24. F. Wolff, *Notre humanité: d'Aristote aux neurosciences* [Our humanity: From Aristotle to the neurosciences] (Paris: Fayard, 2010), 328.

25. Ibid., 328–29. Francis Wolff does, however, acknowledge that "the radical forms of industrial production are morally shocking because, transforming animals into machines for making meat, they violate the implicit contract of domestication (quid pro quo, use for use) which has generally existed between humans and the animals in their service."

26. Ibid., 329–30.

27. Ibid., 313.

28. M. Gibert, *Voir son steak comme un animal mort: Véganisme et psychologie morale* (Montreal, Canada: Lux Éditeur, 2015), 173.

29. Wolff, *Notre humanité*, Kindle edition, 767.

30. Regan, *La philosophie des droits des animaux*.

31. Í. Kant, *Leçons d'éthique* [Lecture on ethics] (Paris: Le Livre de poche, 1997), 391–93. Translation modified by Enrique Utria, translator of Tom Regan, based on Kant's "Von den Pflichten gegen Tiere und Geister" [On our duties toward animals and spirits], in *Eine Vorlesung Kants über Ethik* [Lecture on ethics], ed. P. Menzer (Berlin: Rolf Heise, 1924). Adapted in P. Singer and T. Regan, *Animal Rights and Human Obligations* (Longman Higher Education, 1976), chap. 1, note 2.

32. P. Janet, *Éléments de morale rédigés conformément aux programmes officiels de 1866* [Elements of morality formulated in accordance with the official programs of

1866] (Paris: Ch. Delagrave, 1869), chap. XI, § 2, 185–92. Cited in Jeangène Vilmer, *Anthologie d'éthique animale*, 177.

33. See in particular the presentation by the American philosopher Joel Feinberg: "The Rights of Animals and Unborn Generations" [1971], trans. H.-S. Afeissa in *Philosophie* 97 (2008): 66–71. Cited in Jeangène Vilmer, *Anthologie d'éthique animale*, 284–85.

34. Regan, *La philosophie des droits des animaux*, 371.

35. For example, by referring to Kant's categorical imperative.

36. Midgley, *Animals and Why They Matter*, 6.

37. J. H. Moore, *The Universal Kinship* (Chicago: Charles H. Kerr, 1906), 277.

38. P. Rouget, *La violence de l'humanisme: pourquoi nous faut-il persécuter les animaux?* [The violence of humanism: Why must we persecute animals?] (Paris: Calmann-Lévy, 2014), Kindle edition, 867.

39. Ibid., 1090–1094.

40. According to B. Cyrulnik, É. de Fontenay, P. Singer, K. L. Matignon, and D. Rosane, *Les animaux aussi ont des droits* [Animals have rights too] (Paris: Le Seuil, 2013), Kindle edition, 3184.

41. See E. Reus, "Quels droits politiques pour les animaux? Introduction à *Zoopolis* de Sue Donaldson et Will Kymlicka," *Les Cahiers antispécistes*, no. 37 (May 2015).

42. S. Donaldson and W. Kymlicka, *Zoopolis: A Political Theory of Animal Rights* (Oxford: Oxford University Press, 2011).

43. Ibid. *Zoopolis*, 98.

44. Ibid., *Zoopolis*, 40.

45. Cited in É. de Fontenay, *Sans offenser le genre humain: Réflexions sur la cause animale* [No offense to the human species: Reflections on the animal cause] (Paris: Albin Michel, 2008), 115.

46. Articles 526 and 524.

47. Respectively articles R.653-1, R.655-1, R.654-1, and R.521-1 of the penal code. These modifications of the penal code and the rural code were carried out thanks to the efforts of Senator Laurent.

48. For more details, see *Les cahiers antispécistes* [The anti-speciesist journal], nos. 30–31 (December 2008).

49. A. Goetschel, in his speech "Le Droit de l'Animal" [Animal rights], at a conference organised by Ecolo-Ethik in the French senate, February 7, 2014.

50. J.-P. Marguénaud, "La personnalité juridique des animaux" [Animals as legal persons], in the *Bulletin juridique international pour la protection des animaux (BJAPA) et Recueil Dalloz*, no. 20 (1998): 205. Cited in É. de Fontenay in Cyrulnik et al., *Les animaux aussi ont des droits*, Kindle edition, 2043.

51. É. de Fontenay in Cyrulnik et al., *Les animaux aussi ont des droits*, Kindle edition, 2066–2067.

52. Comments collected by Audrey Garic for *Le Monde*, "Pourquoi les animaux sont toujours considérés comme des biens" [Why animals are always regarded

as goods], April 17, 2014, and "Les animaux reconnus comme 'êtres sensibles,' un pas totalement symbolique" [Animals Recognized as "sentient beings," a totally symbolic step), *Le Monde*, April 16, 2014.

53. Ibid.

CONCLUSION

1. In the United States there are 300 million firearms in circulation, which are the cause of 30,000 deaths per year, of which around 10,000 are murders.

2. In 2012, 370 whales were killed in Iceland. In the case of Japan, which annually kills 1,000 whales, the International Court of Justice, which recently condemned Japan's "scientific fishing," pointed out that only two scientific articles on the subject of fishing, which were of no great value, had been published in that country within the past fifteen years. This shows clearly that in reality the fishing in question is commercial fishing. In Iceland the killing of whales is now carried out only by a single company, Hvalur H/F, whose owner, Kristjan Loftsson, is determined to carry on with whale fishing as a matter of principle because it is no longer profitable as a business. According to a report by the International Whaling Commission, Hvalur caught hundreds of undersized common and boreal rorqual whales and exported their meat to Japan. Some of Loftsson's children are now opposed to this practice, and so we may hope that it will disappear in the not too distant future. Besides Iceland and Japan, only Norway and the Faroe Islands continue to kill whales.

3. M. Kundera, *The Unbearable Lightness of Being*, trans. M. H. Heim (New York: Harper Perennial, 1991), 289.

4. The golden rule—do not do to others what you would not have them do to you—is found in all the great religions and cultures. If in the "religions of the book" this rule concerns only humans, this is not at all the case in other religions and cultures. As early as the fourth to third centuries B.C.E., the *Mahábhárata* of the Hindus tells us: "This is the highest point of duty: do not do to others what you would not wish them to do to you." Buddhism poses the question, "How could I inflict on others what is painful to me?" (Udana-Varga 5:18). Jainism affirms: "Every man should treat all creatures as he would wish to be treated" (Sutrakritanga 1.11.33). Confucianism declares: "What you do not wish for yourself, do not impose upon others." Judaism teaches: "Thou shalt not avenge, nor bear any grudge against the children of thy people, but thou shalt love thy neighbour as thyself" (Leviticus 19:18). Jesus urges us: "Love thy neighbor as thyself" (Matthew 22:36–40). In the sixth to seventh century, Muhammad said: "None of you truly believes until he wishes for his brother what he wishes for himself" (Hadith 13 of Imam al-Nawawi). The Taoists, Zoroastrians, ancient Egyptians, Sikhs, Native Americans, and many other cultures also have forms of this rule. Wikipedia article "Golden Rule."

5. A. Schopenhauer, *The Basis of Morality*, trans. A. B. Bullock (London: Trinity College, Cambridge, 1903), 213–14.
6. B. Russell, "If Animals Could Talk," in *Mortals and Others: Bertrand Russell's American Essays 1931–1935*, vol. 1 (London: Allen and Unwin, 1975), 120–21.
7. On this point, see the presentation of D. Lestel in *L'animal est l'avenir de l'homme* [Animals are the future of man] (Paris: Fayard, 2010), 139.
8. M. Cole and K. Morgan, "Vegaphobia: Derogatory Discourses of Veganism and the Reproduction of Speciesism in UK National Newspapers," *British Journal of Sociology* 62, no. 1 (2011): 142. According to M. Gibert, *Voir son steak comme un animal mort: Véganisme et psychologie morale* (Montreal, Canada: Lux Éditeur, 2015), 134–35.
9. J. Minson and B. Monin, "Do-Gooder Derogation Disparaging Morally Motivated Minorities to Defuse Anticipated Reproach," *Social Psychological and Personality Science*, 3, no. 2 (2012): 200–207. According to Gibert, *Voir son steak comme un animal mort*, 134–35.
10. Gibert, *Voir son steak comme un animal mort*, 134–35.
11. R. Larue, *Le végétarisme et ses ennemis* (Paris: Presses Universitaires de France [PUF], 2015), 255–56.
12. J. Serpell, *In the Company of Animals: A Study of Human-Animal Relationships* (Oxford and New York: B. Blackwell, 1986), 234.
13. A. Hochschild, *Bury the Chains: Prophets and Rebels in the Fight to Free an Empire's Slaves* (Boston: Houghton Mifflin Harcourt, 2006), 7 and 86. Our text is based on extracts from this book compiled and translated by Antoine Comiti, http://abolitionblog.blogspot.co.uk. We thank him for having authorized us to use his work.
14. The latest of which is O. Grenouilleau, *Qu'est-ce que l'esclavage? Une histoire globale* [What is slavery?: A global history] (Paris: Gallimard, 2014).
15. Gibert, *Voir son steak comme un animal mort*, 9–10.
16. E. Lea and A. Worsley, "Benefits and Barriers to the Consumption of a Vegetarian Diet in Australia," *Public Health Nutrition* 6, no. 5 (2003): 505–11. Cited in Gibert, *Voir son steak comme un animal mort*, 184.
17. É. Zola, "L'Amour des bêtes" [The love of animals], *Le Figaro*, March 24, 1896. Cited in J.-B. Jeangène Vilmer, *Anthologie d'éthique animale: apologies des bêtes* [Anthology of Animal Ethics: In praise of animals] (Paris: PUF, 2011), 206.
18. With about 1.2 million hunters, France remains the number one hunting country in Europe. However, the number of hunters in France is diminishing every year. The traditional image of the typical hunter, that is, the farmer who goes out and shoots a rabbit on Sunday, is now a thing of the past. The hunter is more and more a city dweller between 55 and 60 years of age, and farmers now represent only 10 percent of hunters. Since hunting is no longer attracting young people, or hardly, this average age is going up constantly. The motivations expressed by hunters are contact with nature (99 percent), comradery (93 percent), and the maintenance of the land (89 percent). As the

organization Rassemblement pour l'abolition de la Chasse [Assembly for the Abolition of Hunting] asks, if that is the case, what do they need guns for? See http://www.abolition-chasse.org/chasse_chasseurs.htm.

19. According to a study by the General Social Survey, http://gss.norc.org. Cited in S. Pinker, *The Better Angels of Our Nature: Why Violence Has Declined* (New York: Viking Adult, 2011).

20. H. G. Wells, *Une utopie moderne* [A modern utopia] (Paris: Mercure de France, 1907).

21. "L'homme et la souffrance des animaux" [Humans and the suffering of animals], drawn from the "Sermon du 3ᵉ Dimanche de l'Avent" [Sermon on the third Sunday of Advent] [1908] and "La protection des animaux et les philosophes" [The Protection of Animals and the Philosophers] [1936], *Cahiers de l'association française des Amis d'Albert Schweitzer* [Journal of the French Association of Friends of Albert Schweitzer] 30 (Spring 1974): 3–13. Cited in Jean-gène Vilmer, *Anthologie d'éthique animale*, 233–34.

BIBLIOGRAPHY

What follows is a selection of works that will enable the reader to find further information on the subjects treated in this book. All of the bibliographic references, in particular the references to scientific articles, are found in the end notes. An electronic file containing all of these references (*Plaidoyer pour les animaux-bibliographie complète.pdf*) is available on the website www.matthieuricard.org/articles/categories/scientifique.

Ascione, F. R., and P. Arkow. *Child Abuse, Domestic Violence, and Animal Abuse: Linking the Circles of Compassion for Prevention and Intervention.* West Lafayette, IN: Purdue University Press, 1999.

Baratay, É., and É. Hardouin-Fugier. *Zoo: A History of Zoological Gardens in the West.* London: Reaktion Books, 2004.

Barr, S., P. R. Laming, J. T. Dick, and R. W. Elwood. "Nociception or Pain in a Decapod Crustacean?" *Animal Behaviour* 75, no. 3 (2008): 745–51.

Beck, A. M., and A. H. Katcher, *Between Pets and People: The Importance of Animal Companionship.* New York: Putnam, 1983.

Bekoff, M. *The Animal Manifesto: Six Reasons for Expanding Our Compassion Footprint.* Novato, CA: New World Library, 2010.

Bekoff, M., ed., *Ignoring Nature No More: The Case for Compassionate Conservation.* Chicago: University of Chicago Press, 2013.

Bekoff, M., and J. Goodall. *The Emotional Lives of Animals: A Leading Scientist Explores Animal Joy, Sorrow, and Empathy—and Why They Matter.* Novato, CA: New World Library, 2008.

Bekoff, M., and J. Pierce. *Wild Justice: The Moral Lives of Animals.* Chicago: University of Chicago Press, 2009.

Bekoff, P. D. M., and R. Louv. *Rewilding Our Hearts: Building Pathways of Compassion and Coexistence.* Novato, CA: New World Library, 2014.

Boesch, C. "Symbolic Communication in Wild Chimpanzees?" *Human Evolution* 6, no. 1 (1991): 81–89.

Boesch, C., and H. Boesch, "Mental Map in Wild Chimpanzees: An Analysis of Hammer Transports for Nut Cracking." *Primates* 25, no. 2 (1984): 160–70.

Boysen, S. T., and E. J. Capaldi. *The Development of Numerical Competence: Animal and Human Models* [eBook]. New York: Psychology Press, 2014.

Butler, V., "Inside the Mind of a Killer." August 31, 2003, *The Cyberactivist.* www.cyberactivist.blogspot.com. Traduit de l'anglais par David Olivier et publié dans *Les Cahiers antispécistes*, n° 23, December 2003.

Cavalieri, P. *The Animal Question: Why Nonhuman Animals Deserve Human Rights.* Oxford: Oxford University Press, 2003.

Chandroo, K. P., I. J. Duncan, and R. D. Moccia. "Can Fish Suffer? Perspectives on Sentience, Pain, Fear and Stress." *Applied Animal Behaviour Science* 86, no. 3 (2004): 225–50.

Chapouthier, G., and J.-C. Nouet, eds. *The Universal Declaration of Animal Rights: Comments and Intentions.* Paris: Ligue Francaise des Droits de l'Animal, 1998.

Chicago, J., and D. Woodman. *Holocaust Project: From Darkness into Light.* New York: Viking, 1993.

Clutton-Brock, J. *Domesticated Animals from Early Times.* London: Heinemann/ British Museum (Natural History), 1981.

Coe, S. *Dead Meat.* New York: Four Walls Eight Windows, 1996.

Coetzee, J. M. *Elizabeth Costello: huit leçons.* Paris: Le Seuil, 2006.

Corbey, R., and A. Lanjouw, eds. *The Politics of Species: Reshaping Our Relationships with Other Animals.* Cambridge: Cambridge University Press, 2013.

Darwin, C. *The Descent of Man, and Selection in Relation to Sex.* Introduction by A. Desmond and J. Moore. London: Penguin, 2004.

Daub, J.-L. *Ces bêtes qu'on abat: Journal d'un enquêteur dans les abattoirs français.* Paris: l'Harmattan, 2009.

Derrida, J. *The Animal That Therefore I Am.* 3rd ed. Translated by D. Wills and edited by M.-L. Mallet. New York: Fordham University Press, 2008.

Descartes, R. *Discours de la méthode pour bien conduire sa raison et chercher la vérité dans les sciences.* Paris: Compagnie des Libraires, 1724.

Desjardins, R., D. Worth, X. Vergé, D. Maxime, J. Dyer, and D. Cerkowniak. "Carbon Footprint of Beef Cattle." *Sustainability* 4, no. 12 (2012): 3279–3301.

Diamond, J. *Collapse: How Societies Choose to Fail or Succeed.* Rev. ed. New York: Penguin Books, 2011.

Donovan, J., and C. J. Adams. *Beyond Animal Rights: A Feminist Caring Ethic for the Treatment of Animals.* New York: Continuum, 1996.

Douglas, L. R., and K. Alie. "High-Value Natural Resources: Linking Wildlife Conservation to International Conflict, Insecurity, and Development Concerns." *Biological Conservation* 171 (2014): 270–77.

Dresner, S., and S. Siegel. *Jewish Dietary Laws.* New York: Rabbinical Assembly of America, United Synagogue Commission on Jewish Education, 1982.

Dunayer, J. *Speciesism.* Derwood, MD: Ryce, 2004.

Earthlings [documentary film]. Directed by Shaun Monson. Burbank, CA: Nation Earth, 2006. DVD. http://www.earthlings.com.

Eisemann, C. H., W. K. Jorgensen, D. J. Merritt, M. J. Rice, B. W. Cribb, P. D. Webb, and M. P. Zalucki. "Do insects feel pain? A biological view." *Cellular and Molecular Life Sciences* 40, no. 2 (1984): 164–67.

Eisnitz, G. A. *Slaughterhouse: The Shocking Story of Greed, Neglect, and Inhumane Treatment inside the U.S. Meat Industry.* Amherst, NY: Prometheus, 2006.

Elwood, R. W. "Pain and Suffering in Invertebrates?" *ILAR Journal* 52, no. 2 (2011): 175A–84.

Ensminger, M. E. *Animal Science.* Saddle River, NJ: Prentice Hall, 1990.

Feinberg, J. "The Rights of Animals and Unborn Generations" [1971]. Translated by H.-S. Afeissa. *Philosophie* 97 (2008).

Fiorito, G. "Is There *Pain* in Invertebrates?" *Behavioural Processes* 12, no. 4 (1986): 383–88.

Foer, J. S. *Eating Animals.* New York: Back Bay Books, 2010.

de Fontenay, É. *Le silence des bêtes, la philosophie à l'épreuve de l'animalité.* Paris: Fayard, 1998.

————. *Without Offending Humans: A Critique of Animal Rights.* Translated by W. Bishop. Minneapolis: University of Minnesota Press, 2012.

Food and Agriculture Organization of the United Nations (FAO). *Livestock's Long Shadow: Environmental Issues and Options.* Rome: FAO, 2006.

Francione, G., and A. Charlton. *Eat Like You Care: An Examination of the Morality of Eating Animals.* Kentucky: Exempla Press, 2013.

von Frisch, K. *The dancing bees: An account of the life and senses of the honey bee.* 1st American ed. New York: Harcourt, Brace, 1955.

Fry, D. P. *Beyond War: The Human Potential for Peace.* New York: Oxford University Press, 2007.

Goffi, J.-Y. *Le philosophe et ses animaux: Du statut éthique de l'animal.* Nîmes, France: Jacqueline Chambon, 1994.

Goodall, J. *The Chimpanzees of Gombe: Patterns of Behavior.* Cambridge, MA: Harvard University Press, 1986.

————. *In the shadow of man.* Boston: Mariner Books, 2000.

————. *Through a Window: My Thirty Years with the Chimpanzees of Gombe.* Phoenix: 2011.

————. "Tool-Using and Aimed Throwing in a Community of Free-Living Chimpanzees." *Nature* 201 (1964): 1264.

Goodall, J., and M. Bekoff. *The Ten Trusts: What We Must Do to Care for the Animals We Love.* New York: HarperOne, 2003.

Goodall, J., with P. L. Berman. *Reason for Hope: A Spiritual Journey.* New York: Grand Central, 1999.

Greene, J. D. *Moral Tribes: Emotion, Reason, and the Gap between Us and Them.* London: Atlantic Books, 2013.

Grenouilleau, O. *Qu'est-ce que l'esclavage? Une histoire globale.* Paris: Gallimard, 2014.

Griffin, D. R. *Animal Minds: Beyond Cognition to Consciousness.* Chicago: University of Chicago Press, 1992.

————. *The Question of Animal Awareness: Evolutionary Continuity of Mental Experience.* New York: Rockefeller University Press, 1976.

Griffin, D. R., and G. B. Speck. "New evidence of animal consciousness." *Animal Cognition* 7, no. 1 (2004): 5–18.

Haidt, J. *The Righteous Mind: Why Good People Are Divided by Politics and Religion.* London: Allen Lane, 2012.

Hardouin-Fugier, E. *Bullfighting: A Troubled History*. Translated by S. Rose. London: Reaktion Books, 2010.

Harlow, H. F. *Love in Infant Monkeys*. San Francisco: W.H. Freeman, 1959.

Harrison, R. *Animal Machines: The New Factory Farming Industry*. Rev. ed. Boston: CABI, 2013. First edition, 1964.

Hedenus, F., S. Wirsenius, and D. J. A. Johansson. "The Importance of Reduced Meat and Dairy Consumption for Meeting Stringent Climate Change Targets." *Climatic Change* (2014): 1–13.

Heim, A. *Intelligence and Personality*. New York: Pelican, 1971.

Herrnstein, R. J., D. H. Loveland, and C. Cable. "Natural Concepts in Pigeons." *Journal of Experimental Psychology: Animal Behavior Processes* 2, no. 4 (1976): 285.

Herzog, H. *Some We Love, Some We Hate, Some We Eat: Why It's So Hard to Think Straight about Animals*. New York: Harper Perennial, 2011.

Ikhwan al-Safa and L. E. Goodman. *The Case of the Animals versus Man before the King of the Jinn: A Tenth-Century Ecological Fable of the Pure Brethren of Basra*. Boston: Twayne, 1978.

Ingold, T. *Hunters, Pastoralists, and Ranchers: Reindeer Economies and Their Transformations*. Cambridge: Cambridge University Press, 1980.

Jancovici, J.-M. *L'avenir climatique: Quel temps ferons-nous?* Paris: Le Seuil, 2005.

Jeangène Vilmer, J.-B. *Anthologie d'éthique animale: Apologies des bêtes*. Paris: PUF, 2011.

———. *Éthique animale*. Paris: Presses Universitaires de France (PUF), 2008.

Jonas, H. *The Phenomenon of Life: Toward a Philosophical Biology*. Evanston, IL: Northwestern University Press, 2000.

Joy, M. *Why We Love Dogs, Eat Pigs, and Wear Cows: An Introduction to Carnism*. San Francisco: Conari Press, 2010.

King, B. J. *How Animals Grieve*. Reprint. Chicago: University of Chicago Press, 2013.

Kroeber, A. L., and B. Kluckhohn. "Culture: A Critical Review of Concepts and Definitions." In *Papers of the Peabody Museum of Archaeology and Ethnology, Harvard University*, vol. 47, no.1. Cambridge, MA: The Museum, 1952.

Kundera, M. *The Unbearable Lightness of Being: A Novel*. Deluxe edition. New York: Harper Perennial Modern Classics, 2009.

Lambin, E. *An Ecology of Happiness*. Translated by T. L. Fagan. Chicago: University of Chicago Press, 2012.

Lappé, F. M. *Diet for a Small Planet*. New York: Ballantine Books, 1971.

Lévi-Strauss, C. *The Savage Mind*. Chicago: University of Chicago Press, 1966.

———. *Structural Anthropology*. Rev. ed. New York: Basic Books, 1974.

Levine, M. E., J. A. Suarez, S. Brandhorst, P. Balasubramanian, C.-W. Cheng, F. Madia, and V. D. Longo. "Low Protein Intake Is Associated with a Major Reduction in IGF-1, Cancer, and Overall Mortality in the 65 and Younger but Not Older Population." *Cell Metabolism* 19, no. 3 (2014): 407–17.

Linzey, A. *Animal Gospel: Christian Faith as though Animals Mattered*. London: Hodder and Stoughton, 1998.

————. *The Link between Animal Abuse and Human Violence*. Portland, OR: Sussex Academic Press, 2009.

Luke, B. *Brutal: Manhood and the Exploitation of Animals*. Urbana and Chicago: University of Illinois Press, 2007.

————. "Justice, Caring, and Animal Liberation." *The Feminist Care Tradition in Animal Ethics* (2007): 125–52.

Mann, J. *Cetacean Societies: Field Studies of Dolphins and Whales*. Chicago: University of Chicago Press, 2000.

Marana, G. P. *The Eight Volumes of Letters Writ by a Turkish Spy [G.P. Marana] at Paris. Tr. [By W. Bradshaw. Vol.1 Only of the 11th Ed. of the Whole]*. Reprint. Charleston, SC: Nabu Press, 2010.

Marshall, A. J. *Bower-Birds: Their Displays and Breeding Cycles, a Preliminary Statement*. Oxford: Clarendon Press, 1954.

Matsuzawa, T. "Field Experiments on Use of Stone Tools by Chimpanzees in the Wild." *Chimpanzee Cultures* (1994): 351–70.

————. "Sociocognitive Development in Chimpanzees: A Synthesis of Laboratory Work and Fieldwork." In *Cognitive Development in Chimpanzees*, edited by T. Matsuzawa, M. Tomonaga, and M. Tanaka. Tokyo: Springer, 2006.

————. "Use of Numbers by a Chimpanzee." *Nature* 315, no. 6014 (1985): 57–59.

McGrew, W. C. *The Cultured Chimpanzee: Reflections on Cultural Primatology*. Cambridge: Cambridge University Press, 2004.

de La Mettrie, J. O. *La Mettrie: Machine Man and Other Writings*. Edited by A. Thomson. Cambridge: Cambridge University Press, 1996.

Midgley, M. *Animals and Why They Matter*. Athens: University of Georgia Press, 1984.

————. *Beast and Man: The Roots of Human Nature*. London: Routledge, 2002.

Monod, T., and S. Estibal. *Terre et ciel: Entretiens avec Sylvain Estibal*. Arles, France: Actes Sud, 1997.

Monroe, K. R. *The Heart of Altruism: Perceptions of a Common Humanity*. Cambridge University Press, 1996.

Mood, A., and P. Brooke. *Estimating the Number of Fish Caught in Global Fishing Each Year*. July 2010. http://www.fishcount.org.uk/published/std/fishcountstudy.pdf

Morris, D. *The Biology of Art: A Study of the Picture-Making Behaviour of the Great Apes and Its Relationship to Human Art*. London: Methuen, 1962.

Nussbaum, M. *Frontiers of Justice: Disability, Nationality, Species Membership*. Cambridge, MA: Harvard University Press, 2006.

Pan, A., Q. Sun, A. M. Bernstein, M. B. Schulze, J. E. Manson, M. J. Stampfer, and F. B. Hu. "Red Meat Consumption and Mortality: Results from 2 Prospective Cohort Studies." *Archives of Internal Medicine* 172, no. 7 (2012): 555.

Patterson, C. *Eternal Treblinka: Our Treatment of Animals and the Holocaust*. New York: Lantern Books, 2002.

Payne, R. *Communication and Behavior of Whales*. Boulder, CO: Westview Press, 1983.

Pepperberg, I. M., and I. M. Pepperberg. *The Alex Studies: Cognitive and Communicative Abilities of Grey Parrots*. Cambridge, MA: Harvard University Press, 2009.

Pinker, S. *The Better Angels of Our Nature: Why Violence Has Declined.* New York: Viking Adult, 2011.

Plutarch. *Sur l'usage des viandes.* In *Traités de morale*, translated from the Greek by D. Ricard. Paris: Lefèvre Éditeur, 1844.

——, with É. de Fontenay. *Trois traités pour les animaux.* Translated by J. Amyot. Preceded by "La raison du plus fort" (Paris: P.O.L., 1992).

Porcher, J. *Vivre avec les animaux: Une utopie pour le XXIᵉ siècle.* Paris: La Découverte, 2011.

Primatt, H. *The Duty of Mercy and the Sin of Cruelty to Brute Animals.* Fontwell, Sussex: Centaur, 1992. First edition, 1776.

Rachels, J. *Created from Animals: The Moral Implications of Darwinism.* Oxford: Oxford University Press, 1990.

Regan, T. *Animal Rights, Human Wrongs: An Introduction to Moral Philosophy.* Lanham, MD: Rowman & Littlefield, 2003.

——. *The Case for Animal Rights.* Berkeley: University of California Press, 2004. Traduction française d'E. Utria: *Les droits des animaux.* Paris: Hermann, 2013.

Rensch, B. "The Intelligence of Elephants." *Scientific American* 196 (1957): 44–49.

——. "Play and Art in Apes and Monkeys." In *Precultural Primate Behavior*, edited by E. W. Menzel. New York: Karger, 1973.

Ricard, M. *Altruism: The Power of Compassion to Change Yourself and the World.* New York: Little, Brown, 2015.

Richerson, P. J., and R. Boyd. *Not by Genes Alone: How Culture Transformed Human Evolution.* Chicago: University of Chicago Press, 2004.

Rifkin, J. *The Third Industrial Revolution: How Lateral Power Is Transforming Energy, the Economy, and the World.* Basingstoke: Palgrave Macmillan Trade, 2013.

Rockström, J., W. Steffen, K. Noone, Å. Persson, F. S. Chapin, E. F. Lambin, H. J. Schellnhuber et al. "A Safe Operating Space for Humanity." *Nature* 461, no. 7263 (2009): 472–75.

Roe, D., T. Mulliken, S. Milledge, J. Mremi, and S. Mosha. *Making a Killing or Making a Living: Wildlife Trade, Trade Controls, and Rural Livelihoods.* London: IIED, 2002.

Rollin, B. E. *Animal rights and human morality.* Buffalo, NY: Prometheus Books, 1992.

——. *The Unheeded Cry: Animal Consciousness, Animal Pain, and Science.* Oxford: Oxford University Press, 1989.

Rouget, P. *La violence de l'humanisme: pourquoi nous faut-il persécuter les animaux?* Paris: Calmann-Lévy, 2014.

Rousseau, J.-J. *Discours sur l'origine et les fondements de l'inégalité parmi les hommes.* Paris: Aubier, 1973.

Russel, B. "If Animals Could Talk." In *Mortals and Others: American Essays 1931–1935.* London and New York: Routledge, 2009.

Ryder, R. *Animal Revolution: Changing Attitudes towards Speciesism.* Oxford and New York: Berg, 2000.

——. "Experiments on Animals." *Animals, Men, and Morals* (1971): 41–82.

————. "Speciesism Again: The Original Leaflet." *Critical Society* 2 (2010): 1–2.

————. *Victims of Science: The Use of Animals in Research.* London: Davis-Poynter, 1975.

Salt, H. S. "Animals' Rights: Considered in Relation to Social Progress" [1892]. Clarks Summit, PA: Society for Animal Rights, 1980.

Schopenhauer, A., and D. E. Cartwright. *On the Basis of Morality.* Rep Sub edition. Translated by E. F. J. Payn. Indianapolis, IN: Hackett, 1999.

Seidle, T., and H. Spielmann. *Alternative Testing Strategies Progress Report 2011 and AXLR8-2 Workshop Report on a "Roadmap to Innovative Toxicity Testing."* AXLR8 Consortium, 2011.

Semelin, J. *Purify and Destroy: The Political Uses of Massacre and Genocide.* Translated by C. Schoch. New York: Columbia University Press, 2009.

Serpell, J. *In the Company of Animals: A Study of Human-Animal Relationships.* Oxford and New York: B. Blackwell, 1986.

Shabkar. *Food of Bodhisattvas: Buddhist Teachings on Abstaining from Meat.* Translated by Padmakara Translation Group. Boston: Shambhala Publications, 2011.

Shantideva. *The Way of the Bodhisattva.* Rev. ed. Translated by Padmakara Translation Group. Boston: Shambhala Publications, 2006.

Shelley, P. B. *The Complete Works of Percy Bysshe Shelley.* Edited by R. Ingpen and W. E. Peck. New York: Gordian Press, 1965.

Shumaker, R. W., K. R. Walkup, and B. B. Beck. *Animal Tool Behavior: The Use and Manufacture of Tools by Animals.* Baltimore, MD: Johns Hopkins University Press, 2011.

Sidgwick, H. "The Establishment of Ethical First Principles." *Mind* 4, no. 13 (1879): 106–111.

Sinclair, U. *The Jungle.* New York: Signet Classic, 1964.

Singer, I. B. *The Penitent.* New York: Penguin Classics, 2012.

Singer, P. *Animal Liberation: The Definitive Classic of the Animal Movement.* New York: Harper Perennial Modern Classics, 2009.

Singer, P., and T. Regan. *Animal Rights and Human Obligations.* Englewood Cliffs, NJ: Prentice Hall, 1976.

Spinney, L. "When Chimps Outsmart Humans." *New Scientist* 190 (2006): 48–49.

Stich, S. P. "Do Animals Have Beliefs?" *Australian Journal of Philosophy* 57, no. 1 (1979): 18.

Stuart, T. *The Bloodless Revolution: Radical Vegetarians and the Discovery of India.* London: HarperPress, 2012.

Thomas, K. *Man and the Natural World: A History of the Modern Sensibility.* New York: Pantheon Books, 1983.

Toynbee, J. M. C. *Animals in Roman Life and Art.* London: Thames and Hudson, 1973.

Tryon, T. *The Knowledge of a Man's Self.* London: T. Bennet, 1703.

Tuan, Yi-Fu. *The Making of Pets.* New Haven, CT: Yale University Press, 1984.

Tuchman, B. W. *A Distant Mirror: The Calamitous Fourteenth Century.* New York: Ballantine Books, 1991.

Tudge, C. *So Shall We Reap: What's Gone Wrong with the World's Food and How to Fix It.* London: Penguin UK, 2004.

Turner, A. K. "Proposed EU Changes in Animal Experimentation Regulations." *Medical Communications* 18, no. 4 (2009): 238.

Twain, M. *Adventures of Huckleberry Finn.* Berkeley, CA: University of California Press, 2003.

Varela, F. J. *Ethical Know-How: Action, Wisdom, and Cognition.* Stanford, CA: Stanford University Press, 1999.

Voltaire. *Pensées végétariennes.* Edited by Renan Larue. Paris: Fayard/Mille et une nuits, 2014.

de Waal, F. B. M. *The Age of Empathy: Nature's Lessons for a Kinder Society.* New York: Broadway Books, 2010.

———. *The Bonobo and the Atheist: In Search of Humanism among the Primates.* New York: W. W. Norton, 2014.

———. *Good Natured: The Origins of Right and Wrong in Humans and Other Animals.* Cambridge, MA: Harvard University Press, 1997.

de Waal, F. B. M., and F. Lanting. *Bonobo: The Forgotten Ape.* Berkeley, CA: University of California Press, 1998.

Watanabe, S., J. Sakamoto, and M. Wakita. "Pigeons' Discrimination of Paintings by Monet and Picasso." *Journal of the Experimental Analysis of Behavior* 63, no. 2 (1995): 165.

Weary, D. M., L. Niel, F. C. Flower, and D. Fraser. "Identifying and Preventing Pain in Animals." *Applied Animal Behaviour Science* 100, no. 1 (2006): 64–76.

Whiten, A., J. Goodall, W. C. McGrew, T. Nishida, V. Reynolds, Y. Sugiyama, and C. Boesch. "Cultures in Chimpanzees." *Nature* 399, no. 6737 (1999): 682–85.

Wijkman, A., and J. Rockström. *Bankrupting Nature: Denying Our Planetary Boundaries.* New York: Routledge, 2012.

Wise, S. M. *Drawing the Line: Science and the Case for Animal Rights.* Cambridge, MA: Perseus Books, 2002.

Wise, S. M., and J. Goodall. *Rattling the Cage: Toward Legal Rights for Animals.* Cambridge, MA: Perseus, 2001.

Wistrand, M. *Entertainment and Violence in Ancient Rome: The Attitudes of Roman Writers of the First Century A.D.* Göteborg, Sweden: Acta Universitatis Gothoburgensis, 1992.

Wolff, F. *50 raisons de défendre la corrida.* Paris: Fayard/Mille et une nuits, 2010.

———. *Notre humanité: D'Aristote aux neurosciences.* Paris: Fayard, 2010.

———. *Philosophie de la corrida.* Paris: Fayard, 2007.

Wolff, M., and M. Gardener. *The Role of Science for Conservation.* London and New York: Routledge, 2012.

Wyatt, T. *Wildlife Trafficking: A Deconstruction of the Crime, the Victims, and the Offenders.* New York: Palgrave Macmillan, 2013.

Yourcenar, M. *Les yeux ouverts: Entretiens avec Matthieu Galey.* Paris: Le Livre de Poche, 1982.

INDEX

anthropocentric denial/anthropode-
nial, 132–33, 299n52
anthropocentric utilitarians, 171–72
anthropocentrism, 12, 36, 252–53
vs. anthropomorphism, 131–36
See also human exceptionalism; human supremacism; speciesism
anthropomorphism vs. anthropocentrism, 131–36
antibiotic use in livestock, 67, 77
Antonio, Luiz, 51–53
Apollonius of Tyana, 32
Aquinas, Saint Thomas, 14, 15
Aristophanes, 17
Ashoka, Emperor, 31, 281n94
Asian traditions, viewpoint of the, 25–30
Augustine, Saint, 13–14
Austria, 260
automatic emotional reactions, 162

Bacon, Francis, 33–34
bad company, fallacy of, 216–17. See also
good company
Bailly, Jean-Christophe, 50–51
Bandura, Albert, 47–48
Banks, Debbie, 196
Baratay, Éric, 205–6, 224, 226
Baudement, Émile, 73
bear bile farms, 188–89, 196, 227
bears, Asian black, 188–89
Bedichek, Roy, 80
Bekoff, Marc, 127
Bell, Barbara, 246–47
Bencheikh, Soheib, 23
Bentham, Jeremy, 95–96, 160, 181
Bériot, Louis, 190
Bernard, Claude, 168–69
"bestial," 50, 107
Bible, 11–13, 319n4
Bishnoism, 27
Boesch, Christophe, 139
Boeuf, Gilles, 116
bonobos, 245–47
brains of omnivores, vegetarians, and
vegans, 98
Brosnan, Sarah, 245–46
Buddha, 29, 31

Buddhism, 28–30, 161
vegetarianism and, 31–32
Buffon, George-Louis de, 119
Bugnyar, Thomas, 143
bullfighting. See corrida
Burch, Rex, 183
Burgat, Florence, 99–100, 239
Bush, George W., 151
Busquet, Gérard, 33
Butler, Virgil, 83–85

Caetano, Sergio, 219
calves, 81
Cantor, David, 75–76
captive animals, freeing, 227
capture and transport of live animals,
mass losses during, 194–95
carbon dioxide emissions, 61, 62,
68–69, 288n38
carbon footprint, 62–63
Carbonnier, Dean, 258
"care," the hypocrisy of, 77
Caron, Aymeric, 44, 60, 109, 111, 127
castration of pigs, 81
categorical imperative, 160
Catholic Church, 14, 21
Catholic thinkers, 19
cats, 176
illegal trade of, 189–90
cattle, 81–83. See also corrida
Chai, Norin, 225
Chapouthier, Georges, 50, 212–13
Chauvet, David, 90, 129, 132
Chewong, 9
Chicago, Judy, 155
chicken farms, industrial, 45, 49,
79–81, 83
children
bullfighting and, 219
empathy for animals, 228
reactions to meat consumption,
41–42, 51–53
truth from the mouths of, 51–53
chimpanzees
attachment and grief in, 106
genetics and comparison with other
species, 116, 173

KARUNA-SHECHEN
Altruism in Action

In 2000 Matthieu Ricard founded Karuna-Shechen, an international nonprofit humanitarian organization providing healthcare, education, sustainable development, and cultural preservation throughout the Himalayan region. These activities help underserved communities in remote areas that have little or no other access to these vital services.

Karuna-Shechen has developed more than 200 humanitarian projects in India, Nepal, and Tibet. The programs are developed in response to the needs and aspirations of these communities, serving them with respect for their unique cultural heritage and paying special attention to educating and improving the status of girls and women.

Today Karuna-Shechen treats more than 150,000 patients annually through its clinics and outreach programs, educates over 20,000 children in schools it has helped to build, and benefits thousands through its social programs. It was very active in directly helping remote villagers rebuild their lives after the 2015 earthquakes in Nepal. In addition it has built homes for the elderly, equipped remote villages with solar power and rainwater collection systems, and built bridges and schools.

Its cultural preservation programs have helped to renew traditional crafts in Tibet through vocational training, rebuild retreat centers for contemplatives, and reproduce more than 400 volumes of ancient texts.

All of the author's share of royalties from this and his other books and events go entirely to furthering the activities of Karuna-Shechen.

For further information and to support these programs please visit www.karuna-shechen.org or contact usa@karuna-shechen.org.